ELEANOR

and

HICK

PENGUIN PRESS

New York

2016

ELEANOR

and

HICK

THE LOVE AFFAIR

THAT SHAPED A FIRST LADY

SUSAN QUINN

PENGUIN PRESS
An imprint of Penguin Random House LLC
375 Hudson Street
New York, New York 10014
penguin.com

Photograph credits
Unless credited below, photographs are courtesy of the Franklin D. Roosevelt Library
Insert page 2 (top right and middle left): Hennepin County Library Special Collections
3 (bottom) and 6 (top): Bettmann / Corbis
6 (bottom): Marion Post Wolcott / Library of Congress
8 (bottom): Photo by the author

ISBN 9781594205408 (hardcover)
ISBN 9781101607022 (e-book)

Printed in the United States of America
3   5   7   9   10   8   6   4

Designed by Gretchen Achilles

CONTENTS

PART III:

TOGETHER AND APART

PART IV:

THE WORLD AT WAR

PART V:

STARTING OVER

ELEANOR

and

HICK

INTRODUCTION

By the time Franklin Roosevelt was elected president in 1932, his wife, Eleanor, had succeeded in forging an independent life for herself—a life of teaching, writing, and political activism. Now she was about to become First Lady, with all the duties that would entail. In the midst of the victory celebrations, Eleanor was filled with dread about her future.

Lorena Hickok, a top reporter assigned to cover the new First Lady for the Associated Press, was one of the few who noticed Eleanor's unhappiness and took it seriously. Hickok—"Hick" to everyone who knew her—worked patiently to gain Eleanor's trust. By the time she wrote her stories for the AP, Eleanor and Hick had fallen in love. Hick knew both the publishable and the unpublishable reasons for Eleanor's unhappiness. She wrote a profile that was frank about Eleanor's reluctance to become First Lady, but without revealing all the reasons why.

America was in the depths the Great Depression. Banks were running out of money, unemployment was spiraling upward, and there was a very real possibility that the country would erupt in violence. Americans were in desperate need of the leadership Franklin Roosevelt was promising to provide. Eleanor would become FDR's most important partner in the great challenges he faced. She would often act as his conscience, reminding him of the human cost of his political decisions, and urging him to speak out courageously about racism and inequity. But more and more, as FDR waited to assume the presidency, Eleanor found excuses to spend her days and nights with Hick.

It would be hard to imagine a less likely pair than Eleanor and Hick. Eleanor had grown up in a mansion on the Hudson, with nannies and maids, while Hick had worked as a maid in other people's houses, starting at age fourteen, in the bleak railroad towns of South Dakota. Yet despite vastly different circumstances, both women had lonely and loveless childhoods, and both needed the kind of deep caring they gave to each other.

Hick would have loved to settle down with Eleanor for life. It will never be clear if Eleanor could or would have agreed to such an arrangement. Still, she loved Hick in a new and thrilling way. In other times and circumstances, she and Hick might have been able to make a life together, like the other women partners in their circle.

But Hick and Eleanor's intimacy would have to fit in around not only Eleanor's marriage, but also momentous national and world events. After FDR was elected, Hick quietly moved into the White House, where she stayed off and on for the entire thirteen years of the Roosevelt presidency. During those years, Eleanor and Hick managed to form a partnership that transformed their lives and contributed in a major way to important initiatives of the New Deal.

When they weren't together, Eleanor and Hick wrote tenderly of their longing for one another. "Oh! How I wanted to put my arms around you in reality instead of in spirit," Eleanor wrote Hick during the first year of their relationship. "I went and kissed your photograph instead and tears were in my eyes."

"There have been times," Hick wrote from San Francisco after they vacationed together out west in the summer of 1934, "when I've missed you so much that it has been like a physical pain, and at those times I've hated San Francisco because you were not there."

Eleanor loved Hick for many reasons, but it didn't hurt that such a relationship was considered a subversive act within her wellborn family.

Hick was a woman, for one thing. She was also a reporter, a species that FDR's aunt Kassie proudly asserted she had never spoken to in her life. Aunt Kassie, like others in her circle, believed a lady's name should only appear in print at the time of her coming out, her marriage, and her death. Hick had a peaches-and-cream complexion and beautiful shapely legs, but weighed two hundred pounds and dressed without frills, in a tailored style. She reveled in food and drink, played a good game of poker, smoked a lot, including an occasional cigar, and was capable of swearing a blue streak.

Unlike Eleanor, who kept strong emotions under control, Hick let it all out. When she was typing out a "sob story," tears would run down her cheeks; when she wrote a humorous piece, her laughter shook her entire body.

Hick was fun to be with, but she was also tempestuous her letters to Eleanor were often written in a fury about one injustice or another, especially after she went on the road for New Deal relief boss Harry Hopkins to report on the desperate poverty of the Depression years. "This valley is the damnedest place I ever saw," she wrote Eleanor from El Centro, California. "If you don't agree with them, you are a Communist, of course." And another time, when the Red Cross was withholding warm clothes for an emergency: "Good God, I wonder what constitutes an emergency in the eyes of the old ladies who run the Red Cross!"

Eleanor's upbringing would never allow her to express herself so emphatically. But Hick's embrace gave her the courage to open up, more than she ever had before, about her true feelings. "I'm back at my worst verge of tears condition which I hoped I could eliminate this summer," she wrote Hick in August 1935. "I only hope no one else realizes it and I don't think they do for I look well."

Eleanor and Hick's epistolary relationship was a rare and remarkable thing. They poured out their longing in thousands of letters. But they also used the letters to tell the stories of their time. Hick's journalistic training served her well as she reported on the terrible human cost of the Depression: she was good at gathering facts, good at getting people to talk, and good at vivid storytelling. Officially, she was reporting to Harry Hopkins. But she told Eleanor all the same stories—and some extra ones—in her long and detailed letters. The letters and reports added urgency to Eleanor's advocacy for people in need, and sometimes even made it to the president's desk. At other times, Hick described situations so harrowing that they sent Eleanor into action. One of Hick's reports about coal-mining families in West Virginia impelled Eleanor to hop in her roadster and drive down and see for herself. Not long after, she and others drew up plans for Arthurdale, a homestead community to house the mining families. Arthurdale was the first of the many resettlement projects for destitute families built by the Roosevelt administration. It started with a report from Hick.

Eleanor's letters to Hick are a kind of reportage themselves, chronicling her life in the fishbowl of the White House—more honest by far than her published accounts. They came so frequently that Hick, out in the field reporting on the lives of poor people, asked Eleanor to use special plain stationery. The embossed gold letterhead of the White House was an embarrassment when it arrived at a post office in Bemidji, Minnesota, or Jesup, Georgia. Eventually, Eleanor's long and detailed descriptions of her days in the White House led Hick to suggest she take her story to the world. "My Day," the daily column that brought Eleanor Roosevelt into the homes of America, grew directly out of the private diary reports that she first sent to Hick.

Eleanor became a word-producing marvel: she wrote her column six times a week from the 1930s until almost the end of her life. She also wrote memoirs that purported to be the story of her life. These, it must be said, are more fiction than fact when it comes to Eleanor's feelings about her marriage, her mother-in-law, her troubled children, and her life in general. The "My Day" column and the memoirs are useful as a record of events, but they paint an unreal picture of the emotional life of Eleanor Roosevelt. The letters between Eleanor and Hick tell a truer and more compelling story—not just of Eleanor but also of the lesser-known but brilliant journalist and chronicler of the Great Depression, Lorena Hickok.

Eleanor and Hick exchanged well over thirty-three hundred letters, starting when they fell in love, in 1932, and ending not long before Eleanor's death thirty years later. Hick died in 1968, five and a half years after Eleanor. Entrusted by Eleanor with both sides of the correspondence, Hick debated with herself and others about their final disposition. Some of Eleanor's loyal friends thought all the letters should be burned, to protect the First Lady's reputation. Hick did destroy some of the most explicit ones. She tried retyping others, leaving out the passionate parts. Fortunately for posterity, she soon gave up that effort, which was draining the correspondence of all life. In the end, she chose to donate the letters to the Roosevelt Presidential Library in Hyde Park, New York, with the stipulation that they could not be opened until ten years after her death.

On schedule, in 1978, a journalist named Doris Faber, a prolific writer of young adult books about prominent Americans, happened upon the letters. She was shocked and dismayed by what she found. "How could any reasonably perceptive adult deny that these were love letters?" she asked rhetorically. "And that a love affair, with at least some physical expression, had existed between this woman reporter and Eleanor Roosevelt. Unthinkable!" In "something like a classic state of shock," Faber asked the Hyde Park librarian why the collection couldn't be "locked up again, at least for another several decades."

Faber faulted Lorena Hickok for donating the letters and allowing the world to see them. She suggested that Hick had been seduced, in lonely old age, by the library's archivist. She claimed that Hick had acted out of "an uncontrollable craving for posthumous fame." Finally, Faber was persuaded that the story was going to come out, in more sensational form, if she didn't tell it.

The resulting book, *The Life of Lorena Hickok: E.R.'s Friend*, was published in 1980. Doris Faber was a thorough researcher, and brought together valuable information from friends who have since died. But the "very mixed emotions" with which she undertook the project muffled a story that deserves to be fully told—and celebrated. Instead, she sought to reassure readers that "the Eleanor Roosevelt who emerges in the Hickok

Papers does not, to any significant extent, differ from the First Lady of the World we already know." By 1980, when the book came out, there were already some outspoken lesbian women who yearned for more. Kathy Riley lamented in the journal *Big Mama Rag* that Doris Faber was the one who got to the letters first. It was "a crime," she wrote, "akin to turning over Sappho's poems to medieval Christian theologians."

Yet there were others who criticized Faber for even suggesting that Eleanor Roosevelt might have had an intimate relationship with another woman. One of them was Helen Gahagan Douglas, the very progressive Democrat who spoke out against McCarthyism, and was accused by Richard Nixon of being "pink right down to her underwear." She refused to cooperate with Faber once she learned that there might be even a hint of intimacy between Hick and Eleanor. In 1980, homosexuality aroused fear and hostility, even in a woman who had championed migrant workers and African American soldiers.

By the time I began reading the letters at Hyde Park six years ago, a great deal had changed. Blanche Wiesen Cook had presented the intimate relationship between Eleanor and Hick in a new and entirely sympathetic light in 1999, in the second volume of her groundbreaking biography of Eleanor Roosevelt. In our own time, love between two women seems neither shocking nor shameful to me or to many others.

Yet I still encounter people who are reluctant to believe that Eleanor Roosevelt was passionately involved with another woman. "Eleanor Roosevelt?" they will say. "Really? A lesbian relationship? A *physical* lesbian relationship?"

I suspect that people react this way because they have a fixed idea of Eleanor Roosevelt, with her flowered hat and her purse and her sensible shoes, slightly bent forward as she marches off to make the world a better place. *That* Eleanor Roosevelt dwells in a world that transcends all the longings, hurts, and excitements of passion. But that public persona masked the real Eleanor—as her letters to Hick make abundantly clear.

The letters between Eleanor and Hick are less remarkable now for their shock value than for the moving and poignant story they tell of two women who loved each other intensely and deeply. Women who loved women surrounded both of them, and showed the way to a freer life. For Eleanor Roosevelt especially, who was required to marry within narrow boundaries of class and wealth, the possibility of such love was liberating. When she found it, with Hick, it changed her life, and Hick's, forever.

PART I

UNEXPECTED

LOVE

CHAPTER ONE

BEGINNING TO TRUST

BY THE TIME FRANKLIN DELANO ROOSEVELT was nominated for president, in August 1932, some doubted whether a survivor of polio, paralyzed from the waist down, had the strength to conduct a vigorous campaign, let alone lead the country out of the worst economic depression in its history. Even his advisers were worried. FDR came up with a defiant answer to all of them: a nine-thousand-mile, twenty one-day trip through seventeen midwestern and western states aboard the Roosevelt Special.

It was a trip perfectly suited to both FDR's temperament and his physical limitations. As soon as the train came to a stop, FDR stepped out on the rear platform, gripping the arm of his son Jimmy. The railing cut off sight of his lower body, so the public saw only his broad shoulders and chest as he delivered his one-minute address. "It's nice to be back in Dubuque," he would begin, flashing his wide smile, adding, "I'm just here to look, learn, and listen." His speech was patrician, but his message was friendly, and his physical courage buoyed his worried listeners.

Between stops, FDR had only to look out the train window to see just how bad things had become. In Chicago, there were blocks of lifeless factories, overgrown parks, and rows of vacant stores with blackened windows. Shantytowns, clustered along the railroad tracks, sent up smoke from cooking fires. In the rich farm country of Iowa and Ohio, the farmhouses were unpainted, the fences were crumbling, and food was rotting in the fields. By the time the Roosevelt Special reached Seattle, Roosevelt had reason to speak "in the name of a stricken America and a stricken world."

Even in such terrible times, however, Franklin Roosevelt managed to enjoy himself. He loved everything about campaigning, from the enthusiasm of the local crowds to the sparring with the newspaper "boys." FDR's sitting room was open to all comers: local politicians got on and off, and close advisers and future cabinet members huddled late into the night, plotting a future course for a country in crisis. FDR enhanced his listening and learning with healthy doses of jokes, storytelling, poker, and booze.

Eleanor Roosevelt waited until the return journey from the West Coast to join the Roosevelt Special. She didn't share her husband's enthusiasm for the cheering admirers on the campaign trail. "It seems undignified and meaningless but perhaps we need it!" she once confided. She wasn't comfortable with the jocular atmosphere around FDR, either. Try as she might, Eleanor didn't always get the jokes and was uncomfortable with the teasing. On her honeymoon, she had refused to join a bridge game that involved money, because she had been raised to think it was improper. Drinking, especially, made her uneasy. She had her own reasons for disliking even the smell of alcohol: her father had drunk himself to death, and it now looked as though her brother was going down the same path.

Eleanor had plenty to say about policy issues. But the politicians and brain trusters who surrounded Franklin rarely thought to include her in their discussions. The exception was Louis Howe, a wizened little man with a scarred face and bulging eyes who had been a true believer in FDR's greatness since they met in 1911. Eleanor Roosevelt had been repelled by Howe in the early days: he was an inelegant chain-smoking newspaperman, the sort of person she had been brought up to avoid. But Howe's attentions to her in 1920, when FDR was running for vice president on the ill-fated Democratic ticket, went a long way toward changing her mind. When Franklin was stricken with polio on Campobello Island, Eleanor and Louis became a team. They were the only ones who believed that FDR had a political future in those years immediately following the diagnosis. Howe came to understand then that Eleanor could keep Roosevelt aspirations alive while FDR recovered. He urged her to lower her high-pitched voice and suppress her nervous giggle when she spoke in public, and he encouraged her to get more involved in New York politics. In time, he even had the idea that Eleanor should run for president herself.

For Louis Howe, the trip on the Roosevelt Special was a dream come true: he'd been working toward the presidential run ever since Franklin Roosevelt first served in the New York state legislature. Shrewd political operative that he was, Howe was confident that the Hoover campaign was doomed and that FDR was about to become the next president of the United States.

Eleanor Roosevelt didn't want to believe it. The spark that Howe had ignited in her had led to a new, independent life. She was the cofounder of a craft workshop called Val-Kill Industries, a cofounder and teacher at a girls' school, and an activist with other women in New York politics. What's more, she knew a fair amount about the ceremonial burden involved in being First Lady: her aunt Edith had been an exemplary one for her uncle Theodore. She didn't want any part of it. She had been as passionate as Howe about FDR's political rehabilitation. But she didn't share his excitement now, as the Roosevelt Special gained momentum.

It was comforting, under the circumstances, when the campaign train went off on a side rail so that she could pay a visit to an old friend who would understand and sympathize. Eleanor and Isabella Greenway had endured "coming out" as debutantes in consecutive years—both looked upon it as more duty than pleasure—and Isabella had been a bridesmaid in the Roosevelt wedding, staying by Eleanor's side as they organized the myriad presents and even composing some of the thank-you notes. Since then, Isabella had married Robert Ferguson, an old family friend, and moved with him to Prescott, Arizona, in hopes that the dry climate would cure his tuberculosis.

Since Eleanor and her husband kept friends forever, it was natural for them to take a day off from the campaign trail, away from press and public, to visit Isabella and her husband in Prescott. Journalists were more obliging in those days: photographers agreed not to take pictures that included FDR's wheelchair. No picture of FDR in a crablike position, as his prone and helpless body was lifted in and out of his automobile, ever made the newspapers. Giving the family a day off to visit friends was all right with them.

What did surprise and rankle the reporters, though, was that an exception was made for one rookie *Chicago Tribune* reporter named John Boettiger, who for some reason was asked to come along on the private visit. No one resented this slight more than Lorena Hickok. Hick was the only female reporter on the Roosevelt Special and one of the top female reporters in the country, and she'd gotten there by fighting for stories. "Most women," fellow reporter Walter B. "Rags" Ragsdale noted, "were society editors or worked the social beat. The rarities were women who fought and scratched their way to the street as regular reporters." Another reporter who knew her well noticed that a red rash tended to develop on the back of Hick's neck if she thought she was getting cheated out of a plum assignment.

Hick had already complained when she discovered that all the men on the Roosevelt Special had compartments or drawing rooms in which to sleep and work, while she was stuck with a small berth up toward the engine, in the neighborhood of the local reporters. So naturally she was furious about John Boettiger, an inexperienced reporter, getting special treatment. She decided to complain to Eleanor Roosevelt about it.

Hick didn't expect the reaction she got: Eleanor Roosevelt invited her to come along too. Hick was intrigued, and a little puzzled. Eleanor had kept her at a distance in the past. When she had interviewed Eleanor at the governor's mansion, she had been invited up to the drawing room for an elegant tea, poured from a silver pot. On that day, like all others, Lorena Hickok dressed to be taken seriously: a soft silk shirt collar over a suit jacket and a skirt, of course. She was a presence. Her legs were shapely, her shoes sensible. She had a round face with a strong, determined jaw, and

intense, penetrating eyes. At five foot eight, she was broad without look
ing fat.

Though hardly a fashion plate herself, Hick had felt sorry for Eleanor.
She could tell that Eleanor felt homely, despite her warm blue eyes and
winning smile. She dressed abominably, in Hick's view: her skirt was too
long, her blouse was a terrible green, and she wore a hairnet with an elastic
that cut into her forehead. She had inherited the protruding front teeth of
the Teddy Roosevelt branch of the family.

Yet Eleanor had a natural elegance when she moved. Hick was struck
by her long slender hands and the graceful way she manipulated the tea
things. At tea that day, Eleanor kept everything friendly but bland. Hick
had a strong impression that the governor's wife didn't trust her. That was
why she was surprised when Eleanor asked her to come along to Prescott:
something had changed. Hick, ever the reporter, soon figured it out: it all
had to do with a long conversation she'd had late one night with Eleanor's
secretary, Malvina Thompson, as the two of them kept each other company on the Roosevelt Special.

Malvina Thompson, known to everyone as Tommy, was much more
than the usual secretary: she was Eleanor's fiercely loyal friend and traveling companion, always willing to work at Eleanor's demanding pace. The
two had met while both were working on Al Smith's 1928 presidential
campaign. Afterward, Tommy became secretary to Louie Howe, but she
worked on the side for Eleanor. By the time FDR was elected governor of
New York, Tommy and Eleanor were a full-time team. Tommy was married until 1939, and had another man in her life after that. But most of her
waking hours were devoted to the woman she called "Mrs. R." Tommy
and Hick had a lot in common: they were born the same year, came from
the working class, smoked, drank, and held strong opinions. It was natural
for them to gravitate toward each other when work was done.

The train moved along at a measured pace during the day, when FDR
was sitting up in his custom-built chair in the parlor car. If it went too
fast, the jerks and jiggles made it hard for him to steady himself for read-

ing and conversation. At night, the engineer made up for lost time, hurtling though the dark. It may have been a train whistle late one night that prompted Tommy Thompson to share a childhood memory with Hick about her father, who had worked as a locomotive engineer on the railroad. He would sound three short blasts on the train whistle in a private salute as the train roared past the family's apartment windows in the Bronx.

It was such a touching idea, and so at odds with Hick's own childhood memories, that it prompted her to open up to Tommy about her painful past. Hick's mother had died when she was thirteen, leaving her to deal with her violent, abusive father. Within a year, he remarried, and the stepmother kicked her out of the house. From age fourteen on, she had had to make her own way in the hardscrabble pioneer towns of South Dakota, living in other people's houses as a hired girl.

When Eleanor heard Hick's story from Thompson, it changed her view of the tough AP reporter. Because her own life had been scarred by loss and disappointment, she was drawn to others who had suffered and struggled. After that, she began to suspect what Hick's fellow reporters already knew. There was the surface Hick: blasé and shock-proof, a tough-minded reporter who knew how to drink and smoke with the boys, and who fought for her rights. Then there was the tender-hearted and sometimes shy Hick underneath, who bore witness to the suffering of ordinary people in those terrible times.

Long before she joined the AP, back when she was a reporter for the *Minneapolis Tribune*, Hick could be relied on to find and tell the most vivid stories of hardship: long, detailed pieces about girls who came to Minneapolis from little farm towns and got into trouble, about an injured worker who decided to crawl under a bridge and starve to death, about an organ grinder whose monkey was stolen.

Hick was still looking for such stories on the campaign trail. Her fellow reporter Rags Ragsdale would often cover FDR's whistle-stop speeches while Hick circulated in the crowd and talked to people about their lives. "Many times, she came back aboard the campaign train," Ragsdale remembered, "fuming and almost tearful over a hard-luck story she had picked up from someone in the crowd."

There were unending hard-luck stories. During a stopover in Topeka, Kansas, Hick watched Franklin Roosevelt address thousands of "deeply tanned, grim-faced farmers, some so ragged that they reminded one of pictures of starving Mongolian peasants in the rotogravure sections of the Sunday papers. They did not cheer. They did not applaud. They just stood there in the broiling sun, silent, listening."

After her day with Eleanor in Prescott, Hick realized why rookie reporter John Boettiger was getting special treatment: he was having an affair with the Roosevelts' oldest child, Anna, who was unhappily married to Curtis Dall. Not long after, both Anna and John would divorce in order to marry each other.

The divorce was fodder for the gossip columns when it finally happened. But when Hick came back from her day with the Roosevelts and briefed her fellow reporters, she talked about the ranch and the barbecue, not the affair. It was the first of many family secrets she would keep.

The more important discovery Hick made that day was that Eleanor Roosevelt was at least as fascinating as her husband. "Lorena was as excited as I ever saw her when she came back," Ragsdale remembered. "From this time forward it became hard for her to write with the usual AP restraint about Mrs. Roosevelt."

In the past, Hick had avoided writing about politicians' wives: fashion, teas, and charity events were women's page stuff, and she'd escaped that long before, during her initiation at the *Milwaukee Sentinel*. Eleanor, in turn, resisted the curiosity of reporters, especially if it touched on anything personal. Her grandmother had taught her that it was unseemly to appear in the public eye. "I gave as little information as possible," she explained in her first memoir, "feeling that that was the only right attitude toward any newspaper people where a woman and her home were concerned."

Eleanor had good reason to be wary of all reporters. As the Boettiger

incident would make clear, things went on in the Roosevelt household
that needed to be kept away from the scandal-loving press. What's more,
Eleanor disliked the usual portrayals of the devoted political wife at least
as much as Hick hated writing them. In Eleanor's case, as Hick would
soon discover, that ceremonial role was a façade that had little to do with
who she really was.

At first, Hick cared only a little about Eleanor's reticence. FDR, not
Eleanor, was the story, and he relished Hick's attention. In April 1932,
months before he became the Democratic candidate for president, he invited her up to Hyde Park for a daylong charm offensive.

The big house at Hyde Park was a living museum of FDR's branch of
the Roosevelt family. In 1915, FDR himself had worked on plans to double
the house's size to accommodate his growing family. The enlarged version
of Springwood, as the mansion was called, was full to overflowing with
the family collections of books, nautical prints, and paintings. There were
also portraits of Roosevelt and Delano ancestors hanging on the walls,
along with porcelain and curios from China, where the Delanos made their
fortune as traders. Very little in the house was connected to Eleanor's history: she had grown up in her grandmother Hall's mansion farther up
the Hudson. The Roosevelt house she knew and loved was Sagamore
Hill on Long Island, the home where Theodore Roosevelt, her father's
older brother, lived with his large family and the souvenirs of his adventurous life.

FDR and Hick sat before the fire in the big house at Hyde Park and
talked politics as Eleanor listened, knitting. Then FDR took Hick out in
his hand-controlled roadster for a tour of the estate, pointing out the hill
where he sledded as a boy, the Christmas trees he was growing to renew
the impoverished soil, and the stone cottage, at nearby Val-Kill, which he
designed "for my Missus." It was, he noted, conceived in the Dutch colonial style of his ancestors.

Hick toured the cottage with the "missus" and learned of the small
furniture-making company Eleanor was part of. Eleanor and her women
friends had founded Val-Kill Industries with the idea of providing local

farmers with craft skills. The little workshop turned out colonial repro-
duction furniture and pewter.

It could not have escaped Hick's notice, as Eleanor and her two friends
took her around the small factory, that they made an unusual trio. One
was Nancy Cook, a carpenter who had used her skills to fashion artificial
limbs during World War I, and the other was Marion Dickerman, the
head of a girls' school in New York City. Both were avid Democrats and
hardly the "ladies who lunch" whom Hick tried her best to avoid. Probably she also realized that Cook and Dickerman were a couple. Hick must
have been intrigued by Eleanor and her unconventional friends, but she
left them out of her AP piece. Instead, she emphasized FDR's admirable
efforts to restore the soil on his property.

Hick became more interested in Eleanor during the Democratic convention in 1932, while she was keeping vigil with fellow reporters outside
the governor's mansion in Albany, waiting for the delegates to settle on a
candidate. It was a noisy and contentious convention, and the outcome was
still unclear when FDR held a press conference on the first day of July.
Hick noticed that he was lively and buoyant, joking and laughing even
more than usual. His mood suggested what was later confirmed: a deal
was in the making. But what she also noticed that night was that Eleanor
looked despondent. "That woman is unhappy about something," Hick
told her Albany counterpart after they left. It was the only really vivid
memory she carried away from the press conference. Yet it didn't show up
in the story she filed at the time.

By the time she got off the Roosevelt Special in Buffalo, Hick had
figured out that covering Eleanor Roosevelt had the potential to be much
more than churning out the standard First Lady coverage of the past. So
when the AP reporter who was assigned to Eleanor left, Hick began ac-
tively lobbying for the job. She wired her boss, AP city editor Bill Chapin,
"THE DAME HAS ENORMOUS DIGNITY, SHE'S A PERSON." In Octo-
ber, Chapin finally gave her the green light. "She's all yours now, Hickok,"
he told her. "Have fun!"

Hick became Eleanor's appendage. She spent her afternoons sitting outside her office in New York, trying to guess what was going on behind closed doors. She went to every one of her public appearances. On the night of Eleanor's forty-eighth birthday, there was a small dinner party celebration with close friends. Hick, of course, was not invited. But she did manage to hear Eleanor comment that it was "good to be middle-aged. Things don't matter so much. You don't take it so hard when things happen to you that you don't like." The remark intrigued Hick. But it didn't seem like newspaper copy.

Hick was invited—or invited herself—on Eleanor's marathon campaign journey around New York State two weeks after the birthday party. Over five days at the end of October, Eleanor spent a total of fifty hours on the train. "Most of the time," Hick's AP story reported, "Mrs. Roosevelt was accompanied only by one woman companion." That woman companion was the author of the story, Lorena Hickok.

On the campaign trail during that trip, Eleanor operated by complicated rules. On one hand, she refused to make campaign speeches for Franklin, because she didn't think it was appropriate for the wife of the candidate to appeal to voters on his behalf. On the other, she did speak out enthusiastically in support of gubernatorial candidate Herbert Lehman, because, as she explained, he was a good friend of the family. In other words, it was personal not political—a distinction, in Eleanor Roosevelt's case, without a difference.

Hick noted that Eleanor vacillated between the private and public persona from one day to the next. In Syracuse one evening, she warned an audience of Democratic women that the coming winter was likely to be "desperate" and that the Republicans had no answers. "If you and I were hungry, I doubt whether we'd be so patient as these people have been so far." Then the next day, she insisted that she was just the candidate's wife and didn't talk politics.

There were still more surprises and contradictions to come. Eleanor paid a visit to her husband's former bodyguard Earl Miller and his new wife in Elmira, New York. The Millers had been married not long before

at the Roosevelt estate at Hyde Park. But this too was far more complicated than it appeared on the surface.

Earl Miller and Eleanor Roosevelt had an affection for each other that
made some suspect they were lovers. At the very least, it was a lively flirtation. Earl, a fit and handsome athlete thirteen years her junior, had encouraged Eleanor in new, bold pursuits: riding horseback with her and
teaching her to dive, to play tennis, to fire a pistol, and even to take part
in silly home movies when he visited her at Val-Kill. Eleanor, for her part,
lavished attention on Earl, helping him set up house and listening to his
tales of romantic woe.

Some had suggested that this marriage, which began to go sour very
quickly, was a sham, staged only to put off the gossips and protect the
woman Miller called "Lady." Later, there was a second unsuccessful marriage. That time there was a threat that Eleanor Roosevelt would be named
as a co-respondent in divorce proceedings. Miller's special friendship with
Eleanor might have become a scandal if it got the attention of the wrong
people. Once again, Hick was witness to a potentially damaging family
secret; once again, she kept it to herself.

Eleanor had no sooner returned from her New York State tour than
she learned that FDR's personal secretary for the last twelve years, Mar-
guerite LeHand, known as Missy, had lost her mother. Immediately she
made plans to get back on the train and accompany Missy all the way to
the mother's home in Potsdam, New York, up near the Canadian border,
for the funeral. Hick came along, of course.

On the long train ride to Potsdam, Hick learned about yet another
unusual aspect of the complicated emotional landscape of the Roosevelt
marriage. Missy was not just a personal secretary to FDR. She had become
in fact a sort of second wife. She had lived in the governor's mansion for
the previous four years, and she would go on to live in the White House
for much of Roosevelt's presidency. A tall, stylish woman in her thirties,
with gray eyes and a long face, Missy was a highly efficient secretary completely devoted to carrying out "Effdee's" wishes. She was also the one who

kept FDR company, who listened to his jokes and shared in his cocktail hour, the one who came into his bedroom in the morning to plan for the day, and who sometimes could be seen sitting on his lap when work was done. She might have been a lover.

Quite understandably, there were times when Eleanor resented Missy, especially since she was not the first personal secretary to become her husband's intimate companion. Nonetheless, Eleanor insisted that she was very fond of Missy. This fact says not only a great deal about Eleanor, who tried hard to love almost everybody, but also about the evolution of the Roosevelt marriage. Certainly, Eleanor no longer wanted to play the role that Missy did in her husband's life. Some months before, in a magazine piece entitled "Ten Rules for a Successful Marriage," she had observed that a husband "may have many other helpers besides his wife, particularly if his interests are varied and broad."

It would be hard to imagine a man with more varied and broad interests than Franklin Delano Roosevelt. He was a lover of people of all kinds. He relished politics and was a brilliant player of the game. But he loved many other things as well: every kind of boat, including those he sailed and the boat models he constructed out of tiny pieces of wood; trees of all kinds, including the virgin timber and the new spruces he nurtured on his eleven-hundred-acre estate at Hyde Park; his stamp collection, which he fussed over in quiet moments; the pleasure of a good stiff drink, preferably mixed by his own hand. FDR liked to enjoy all of these things without fear of disapproval, in the company of an agreeable woman. Missy, though she had her own opinions, was such a woman. Eleanor, though she may have tried to fulfill that role in the early years of her marriage, most certainly was not.

One thing became clear to Hick during her weeks as Eleanor Roosevelt's constant companion: the complete story of her life couldn't be told without hurting her and her family. It was going to take a skilled and careful hand to introduce this unusual woman to the public. Lorena Hickok, who had her own secrets, was ideally suited to the job.

At some point during their journeys, Eleanor must have sensed this.

By the time the two of them returned from Potsdam on the train, Eleanor was no longer treating Hick as a dangerous journalist. In fact, she was beginning to see her in an entirely different light: as the person who might be able to fulfill her longing for affection and understanding at a daunting moment in her life.

There was only one room for the two of them on the train, a drawing room with a single berth and a long narrow couch. Eleanor insisted on giving Hick the berth and taking the couch for herself. "I'm longer than you are," she explained. "And," she added with a smile, "not quite so broad."

They talked long into the night, sharing stories of their childhoods— seemingly so different but alike in their misery. Hick told Eleanor about her violent and abusive father and her teenage years as a maid in other people's houses. Eleanor told Hick about her disapproving mother, about the tragic death of her father, whom she adored, about life in the home of her strict grandmother, and about the aunts who called her "the ugly duckling."

Hick asked, "May I write some of that?"

Eleanor replied, "If you like. I trust you."

CHAPTER TWO

ELEANOR ACCORDING
TO HICK

MOST DAYS, LORENA HICKOK banged out her stories in a sea of noise, in the wide-open newsroom of the AP bureau in midtown Manhattan. The clackety-clack of the teletype machine was constant, overlaid with the voices and chattering typewriters of several dozen writers and editors. Sunday watch was the exception. When Hick drew that assignment, she could bring her favorite companion, a large German shepherd named Prinz, along with her. Hick was always happier with Prinz by her side. Her return to him after a day at the office precipitated an orgy of baby talk and slobbery dog kisses.

Hick lived at 10 Mitchell Place, near the East River in Manhattan, in a new building, a thirteen-story apartment house in Tudor Revival style, with herringbone brickwork, diamond-shaped leaded windows, and a big welcoming fireplace in the mahogany-paneled lobby. It stood as a kind of defiant challenge to its grim surroundings. The Turtle Bay neighborhood around it was the underbelly of the city: a maze of breweries, laundries, and slaughterhouses that made it the sootiest district of Manhattan. As the Depression deepened, a shantytown developed along the river, not far from Hick's door. Sometimes she would walk down there with Prinz and chat with the inhabitants.

But when Hick drew Sunday watch, she and Prinz emerged together into the gritty neighborhood, crossed under the shadow of the elevated trains at Second and Third Avenues, and made their way west to the cleaner and brighter world of Madison Avenue and the AP. There, they took the freight elevator to the sixth floor and the nearly deserted press-room. While Hick worked, Prinz roamed, pausing occasionally to flop down near her desk.

A young reporter named Gardner Bridge once shared Sunday watch with Hick, and remembered encountering Prinz. He also remembered, after FDR was elected, how quickly and easily Hick seemed to turn out her profile of Eleanor Roosevelt while he, writing a parallel six-part series about FDR, had to do research before he could even begin. "Hick batted out her three pieces with hardly any recourse to the files—she knew her subject that well. I had to spend a day in the library before I could even start writing." Hick, of course, had spent time too: those many hours with Eleanor on the train, gaining her subject's trust.

The portraits of Franklin and Eleanor that went out on the AP wire reflect the difference. Bridge, if he interviewed FDR at all, accepted the president's upbeat version of events without question. In general, he told FDR's story as a journey from triumph to triumph in six episodes, starting with Franklin's privileged birth, moving on to his first memory of surviving a shipwreck at sea, followed by an idyllic childhood at Hyde Park climbing trees and shooting birds for his collection. In Bridge's account, FDR was a sportsman at Groton, where he quickly made friends, and a very successful student at Harvard, where he edited the *Harvard Crimson*.

The reality was much different: FDR came late to Groton, and didn't fit in easily with the established cliques. Nor was he much of an athlete: he wound up managing the baseball team rather than playing on it. His rejection from the exclusive Porcellian Club at Harvard left a permanent scar.

Bridge continued his triumphal version of the story: FDR successfully challenged Tammany as a New York State legislator, then followed in his uncle Theodore Roosevelt's footsteps as assistant secretary of the Navy. Here, it is suggested, Roosevelt often had to take charge. In fact, FDR's boss, Josephus Daniels, was unusually forgiving of his young acolyte, who took some questionable liberties. The defeat of the Cox/Roosevelt presidential ticket in 1920 merited only a paragraph. As for polio, which FDR contracted in 1921 and which deprived him of the use of his legs, "neither Roosevelt nor any member of his family has ever publicly acknowledged his condition to be affliction [sic]. Rather they have taken the attitude that it makes him better fitted for desk work."

The upbeat presentation of FDR's polio and paralysis was the one thing on which Eleanor and FDR were in lockstep: "He was grand about his illness you know," Eleanor told Hick. "In fact, never once have I heard him say that what happened to him was hard, or disagreeable, or out of the ordinary."

Such astonishing cheerfulness in the face of a bleak reality may have been what Americans needed in 1932. Like the theme song of the campaign, "Happy Days Are Here Again," it carried denial to new heights.

Aside from its rosy presentation of FDR's life, the most striking thing about the Gardner Bridge series is Eleanor Roosevelt's absence. She comes up only once, and then in the context of her being a Roosevelt marrying a Roosevelt, at a wedding presided over by her uncle Theodore Roosevelt, then president of the United States. TR is quoted as saying, "Well Franklin, there's nothing like keeping the name in the family."

Bridge's six-part series on FDR made for dull reading when compared to Hickok's on Eleanor. Hick's articles managed to keep Eleanor's important secrets while still revealing the unhappiness Hick had observed during the campaign. In Hick's pieces, the separate lives of Eleanor and FDR became even more obvious. FDR was mentioned only twice: once in reference to his polio, and once in describing the late-night meetings at the governor's mansion, which filled the library with so much smoke that she had to move the children's room to another part of the house.

"If I wanted to be selfish," said Eleanor in Part I, "I could wish he had not been elected." She "never wanted to be a President's wife, and I don't want it now. . . . For him, of course, I'm glad—sincerely, I couldn't have wanted it to go the other way. . . . Being a Democrat, I believe this change is for the better."

"And now," she concluded, "I shall have to work out my own salvation."

Throughout her career, Hick specialized in grabbing the reader with the unexpected. This was no exception. The new First Lady was not going to be satisfied with the role of helpmeet, cheering her husband on? She was pleased with his victory as a *Democrat*, not as a wife? She was looking for a separate life, for her "own salvation"? Such an independent attitude in a First Lady was heresy.

In fact, Eleanor went on to insist, she wasn't going to be a First Lady at all, but "plain ordinary Mrs. Roosevelt." Here was part two of Eleanor Roosevelt's one-two punch. She was going to be independent. But she was also going to be humble.

With clear delight, Hick elaborated on this second dimension: "The next mistress of the White House," she wrote, "thinks people are going to get used to her ways, even though she does edit a magazine, wear $10 dresses and drive her own car." She ate at drugstore counters, unless she was taking someone to lunch. Also, Mrs. Roosevelt didn't really own her own automobile—only a third of one. The blue roadster belonged to the "furniture factory" of which she was one-third owner. "Sometimes she borrows it and she loves to drive it—fast."

In general, she was a "whirlwind" who got along on six hours' sleep and walked with a "long swinging stride" that made her hard to keep up with, even when she was in heels. Hick was writing from firsthand experience. When they were together at Hyde Park, Eleanor sometimes wore golf shoes. When that happened, Hick found it "practically impossible" to keep up with her.

"I had an odd sort of childhood really," Eleanor said. She told of losing her mother when she was eight, her father when she was ten, of being raised strictly by her maternal grandmother, before going off to a boarding school in London, where she got her first taste of freedom under the enlightened tutelage of a French woman of letters, Marie Souvestre.

Not long after her return and her debut, she married. "For the next ten years it never occurred to me to do anything outside my own home. My children were born—six in ten years." Revealing her privileged background, she noted that she kept the same trained nurse for all of them, and learned from her that "work could be fun," adding, "I still love to make a bed."

During World War I, Eleanor discovered volunteer work she loved, and she continued—with an interruption during FDR's polio crisis—to volunteer. In recent years she had become very involved with the Democratic women's organization in New York; she was also doing a series of radio broadcasts, teaching a class at Todhunter, a girls' school in New York, and editing a parenting advice magazine called *Babies, Just Babies*.

She took up these activities because she needed to make money. This in itself was controversial: a wife, and especially one from a privileged background, was not supposed to work for money. Her husband did that.

The question of whether a woman should work after marriage would come up over and over again in Eleanor's ongoing dialogue with the women of America. Later, Eleanor would defend married women's right to pursue their own fulfillment in work. But at this early stage, Hick's profile provided Eleanor with a good justification for making her own money. She wasn't earning for her own needs, but because she liked to have it in order to give it away. "I don't know where it goes exactly," she said with an amused expression in her eyes, "but I have a lot of fun doing things with money.'"

Now that FDR had won, Eleanor Roosevelt was going to have to give up some of the work she loved most and spend more time in a ceremonial role, doing what she and Hick came to refer to as "being Mrs. R."

"Sometimes," she told Hick, "I daresay I shall feel a little as one of my boys —after I had lectured him on the responsibilities incumbent on the sons of a man in public life—felt when he said: 'Wouldn't it be fun to do things just because you wanted to do them?'"

Hick's AP series managed to give the public a taste of a woman who was going to do things differently, while also lovingly protecting Eleanor from those who might do her harm. Hick's admiration for her subject permeates the stories. But so does her well-honed understanding of conventional expectations. There is no mention of the fact that Eleanor's father drank himself to death. Of course there is no mention of any problems in the Roosevelt marriage, or of the looming divorce of daughter Anna.

Nothing is mentioned either of the oppressive reign of Eleanor Roosevelt's mother-in-law, Sara, at the big house at Hyde Park, nor of the unconventional lifestyle of many of Eleanor's closest women friends. The Val-Kill cottage at Hyde Park, for instance, was a hideaway created and used by Eleanor and life partners Nancy Cook and Marion Dickerman, with only occasional visits from the rest of the Roosevelt family. Yet according to Hick's story, Eleanor and Franklin built the Val-Kill cottage "in order that the children might learn to live without servants."

Hick's AP series was not untruthful—merely selective. It was an act of devotion.

ON NOVEMBER 8, 1932, Franklin Roosevelt won the presidency with 57.4 percent of the vote, carrying forty-two of forty-eight states. Many saw the victory coming long before election day. But Eleanor insisted on hanging on to her freedom right up to the very last minute.

On the night before the election, she played her wifely role at Hyde Park as FDR addressed a friendly hometown crowd. "With your help and your patience," he told his constituents at a rally in Poughkeepsie, "and your generous goodwill, we will do what we can to mend the torn fabric of our common life."

As the Roosevelt party left the event, Eleanor announced that she was going to drive to New York City so that she could be on hand early the next day to teach her class at the Todhunter School. Eleanor told an interviewer she "liked teaching better than anything else I do." She was cofounder and an associate principal of Todhunter, working alongside Marion

Dickerman, who was principal. In the four years since the school opened, she had become a lively and beloved teacher of history and current affairs. One of her courses, aptly named "Happenings," required the girls, all from privileged backgrounds, to visit Ellis Island and model tenements, and to read periodicals instead of textbooks.

FDR was generally supportive of Eleanor's independent undertakings. But on this night, he objected. It was raining out. The roads would be slippery, and it would take several hours to make the seventy-five-mile trip. Eleanor persisted, determined to go on with her life despite the looming victory. Finally FDR agreed when it turned out that Hick, who was never far from Eleanor's side, could go along "to keep you awake." Having won that battle, Eleanor promptly faced another: a woman reporter from a competing press association wanted to come along.

"I'm sorry, but there isn't room," said Eleanor.

The reporter pressed on, asking to ride in the rumble seat.

Eleanor was adamant. "And off we went," Hick remembered, "leaving the woman in the parking lot."

In the car that night, Hick lectured Eleanor on press relations. "You aren't going to be able to do that sort of thing after tomorrow," she told her. "That girl is furious and I can't say I blame her."

"I couldn't crowd her in here with us," Eleanor declared. "It's not a very good night for driving, and I'll need elbow room.

"And besides," she added, "what makes you so sure Franklin is going to be elected?"

Hick thought she detected "something almost like a note of hope" in her voice.

With Hick in attendance, Eleanor taught her classes in history and current events at Todhunter, making no mention of the election. Toward the end of class, a student piped up, "We think it's grand to have the wife of the President for our teacher."

"But I'm not the wife of the President yet," she replied.

After the class, Eleanor drove back up to Hyde Park and voted at Town Hall, then rode with her husband down the Albany Post Road to

New York City to await the final returns. Hick was riding behind the Roosevelts in the cavalcade of press cars. But in New York City, she joined the couple's inner circle at a buffet supper at their home on 65th Street. As always with the Roosevelts, it was a large inner circle, including their many relatives and friends, as well as some newspaper people. Hick arrived with the handful of women who had now been assigned to cover the First Lady.

Eleanor greeted the newswomen at the door. "When I came in," Hick remembered, "she kissed me and said softly, 'It's good to have you around tonight, Hick.'"

LORENA HICKOK AND ELEANOR ROOSEVELT had grown up believing they were homely women, admiring inordinately the beauty and glamour of others. Lorena, at fifteen, was enchanted by the daughter of the local hotel owner in Aberdeen, South Dakota: she had beautiful dresses, with hair ribbons to match, and she was "the first person ever to become an inmate of . . . my imagination." The first sentence of Eleanor's memoir of her childhood describes her mother as "one of the most beautiful women I have ever seen." Eleanor considered it a great privilege to spend time in her mother's bedroom, watching her prepare for a triumphant evening out in New York society.

"Attention and admiration were the things through all my childhood which I wanted," Eleanor wrote, "because I was made to feel so conscious of the fact that nothing about me would attract attention or would bring me admiration!"

On this night, in Lorena Hickok's eyes, Eleanor Roosevelt became one of the beautiful ones, the object of the attention and admiration she had longed for. It was the first time Hick had seen Eleanor in evening clothes, and she was stunned by the change in her appearance. She stood beautifully tall, slender and erect in a long white gown, "made of some soft material like chiffon," with a short train. Hick thought Eleanor looked like a queen.

Later that night, the Roosevelt contingent moved on to the Hotel Biltmore to wait for the election results. Special telephone and telegraph wires had been installed to bring the latest news to the Roosevelt suite. The grand ballroom on another floor was overflowing with supporters watching a big board flash the returns as they came in. As the night wore on and victory seemed assured, the excitement built: the corridors were filled with celebrants shouting and congratulating one another. A great clamor arose for Eleanor to give a press conference, and she reluctantly agreed, only to be barraged with too many questions. "Through it all," Hick remembered, "she kept smiling, but once she looked directly at me. She shook her head, ever so slightly, and the expression in her eyes was miserable.

"I was reminded of a fox," Hick wrote, "surrounded by a pack of baying hounds."

CHAPTER THREE

JE T'AIME ET JE T'ADORE

WITH STRONG MAJORITIES in both houses of Congress, FDR had a mandate to quickly and decisively address the economic crisis facing the nation. Unfortunately, he was constrained by an antiquated law: inauguration wouldn't take place until March.

During the four-month interregnum, the national emergency escalated to new heights. But lame-duck president Herbert Hoover lacked power and imagination, and the incoming one refused to be associated with Hoover's ideas or to reveal many of his own. Neither seemed to have solutions commensurate with the desperation of ordinary people, chronicled daily in newspaper headlines and bleak photographs.

That December, eight thousand men showed up every day at the New York docks looking for work—which was unavailable because there was almost no foreign trade. Over a thousand hunger marchers threatened to occupy Cumberland, Maryland, and were held back by troops and vigilantes. When it snowed in New York, twenty thousand men came looking for a few days' work shoveling; at one site, thousands lined up for eighty-one jobs. On December 25, William Borah of Idaho, Republican dean of the U.S. Senate, declared that "this Christmas belongs to the poor, the needy. For unnumbered millions it is a season of severe privation, of deep anxiety."

Roosevelt's public pronouncements sounded the right notes. At Thanksgiving, he issued a governor's proclamation urging citizens to remember the "destitute, homeless or forgotten of their fellow men." In December he declared that the inaugural ceremonies would be simple, in keeping with the times. But most of the headlines concerned FDR's refusal to endorse the sitting president's ideas, particularly on the issue of repayment of European debt, which Hoover viewed as central to economic recovery: ROOSEVELT NONCOMMITTAL IN PARLEY; ROOSEVELT OPPOSES DEBT COMMISSION; ROOSEVELT BARS BIPARTISAN DEBT ACTION, DECLINES TO COOPERATE IN NAMING BOARD, and so on.

When Hoover and his advisers met with FDR, they came away unimpressed. Hoover himself refused to be photographed with FDR, declaring he had "too much respect for myself."

Press treatment wasn't much kinder. Arthur Krock reported in the *New York Times* in December that prominent Democratic members of Congress were worried about FDR's inaction, feeling it was "high time to begin." It was starting to look as though Walter Lippmann had been right when he described FDR during the campaign as "a pleasant man who, without any important qualifications for the office, would very much like to be president."

On February 3, FDR added fuel to the critics' fire by leaving for an eleven-day fishing trip on board the *Nourmahal,* one of the largest private yachts in the world, in the company of its owner, his friend Vincent Astor, one of the richest men in the world. The symbolism could not have been worse. For the next twelve days, FDR demonstrated his remarkable ability to pursue pleasure in the midst of a world of trouble.

Meanwhile, Eleanor and Hick were engaged in their own voyage of discovery, venturing into each other's very different New York worlds. Probably they saw a play or two together—Eleanor never missed a chance to go to the theater when she was in New York. Hick visited the Georgian mansion on 65th Street off Fifth Avenue, the Roosevelts' New York City home in the years since they married. It was, as Hick learned, a shared arrangement: two six-story town houses, one for Sara Roosevelt and one for her son and his wife, built and furnished by Sara as a gift to the newly-weds. Sliding doors connected the two, and Eleanor never knew when to expect a surprise visit from "Mama."

One night, Hick took Eleanor to one of her favorite restaurants, an Armenian place downtown. Afterward, they shared a cab. Hick got off in midtown at the AP offices, and Eleanor continued to her town house on 65th Street. But as soon as Hick arrived at the AP, the night editor shouted, "Where's Mrs. Roosevelt?"

"On her way home in a cab," Hick replied.

The editor told Hick to get up to her place in a hurry. "Some crackpot in Miami just tried to shoot her husband!"

FDR had sailed into Biscayne Bay earlier that day on the *Nourmahal* and made a brief appearance at a Miami park before traveling back to New York. He spoke for less than a minute to the small crowd, then greeted Chicago mayor Anton Cermak, who happened to be in Miami on vacation.

Giuseppe Zangara was a thirty-two-year-old unemployed bricklayer from New Jersey who had been attempting for years to assassinate some-one important: once it had been the king of Italy, later it was President Hoover. That night it was Roosevelt.

When Hick arrived at the town house, she found Eleanor sitting at the foot of her husband's bed, looking pale. "This is what it's like to be in public life, Hick," she said. Louis Howe was there too, trying to get through to Miami. Finally the phone rang. FDR himself was on the other end of the line, assuring them that he was fine, though he had a few sore ribs from being sat on by his large bodyguard, Gus Gennerich. He asked Eleanor to pass on the news to his mother.

Zangara had fired five shots. One hit the convertible, inches away from Roosevelt, several wounded bystanders, and one hit Mayor Cermak. FDR was unharmed, but he took Cermak into his car and held him and talked to him all the way to the hospital, stayed with him for two hours, and displayed the unruffled fearlessness that was a Roosevelt tradition.

Tragic as the evening was for Cermak, who ultimately died of complications from his wound, it set a new tone for the administration-in-waiting and particularly for Roosevelt himself. "To a man," wrote *Time*, "his country rose to applaud his cool courage in the face of death. He is a martyr president at the start of his term."

Eleanor had been dismayed by Franklin's decision to go sailing with his rich friend in such hard times. But now she gave him credit for courage. "That drive to the hospital must have been awfully hard on Franklin," she told Hick. "He hates the sight of blood."

AFTER THE ASSASSINATION ATTEMPT, FDR urged his wife to travel with bodyguards. But she refused, insisting, "I'm not that important." She announced that she would be taking the train that night to Ithaca, as planned, to keep a speaking engagement the next day at Cornell. She would be, the *New York Times* reported, "accompanied only by her maid." The "maid," as it turned out, was Lorena Hickok. Hick must have enjoyed the immense irony of being called the maid: she had worked as a "hired girl" for much of her adolescence, and hated every minute of it.

Yet the *Times* reporter's confusion was understandable. It was becoming increasingly unclear—to other reporters, to her bosses, and to Hick herself—what exactly her role was. She was still an AP reporter covering Eleanor Roosevelt, but it was more and more obvious to everyone that she had special status. When Eleanor held a press conference with the women who would be covering her over the next four years, Hick was not among them. Because she and Eleanor had become "very good friends," as Hick explained, she always knew Eleanor's plans in advance and met her alone before or after the meeting with the rest of the press.

"Very good friends" is an understatement: Eleanor Roosevelt and Lorena Hickok were falling in love. In the beginning, Hick had stuck close to Eleanor because she was a dogged and determined reporter. But Eleanor now *wanted* Hick by her side—always. A secret intimacy had developed between them. When they had to part, their final words to each other were "je t'aime et je t'adore."

Their loving feelings may have originated that night on the train, when Eleanor took the long narrow bed and Lorena took the wide one. Eleanor had given Hick a small part of her story then, and she already knew a little about Hick's painful childhood from Tommy. Over the next four months, as they traveled together, dined together at each other's homes, went to the theater together, they had begun to share the hidden parts of themselves—the parts they couldn't tell anyone else.

Both Eleanor and Hick had painful secrets—Hick because she was a lesbian, in a time when her kind of love was considered immoral and shameful, and Eleanor because she had to pretend she was happily married. Hick now dared to tell Eleanor about Ellie, the Minneapolis woman who had been, until she met Eleanor, the great love of her life. Eleanor listened with the tenderness that was her special gift. She in turn told Hick how unloved she felt in her marriage and how disappointed she was in the "great man" everyone else idolized. It was a reckless act on her part: Hick was, after all, a reporter still. But by this time Eleanor understood that Hick loved her too much to betray her. In their many hours together, she told Hick the story that explained, more than any other, her dread of Washington. Her return there evoked painful memories of the injury she could not forgive or forget: Franklin's affair with Lucy Mercer.

Life had improved for Eleanor during the years FDR served in the state legislature in Albany, where her mother-in-law no longer ruled the roost. When she and Franklin were apart, they exchanged affectionate letters. "I do wish you were here," Franklin wrote her from a sailing trip in the Bahamas shortly before the move to Washington. "It is hard enough to be away from the chicks, but with you away from me I feel too very much alone and lost. I hereby solemnly declare that I *refuse* to go away the next time without you. . . . I can't tell you how I long to see you again."

After Woodrow Wilson was elected in 1912, FDR was rewarded for his political support with an appointment to the position of assistant secretary of the Navy—a post previously held by his fifth cousin, Theodore Roosevelt, and eminently suited to a man who loved the sea. Eleanor packed up the family and moved to Washington.

Though she was still in her childbearing phase—FDR Jr. was born in August 1914, and John, the last child, in March 1916—Eleanor succeeded in becoming an exemplary Washington wife. On the advice of her elders—particularly Theodore Roosevelt's sister, the politically savvy Auntie Bye—she made hundreds of calls on the wives of congressmen, cabinet members, and Supreme Court justices. She was a star at diplomatic affairs, where her language skills allowed her to converse and translate. She hosted frequent dinners and impromptu lunches at the Washington house the Roosevelts inherited from Auntie Bye. The tall and willowy Eleanor, with her beautiful hair stacked high on her head, and her handsome and charming husband, Franklin, were seen as an attractive couple with a promising future in national politics.

Assisting Eleanor in her various endeavors, starting in 1914, was a young Washington belle named Lucy Mercer, a social secretary who seemed ideal for the position: she was pretty, efficient, willing to work overtime, and good at anticipating what needed to be done. She got along splendidly with the Roosevelt children as well.

But within a couple of years of the Roosevelts' arrival in Washington, evidence began to accumulate that FDR, a notorious flirt, was focusing more than casual attention on his wife's young and beautiful secretary. FDR was seen on several occasions in the company of Lucy Mercer. He even went to dinner with her at the home of Eleanor's devilish cousin, Alice Roosevelt Longworth, who was envious of her father Theodore's affection for Eleanor and liked to make trouble when she could.

For a long time, Eleanor tried to look the other way. But when FDR returned home from an official trip to Europe ill with flu, she discovered packets of love letters from Lucy Mercer in his suitcase. She could keep silent no longer.

Eleanor offered Franklin his freedom. But divorce would have been political suicide in 1918, as FDR's political mentor Louis Howe pointed out. Sara Roosevelt threatened to cut her son off altogether if he deserted his wife and children for another woman. It was, in her view, simply not done. So Eleanor and Franklin settled on the alternative. FDR promised never to see Lucy Mercer again, and he and Eleanor agreed to live amicably, if not passionately, side by side.

Eleanor never fully recovered from this betrayal. She held on to her resentment for the rest of Franklin's life. Her growing confidence suffered a severe setback. There would be other flirtations and affairs—even after FDR was struck with polio—but none wounded her in the way that first one did.

Coming back to Washington, fifteen years later, brought back that most painful of memories. It may also have aroused the suspicion, which proved to be justified, that Franklin would attempt to see Lucy again, despite their agreement and despite Lucy's marriage to Winthrop Rutherfurd, a wealthy older man.

Hick, whose emotions were always close to the surface, listened to this story with indignation. Conventional marriage, happy or unhappy, had never been an option for her—though she once wondered, in a letter to Eleanor, whether her life might have been easier if she had been capable of it.

But during her years at the *Minneapolis Tribune*, Hick had been as good as married, to Ella Morse, the woman she called "Ellie" and who called her, in return, "Hickey Doodles." Ellie was tiny, with a soft voice, gray-blue eyes, and a shy manner. She had a passion for great literature and a gift for friendship. She also had a defective heart, but that didn't seem to affect her love of a good time. "Friends," Hick explained, "were as necessary to her as the oxygen that pumped the blood through her labored, valiant heart."

Ellie's father, a wheat and real estate baron, provided his daughter and her special friend Hick with an apartment at the modern Hotel Leamington in Minneapolis. It was the first time in Hick's life that she could claim to have a happy home. Ellie learned to cook to please Hick. The couple adopted a stray cat and named him François Villon, after the fifteenth-century poet, thief, and vagabond. Hick could be found polishing the Morse family's heavy silver as Ellie read Shakespeare aloud. Ellie, who attended Smith, loved Charles Dickens, and was inclined to quote passages from *Alice in Wonderland*. She and Hick, also an autodidact, gave parties together to celebrate Dickens's birthday.

After Ellie received her inheritance and Hick was diagnosed with diabetes, they decided to move to California together. The climate might be healthier there, and Hick could perhaps turn herself into a novelist. What happened instead was that Ellie fulfilled her own lifetime ambition of finding a husband. She left Hick, after eight years, to marry a high school friend. Hick was devastated.

It would have been too painful to return to Minneapolis, with all its happy memories, though Hick surely could have gotten her job back at the *Minneapolis Tribune*. Instead, she took the train across the country to New York City, where she went to work for the *New York Daily Mirror*, a tabloid owned by the notorious William Randolph Hearst. It was 1928, and Al Smith was running for president on the Democratic ticket. Hearst's editors, willing to do anything to defeat Smith, hit upon (or created) the story of the kidnapping of a Smith College student named Frances St. John Smith. The kidnapping had nothing to do with Al Smith's presidential campaign. But it generated the desired headlines: SMITH TERROR, SMITH HIJINKS, SMITH SCANDAL. Hick was sent to Smith College to look for stories that could generate more Smith headlines. Fortunately, she was soon able to move on from the *Mirror* to the Associated Press, a trusted national reporting service for member papers all over the country. In the beginning, her boss at the AP referred to her as "that girl" and sent her off to cover the unexciting deliberations of the Democratic National Committee. But over the next three years, she worked her way up to important assignments, including the genuinely sensational kidnapping of the baby of aviator Charles Lindbergh.

Hick's success as a journalist didn't carry over into her personal life. She had other brief affairs after the breakup with Ellie. But there were times when, in her loneliness, she misjudged the situation, as happened with fellow journalist Katherine Beebe. The two women were both working at the AP at the time, sharing a room as they covered the Lindbergh kidnapping. Hick was ill and Beebe took care of her. Then, to Beebe's surprise, Hick "made for me."

"It knocked me off my base," Beebe remembered. When Hick realized her mistake, she apologized. "You were just so sweet to me that it undid me," she explained. She went on to talk about her "tendency."

Beebe confessed she didn't know "what women do."

Hick answered, "No, and you don't want to know."

They remained friends but "never another word was said about it."

Hick maintained friendships with a wide array of journalists, theater people, and politicians from various phases of her life. But after Ellie, she lived most of the time alone, except for Prinz. One year, she sent her friends a Christmas card with a perky drawing of a young Prinz, with one ear cocked, above the greeting "A Very Merry Christmas to You and Yours from Me and Mine." Now she was in love once more, with the woman who was about to become First Lady.

FOR THE MOST PART, FDR felt the same way about Hick that he did about Eleanor's other women friends. As long as the press and public didn't notice anything irregular—and it is remarkable that they almost never did—he was happy to have Eleanor go about her own separate life, just as he went about his. He also appreciated Hick's coverage, which depicted his wife as charmingly, rather than shockingly, unconventional.

In December 1932, when she took the 3:18 a.m. train from Albany to New York City to greet her son Elliott's new baby, Mrs. Roosevelt had to borrow pocket money from the Secret Service man. In January, when she traveled to Washington to visit Mrs. Hoover, she turned down a limousine in order to walk over from the Mayflower Hotel to the White House. In February, Mrs. Roosevelt chose her wardrobe for the inauguration in one afternoon—everything in blue for mixing and matching, and removable sleeves to allow one dress to be used on more than one occasion.

Someone decided to call the shade she chose "Eleanor blue," in a nod to the tradition of First Ladies as fashion trendsetters.

FDR found nothing to object to in any of this coverage. But on February 13, a story appeared that enraged him: WIFE OF NEXT PRESIDENT TO DRIVE ALONE TO CAPITAL read the headline. "Accompanied by her two dogs, Mrs. Franklin Roosevelt plans on March 3 to drive her own car, a roadster, to Washington, where the next day she will begin her career in the White House." Mrs. Roosevelt explained that someone would have to take the dogs—a Scottish terrier named Meggie and a police dog named Major. She liked to drive, and it gave her a chance to get away. "These first few weeks in Washington are going to be strenuous," she pointed out. What she didn't say in the article, authored of course by Hick, was that Hick was going to be at her side.

FDR strenuously objected. It was the only time, Roosevelt adviser Raymond Moley said, that he heard FDR complain about his wife's independence. It was a matter of appearances: he wanted the entire family to travel together to Washington, on the train. Eleanor acceded to his wishes. In typical Roosevelt style, the train party numbered in the dozens: the whole family, of course, including mother Sara, as well as FDR's cabinet designates, political advisers, and close friends. Eleanor also brought her retinue: Hick came along and watched over the dogs, as did Nan Cook, Marion Dickerman, Earl Miller, and several others.

But as soon as the Roosevelt party arrived at Union Station, Eleanor returned to her previous plan—to be alone with Hick as she faced the ordeal of her return. Before they separated at the train station in Washington, Eleanor made sure Hick would come to the side entrance of the Mayflower Hotel early the next morning. She wanted to take her along on a pilgrimage "to something that used to mean a very great deal to me when we were in Washington before."

As soon as Hick's cab pulled up the next morning, Eleanor slipped quickly out the door of the Mayflower and told the driver to go to Rock Creek Cemetery, directing him, when they arrived, through a maze of narrow roads to a semicircle of small shrubs surrounding a hexagonal plot.

She led the way to a stone bench facing a towering bronze figure, so heavily shrouded that its face was almost hidden in darkness.

After a long silence, Eleanor said, "In the old days, when we lived here, I was much younger and not so very wise. Sometimes I'd be very unhappy and sorry for myself. When I was feeling that way, if I could manage it, I'd come out here, alone, and sit and look at that woman. And I'd always come away somehow feeling better. And stronger. I've been here many, many times."

The spectral figure was created as a memorial to Henry Adams's wife, Clover, who committed suicide in a particularly terrible way, by ingesting the chemicals she otherwise used in her work as a photographer. The sculptor, Augustus Saint-Gaudens, called the work *The Mystery of the Hereafter and the Peace of God That Passeth Understanding*, but it is more often referred to as *Grief*. Eleanor had visited the statue alone in the past, obeying her grandmother's dictum that strong emotions should only be expressed in private. Bringing Hick along to see the statue was an act of great trust and affection.

Saint-Gaudens used both men and women as models for the sculpture, and the stoic face, with its cast-down eyes, transcends gender. "All the sorrow humanity had ever had to endure was expressed in that face," Hick wrote afterward. "I could almost feel the hot, stinging unshed tears behind the lowered eyelids."

Later that day, back at her hotel, Hick got another call from Eleanor. Franklin was tied up, she told Hick, working with James on the final draft of his acceptance speech. "The other children are all out, and I'm alone. Would you mind coming over and dining with me?"

At the Mayflower, Hick made her way through a lobby swarming with reporters eager for small bits of information. But she was no longer part of the melee. The Secret Service men were expecting her, and showed her to a special elevator that whisked her up to the Presidential Suite. Neither Eleanor nor Hick had much appetite for dinner that night, knowing as they did that the fate of the nation depended on Franklin Roosevelt, who was working on his speech in the sitting room next door.

In recent days, the financial crisis had gotten still worse. The wealthy feared that FDR would ruin them, and were fleeing the market. Everyone else hoped the new president would rescue them from financial ruin. Days before the inauguration, banks closed in waves—first in Ohio, then New Jersey, Arkansas, and Maryland. Late that night, as FDR honed the draft of his speech, governors in New York and Illinois decided to close down their banking systems. By the next day, thirty-four out of forty-eight states had shut down their banks. People couldn't buy milk or bread or gasoline. Cars were abandoned, out of gas, in the middle of the road. Riots seemed imminent in several cities. Everything now depended on FDR's ability to calm a situation bordering on mass hysteria.

Late in the evening, FDR sent the final draft of his speech next door to his wife. Eleanor read it aloud to Hick. Eleanor thought it "a good speech, a courageous speech." As Hick listened to the now-famous words "the only thing we have to fear is fear itself," it occurred to her that she was right in the middle of what, that night, was the biggest story in the world. She could have slipped out to the telephone and given the AP the essence of it, with a few choice quotations. If she had, it would have been the biggest scoop of her career. But she didn't slip out. Instead, she slipped off her dress and shoes and put on the dressing gown Eleanor handed her. By the time Eleanor returned from saying good night to her husband, Hick was asleep in the bedroom of her friend, who had become more important to her than any scoop.

The next day, Hick became the first reporter to interview a First Lady at the White House on Inauguration Day—a rare opportunity that infuriated the Washington press corps. But Hick didn't feel at all triumphant: in fact, she reverted in her story to an old, self-mocking persona she had assumed in her cub reporter days. An usher appeared and told her that Mrs. Roosevelt wanted to meet with her in the sitting room. "Stepping out of the elevator, I slipped on the waxed floor, turned an ankle, and nearly fell. . . . Limping, but on tiptoe, I followed the usher." Hick never managed to describe much beyond her awe and discomfort at being in the White House, in the presence of the president and First Lady at a historic

JE T'AIME ET JE T'ADORE

moment. The story is long and overinflated—completely unlike Hick's earlier writing about Eleanor.

Years later, Hick would claim that she "ceased to be a reporter" on inauguration eve, when she heard FDR's entire speech and didn't do a thing about it. But in fact, her reporter role had begun to erode months before, fading as her affection for Eleanor Roosevelt grew. She continued to work for the AP for another three and a half months, covering the tax-fraud trial of banker Charles E. Mitchell, because she understood it better than anyone else at the bureau. Occasionally she wrote a light feature piece about the First Lady.

Increasingly, however, her name appeared in the body of the stories rather than in the byline. She was "Miss Lorena Hickok of New York," accompanying Eleanor Roosevelt as "a friend" or "a companion." In June, she resigned from the AP. On July 26, she was identified in one story as "Miss Lorena Hickok, a former New York newspaperwoman."

It had taken Hick seventeen years to move from the society pages of the *Milwaukee Sentinel* to a top spot in the New York offices of the Associated Press, where she had "achieved standing . . . that no other woman had matched." It was slowly dawning on her, and on Eleanor too, that all of that was now in jeopardy.

Late Monday night, after Hick had left for New York following the inauguration, Eleanor sat down to write her a letter: "Hick, my dearest," it began, "I cannot go to bed tonight without a word to you . . . you have grown so much to be a part of my life that it is empty without you even though I'm busy every minute."

The letter ended, "O! darling, I hope on the whole you will be happier for my friendship. I felt I had brought you so much discomfort and hardship today and almost more heartache than you could bear and I don't want to make you unhappy. All my love and I shall be saying to you over thought waves in a few minutes—

"Good night my dear one
Angels guard thee

[47]

God protect thee
My love enfold thee
All the night through."

The letter, the first of thousands that Eleanor and Hick would exchange over a lifetime, was dated March 5, 1933. Two days later, Hick would turn forty. Her old life as a newspaper reporter was over. As of that moment, she had no idea how she would live her new one. But she knew she wanted to live it with Eleanor Roosevelt.

CHAPTER FOUR

LORENA

IN 1907, WHEN LORENA HICKOK was fourteen, she went to work in a bindery in the little town of Bowdle, South Dakota. The job lasted only a few days, because she couldn't master the machine. But the forelady, trying to teach her how to use it, addressed her as "my dear." Those words worked their magic on the motherless Lorena. "I can still feel the warm glow that suffused my lonely, adolescent heart," she remembered years later. "But at quitting time she fired me!"

Hick told this story in her autobiography to illustrate that she learned early in life "never to expect love or affection from anyone." But the truth was that she never ceased to melt when she was treated kindly. Despite many rejections, and the cruelty she experienced through much of her childhood, she hung on to the hope of a different future.

Never once did her father beat her, Hick remembered, "when I didn't mutter, inaudibly behind my gritted teeth: 'You wouldn't dare do this to me if I were as big as you are.'" By the time she was fifteen, Lorena had vowed that she was "not always going to be an underdog." In 1932, as a respected national reporter, Hick was no longer an underdog—in fact, she was closer to being a top dog. But Eleanor's affection touched a longing even more powerful than her determination to succeed in her career.

Alice Lorena Hickok was born on March 7, 1893, in the little town of

East Troy, Wisconsin. Her mother, Anna Waite, was already thirty-seven when she married Addison Hickok, a buttermaker in rich dairy country. Anna's family had a thriving farm, and she herself was not without resources: she was working as a seamstress at the time. The family disapproved of the marriage from the start—a fact that no doubt stiffened Anna's resolve to make it work.

Hick's happiest memories were of life on the farm, and especially of farm animals. "I cannot remember when I decided that I liked animals better than people," she wrote years later, "but all my life I have felt more at ease with them." She put her doll in the pig trough so it could eat along with the piglets, and she spent time trying to figure out what the hens were saying to each other in the chicken coop. "That animals could and did talk among themselves I had not the slightest doubt. It never even occurred to me that they couldn't." She sensed that animals' judgment was "based on something deeper than what you look like, how you are dressed or how you rate with your fellow humans."

When Lorena was eight, the family left farm life behind, and her father began a desperate odyssey, trying and failing at one job after another in the small prairie towns of northeastern South Dakota. Lorena's childhood became "a confusing, kaleidoscopic series of strange neighborhoods, different schools, new teachers to get acquainted with, playmates whom I never got to know very well."

South Dakota had its own kind of treeless beauty. The ceaseless wind created great snowbanks during the harsh winters and rippled the wheat in summer. The vast open plain, stretching to the horizon in all directions, made everything seem possible. Hick would fondly remember the glorious sunsets of South Dakota all her life. But the little towns were dreary places, by-products of Milwaukee's railroad drive westward. Most consisted of one main street of single-story wood houses, no more than a few blocks long, with saloons that rowdy cowboys came to on Saturday night to get drunk. Shooting stray cats was a favorite pastime of the locals.

The wheat farmers, German-speaking refugees from Russian lands, were a tamer lot than the cowboys. Hick and her friends were fascinated by the "Russian" women, who would sit along the edge of the board side-walk and nurse their babies. But her mother, and the other settlers from "back East," strongly disapproved of such unrefined behavior.

Hick described her father as "the most undisciplined person I ever knew"—a mild way of characterizing a man who seemed to go through life in a permanent rage. "He was always losing his temper and whipping horses, beating us children—especially me—getting into fights with his employers and losing his job." One of her early memories was of her father thrusting the tips of her fingers into her mouth and making her bite them, "holding my jaws together with his big, strong hands, until the tears rolled down my cheeks," supposedly to cure her of biting her nails.

Another time, her mother took her into the bedroom and held her on her lap, weeping. "From without came whistling, crackling sounds and yelps of pain from my puppy." Hick's puppy Mayno had been chasing wag-ons, and her father was beating him with a horsewhip. It was the first time Hick remembered being angry herself. When she and her two younger sisters dawdled one morning with a new kitten, their father took the kitten and dashed its brains out by throwing it against the barn, where they would pass the remains on the way to school. Later that day, Lorena re-turned to bury it in a shallow grave.

Lorena's mother wept a great deal, but didn't seem able to stand up to her husband. Once, after he beat Lorena with the stave from a butter keg, leaving black-and-blue marks all over her back and legs, she heard her mother objecting. Another time, when he knocked her down, her mother asked, "Do you mean to kill the child?" But Hick learned early on "not to look to my mother for protection from my father."

Reading became young Lorena's salvation. She loved strong heroes like Jesse James. Ben Hur "thundered triumphantly into the world of my imagination, followed rapidly by an assortment of strange, colorful, and incongruous characters." Once, she got to see a performance of *Uncle Tom's Cabin*. "I got so excited when Little Eva, a child about my own age, with long, golden curls, went up to heaven in her little white nightie . . . all the slaves moaning in the background, that I became ill and had to be dragged out to the washroom." Lorena's lifelong passion for the theater may have been born that night.

Music was a companion from early on. "Ever since I can remember," Hick wrote in her unpublished autobiography, "through almost every waking hour, music has run through me, somewhere in the back of my throat." Unfortunately, Lorena's contralto voice, which seemed made for church solos, was the source of one of her worst conflicts with her father as she approached adolescence. Tall for her age, and convinced she was "hopelessly ugly," she hated to perform in public. Her stubbornness about performing infuriated her father. He gave her one of his worst whippings because she refused to sing a solo one evening in church.

Life was especially hard for Hick's mother in the dusty little towns along the rail line in South Dakota, so far from the green dairy country of her Wisconsin past. Hick remembers one excursion with her mother to what was supposed to be a lake but turned out to be "a mud hole filled with rushes and surrounded by a grove of dusty cottonwoods." Hick's mother sat in the surrey, the reins in her hands, and "cried as though her heart were breaking."

The family's situation grew even worse when they arrived in the little town of Bowdle, "the dustiest and dreariest of the Dakota towns my mother was to know." Progress in Bowdle, as measured by the *Bowdle Pioneer*, consisted of churches outnumbering saloons, four to three. There was one cement sidewalk crossing muddy Main Street, a street sometimes filled with herds of steers driven into town to board railroad cars and travel east to market.

Hick was thirteen when her mother died in Bowdle of a stroke. "A very sad death occurred at 1 o'clock A.M. Sunday," the *Bowdle Pioneer* reported, "taking from the home—a mother—and what could be more sad than to leave a husband with three young girls in the home." The sentiments were especially true in this case: Lorena's two younger sisters, Ruby and Myrtle, were swiftly sent off to live with relatives, and before long Lorena found herself unwelcome in her father's house. The housekeeper who took over from her mother soon became Addison Hickok's second wife. Within the year, she informed Lorena that she had better find another place to live—and quickly.

Fortunately for the fourteen-year-old Lorena, she had formed a close friendship with a schoolmate, Lottie McCafferty, who found her a job working in the house of a kind Irish couple with two young children. That was one of the better jobs. After that, young Lorena worked in a mice-infested boardinghouse in nearby Aberdeen and in a run-down rooming house where railroad workers stayed at the edge of town. At the rooming house, she put a chair against the door to keep out male intruders. After that, she worked in an unhappy home she called "the house of discord" and in a farm kitchen, where she had to rise before dawn and work frantically to feed the threshers.

As she rode the train back to Bowdle after leaving the job on the farm, a chance encounter changed Lorena's life. As she was about to enter the coach, she saw her father. She slipped into the next car, hoping to avoid him, but he had spotted her. He followed her and sat down in the seat beside her. He was wearing his "town clothes" and his brown derby—part of an attempt to further himself in the world—but he looked ill at ease in them. He started in on Lorena, berating her for being an "ungrateful daughter." But Lorena noticed, as he continued his tirade, a subtle change in his attitude toward her; there had been a shift in the balance of power between them. "I felt . . . a new and wonderful exhilaration. That change in his attitude gave tacit recognition that I was no longer a child, to be cuffed about and beaten. He would never strike me again. I was grown up!"

Lorena got off the train at Bowdle. Her father remained on board. She was fifteen years old, and she never saw him again.

There were a few bright spots in Lorena's hard young life. One was her friendship with her Bowdle schoolmate Lottie, with whom she corresponded for the rest of her life. Another was a first crush on the daughter of the owner of the Aberdeen Hotel, an elegant oasis of dark carved wood and carpeted floors on a Main Street of shoot-'em-up saloons. The girl's name was Elizabeth Ward. Elizabeth's hair ribbons were "great, crisp silken butterflies that matched her dresses.

"Her dresses fitted her, they were new and clean, and she had so many—a different dress for each school day! I used to stare at her for long minutes when I thought she wasn't looking, and she was the first living person ever to become an inmate of the world into which I retired with my imagination." By that time, Lorena's own appearance was "exceedingly shabby." Her hands were red and chapped, her hair unkempt, and she remembers "stuffing wads of paper into the soles of my shoes that winter because the snow and pebbles hurt my feet." Her school attendance depended entirely on the demands of her work at various jobs.

Fortunately, an unlikely trio of kind women, along with one wise male teacher, came along at crucial moments and saved her from spending her entire life as a maid in other people's houses, lacking even a high school education. Perhaps it was her touching hunger for affection that made them want to help. When caring adults intervened, she responded—wholeheartedly.

The first to help her was a Mrs. Dodd, a friend of Lottie's family who was looking for household help. Mrs. Dodd "lived in the cleanest house I had seen since my mother died." It wasn't just the house, though. "I can close my eyes now," Hick wrote some forty years later, "and still experience the wonderful feeling of serenity that came over me as I walked into it for the first time."

Mrs. Dodd, a grandmother raising a child, was "one of the gentlest, most patient women I have ever known." She went to work on Lorena's appearance. "My resentment simply melted away under her warm, soothing personality." Mrs. Dodd gave Lorena scented soap for her bath and "a can of cool clean smelling talcum powder." She taught her how to shampoo her hair and care for her hands. Mrs. Dodd also instructed her on how to do housework more efficiently, and "even praised me when I did things right."

It may have been Mrs. Dodd's influence that made Lorena decide she needed go back to school. She returned to Bowdle from Gettysburg, the small town where Mrs. Dodd lived, reenrolled in ninth grade, and took a job—not for wages but for room and board. The school in Bowdle consisted of a principal and two teachers, instructing all the children of the town in one lone frame building surrounded by a bare playground. But the principal, a "tall homely Scandinavian" who was "the most unappreciated man in town," saw something in Lorena. "It was he who first began to cultivate in me a taste for good literature and good music." After she wrote an insulting verse about him—"His eyes are green, his hair is white, / His nose is crooked, he's a fright"—he responded by making her the class poet, "remarking drily that I seemed to have an aptitude for verse."

Lorena lived with a couple who were the "upper crust" of Bowdle and expected the hired girl to contribute to keeping a perfect house. "Every waking minute outside of school hours," Lorena remembered, "belonged to Mrs. Bickert." In the morning, work kept her so long that she had to run to school. In the evening, she helped with laundry and carried coal to heat the range. There was no time for schoolwork.

The final straw came when Lorena was chosen to represent Bowdle High School in a declamatory contest. When a rehearsal made her late coming home, Mrs. Bickert delivered "one of the worst tirades I had ever been forced to listen to" and announced that Lorena was to scrub the kitchen and pantry the next morning, no matter how late she was for school. "I carried out her orders the following morning, missed a half day of school, and quit, after actually finding the courage and the words to talk back to Mrs. Bickert."

In desperation, Lorena went to see Mrs. Tom O'Malley, a woman "held in low esteem by the good women of Bowdle." A seventy-year-old whose husband had run a local saloon, she dressed in outrageous costumes, wore a wig, painted her face, and sometimes drank herself into a stupor. She was, Lorena wrote fondly, "an elderly and somewhat frayed bird of paradise stalking defiantly about a barnyard populated by little brown hens."

Lorena had a soft spot for Mrs. O'Malley, who had stopped her one day on the street shortly after her mother died and talked to her gently and sympathetically. Now it was Mrs. O'Malley who took her in.

In her sober moments, Mrs. O'Malley devoted herself to several projects. One was hunting around the barn for a cache of money she suspected

Mr. O'Malley had hidden from her. The two women—one young, one old—spent hours out there, going through old boxes of letters and finery and talking about Mrs. O'Malley's colorful past.

The other project was Lorena's future. Mrs. O'Malley decided the sixteen-year-old should get married. Bowdle in those days was full of young men working on the railroad, and Mrs. O'Malley zeroed in on one of them and invited him to dinner. That led to a date. Lorena, arrayed in one of Mrs. O'Malley's "lacy confections," went with the young man to the movie and the drugstore for ice cream. When a prolonged whistle sounded, calling the railroad workers to an emergency somewhere along the line, she went down to the station to see him off. As he was about to leave, Lorena's date grabbed her and kissed her. Lorena responded by slapping him with all her might. At that point Mrs. O'Malley gave up on matchmaking. But she didn't give up on helping Lorena find her way.

It is a tribute to Lorena's intelligence that she scored well on a test that would have allowed her to teach in a country school, despite her spotty education. She was sixteen, but could pass for the required age of eighteen. She might have gotten the job, but an older girl came along and edged her out. Undaunted, Mrs. O'Malley began quizzing Lorena about her mother's relatives: wasn't there someone, she wanted to know, who could take Lorena under her wing? There was: the "tiny, dainty and lame" woman Lorena called Aunt Ella. Aunt Ella, who was actually her mother's cousin, was "the first human being I ever loved. . . . She never scolded, and I could talk to her, confident and relaxed. She seemed to understand me, to be interested in what I was saying. . . . I thought she was the most beautiful woman in the world."

Aunt Ella and Uncle Sam lived in Chicago, in very comfortable circumstances, and had tried to keep in touch with Lorena after her mother's death. But young Lorena had "a horror of family authority, of being bossed. . . . I never answered her letters."

Finally, Mrs. O'Malley managed to worm Aunt Ella's address out of Lorena and write her a letter. A letter came back immediately, enclosing a check for Lorena's train fare to Chicago. Mrs. O'Malley plunged enthusiastically into the task of dressing Lorena Hickok for her great adventure.

On a hot August day in 1909, Lorena boarded the train dressed in a new blue suit and "one of the strangest hats ever turned out by Mrs. O'Malley," on her way to another world. It was dusk in the busy Chicago station when the sixteen-year-old, "solemn and tongue-tied," emerged from the train, wearing a now-rumpled blue suit. A tiny woman in an immaculate gray ensemble limped forward to greet her.

"The hands she held out in greeting," Hick remembered, "were encased in spotless chamois gloves. It was the first time I had ever seen a pair of real chamois gloves."

AUNT ELLA WATCHED OVER Lorena all through high school and college. She first sent her to live with another aunt, in Battle Creek, Michigan, where she finished high school in three years. Then, with Aunt Ella's support, Lorena tried twice to attend Lawrence College in Appleton, Wisconsin, first for a year and then, a second time, for a semester. She was a very bright girl, the president of Lawrence assured Aunt Ella, but there were gaps in her record—it was "simply a question of . . . developing habits of regularity and faithfulness." He must have offered a more detailed explanation, however, because Aunt Ella sent "Rena" a gentle reprimand. "Now my dear girlie you know my faith in you, I do sincerely believe that next year you will rank among the very best in college. . . . Please try *very, very* hard to overcome getting angry that is the cause of many diseases." Later, Lorena told friends that she had been deeply hurt and angry when no sorority invited her to join. She summarized her experience in her autobiography: "discover I'm complete misfit there and give up."

In 1912, at age nineteen, Hick began working as a cub reporter at the *Battle Creek Journal*, covering the visits of celebrities to the sanitariums of Kellogg and Post. It may have been the example of Edna Ferber, whose novels were just beginning to attract attention, that led Lorena, at twenty-one, to look for newspaper work in Milwaukee. Ferber had also attended Lawrence, then honed her skills at the *Milwaukee Journal*, writing stories of everyday life that later made their way into her novels. Now Lorena began to do the same thing.

Defiantly, she took the pen name "Lorena Lawrence," derived from the place where she had felt unwelcome, and began to write funny feature stories with herself in the lovable misfit role. Lorena Lawrence got one of her first bylines for a story about a dark and handsome musical impresario from Spain who announced that he was looking for a wife. "Girls!" the headline shouted. "Here's Your Chance to Get a Husband!"

"I won't do," the young Lorena wrote. She went on to catalog her faults: too tall, ten pounds overweight, and "too radical a suffragist." But according to the story, the handsome genius from Barcelona liked Lorena's blue eyes—one of his requirements—and warmed to her when he discovered her musical tastes.

In real life, of course, Lorena Hickok preferred women to men. But Lorena in her reporter role pretended to be smitten but magnanimous: "Being a big hearted, unselfish woman," she wrote, "I am willing to give other Milwaukee girls a chance."

The story about the eligible Spaniard was followed by another, about an attempt to interview the celebrated soprano Geraldine Farrar. After a muddy slog through a trainyard, she succeeded only in meeting Farrar's dog Wiggles and ruining her best suit.

Some stories were more poignant than humorous. Dame Nellie Melba's rendering of "Songs My Mother Taught Me" reminded her of her own mother. She wrote, "I would die for Melba—big-souled, warm hearted Melba—Melba who kissed me!" The admiring story she wrote about another diva, Ernestine Schumann-Heink, resulted in the gift of Schumann-Heink's ring and a lifelong friendship.

Lorena Hickok was twenty-five, and still trying to get a college degree, when she moved to Minneapolis. During the day, she was a student at the University of Minnesota, making her way from class to class as Alice L. Hickok. At night, she worked as a reporter for the *Minneapolis Tribune*,

interviewing the university president about the alarming spread of Spanish flu on campus. It wasn't long until the student, Alice L. Hickok, left
college behind and became Lorena Hickok, a full-time and prolific reporter who finally began to put her preferred name on her stories.

At the *Tribune*, Lorena found a home. She became "Hick," a favorite of
editor Charlie Dillon, who was fondly addressed by everyone as the "Old
Man," or OM. She was a regular at the various haunts on Newspaper Row,
a cross section of newspapers, bars, and theaters that drew a rich collection
of Minneapolis newspaper people, artists performing at the Metropolitan,
and sports enthusiasts who gathered to watch for scores of Minnesota
football games announced on a banner reeled out over 4th Street. Hick
partook of it all, and wrote about it all. She never went back to college.

There were a whole series of stories written in the "girl reporter" mode,
as she tried, awkwardly and disastrously, to play golf, box, and understand
those mysterious male games of baseball and football. Some of the stories
came with comic illustrations of Hick, looking fatter than she actually
was. There was a hilarious piece in which Hick spelled the department
store Santa and got stuck in the display chimney. "Santa, who has been
overworking of late and going without a good many breakfasts and lunches
on account of the Christmas rush, has to wear a pillow stuffed in front. I
didn't."

Tucked in among the frivolous features were stories in which Hick
showed her empathy for outcasts of every kind. She wrote touchingly of
the humiliating life of midgets: a thirty-two-year-old told of having a
young woman pick him up at a water fountain and ask, "Does him want
a dink of water?" A diminutive married woman described waking up on a
train ride and finding herself being cuddled in the arms of a strange man
who thought she was a lost child.

Another time, Hick wrote with "a lump in my throat" about a fifteen-
year-old girl who had run away from sexual abuse at home. "I guess I've
gone through too much to be afraid of anything," the girl told Hick from
her cell in the city jail.

"What sort of things do you mean?" Hick asked.

"Out of her wise blue eyes," Hick wrote, "she gave me a knowing look."

Hick wrote of a World War I veteran, desperate for work, who showed up at an interview with a bulge in his overcoat. The bulge turned out to be a very young baby. His wife was dead, he explained, and he had no place to leave the infant.

Toward the end of her nine-year tenure at the *Tribune*, Hick's career took a surprising turn. After being the "girl reporter" who didn't know a thing about sports and who called football practice a "rehearsal," she suddenly began writing colorful and savvy pieces about the University of Minnesota Gophers and their chances against their Big Ten rivals. "We dispatched . . . the Invincible Illini," she writes, "trailing their proud banner in the dust." And in a report from Ann Arbor, Michigan, before the all-important game against the Wolverines: "Even here in enemy country tonight they say the chances are even." Among fans and players, she acquired the nickname "Auntie Gopher."

It was going to require another transformation for Hick, the over-the-top sportswriter, to become a sober national reporter for the Associated Press, covering big stories like corruption in Tammany Hall, the Lindbergh baby kidnapping, the decline and fall of New York mayor Jimmy Walker, and the rise of a promising new politician, Franklin Delano Roosevelt, to the New York governorship. But Hick, on the comeback in 1928 after her breakup with Ellie, badly needed a professional success after the disappointment she had experienced in California. Just as she had taught herself to write long pieces that touched her readers' hearts, she now mastered the kinds of short, fact-laden dispatches required by the AP. Yet even there, she excelled at finding the human angle: when the steamship *Vestris* sank in 1928, killing more than one hundred passengers, Hick was the first to get to the lifeboats carrying survivors as they arrived in New York. She managed to snag a great storyteller who gave her a minute-by-minute account of his ordeal. "I guess there's just one more thing," Paul A. Dana told Hick as he concluded his account. "About two minutes after we were hoisted aboard the American Shipper [which rescued survivors], a dead body floated alongside. And two sharks." Hick's piece ran above the fold in the *New York Times*.

Hick's ability to get the *real* story served her well once again when she was assigned to cover Eleanor Roosevelt. But then, paradoxically, that same ability began to get her in trouble with her bosses. As she and Eleanor grew closer and closer, she began to know too much. It hobbled her at every turn. Eleanor had told her, for instance, of the havoc alcohol had wreaked in her immediate family. Her father and two of her uncles destroyed themselves with drink, and her brother was well on his way to doing the same. It was the reason, she explained to Hick, that she couldn't even bear the smell of alcohol. It was the reason she had been until recently a strong supporter of Prohibition.

But other reporters, not knowing this, completely misinterpreted a comment Eleanor made about Prohibition on the campaign trail. Eleanor noted that the law was so widely disregarded as to be a joke, adding that "nowadays a girl who goes out with a boy needs to know how to handle her gin." It was an attempt to sound nonchalant about something she didn't feel at all nonchalant about.

Eleanor was roundly criticized in the press for having a cavalier attitude toward drinking. Hick's bosses criticized her, in turn, for not writing a follow-up story about the comment. They even docked her pay. "I've been in a devil of a mess here," Hick confided to fellow reporter Bess Furman, "over getting beaten on a story. . . . Trouble with this outfit is that they're spoiled. Think they have to have a beat on every story."

Bess Furman and her fellow reporters knew by that time that Hick was leaving the AP because she was in love with Eleanor Roosevelt. "Well, it won't be long now," Hick wrote Bess, "before she'll be yours to worry about, not mine."

CHAPTER FIVE

ELEANOR

WHEN SHE WAS YOUNG, Eleanor always listened for the door to open when her father arrived home, then slid down two flights of banisters into his waiting arms. "With my father," she remembered, "I was perfectly happy." She remembered dancing with him, "intoxicated by the pure joy of motion, twirling round and round until he would pick me up and throw me into the air and tell me I made him dizzy!"

Elliott Roosevelt adored his "pretty, companionable little daughter." He called her "Little Nell"—a nickname that Eleanor believed he took from Dickens's *The Old Curiosity Shop*. But Elliott Roosevelt himself was called "Nell" within the family, so his Little Nell also shared her father's name.

When her father was away, Eleanor daydreamed about him and awaited his return. She worked hard to live up to his expectations—practicing riding with the pony he sent, and trying, because she knew it would please him, to get along with Mademoiselle, the French governess she despised. She remembered for the rest of her life the times she disappointed him. Once, in Italy, when they were riding donkeys down a steep path, she became frightened and refused to follow him. She never forgot his reproach. In the Roosevelt family, lack of courage was a badge of shame.

When he was young, Elliott Roosevelt had sometimes outshone his older brother, Theodore, in the ongoing athletic competition that characterized family life at Sagamore Hill. But as they grew older, the brothers' paths diverged. Theodore left for Harvard and embarked on a career in politics. Elliott, always seen in the family as the sweeter and gentler brother, began to have fainting spells and proved unable to compete academically. His father sent him off to ride and hunt on the Texas range. After that, he continued a life of adventure by hunting big game all around the world. When he returned home, he took up polo and began spending his time in New York Society—spelled, as Eleanor noted in her memoir, with a capital S. Alice Hall, who could trace her lineage to signers of the Declaration of Independence, was one of the most beautiful women in her social set: the poet Robert Browning asked to simply gaze upon her when she was having her portrait painted. She and Elliott married in 1883; within a year, she gave birth to their first child, a daughter named Anna Eleanor.

Eleanor's mother came to consider her daughter a disappointment, since she had neither the beauty nor the personality to succeed in Society. "She is such a funny child," her mother said in her presence, "so old-fashioned, that we always call her 'Granny.'" It was a comment that made Eleanor want to "sink through the floor in shame." Her mother's disapproval made Eleanor long for her father's loving arms.

But the father she adored was rarely present. Due to his alcoholism and erratic behavior, he was forbidden by family fiat from living at home during much of Eleanor's childhood. In his absence, her loyalty to him only intensified. She knew nothing until much later of the other women in his life, and of the family's alarm about the possibility of scandal when his mistress bore a child. Eleanor even refused for some time to believe that her father was an alcoholic. Even when she edited and published his letters, around the time she became First Lady, she claimed that his illnesses, and the pain from a polo injury, had led him to drink.

Hunting Big Game in the Eighties: The Letters of Elliott Roosevelt, Sportsman was Eleanor Roosevelt's attempt to rehabilitate the man she loved so much. Elliott's tender side does come out in the letters to his Little Nell. But there is cruelty as well in his description of his adventures with other children during his exile in Virginia, riding over the broad fields at sunrise with horses, ponies, and fox terriers. "We rarely fail to secure some kind of game, and never return without roses in the cheeks of those I call now, my children." He added, "Do you continue to ride? Learn the right way so I will not have to teach you all over again."

No wonder Eleanor continued to ride horseback during her years in the White House. No wonder, too, that she often expressed her strongest emotions in letters, to Hick and to others she loved. During those long periods when her father was forbidden to visit her, his letters were her sustenance.

Hunting game, first out west and then in the Far East, seems to be the one passion Elliott Roosevelt hung on to through all the turmoil of his life. He wrote his mother proudly from Ceylon that he had "got two elephants," and made a present to her of "my big tiger skin." Eleanor proudly wore an oversized and clunky necklace of tiger's teeth brought back by her father from his adventures.

When Eleanor saw her father again, at age eight, after her mother died, he told her that now that her mother was gone, "he and I must keep close together. . . . Somehow it was always he and I. I did not understand whether my brothers were to be our children. . . . There started in me . . . a feeling which never left me—that he and I were very close together, and some day would have a life of our own together."

It must have been during this period that Eleanor developed the ability to walk at a clip that left others in the dust. She remembered walking with governesses, French maids, and German maids who were always trying to talk with her. "I walked them off their feet. . . . I wished to be left alone to live in a dream world in which I was the heroine and my father the hero. Into this world I retired as soon as I went to bed and as soon as I woke in the morning, all the time I was walking or when anyone bored me." Her father died two years after her mother, from complications of alcoholism. Eleanor refused for some time to accept that he was gone.

Eleanor's dream world was much warmer than the place she actually inhabited after her mother died: her maternal grandmother's mansion on the Hudson, north of Hyde Park in Tivoli, New York. Eleanor's grandmother was a severe Victorian who "so often said 'no' that I built up a defense of saying I did not want things in order to forestall her refusals and keep down my disappointments." Grandmother Hall strived to maintain the routine set by her late husband: family prayers morning and evening and religious reading on the weekends. Young Eleanor remembered having her weekday book taken away from her and replaced with a "Sunday book" after church, only to have that one taken away on Monday until the following Sunday. She also had to teach Sunday school each week to the coachman's daughter, and recite the hymn and collect to her grandmother.

Some of her happiest memories were of times spent with servants in the house: ironing hankies and napkins alongside the "cheerful woman" who did the laundry, or lingering in the butler's quarters with Victor, who was kind to her and taught her how to wash dishes. When she was sent to bed without dinner for some infraction, the maid sometimes managed to send up a tray of food for her. Perhaps these happy times explain in part her attraction to rough-edged working-class types like Lorena Hickok and Earl Miller later in life.

She also took refuge in the third-floor rooms of her two young aunts, who were caught up in romances and gossip about their social set. But she had almost no playmates her own age, and she lived in fear of her governess Madeleine, who punished her cruelly for small misdemeanors: if her darning was imperfect, Madeleine would cut it out and make her do it over again. At night, Madeleine took out her resentment on Eleanor by pulling her hair mercilessly as she brushed it.

Meanwhile, her two Hall uncles, Eddie and Val, were becoming wild and erratic alcoholics. Eddie once fired a shotgun out an upstairs window at guests visiting Tivoli. There is no way of knowing if her uncles' behavior ever became physically dangerous or sexually abusive to Eleanor. But according to a friend of the family, three strong locks appeared on Eleanor's door during the time she lived in Tivoli. She later wrote that this experience of her unpredictable uncles led her to "an almost exaggerated idea of the necessity of keeping all of one's desires under complete subjugation."

If it had been up to her grandmother, Eleanor might never have escaped from Tivoli. But Auntie Bye, her father's independent sister, encouraged Grandmother Hall to send Eleanor to a school near London called Allenswood, run by a remarkable Frenchwoman named Marie Souvestre.

Auntie Bye was an important role model for Eleanor. Unlike her mother, Bye was not a beauty or a candidate for high society; she had a spinal deformity that made her lame and very thick through the shoulders. But she was highly intelligent and animated, always the center of any group she socialized with. Her house in Washington was a political and social magnet during her brother Theodore Roosevelt's administration.

Auntie Bye had been a student at the school of Mademoiselle Souvestre when it had been based in Paris. It was that family history that convinced Eleanor's grandmother to send Eleanor, at age fifteen, to Allenswood, where Souvestre had reestablished her school after escaping the turmoil of the Franco-Prussian War.

Had Eleanor's grandmother looked into the credentials of Mademoiselle Souvestre, she might have kept her granddaughter at home. Souvestre, daughter of the French novelist Émile Souvestre, was a professed atheist and a progressive who sided with the Dreyfusards against anti-Semitism and even dared to criticize the imperialist excesses of the British during the Boer War. She was also a lesbian: her life's companion was the school's Italian teacher, Mademoiselle Samaia, who waited on her hand and foot, and tended to be jealous of Mademoiselle Souvestre's favorite pupils. Most important, Souvestre was a feminist who expected girls to think for themselves.

Marie Souvestre's wavy hair was white by the time Eleanor met her, and pulled tightly back from her handsome face. She had a high-domed forehead and beautiful eyes that could, as Eleanor wrote, "look through you." "She always knew more than she was told." Her judgment could be severe: Eleanor remembered her taking a girl's paper and tearing it in half in disgust because the work was "shoddy." Many of her students found Souvestre formidable. But one remembered that she had an "infectious ardor" that was "the secret of her success as a schoolmistress. . . . She communicated a Promethean fire which warmed and coloured their whole lives."

Surprisingly, though she had often been intimidated in the past, Eleanor was completely unafraid of her new teacher. Fluent in French, she became an immediate favorite of Mademoiselle Souvestre's and was soon sitting across from her at dinner—a prized position—and listening in on the lively talk of the headmistress's visitors. Beatrice Webb, a Fabian socialist who sparred with Mademoiselle Souvestre on a visit to the school, described the way "every idea is brought under a sort of hammering logic, and broken into pieces unless it be of very sound metal."

Mademoiselle Souvestre came to adore Eleanor, whom she called "Totty." In a letter to her grandmother, Souvestre praised Eleanor's "purity of heart, the nobleness of her thought," her "intelligent interest in everything," and her ability to influence others "in the right direction."

At Allenswood, Eleanor made the first team in field hockey, danced, played games, and developed strong friendships. When one of her closest friends, a girl she called Jane in her autobiography, threw an inkstand at a teacher and was about to be expelled, Eleanor even exploded in a fit of temper—a rare loss of control that was, given her past inhibitions, a sign of progress.

Her new confidence extended to her looks: she dared, with Souvestre's encouragement, to have a Parisian dressmaker fashion a dress for her. "I still remember my joy," she wrote years later, "in that dark red dress." For Eleanor, whose own mother had found her a disappointment, the motherly affection of Mademoiselle Souvestre was a great gift.

It seems unlikely that Eleanor's relationship with the seventy-year-old Souvestre went beyond warm hugs and kisses. But another student, who attended Allenswood thirty years earlier, wrote a roman à clef about falling in love with a younger Mademoiselle Souvestre—not, she insisted, just a schoolgirl crush but a true powerful physical and emotional passion for another woman. *Olivia* was written in 1933 and published anonymously sixteen years later by Leonard and Virginia Woolf's Hogarth Press. It was later revealed to be the work of Dorothy Strachey Bussy, who was bisexual. She had been a student at the school, and was a teacher of Shakespeare there in Eleanor's time. Bussy presents a conversation, in *Olivia*, between an exemplary student, a girl named Laura and another girl, Olivia. The two talk about the beloved headmistress.

"Do you love her?" Olivia asks her admirable friend Laura.

"Oh," replies Laura, "you know I do. She has been the best part of my life."

"And tell me this, Laura. Does your heart beat when you go into the room where she is? Does it stand still when you touch her hand? Does your voice dry up in your throat when you speak to her? Do you hardly dare raise your eyes to look at her, and yet not succeed in turning them away?"

"No," said Laura. "None of that."

Was Eleanor more like Laura, admiring and adoring her teacher without the passion Olivia describes? Or did she experience the erotic feelings that consumed Dorothy Bussy's stand-in, Olivia, despite Mademoiselle Souvestre's advanced age? When *Olivia* was published, nearly fifty years after their schooldays together at Allenswood, Eleanor and her schoolmates seemed to take Bussy's homoerotic re-creation of the school in stride. "I am glad you liked *Olivia*," classmate and lifelong friend Marjorie Bennett Vaughn wrote after hearing from Eleanor about the book. "It seemed to take me back so far."

Eleanor may have had her share of passionate crushes on other girls at the school—the intensity of her defense of the wayward "Jane" suggests that that might have been one. "There were perhaps eight other girls in our class," she wrote years later, "but as far as I was concerned there was no one but Jane. . . . Her glamour . . . is still with me, so that I would give much to see her walk into my room today."

Eleanor was also the object of others' crushes. Her cousin Corinne Roosevelt Robinson, who followed her to Allenswood, remembered the Saturday ritual of going into the nearby town of Putney and buying books and flowers. "Young girls have crushes," she wrote, "and you bought violets or a book and left them in the room of the girl you were idolizing. Eleanor's room would be full of flowers because she was so admired."

Eleanor accompanied Mademoiselle Souvestre to Europe on three different occasions. They visited Florence, Rome, Pisa, Marseilles, Biarritz, and Paris together. Souvestre asked Eleanor to take charge of all the train scheduling and to pack and unpack the bags. She encouraged her young acolyte to take her Baedeker and go out alone to explore Florence and Paris. "I really marvel now at myself," Eleanor wrote years later. "I was totally without fear in this new phase of my life."

Souvestre was spontaneous: she once made a split-second decision to get off a train in Italy to visit a friend. "We simply fell off onto the platform," Eleanor remembered, "bag and baggage, just before the train started on its way. I was aghast, for my grandmother, who was far from Mlle. Souvestre's seventy years . . . would never have thought of changing her plans once she was on the train."

Eleanor would have thrived in college. But her old-fashioned grandmother believed that higher education was a liability in the all-important task of marrying well. Eleanor almost had to leave Allenswood after two years, because her grandmother got a report that she had been seen walking unchaperoned in a European city. Eleanor managed to appease her by finding a woman chaperone to sail back to England with her for a third year at the school.

Then it was over: Grandmother Hall insisted that she leave school and "come out" as a debutante, like her mother and aunts before her. It was wrenching for both student and teacher. Mademoiselle Souvestre "had become one of the people whom I cared most for in the world," Eleanor wrote, "and the thought of the long separation seemed very hard to bear." Souvestre, for her part, wrote to Eleanor, "I miss you every day of my life."

There can be no doubt that Marie Souvestre was Eleanor Roosevelt's second great love, after her father. She kept Souvestre's portrait on her desk for the rest of her life.

After Allenswood, Eleanor's coming out in New York Society proved to be "utter agony." She still felt "deeply ashamed" that she was "the first girl in my mother's family who was not a belle." She much preferred teaching dancing and exercises to young girls at the settlement house on Rivington Street, where she didn't need to worry about filling her dance card.

At the Hall family town house in New York, Eleanor was surrounded by turmoil. Her aunt Pussie shut herself in her bedroom for days on end, weeping over disappointments in love, and her uncle Val arrived periodically from Tivoli "to go on a real spree."

Eleanor's decision to marry Franklin Roosevelt, her fifth cousin once removed, came at this time of diminished confidence and domestic confusion. "Though I was only nineteen," she wrote later, "it seemed an entirely natural thing and I never even thought that we were both rather young and inexperienced." Her grandmother asked her if she was sure she was really in love. "I solemnly answered 'yes,' and yet I know now that it was years later before I understood what being in love was or what loving really meant."

Franklin was an enthusiastic amateur photographer in this period, and he took admiring photographs of Eleanor. In one, she sits tall and composed in the stern of a rowboat, her lovely hands folded, her beautiful ash blond hair piled high, her large eyes wistful. Franklin must have perceived Eleanor's intelligence and enjoyed her ability to listen and sympathize. Eleanor was also Theodore Roosevelt's niece, which added to her appeal for the ambitious Franklin.

Within a year of her debut, Eleanor was engaged to Franklin. They married two years later, and she became pregnant with her first child a year after that. "For ten years," she wrote, "I was always just getting over having a baby or about to have one." From 1906, when Anna was born, until World War I, her life revolved around her duties as a mother to five children and a political wife whose only job was to smooth her husband's path. Her mother-in-law ruled at home, and she depended heavily on the expertise of nurses.

In Washington, Eleanor watched without protest as her husband partied and flirted with other women. Eleanor's cousin Alice Roosevelt Longworth enjoyed telling the story of one Washington night when Eleanor looked particularly foolish. At around 10 p.m., she left a lively party, only to arrive home and discover that she had no key. Six hours later, FDR arrived with friends, in high spirits, and found Eleanor sleeping on the front step. She hadn't wanted to disturb the servants, she explained, or return to the party. "I knew you were all having such a glorious time, and I didn't want to spoil the fun."

Eleanor worked hard, no doubt too hard, at being the conscientious wife. "I still lived under the compulsion of my early training. . . . I looked at everything from the point of view of what I ought to do, rarely . . . what I wanted to do." She was "appalled by the independence and courage" of less dutiful women. When her husband came out in favor of women's suffrage, she was "somewhat shocked."

But then Eleanor began to shake off the constraints of the dutiful wife role. In her memoir, she attributes her transformation to the war, and to her discovery that she could be effective as a volunteer. The usual round of teas, luncheons, and dinners no longer seemed possible in a world of so much suffering and need.

She began to spend long days volunteering: organizing the Red Cross canteen, knitting and encouraging others to knit, serving coffee and sandwiches to the troops at Union Station. She visited the wounded and the shell-shocked in hospitals. She raised money to build a recreational center for the wounded. She also learned to drive so that she could participate in the Red Cross motor corps. "All my executive ability came into play," she wrote.

Another reason for Eleanor's new independence was the discovery, in 1918, of Franklin's affair with Lucy Mercer, a betrayal that demonstrated the limitations of trying to be the dutiful and selfless wife. This revelation surely contributed to what Eleanor called "the budding of a life of my own."

Back in New York, after the painful Washington years, Eleanor began to spend time with a group who represented the path not taken: college-educated women who had worked for women's suffrage and who, after the passage of the Nineteenth Amendment giving women the right to vote in 1920, were involved in educating and empowering the new female electorate. For Eleanor, who hadn't even been sure of her position on suffrage, these women were a revelation.

Esther Lape and Elizabeth Read were "partners," a phrase that friends understood to mean they were a loving couple. If they had a sexual relationship, they probably didn't name it or talk about it. Homosexuality was viewed in the wider world as both shocking and criminal. But among Eleanor's political friends, such lifetime liaisons were common.

Several evenings a week, she took the Fifth Avenue coach from the Roosevelt town house on East 65th Street to the unconventional home of Esther and Lizzie in Greenwich Village. In the house on 65th Street, there was virtually nothing Eleanor could call her own—her mother-in-law, Sara, had purchased every stick of furniture and supervised the hanging of every picture and drape. Even though the house on West 11th Street belonged to her friends, it felt much more like home.

Politics were the ostensible reason for Eleanor's meetings with Esther and Lizzie, who for some time published a weekly newsletter called *City, State and Nation*. Together, they worked on solidifying and publicizing the work of the newly formed League of Women Voters. But politics were only part of it. Esther and Lizzie lived with a great deal of style. Lizzie was the more casual of the two: she had a strong, athletic body, and favored tailored suits with string ties, sensible walking shoes, corduroys, and knickers with high-laced hunting boots. Esther, on the other hand, dressed in patterned silks and satins and wore red velvet at Christmas.

Esther and Lizzie had a doormat at their country home in Connecticut emblazoned with the words "toujours gai" and a slogan over the door that read "give me beauty of the inward soul." In their brownstone on West 11th Street they insisted on beauty: cut flowers filled the rooms, and elegant meals were accompanied by champagne. After dinner came the pièce de résistance for Eleanor: long evenings spent reading French poetry aloud, evenings that reminded her of her happiest girlhood moments listening to Mademoiselle Souvestre.

"Their interests played a great part," she wrote later, "in what might be called 'the intensive education of Eleanor Roosevelt' during the next few years."

Eleanor's journey toward independence was interrupted quite suddenly in the summer of 1921, during the family vacation at the Roosevelt compound on Campobello Island, off the coast of Maine, in Canada. On August 10, Franklin took the family out sailing, joined in putting out a forest fire they came upon, went for a swim in a pond on the island, then raced everyone back to the house; it was an exuberant day of activity that typified family life at Campobello. But the next day, one of FDR's legs began to drag, and soon his entire body from the chest down became paralyzed. For a few terrifying days, no one understood what was wrong. A specialist diagnosed polio.

Life changed for everyone in FDR's inner circle. Eleanor became a tireless nurse, soon joined by FDR's devoted adviser Louis Howe. Sara Roosevelt, who was in Europe, rushed to the island as soon as she got the news. Everyone, she noted, was being "cheerful" by the time she arrived, so she joined in the charade. But there was nothing to be cheerful about. First there would be the agonizing trip, on a stretcher, in a boat, and then in a private railway car, back to New York City. Then there would be months in New York Presbyterian Hospital and more months in a back bedroom at the 65th Street town house, followed by a long stay in Hyde Park.

FDR worked hard to get better, exercising and trying out various treatments. But even though he developed great upper-body strength, he didn't succeed in recovering the use of his legs. He discovered some things, however, that made him feel better. In 1924 he visited a run-down spa in Warm Springs, Georgia, with Missy and discovered he could stand nearly on his own in the warm buoyant water. After that, he visited Warm Springs frequently and hatched plans to expand and improve the place. He also loved to be out on houseboats in southern waters, fishing, drinking with pals in defiance of Prohibition, and moving about the deck by pulling himself along with his arms, free from the scrutiny of strangers. The sun and the swimming and the tropical Florida climate seemed to do him good.

Eleanor had always been a poor sailor, and her letters to her friends from Florida were testimony to just how little she enjoyed life on the houseboat. Writing to a friend from Key West, she reported that Franklin was loving it "as much as ever," while she was sleeping on deck with a "large bottle of Citronella" to keep off the mosquitoes. At one point they were marooned in a swamp with a failed engine. The citronella had not worked: she had so many mosquito bites on her face that she looked as if she had smallpox. She found Florida "queerer each year" and didn't understand why people would want to settle there, and she had no patience whatsoever for the "lazy life one leads" on board a boat. She was happy to leave and make room for Missy.

After the early months, when she was involved in nursing and encouraging FDR, Eleanor's life diverged more than ever from her husband's. While he was relaxing in the sun, she began, with Louis Howe's encouragement, to spend more and more of her time working for Democratic causes: writing, campaigning, and even speaking.

Eleanor's political activism led to a new and important friendship with Nancy Cook, head of the Women's Division of the New York Democratic Committee, and Nancy's life partner, Marion Dickerman. Nan and Marion were in graduate school together at Syracuse University, and became partners not long after. Nan, curly-haired, boyish, and intense, was seven years older than Marion, who had a long, serious face with downturned eyebrows and mouth and was the quieter and more measured of the two. But both were women of action, passionate suffragettes who signed up for Red Cross duty in a London hospital during World War I. Nan, who was a gifted craftsperson, used her carpentry skills to fashion artificial limbs for wounded soldiers. The moment they returned from England, Marion was recruited by women activists to run for the New York Assembly on the Democratic ticket. She took it on and survived, despite vicious red-baiting and misogyny. Her Republican opponent won, but the challenge was successful in snuffing out his hopes for higher office.

Eleanor became bolder too, following Nan and Marion's example. She ordered matching tweed suits with knickers for herself and Nan, much to the disapproval of her elders. One day she sat for hours with her knitting on the porch of a county chairman who was avoiding her, knowing he was inside and would eventually have to come out and face the music. In 1924, when Democrat Al Smith campaigned for governor against Republican Teddy Roosevelt Jr., Eleanor, Marion, and Nan rode around New York State in a car with a three-dimensional steaming teapot on the top. It was, she later admitted, a "rough stunt"—intended to associate Teddy Roosevelt Jr. with the Teapot Dome scandal, in which a member of Republican president Warren Harding's cabinet accepted bribes in exchange for leases on oil-rich western lands. Eleanor described her cousin Teddy as a reasonably nice young man "whose public service record shows him willing to do the bidding of his friends." Eleanor's campaign against her own kin caused lasting resentment in the Teddy Roosevelt branch of the family. By the time Al Smith won the election, Eleanor, Marion, and Nan had become fast friends and frequent companions.

One fall day in 1924, the three of them were picnicking with FDR and younger sons John and Franklin Jr. on a stream called Val-Kill, about two miles from Springwood, the Delano/Roosevelt family mansion. Eleanor noted that her mother-in-law was about to close up Springwood for the winter, as she did every year, and move to the town house in Manhattan. She mentioned how nice it would be to have a country place to come to in winter after the big house was closed down.

FDR took up the idea immediately. The land they were picnicking on belonged to him, not his mother, he told the gathering, and he would happily lease it for life to the threesome of Nan, Marion, and Eleanor. They could build a year-round cottage of their own there, a place free from the formalities and obligations of the big house. The Val-Kill stream could be dammed to make a swimming pool, and the whole place could be called Val-Kill. Nan Cook drew up the first plans for Val-Kill cottage. But before long, FDR, who loved to design buildings, took over. He engaged Henry Toombs, a local architect, to plan a stone house in Dutch colonial style for "my missus and some of her political friends."

A year and a half after the picnic where the idea was born, the stone cottage at Val-Kill was finished. On New Year's Day 1926, everyone gathered in the airy living room, sitting on nail kegs around a makeshift table, to celebrate with a first meal. Even Sara Roosevelt was there. Franklin presented Marion Dickerman with a children's book he had found, entitled *Little Marion's Pilgrimage*, and signed it "from her affectionate Uncle Franklin. On the occasion of the opening of the Love Nest on the Val-Kill."

In the early years, Val-Kill was a beloved place for all three women. Eleanor stayed there as often as she could, going over to the big house only for official duties. At Val-Kill, she was an equal partner in shared enterprises: working on political issues with Nan, as head of the Women's Division of the New York Democratic Party, and on educational plans with Marion, who was about to take over the Todhunter School, with Eleanor's support. Franklin came to visit, as did the children. But Val-Kill belonged to the threesome. Eleanor embroidered towels for the cottage with the initials EMN.

Even before the cottage was finished, Nan had begun to talk about the possibility of a workshop where she could return to the carpentry she loved. She was intrigued by the idea of creating authentic reproductions of colonial American furniture. Soon the plan expanded into a project named Val-Kill Industries, which would produce furniture for the general public. Val-Kill Industries operated first out of a small shop in the cottage and later in a separate building on the property. Under Nan's supervision, pieces were carefully turned, and joined with wooden pegs. Most were made in hardwoods and burnished by hand before being stamped with the Val-Kill hallmark. In the beginning, the women had the idealistic goal of employing local farmers in the off-season, thus discouraging flight to the cities. Ultimately, however, recent European immigrants with carpentry skills were hired to do the work. At its peak, the cottage industry employed as many as twenty people. Eleanor was in charge of marketing, and hosted a small exhibit of the finished pieces at her town house in Manhattan in the spring of 1927. FDR was among the project's very first customers: he used Val-Kill pieces to furnish the Little White House at Warm Springs.

FDR had first visited Warm Springs with Missy in 1924, and eventually envisioned a whole complex of buildings to accommodate the presidential party and friends, as well as fellow polio victims seeking treatment and rehabilitation. Henry Toombs would also design Warm Springs, including FDR's cottage, which became known as the "Little White House." The modest clapboard cottage, with a porch in the shape of a ship's prow, looked out over a stand of Georgia pines. A central living and dining room separated the two bedrooms: one for FDR and one for Missy. A connecting bath linked FDR's bedroom to a tiny third bedroom that belonged to Eleanor. But Eleanor, when she did visit Warm Springs, preferred to stay in one of the other cottages on the campuslike property.

FDR loved Warm Springs: it was the one place in the world where he didn't have to hide his disability, and where he could race around on the dusty roads in his hand-controlled Model T. Eleanor, on the other hand, went there reluctantly, most often for Thanksgiving. She preferred to be with her friends at Val-Kill.

The friendship between Eleanor, Marion, and Nan, which began in 1922, was at the center of all three women's lives for a decade. The trio went on camping trips together, pitching a tent and savoring Nan's cooking, prepared on a portable stove over an open fire. Because Nan and Marion seemed to have an easy rapport with her younger sons, Franklin Jr. and John, Eleanor often brought them along on the camping adventures. The three women spent time together in Campobello as well, boating, swimming, and reading aloud by the fire. In 1929, they even toured Europe together, with Franklin Jr. and John in tow.

On the surface, it looked as though nothing had changed in the spring of 1933. Eleanor went on vacation as usual with Nan and Marion, traveling through upstate New York and Vermont and Maine before crossing by boat to Campobello. But this time she made the trip with Nan and Marion in June, all while planning to repeat much of it with Hick in July. She wrote Hick that she now knew the prettiest roads and the best places to stop. She wondered if Hick would love Campobello as she did. "Hick dearest," she wrote from Maine, "this has been the most glorious day, and the best of it you and I will be doing together next month."

Even though Eleanor would be retracing her steps, the July trip with Hick was going to be very different. As close as Eleanor was to Nan and Marion, there had never been any doubt that they were the couple and she was the third person, caring but not committed. Eleanor's relationship with Hick was different. Hick was wholeheartedly in love with Eleanor, and Eleanor, in her letters and in their times together, seemed to feel just as passionately about Hick. This was something new for a woman who had learned early to keep her "desires under complete subjugation." Eleanor was usually uncomfortable with physical intimacy. She had long ago given it up in her marriage, and she rarely allowed it with her children. On this trip, she and Hick were going to be together as a couple, all day and all night. There would be no buffers—no friends, no relatives, and very few official appearances. Of all the many brave things Eleanor Roosevelt did over her lifetime, going off with Hick—and only Hick—on a three-week car trip may have been one of the bravest.

CHAPTER SIX

GETAWAY

ON THE FOURTH OF JULY 1933, Eleanor Roosevelt took a small fast boat out to the USS *Indianapolis* to play "Mrs. R." one more time as the fireworks lit up the skies over the Potomac. Then she and Hick hopped into her Buick roadster and headed for upstate New York. From there, they intended to meander at their leisure in the mountains of New England, then cross the border into French-speaking Quebec, staying first in luxury at the Château Frontenac, then driving along dirt roads to explore the sparsely populated beaches and tiny fishing towns of the Gaspé Peninsula.

The first six months of FDR's first term had been an unsettling time for both Eleanor and Hick. Eleanor had worries about her children, which she related in detail to Hick. Hick, for her part, was distressed about leaving the AP and worried about her professional future.

"Poor Hick," Eleanor had written in June, "I know how you hate to leave the life. I do hope there will be enough interest in the next years to compensate." There was talk of Eleanor's agent signing Hick up to write some articles for *McCall's*, or a profile of the White House butler, Ike Hoover. But such assignments couldn't make up for what Hick was leaving behind: the news business was the closest thing to a true home she had ever had.

It isn't surprising, given how much newspapering had meant to her, that Hick felt tearful after she left Eleanor to go back to her job in New York. It must have been easier, when she and Eleanor were together, to convince herself that she was doing the right thing in leaving it all behind.

"I couldn't bear to think of you crying yourself to sleep," Eleanor wrote five days after Hick left her in Washington. "Oh! how I wanted to put my arms around you in reality instead of in spirit. I went and kissed your photograph instead and the tears were in my eyes. Please keep your heart in Washington as long as I'm here for most of mine is with you!"

It was Eleanor who finally engineered a solution of sorts for Hick: a job with Harry Hopkins, head of New Deal relief programs. The new job would take care of money worries, which were never far away in Hick's life, and, most important, allow her to be near Eleanor in the White House between her field trips.

The Roosevelt White House was an astonishingly hospitable place. FDR's close adviser Louis Howe lived there until nearly his dying day, and later, when Harry Hopkins assumed many of Howe's duties, he too moved into the White House, with his daughter Diana. After Hopkins remarried, in a ceremony in the Oval Office, his new wife moved in too. Missy lived on the third floor. Now Hick was going to become another of what the staff referred to as "permanent guests." Eleanor and Franklin invited many others as well, to stay for a night or two. Hick's aunt Ella, who had rescued her and watched over her education, was invited to spend a weekend with her family at the White House, including a dinner with the president. Eleanor gave her husband explicit instructions to "behave" himself with Hick's "Republican relatives" from Illinois. "Don't you say anything to shock them," she told him. Aunt Ella, who was in her seventies, was usually shy and soft-spoken. So Hick was amazed to see her aunt, who was seated next to the president, laughing and "having a grand time." "Never in all the years I knew him did I see Franklin Roosevelt put forth more charm than he did that evening," Hick wrote.

Alexander Woollcott, the actor and bon vivant who inspired a comedy called *The Man Who Came to Dinner*, actually stayed at the Roosevelt White

House while he was playing the role of a guest who comes to dinner and never leaves. After seeing the play, Eleanor insisted in her newspaper column that "Mr. Woollcott is one of my favorite guests and I hope he will always consider himself not only welcome, but sought after." This warmth defined the early days of the Roosevelt presidency.

The chance to live near Eleanor and even to work with her on the problems she encountered was what made the job with Harry Hopkins appealing to Hick. But there were things about it that were going to be difficult. She was going to have to put her beloved Prinz in a kennel and embark on a strenuous travel schedule, all while raising doubts, in her own mind most of all, about whether she was only getting the job because of her relationship with the First Lady. What's more, she didn't know how she was going to get around, since she didn't drive. Trains and buses could only take her so far. To really examine and report on ordinary people's lives outside the cities, she was going to need a car, driven by her or someone else.

Hick's consolation as she faced this daunting new challenge was the conviction that she was loved—and needed. "Remember no one is just what you are to me," Eleanor wrote Hick around this time, and "I've never enjoyed being with anyone the way I enjoy being with you."

Eleanor's love for Hick had freed her to express herself with unprecedented boldness. Though she cared a great deal about her children, she had never been good at showing it. Hugging and kissing didn't come easily to her, and she was not very sympathetic with their ailments. Illness, in her view, was something to be got over, as quickly as possible.

But Eleanor lavished her concern and affection on Hick in a way she never had been able to do with her own family. She worried about Hick's diabetes, her teeth, her minor illnesses. "I am so glad your cold is better," she wrote her that spring. "You are sadly mistaken if you think I'd let you have the 'flu' without me!"

There were spontaneous hugs too, as never before. "My dear if you meet me, may I forget there are other reporters present," she asked Hick, "or must I behave? I shall want to hug you to death. I can hardly wait."

Most important, she wrote and talked to Hick about everything—no holds barred. "I never talked to anyone," she confided. "Perhaps that was why it all ate into my soul."

Hick, who had never married nor borne children, who had no pedigree and no family legacy to carry on, was now the person to whom Eleanor told all her worries about her unhappy and troubled children, about her flirtatious and vacillating husband, about her out-of-control brother, and about her struggles with "Mama," her domineering mother-in-law, and with Aunt Susie and all the Hall and Roosevelt relatives who were so quick to judge her.

In her letters to Hick, Eleanor fretted about Anna, who was trying to escape her unhappy marriage. "Poor kid, blind faith in a kindly providence keeps her up, but I fear a break." FDR rather poignantly urged Anna to go slow with ending her marriage, telling her that many people who were in love saw each other rarely and "got on very well in the end without love." Eleanor, on the other hand, was cheering for Anna and her new love, John Boettiger.

No doubt both Franklin and Eleanor had the Lucy Mercer affair in the back of their minds. For Eleanor, it was a good reason to divorce rather than stay in an unhappy marriage. FDR, on the other hand, thought it was possible to keep up appearances and manage a love affair on the side, as he had done.

More painful to Eleanor than Anna's complicated personal life was the irresponsible behavior of the Roosevelts' second son, Elliott, who suddenly announced that March that he was taking off for the Texas range to find himself, leaving his wife, Betty, and five-month-old baby behind and demanding that his mother talk to Betty about a divorce. "I'm to talk to Betty and find out their future," she wrote Hick. "Oh, dear! I'd like to run to you. I want to lean on you."

Elliott did finally meet Betty face-to-face, after FDR told him he must, and Eleanor traveled out to Phoenix to confront him and at the same time meet the woman he now planned to marry. "I went over everything with Elliott—finances, business, drinking," she wrote Hick in one of her many communications on the subject. But Elliott's behavior forced the parents to pick up the pieces, depositing money in his overdrawn bank account and taking Betty and the baby into the White House. Eleanor assured her daughter-in-law that she was welcome to stay and that Bill was "our grandchild, whatever happened." Betty was self-controlled, but very pale and unhappy. "My heart aches," Eleanor wrote Hick.

Around the same time, family friends came to see Eleanor to talk with her about her brother Hall's escalating alcoholism. "I am acutely conscious of it," she wrote Hick, "but impotent to do a thing, for he is another of life's undisciplined souls."

All of this left Eleanor deeply unhappy. She felt responsible, she confided to Hick, for Anna's and Elliott's problems, and accused herself of being "a pretty unwise teacher." Five days later, she wrote that her "zest in life is rather gone for the time being. If anyone looks at me, I want to weep."

The great escape in the Buick roadster could not have come at a better time. For Hick, it was a pause before the momentous change in her life's direction, not to mention a chance to be with the woman she now cared for so deeply. For Eleanor, it was an opportunity to escape from all her worries about her children and go on a lark with the woman she loved to be with. It was something she had rarely been able to do in her duty-bound life.

Right at the start, however, it looked as though the whole trip was going to be spoiled by security issues. The Secret Service wanted to come along. They feared the two women might be kidnapped, just as the Lindbergh baby had been not long before. But Eleanor and Hick made a joke of the idea: where would the kidnappers put the two of them—one nearly six feet tall and the other weighing nearly two hundred pounds? They wouldn't fit into any trunk. Besides, they'd been looking forward to their private getaway for months: they weren't about to bring along a Secret Service agent. Eleanor agreed to keep a gun in the glove compartment. Since she didn't load it, the weapon was more or less useless.

Thirty years later, Hick remembered the immense pleasure of that road trip: the spontaneous sleepover at a farmhouse in the woods, the beautiful drive down the chain of islands in Lake Champlain, and, above all, the laughter. In Quebec, when a religious shrine required a head covering, Eleanor knotted the four corners of her hanky and pinned it on Hick's bare head. "I must have looked funny," Hick remembered, "for I can still see her, laughing until she cried!" When Eleanor wanted her way, she would threaten to tickle Hick. "I was so ticklish that all she had to do to reduce me to a quivering mass of pulp was to point her fingers at me."

As it turned out, the Secret Service needn't have worried about the First Lady's safety. For the first and last time, Eleanor and Hick enjoyed anonymity for nearly their entire trip. In the small French-speaking towns of the Gaspé Peninsula especially, no one seemed to have received the news that Franklin Roosevelt was the new president of the United States. People were more interested in Eleanor's roadster than they were in its driver and her passenger. That was fine with Eleanor: she was pleased with the car herself.

Eleanor was a careful, frugal manager who worked to reduce White House expenditures by 25 percent, and spent as little time and money on clothes as possible. She even advised women to follow her practice of "try[ing] on all of last year's things so as to ascertain whether they will still be sufficiently in fashion to keep . . . from being conspicuous in wearing them." When it came to choosing her own personal car, however, Eleanor broke her own rules. Her sporty light blue Buick convertible, with chrome bumpers, chrome grille, and rumble seat, was a dashing—and conspicuous—symbol of independence, and a dramatic departure from the somber black limousines of First Ladies past.

The automobile set Hick and Eleanor free, just as it had loving women before them. Eleanor's good friend Molly Dewson, a savvy Democratic political operative, might have been the model. She and her life partner, Polly Porter, were enthusiastic car travelers, shipping their Willys-Knight across the ocean to explore the Dutch and French countryside one summer, motoring through Tunis and Algiers another. Eleanor and Hick had more modest plans. But there was pleasure in simple things, because they were doing them together.

Evenings were spent with *John Brown's Body,* an epic poem about the Civil War by Stephen Vincent Benét, with a large cast of characters: slaves, rebels, Yankees, Abraham Lincoln, and of course John Brown, the visionary who was hanged for attempting an insurrection to free the slaves. Eleanor read and Hick listened adoringly: Hick always maintained that Eleanor read poetry better than anyone else she'd ever known. Then, since John Brown's New York farmstead wasn't far off their route, they paid a visit to his grave.

Eleanor had learned to drive in her early thirties, under the guidance of the family chauffeur. An early swipe of a Hyde Park gatepost and a backward roll into the woods made her the butt of jokes from the men in the family. But she applied the same determination to learning to drive that she did to swimming and diving, horseback riding, and speaking in public. When she and Hick arrived late at the famous toll road up to the top of Mount Mansfield in Vermont, she defiantly took it on—despite a dire warning from a policeman that it was dangerous to drive the zigzagging, steep, mostly unpaved road in the dark. In the morning, the two of them rose early at their small hotel and watched with special satisfaction as the sun spread over the mountaintop while all below were still in darkness.

Late in the journey, as they passed through a small Maine town, someone recognized Eleanor and a crowd began to gather. Hick, who had gone without a hat for the whole trip, was sunburned and slathered in white cream. Eleanor's lower lip had gotten burned and swollen to twice its size. Neither of them had any wish to be greeted by the crowds lining up along the main street. Evasive action was required. Eleanor, confused and desperate, ran into a traffic standard and came out with an exasperated "Damn!" Hick was astonished: "It is a word I had never heard her use before, nor did I ever again in all the years we were friends." With some "highly skilled maneuvering around several corners," Eleanor escaped the crowd

ELEANOR AND HICK

and got out of town fast, driving into the potato country of Aroostook County.

It was getting dark by then, so they stopped at a pristine white farmhouse with a sign welcoming tourists. When the lady of the house learned they were not just any tourists but Mrs. Roosevelt and a friend, she seemed distressed. "You can be sure of one thing," Eleanor told Hick when they went out for a walk. "Those people did not vote for Franklin!"

A little later that evening, as Hick and Eleanor sat on the front porch swing, the farmer came out to sit on the steps. Hick watched in astonishment as Eleanor, who had spent only a few moments going through the Maine newspaper that morning, began to recite potato prices and discuss potato crops with the farmer "as easily and confidently as though she had spent her whole life raising potatoes in Aroostook County, Maine!" The farmer and his wife ended the evening as their great friends, sharing doughnuts and milk with the two of them in the kitchen.

Hick and Eleanor's private adventure ended with an important public event: a speech by Eleanor before seven thousand women of the Chautauqua Women's Club in the Amphitheater at Chautauqua, New York, the original site of the eponymous movement, which brought culture and entertainment to gatherings around the country in the late nineteenth and early twentieth century. Mrs. Roosevelt, according to a local report, pulled up at the wheel of her blue roadster, with Miss Lorena Hickok in the passenger seat. She carried her own two bags, and one of them had knitting needles sticking out. The *Home Book of Verse* was tucked under her arm, and Hick was by her side. Hick was described as a "personal friend of Mrs. Roosevelt," formerly an AP reporter and now an employee of the federal government.

Eleanor Roosevelt never wrote out her speeches. But she and Hick must have talked about this one as they made their way west from New England to New York. It was a bold speech, calling for a "new social order" in which women and men would work cooperatively. "I feel that we should all enlist in the army of peace," she told the congregants. The rise of Hitler was unspoken, but was a growing concern among women she

[88]

had worked with in the suffrage and peace movements in the past. Though she emphasized that men's and women's organizations should cooperate "until our interests merge," she also suggested that women would "set new values and give to us a new social justice, a wider mental and spiritual outlook."

Back at the White House after the trip, Eleanor and Hick told FDR all about their great adventure at a three-person dinner. Hick, who had already observed Eleanor at work with the potato farmer and his wife, now saw how well practiced she was at serving as her husband's eyes and ears. Eleanor observed things that Hick hadn't noticed at all. She guessed at the prosperity of a family, for instance, by looking at the washing hanging on a line in the backyard.

The job that Eleanor had been doing for years for her husband was about to be Hick's job as well. Hopkins's charge was to "go around the country and look this thing over." He didn't want "the social-worker angle," and he didn't want statistics. He just wanted Hick's own reaction, "as an ordinary citizen. . . . Tell me what you see and hear. Don't ever pull your punches."

Hick's other audience was going to be Eleanor, who would see all the reports as well as the detailed letters Hick wrote to accompany them. Eleanor's reactions would influence Hick's reports from the field. At the same time, Hick would become Eleanor's best adviser in dealing with the press and public. Increasingly their lives were becoming intertwined—not just on vacation but during all the days in between.

PART II

BECOMING
A TEAM

CHAPTER SEVEN

PARTNERSHIP

NOTHING IN LORENA HICKOK'S impoverished childhood prepared her for the mining camps of West Virginia, where she traveled on her first assignment for Harry Hopkins in August 1933. In South Dakota, her family lived for a summer on potatoes and tomato gravy while her father was away looking for work. But poverty in the vast open spaces of South Dakota, where the sun shone and the sky was blue, didn't compare with the hopelessness she felt in the dark hollows of West Virginia, on the edge of steep mountains.

The worst conditions were in the coal camps along the narrow Scotts Run valley, not far from Morgantown, where filthy water ran down gutters along what passed for a street. It was the same water that was used for drinking, cooking, and washing. Ramshackle houses, black with coal dust, crowded either side. Rats scampered around in the night. Children went to sleep hungry every night on piles of "bug-infested rags" spread out on the floor.

The acute poverty shook Hick to the core. "I have the sense of having lost my individuality," she wrote Eleanor. "What happens to any of us as individuals, what we think or desire or hope to do seems so trifling in the face of what I'm seeing these days."

Soon after, Eleanor traveled to West Virginia to join Hick and see for herself. The First Lady's visit surprised everyone but Hick, who had known about it even before she set out. It was a chance for Eleanor and Hick to be together, but it also allowed Eleanor to see the situation firsthand. But there was a practical reason for the trip as well. For a few days at least, Hick would have a way to get around.

Hick had never learned to drive. She grew up in surroundings where almost no one owned a car, and worked as a journalist in cities where she didn't need one. But just to reach the small towns and rural areas that were her new territory, she was going to need to drive or be driven. So Eleanor, eager to offer support to her special friend, hopped into her blue roadster in Washington and set out for West Virginia alone, avoiding not only the Secret Service but also journalists and the curious public. She slipped into Morgantown and met up with Hick without fanfare. Together they drove on to the mining camps, where she was determined to be seen as just another social worker. Her disguise was a simple short-sleeved white blouse, blue linen skirt, and crush hat, along with good walking shoes.

In the beginning, it worked. She parked her roadster and traveled instead in the Quakers' battered cars. Leading the way, along with Hick, was a dedicated Quaker activist named Clarence Pickett, soon to become an important ally. The Quakers were already working with some destitute families in the mining camps around Scotts Run. Two women working for the Quakers, Alice Davis and her partner, Nadia Danilevsky, were encouraging out-of-work mining families to do subsistence gardening—a huge challenge on the steep hillsides—as well as canning and carpentry.

But as Eleanor's retinue proceeded up the winding dirt roads of Cheat Mountain, people began to hear the news. Sometimes there were cheers, and sometimes people just stood outside their houses and stared. At first, when she got out and greeted people, they were too shy to do more than mumble. But just as she had talked potatoes in Aroostook, she spoke with them of everyday things and slowly began to elicit their stories.

At one house, a miner showed the First Lady his paycheck, which came to less than a dollar a week after the company deducted his bill at the company store. There were six children in the house who took scraps from a single bowl on the table, "the kind you or I might give to a dog," Eleanor wrote. "That was all they had to eat."

Two of the children were standing at the door as she left. The little boy held a white rabbit in his arms, which was obviously a cherished pet. The little girl was very thin and had a gleam in her eye as she looked at her brother. "He thinks we are not going to eat it, but we are," she said.

It was rare for these families to have sheets or dishes in their houses, let alone furniture. So when Eleanor entered a neatly kept house with crocheted curtains and several chairs, she complimented the Slavic woman she met, who smiled broadly as she hastily dried her hands. She told Eleanor that when they first came they had only soapboxes to sit on.

There were visits to a carpentry shop, where Eleanor took special interest in the furniture making because of her experience with Val-Kill Industries, and to the community garden. At one point, when she couldn't make it through the woods to a camp in her battered sedan, she parked it in a field and walked along with her party for more than a mile so she could talk to the miners and their families. All of this was done with great gusto. "She made us feel she was one of us," a worker reported. At the end of the day, an official on the tour paid the First Lady the compliment of pronouncing her "a swell guy."

By the time she left Morgantown, the news of Eleanor Roosevelt's visit had become a huge banner headline in the *Dominion News*. MRS. ROOSEVELT VISITS MINES HERE, it read. But she had the satisfaction of slipping out of the home of her hosts, superintendent of mines Glenn Work and his wife, without anyone sticking a camera in her face. Just before she left, the phone at the Works' house rang and she answered.

"Can you tell me when Mrs. Roosevelt is leaving?" inquired the caller.

"Why, she may be going while I am talking to you at this very minute," replied the First Lady slyly.

THINGS HAD NOT ALWAYS been this bad in mining country. The enormous demand for coal during World War I lured many families off the farm into promising jobs in the pits. There were immigrants from nineteen different countries working in the mines of Scotts Run at its height. There were also black families there, many of whom had escaped worse conditions in the South to work in the mines. But then came the postwar bust, and a depression that took hold well before the national collapse. Mine operators' greed, along with dwindling demand and the depletion of the rich coal vein that had created Scotts Run, left these families bereft and desperate. Work came sporadically, under worse and worse conditions, and the owners often took much of the money miners earned to pay off debts they had incurred at the company store, or even to pay for the oil for their headlamps. Under these circumstances, the work of the Quakers, as Clarence Pickett observed, was like trying to sweep back the ocean.

Eleanor Roosevelt, however, was undaunted. One of the things she learned on her visit was that the women didn't have enough jars for canning. Within days of her return to Washington, a freight car filled with canning jars arrived in Scotts Run. The jars were a down payment of sorts on a much bigger scheme: a whole new village for at least some of these stranded mining families, where they would combine self-sustaining farming with work in industry, away from the danger and black soot of the mines. This was an idea FDR and Eleanor had talked about for some years. Within the week Hick wrote to Eleanor from the southern counties of West Virginia, "I think the President would be interested in the attitude of this whole West Virginia mining population on going back to the land." Relief officials in Charleston begged Hick to find out in Washington if there was a way to get some of the miners out onto the land. They thought hundreds would respond, since the great majority of the miners came down out of the hills in the mining boom and were actually raised on the farm.

Arthurdale was the very first embodiment of this New Deal dream. It was built on a 1,028-acre farm in Preston County, West Virginia, just eighteen miles from Scotts Run, that had been the property of a gentleman farmer named Richard Arthur. Having fallen on hard times, Arthur sold the land to the Department of the Interior for $45,000.

With the encouragement of FDR, and the teamwork of Eleanor and Louis Howe, the town came into being quickly. By July 1934, less than a year after Eleanor's first visit to Scotts Run with Hick, 50 homesteads were completed and 50 stranded mining families had new homes not far from their old ones, with running water, indoor plumbing, and enough land for subsistence gardening and husbandry. Before it was all over, there would be 165 families living in Arthurdale. The town would include a clinic, funded by Eleanor and the wealthy friends she persuaded to help, including Bernard Baruch, as well as an innovative school and an active carpentry shop. Mrs. Roosevelt would become a regular visitor to Arthurdale, joining in square dances at the community center and speaking at high school graduations. She stayed in touch with the villagers for the rest of her life.

Howe told Hick, "You and Eleanor ought to get a great sense of satisfaction. You really started something."

Even though FDR had talked of the resettlement idea before, it was Hick's fieldwork that inspired action. She was the one who escorted Eleanor around Scotts Run. She was the one who introduced her to Clarence Pickett, whom Eleanor then recruited to oversee the project. She even pointed to Prescott County as a possible location. Over the course of the Roosevelt presidency, the Arthurdale experiment would be repeated in many different guises all around the country. Some communities would follow the Arthurdale model closely, resettling stranded communities like Scotts Run. Others would be formed around an industry, or as cooperative farms. Still others would require families to pick up and move great distances: in 1935, 203 farm families moved from Minnesota, Wisconsin, and Michigan to the fertile Matanuska Valley in Alaska. All told, the homestead project produced 10,938 new homes at a total cost of about $108 million. The projects were a frequent target of criticism, because in most cases they failed to be self-sustaining. But for the families who moved into them, they were often akin to a gift from heaven.

On a visit to Arthurdale not long after the first houses were finished, Eleanor stopped by the new four-room home of a couple with three young daughters. Their house and all their belongings had been washed away in a landslide, and they had been living in a two-room windowless building before moving to the little white house in Arthurdale. "It is Paradise for us," the woman of the house told Eleanor. No wonder the citizens of Arthurdale referred to Eleanor Roosevelt as "our angel."

Hick and Eleanor had different roles to play in the New Deal undertaking. Eleanor could bestow gifts and work on ambitious projects like Arthurdale. But Hopkins had instructed Hick right at the start that she was to be a reporter, not a social worker. She was to listen, not to act. Most of the time, she was happy in that role. "I seem . . . to have become a kind of wax record for the recording of other people's ideas and complaints and hopes," she wrote Eleanor. "And it is the most interesting thing that has ever happened to me in all my life."

Hick wrote parallel and overlapping reports: an official typed one for Harry Hopkins and another less official one for Eleanor, written in ink in her clear and flawless script. Much of the material was the same. But the letters to Eleanor had little soft touches absent in reports to the man she called "the boss."

After Eleanor left Morgantown that first time, Hick took a bus over bumpy roads "through some of the loveliest mountain scenery I've ever beheld" to the southern counties of West Virginia, where conditions were even worse. Two miners died in a mine explosion while she was there, and she observed miners who had calluses on their backs from working in coal veins only thirty inches in diameter. When she described this to Eleanor she added that the miner would be "bent double—almost in the position in which he lay in his mother's womb, before he was born."

With Eleanor, too, she felt freer to blow off steam: "Oh, I get so burned up over the whole business!" she ranted. She hated the talk of miners as extravagant, spending their money too freely when they had it and also having too many children. "Well, what the hell is there in life for them except food and cohabitation. Ah, all that kind of talk makes me sick." None of this went into the Hopkins reports.

But the terrible things Hick saw made her want to shed her role as reporter and do something. In Logan County, she encountered three mining families living in an abandoned schoolhouse with no windows. The men were able-bodied, but had been fired for refusing to join the company union. She saw sick little children there, including one baby with rickets and a bloated stomach. This time, she did act: she arranged to have the baby taken to a doctor in town.

Other times, she passed on a story to Eleanor, knowing that her friend could do things she couldn't. There was the case of the wife of a disabled miner, who had harvested (and here we see Hick's prodigious note-taking abilities) "35 bushels of pole beans, three and a half bushels of onions, enough tomatoes to can 17 gallons . . . enough beets to can nine and a half gallons; more than 15 gallons of cucumber pickles and a large and varied assortment of other vegetables, including parsnips, cabbage, carrots, lettuce, radishes, and spinach." This woman was the mother of two "grand looking boys," and she didn't want them to go into the mines. She told Hick that her dream was to get a couple of acres somewhere and a cow and a couple of pigs and a few chickens. She added that "we'd be pretty well fixed right now if we could get hold of a couple of pigs." Hick wrote Eleanor, disingenuously, "Gosh, how I'd like to give her those pigs! She's certainly earned them. I wonder if we could any way."

On August 25, around the time Hick left West Virginia, Eleanor sent a letter from Hyde Park that confirms she got the hint: "I talked to you," Eleanor wrote, "and know that you acquired the pigs!" It was the kind of thing she loved to do, for strangers and friends alike.

That September, as Hick got ready for a monthlong field trip around the Northeast, Eleanor came through again, this time with a secondhand Chevrolet convertible and an unemployed young man who would travel with Hick and teach her to drive. It's unclear how much say Hick had in this decision, but she did insist on paying Eleanor back for the purchase, in installments—as a matter of pride. Eleanor and Hick agreed to call the car "Bluette."

"I am glad relief conditions are good in N.Y.," Eleanor wrote soon after, "but even more glad that Bluette works so well, and that the boy is a good teacher and pleasant to be with."

A letter to Harry Hopkins's secretary, Kathryn Godwin, confirms that Hick did learn to drive—a challenge at age forty in the time of gearshifts. "Sorry the report is so late," she wrote Godwin, "but learning to drive that darned automobile has left me pretty much frazzled every night. Getting the hang of it, however." Hick came to love driving: five years later, she wrote Eleanor that she'd rather drive than do almost anything else.

As Hick traveled farther and farther from her new home, the White House, Eleanor's daily letters became her lifeline. When they didn't come, she protested. Writing from Rochester, New York, that September, she described herself to Eleanor as "the forgotten woman."

"It's the first time I've had to go three weeks without seeing you and the first time I've gone this long without a letter. There, there, Hickok! Be good. And reasonable."

"Of course the long separation has been harder on you," Eleanor observed at one point, "because so much of the time you've been with strangers." But she too lived for Hick's letters: "Hick dearest," she wrote, "no letter today, but I was spoiled yesterday so I will just read over all those I had yesterday!"

In late October, Hick set out on a long trip to the Midwest, revisiting the heartaches and triumphs of her early years. In Minneapolis, she stayed at the Hotel Leamington, where she and her great love Ellie had lived together so happily during her years at the *Minneapolis Tribune.*

This time, she used her connections from her days on the *Tribune* to get "the dope," as she called it, on Minnesota—dope that included a lengthy interview with its left-leaning governor, Farmer–Labor Party firebrand Floyd Olson. "Floyd Olson really is a remarkable man," she wrote Hopkins. "And sometimes when I am under the spell of his personality, I feel like a dog for ever doubting him." But she warned Hopkins that Olson was terribly ambitious for himself above all else, and wasn't beyond slowing down a New Deal program if he couldn't take credit for it: "Floyd is for Floyd and that's that."

As valuable as the political reporting was, Hick's best writing focused on the bare-bones existence of the ordinary people she encountered in Iowa, the Dakotas, and Nebraska as fall turned into winter. From Bottineau, North Dakota, she wrote to Eleanor of the familiar beauty of the open prairie: "a deep blue cloudless sky and sunlight that brings out all the gold and blues and reds and orchid shades in the prairie landscape. These plains are beautiful. But, oh, the terrible crushing drabness of life here. And the suffering, for both people and animals."

Over and over, in her letters to Eleanor and to Hopkins, Hick emphasized the desperate need for supplies in a place where temperatures could go down to forty below and where "we have between 4000 and 5000 human beings—men, women and children—without clothing or bedding, getting just enough food to keep them from starving." She wrote of two small boys, one about the same age as Eleanor's oldest grandson, Buzzie, running about without a stitch of clothing except some ragged over alls. They had no shoes or stockings, and their feet were purple with cold.

Little had changed in the twenty-five years since Hick left the little towns of her childhood: Aberdeen, Milbank, Summit, Bowdle. Outside the towns stretched miles and miles of "flat brown country. Snowdrifts here and there. Russian thistles rolling across the roads. Unpainted buildings, all going to seed. . . . What a country—to keep out of!"

The stories poured out of Hick: of a proud old couple who had lived for two years on $126; of cattle ranches devastated by plagues of grasshoppers; of "mares, dull-eyed, every rib showing, their scrawny backs sagging, great hollows behind their shoulders, followed by scrawny colts"; of farmers who wanted to work on the roads, but whose teams were too weak to last through the day.

"What a picture you can paint!" Eleanor wrote Hick after reading her letter from Huron, South Dakota. "I nearly wept. If ever under any circumstances you give up writing, I'll flay you, whether I'm here in the flesh or flaying you from some other world!"

As their time apart continued, Eleanor wrote of missing Hick more and more. "Dear heart, I would like to be with you when this letter reaches you," Eleanor wrote as Thanksgiving approached. "If I were free I would meet you in Minneapolis Wed. only my sense of duty keeps me from doing it!" Instead, Eleanor spent Thanksgiving at Warm Springs with FDR and friends, as usual. She wrote Hick that she dreamed Franklin would insist on Hick's coming to make an in-person report at Warm Springs. "I knew it wouldn't be true but it was nice to think about!"

Hick and Eleanor's anticipation of a reunion at Christmas intensified their expressions of passion. "Darling," Eleanor wrote, "the only real news is 'I love you' and two weeks and three days from now you will be here and it makes me all excited inside to think about!"

"Good night, dear one!" Hick wrote six days later. "I want to put my arms around you and kiss you at the corner of your mouth. And in a little more than a week now—I shall!"

"Dear one," Eleanor wrote four days after that, "it's getting nearer and nearer and I am half afraid to be too happy. It's the way I felt as a child when I dreaded disappointment!"

In their letters, which combined their deep affection with their passionate need to make a difference, Hick and Eleanor were often at their best. They were happy when they were part of a shared enterprise, as they were when Hick was out in the field and Eleanor was working her magic back in Washington. But when Hick was at her leisure at the White House and Eleanor was attending to her unending mountain of appointments and family obligations, things often didn't go so well. The reunion that Christmas didn't live up to expectations. Knowing how busy Eleanor would be with family and public events, the two of them planned to spend one evening together, December 22. But when the evening arrived, Eleanor was drawn into a long conversation with her daughter, Anna, who was upset about the public airing of her divorce. Hick, waiting for time alone with Eleanor, grew more and more impatient. Finally, she stormed off, furious, announcing that she was taking the train to New York and would spend the next two weeks with her friends there.

"I went to sleep saying a little prayer," Eleanor wrote Hick on December 23. "God give me depth enough not to hurt Hick again," adding,

"Darling, I know I'm not up to you in many ways but I love you dearly and I do learn sometimes." After they talked, on Christmas Day, Eleanor wrote Hick again. "Dearest one bless you and forgive me and believe me you've brought me more and meant more to me than you know and I will be thankful Christmas eve and Christmas day and every day for your mere being in the world. I'd like to hug you."

Unfortunately, because Hick became custodian of the correspondence, and threw out many of her own letters while keeping Eleanor's, we don't know what she wrote in response to these entreaties. But it's fair to guess that she quickly calmed down, as she did on later occasions, and then castigated herself for being so volatile.

Eleanor wrote to thank Hick for her wonderful presents (underclothes, automobile first aid kit, lemon fork, and a poetry collection). Before long, the two were starting to plot another field trip—this one to Puerto Rico in March, at the time of Hick's birthday. "Franklin said I could ask Harry Hopkins about Puerto Rico," Eleanor wrote her. "I only wonder if I'll be a nuisance for you for of course we can't keep it quiet and there will be reporters and fuss. Would you rather I didn't try to go with you? Be honest, I won't be hurt!"

Hick was all for it, of course.

CHAPTER EIGHT

LA PRESIDENTA AND
THE NEWSHAWK

As Eleanor walked with Hick through the worst slums of San Juan, Puerto Rico, naked children surrounded her, shouting, "La Presidenta." She and her press retinue marched side by side past dilapidated houses built on stilts above polluted waters, and shacks clinging to old fortress walls. In the swamp slums created by the 1932 hurricane, two years before, she peered into a rickety hut built with debris, and instructed the photographer, the one male among the women journalists, to take a photograph. "I want you to get this," she instructed him, "to really show what it is like."

But no photograph could do justice to the desperation of those Puerto Rican slums. "Photographs don't give you the odors," Hick wrote Hopkins. "Imagine a swamp, with stagnant, scum-covered, muddy water everywhere, in open ditches, pools, back up around and under the houses. . . . Pack into this area, over those pools and ditches as many shacks as you can, so close together that there is barely room to pass between them. Ramshackle, makeshift affairs, made of bits of board and rusty tin, picked up here and there. Into each *room* put a family, ranging from three or four persons to eighteen or twenty. Put in some malaria and hookworm, and in about every other house someone with tuberculosis, coughing and spitting around, probably occupying the family's only bed. And remember, not a latrine in the place. No room for them. . . . And pour down into that mess good, hot sun."

Eleanor's prediction that there would be "reporters and fuss" on the trip to Puerto Rico came true. What was supposed to be Hick's investigation of conditions turned instead into a media feast for the women reporters who came along. They focused more on the First Lady than on Puerto Rico's problems. But the trip did draw attention to the extreme poverty on the island, where, as Eleanor pointed out, people had lived through three generations of depression as well as a recent devastating hurricane. It also set the precedent for Eleanor Roosevelt's lifetime of trips abroad, in which she would fight to get the real story in the face of ever-growing celebrity.

Eleanor had brought along her riding clothes with the wildly optimistic idea that she could ride up into the remote mountain areas. When that proved impossible, she agreed to be driven. But, in her usual fashion, she insisted on minimizing pomp: she rode in a small car, marked with the initials of the Civil Works Administration. Nonetheless, one town along the way saluted her with "sirens and aerial bombs" and another with a detachment of soldiers who wanted to lead a procession. "I cannot crawl along at this pace," she protested, and sent them on their way.

Eleanor and the press corps visited a small factory where women were earning $2 for sewing a dozen nightgowns, which would sell on the mainland for $1.95 each. She knocked on the doors of palm-thatched cottages in the banana and coffee forest. At one home, she and her retinue found "only a crying baby with a rooster on her crib."

Despite the grim conditions in much of the country, and despite Eleanor's insistence on visiting people in distress—in a women's prison, a juvenile jail, an insane asylum—there were spontaneous moments reminiscent of her happy days traveling with Hick the previous summer. Eleanor insisted on driving over mountain roads with hairpin turns on the edge of precipices, rather than the safer routes. Spying a cable messenger on a bike along the way, she stopped him in the middle of the road and wrote out birthday greetings to her youngest son, John, back in the United States.

Eleanor and the retinue of journalists celebrated Hick's forty-first birthday on a mountaintop, with a picnic lunch for everyone to share. They arrived back in San Juan at the end of their three-hundred-mile journey just in time for a reception at the Governor's Palace, the magnificent sixteenth-century edifice La Fortaleza. Eleanor's costume for the occasion was duly noted in the exhaustive newspaper coverage: "a flowered chiffon with a spray of pale lavender and native orchids."

The flurry of excitement surrounding the visit of "La Presidenta" drowned out the objections of the Puerto Rican independence movement leaders, who complained that Mrs. Roosevelt was the wife of "Puerto Rico's greatest oppressor." Instead, she was praised for the thoroughness of her investigations. "You can't fool Mrs. Roosevelt," island governor Blanton Winship declared.

If ever there was one event that cemented Eleanor's reputation as bold and unconventional, it was this visit to Puerto Rico, the first ever by a president's wife. In a time when "fear itself" was the enemy, Eleanor's fearlessness, and tirelessness, made great copy for the "news gals" who now covered the First Lady.

The news gals, and all the publicity they created about the First Lady, were Hick's doing. It was she who encouraged Eleanor, so wary of the press in the past, to hold weekly press conferences for women only. It meant that news outlets would have to hire or retain women to cover the briefings. The idea appealed to Eleanor, who liked supporting other women, and to Hick, who had long resented her treatment in the oppressively male newsroom. "I can never be anything better than a second-stringer on a story, leg-man for the guy who does the job," she had complained to her fellow AP reporter Bess Furman in 1930. "And, if there are men available, I can't even be a second-stringer, but third- or fourth-, or fifth-stringer. And it burns me up awfully. God Damn it, I don't want any of their desk jobs or fancy executive positions . . . but if only they'd let me be a *reporter*, dam-

ELEANOR AND HICK

mit, instead [of] sending me out to do blah-blah features and patting me
on the back and telling me I'm a nice girl. . . . Sometimes it hurts like hell.
Sometimes I just get—savage."

The atmosphere at the women-only news conferences was so friendly
that some male reporters, no doubt resentful, came to call the thirty-five
women who attended them "incense-burners." Eleanor passed out candied
fruit, took an interest in the reporters' family lives, and even paid visits to
their new babies.

Bess Furman couldn't get over the fact that she found herself riding in
the White House car, having lunch at the White House table, and receiving Easter lilies from the White House greenhouses. In her purse were
cards of the president and Mrs. Roosevelt. "These things happened naturally," she noted, "one friendly gesture leading to another, on a basis of
day-by-day camaraderie."

The women reporters, in exchange for this camaraderie, were careful
not to write anything that might be embarrassing or awkward. As Eleanor
herself noted to Hick, "I rather think some of the girls are getting [to be]
pretty good champions!" Even the *New York Herald Tribune*, editorially
anti-Roosevelt, wound up running the lengthy Puerto Rican dispatches of
Emma Bugbee, one of these admiring journalists, on the front page.

The plane ride to San Juan was a story in itself: Eleanor's flight coin-
cided with the attempt to initiate airmail service, and there had been ten
small-plane fatalities right around the time of her trip. Eleanor, however,
was a friend and admirer of Amelia Earhart and an enthusiastic and fearless
flyer. "Fog Interrupts Flight," read one headline, "but She Knits On, Unafraid." Eleanor used some of her time in the air to conduct what may have
been the first in-flight news conference.

Bugbee mentioned that Lorena Hickok would be "accompanying" Mrs.
Roosevelt. But, perhaps to allay suspicions of an intimate relationship between the two, she placed emphasis on Eleanor as devoted wife, wearing
"a diamond monogrammed watch, the President's wedding gift to her,
which she always wears pinned to her blouse."

A storm forced Eleanor's plane down in Haiti on her return, so she

traveled the last leg of her journey by boat and train, arriving back in Washington on her twenty-ninth wedding anniversary. "Mrs. Roosevelt," Bugbee wrote, "talked about her wedding as the train sped north. She still wears daily her engagement ring, a large square diamond." Bugbee didn't mention of course that she also wore a ring Hick had given her. Nor that FDR and Eleanor very rarely traveled or spent leisure time together.

FDR was waiting to greet Eleanor at Union Station when she returned. A small crowd had gathered and cheered the couple as they sped off in the White House limousine. The next day, the headline in the *Herald Tribune* read, "President Welcomes Wife Home on Their Wedding Anniversary." A day late, the Roosevelts celebrated their anniversary and their son John's birthday with friends. Hick was in attendance, of course.

Hick was used to the "happy marriage" myth—in fact, she had helped to perpetuate it. What bothered her about the Puerto Rican trip was something else: the role she was assigned in the advance publicity. "It was announced," according to a February piece in *Time* magazine, "that Mrs. Roosevelt planned to visit Puerto Rico in March" and that "Miss Hickok would also go along to look into Mr. Hopkins' relief work there." This infuriated Hick, since it was *she* who was to investigate, and Eleanor's coming along was an afterthought.

"I'm so fed up with publicity," she wrote Mrs. Godwin, Harry Hopkins's secretary, "I want to kick every reporter I see. Which is a bad state for me to get into, since I'll probably be back in the business myself after I get through with this."

Her resentment carried over into the trip itself and made her disagreeable. Even though she stayed with Eleanor at the Governor's Palace and had some private moments with her on the beach in the early morning, the relaxed, intimate time together she had imagined was impossible. Sometimes, she told Godwin, she wished Eleanor Roosevelt were "Mrs. Joe Doaks of Oelwein, Illinois."

What was surely bothering Hick even more about the *Time* article was the subtext. She was described in exaggerated terms as "a rotund lady with a husky voice, a peremptory manner, baggy clothes . . . one of the country's best newshawks." The article went on to say she had become "fast friends with Mrs. Roosevelt" and "gone around a lot with the First Lady." The combination of the physical description of a heavy woman in unflattering clothes with a deep voice, who was commanding, who was not a news hen but a newshawk, and who was also Eleanor's close friend, suggested to readers, even in a time when it was taboo to say so in polite company, that there might be something unconventional and scandalous going on between Eleanor and Hick. To add to suspicions, the Spanish-language press picked up the *Time* story and wrote their own about the "amistad íntima" (intimate friendship) between the two women.

Hick had hoped that Eleanor "would get all the publicity and that I could go fairly quietly about my business." But that was not to be. It was impossible, with all eyes on Eleanor, to do the kind of investigation that made her reports worthwhile: long conversations with politicians, journalists, relief workers, and ordinary people in many walks of life. Hick, who held herself to very high standards, considered her report from Puerto Rico one of her worst.

After the Puerto Rican trip, Eleanor wrote Hick that it got harder and harder to let her go each time, "because you grow closer. It seems as though you belonged near me, but even if we lived together we would have to separate sometimes and just now what you do is of such value to the country that we ought not to complain, only that doesn't make me miss you less or feel less lonely!"

The belief that they were a team, doing important work, helped both women deal with the long separations. "We do do things together don't we?" Hick wrote Eleanor. "And it's fun, even though the fact that we both have work to do keeps us apart."

The weekly press conferences were one of the ways in which Hick helped Eleanor take possession of her role as First Lady. Less obvious, but equally important, was her influence on Eleanor as a writer. There can be no doubt that Hick made Eleanor, through all their talking and corresponding, a better writer over the years. One need only read the preachy first book she published as First Lady, *It's Up to the Women,* and compare it to the second, *This Is My Story,* to discern Hick's influence.

In a sort of Lady Bountiful voice, *It's Up to the Women* lectures to women, both rich and poor, about the challenges of the Depression. "It will do us no harm to look at ourselves somewhat critically," she wrote in her introduction, "in relation to some of the problems that confront us to-day."

Hick encouraged Eleanor to stop preaching and find substance from her own experience instead of from some general ideas about other women—most of whom lived lives vastly different from her own. In *This Is My Story,* Eleanor replaces her grand lady voice with a more genuine, storytelling one. She writes of being sent to a convent in France as a young child: "One of the girls swallowed a penny. Every attention was given her, she was the center of everybody's interest. I longed to be in her place. One day I went to one of the sisters and told her that I had swallowed a penny. I think it must have been evident that my story was not true, so they sent for my mother. . . . She took me away in disgrace." We can imagine Eleanor telling this story, and so many others in *This Is My Story,* to Hick. It has the intimacy of their letters to each other and is a world away from the sanctimonious tone of *It's Up to the Women.*

Eleanor often wrote in a last-minute rush and Hick's editorial comments came too late. But that didn't mean Eleanor wasn't taking them in. She herself had spoken more than once of her ability to listen in on others and acquire new ideas as they "passed through my rather quick mind." In her typical self-deprecating fashion, she described it as a "bad habit." But in this case, it was a habit that greatly improved the quality of the numerous articles and memoirs that Eleanor published throughout her life. Though she didn't often admit it, Eleanor also had a strong competitive streak: she wanted to become as good a writer as Hick.

Eleanor helped Hick in her work too—especially in overcoming one large and potentially damaging blind spot that began to emerge in her reports from the South early in 1934. Hick had no trouble reading and explaining the mood of the country as long as she stayed in familiar territory—the Midwest, New York, and even New England. But that January, Hopkins asked her to travel to Georgia, where Governor Eugene Talmadge was making news by calling the New Deal "a combination of wet-nursin', frenzied finance, downright communism and plain damn foolishness." Talmadge took particular aim at the relief programs, quoting a farm laborer who wrote, "I wouldn't plow nobody's mule from sunrise to sunset for 50 cents a day when I could get $1.30 for pretending to work on a DITCH." FDR replied, "I take it . . . that you approve of paying farm labor 40 to 50 cents per day. Somehow I cannot get it into my head that wages on such a scale make possible a reasonable American standard of living."

Talmadge was an extreme racist. He once told a columnist, "No niggah's as good as a white man, because the niggah's only a few shawt year-ahs from cannibalism." Talmadge's attitude was widespread in the South. But Hick, a midwesterner, didn't sound so very different in her early reports from Savannah.

"Savannah must be a little afraid of the Negroes," she wrote. "More than half the population of the city is Negro—and SUCH Negroes! Even their lips are black, and the whites of their eyes! They're almost as inarticulate as animals. They ARE animals. Many of them look and talk and act like creatures barely removed from the Ape."

Hick didn't write that way about all African Americans. While at the *Minneapolis Tribune*, she had written an admiring portrait of Roland Hayes, the black lyric tenor, who had a childhood not unlike hers, working for his board and a dollar a week in Louisville while attending sixth grade. Hayes, who had performed before the king and queen, was on a quest to find and perform the "purely Negro music of Africa," music not distorted by "our association with white people." Clearly, Hick made a distinction between successful and polished blacks like Roland Hayes and those she encountered in Savannah.

Hick had prefaced her report to Hopkins with the caveat that "the 'Old South' is all brand new to me—it's the first time I've been south of Charlottesville, Virginia and I've been feeling my way about a bit." She no doubt brought her own midwestern prejudices along with her. But in the South, her remarkable ability to mirror the attitudes of others reflected the more extreme distorting effects of racism.

Eleanor had her own blind spots—particularly an upper-class strain of anti-Semitism that shocks the modern ear. In 1925, while on a houseboat with Franklin near Key West, she wrote her friend Esther Lape that "we've had a little Jew business friend of F's on board for 4 days and he's such a good kind little man I couldn't imagine why he annoyed me so much but I decided yesterday it was because he typifies the people who think everything can be done with money! He left us last night and it is a strange relief."

Another time, Eleanor told a visiting writer from South Africa that "the country is still full of immigrant Jews, very unlike ourselves. I don't blame them for being as they are. I know what they've been through in other lands, and I'm glad they have freedom at last, and I hope they'll have a chance, among us, to develop all there is in them. . . . Well, one day, I hope, we'll all be Americans together."

Eleanor showed some of the usual attitudes toward blacks as well: her "My Day" column included a recommendation of a book called *Chocolate Drops from the South*, a compendium of "Negro Humor" in dialect. "Many of us do not appreciate what we owe the Negro race for its good humor and frequently unconscious fun producing ways of saying and doing things," she wrote, and proceeded to quote one of the jokes in dialect. When she used the word "darky" in her first memoir, she was surprised when it caused an uproar.

But right at the time Hick was writing about Negroes as animals, Eleanor was taking on racism in a major way in Washington. Eleanor's greatest virtue was her ability to learn from experience. And the experience of establishing Arthurdale had brought home the prevalence of racism in the United States like nothing before it. In Scotts Run, miners of color and whites had lived alongside each other. But when it came time to found the new colony, whites voiced fierce opposition to including blacks, opposition Eleanor and other planners were unable to overcome.

It was that experience which led Eleanor to invite leaders of the nation's most prestigious black institutions, including the presidents of Howard and Fisk universities, and of the Tuskegee Institute, to a White House conference that January for what turned out to be an "unrestrained" airing of grievances. At the same time, she was working hard, along with Walter White of the NAACP, to gain FDR's support for an antilynching bill, which was introduced to Congress that January. Lynching was still widespread in the South. Between 1901 and 1929, twelve hundred blacks were lynched in the South. There had been twenty-eight lynchings in 1933 alone.

Given her growing concern about racial injustice, Eleanor must have been deeply troubled when she read Hick's report from Savannah. She wrote, mildly, that Hick "should be reading John Brown." Eleanor had read the whole of the Benét poem *John Brown's Body* aloud to Hick on their trip into Canada. Now she was telling Hick she should read it again—surely because she thought Hick needed to be more reflective about the poisonous legacy of slavery in the South.

Two weeks later, Eleanor joined Hick in Warm Springs for three uninterrupted days together. This time, instead of the usual crowd, it was just Eleanor and Hick. Eleanor had reserved one of the private cottages in the woods for "three quiet evenings and breakfasts and I don't know if you realize how nice that sounds to me!" Local papers made note of the presence of the First Lady at Warm Springs, but this raised no suspicions, since it was natural for her to pay a visit to FDR's retreat. No one noticed her companion. It was one of Hick and Eleanor's better reunions—enhanced by the satisfaction of taking over a place where Eleanor had never felt entirely at home.

As usual, the two of them spent their time in earnest talk and reading, probably about the issues of race that were hovering around them in Talmadge country. One of the things that bothered Eleanor most about Warm Springs was that all the patients there were white. FDR, when challenged on the issue, cited local prejudices and helped to fund a polio treatment center at Tuskegee instead of trying to integrate Warm Springs.

Eleanor also lobbied for a school for black children in the area to match the all-white school FDR had funded. A bare-bones brick school for blacks was finally built, partly with WPA funds. FDR wrote a $1,000 check in the end to cover a shortfall. When it opened in 1937, he spoke at the dedication. It was called the Eleanor Roosevelt School, a tribute to the woman whom some longtime white residents of the county considered an intrusive busybody and troublemaker.

A side trip to the homestead of Eleanor's paternal grandmother, Martha Bulloch, in Roswell, Georgia, was no doubt part of Eleanor's educational project. Martha and her family were southerners who sympathized with the Confederate cause—more history to deepen Hick's understanding.

"Hick dearest," Eleanor wrote afterward, "it seems years since we sat and read and read and were alone together. I loved every minute and I am going to live on it during these next few weeks."

Hick wrote Eleanor, "I had a little ache when I unpacked my briefcase and realized that I was in the cottage at Warm Springs, *with you*, when I packed it early this morning."

AFTER HER REFLECTIVE TIME with Eleanor in Warm Springs, Hick became more alert to lurking racial violence. Visiting turpentine farms "hidden away in the pines, cut off from all the world by trees and swamp," she heard an owner complain about the federal government stirring up the Negroes. Most of his employees were "good Niggers," he said, but occasionally he had some trouble. He showed Hick his bruised fist, painted with mercurochrome. Afterward, her guide told her that the man had "killed a couple" of Negroes in his camps.

Another day, as she drove out of Odum, Georgia, Hick saw a man with a blacksnake whip in his hands going into a dooryard. "I've been wondering ever since what he was going to do with it."

In North Carolina, Hick met with prominent black leaders of an interracial commission—businessmen and teachers she described as "very fine Colored people—intelligent, well-educated, cultured. Little by little, they are probably getting somewhere but it's awfully slow." They talked about a subject close to her heart: the exploitation of household servants. The black leaders were proposing a training program to get wages up: many maids now worked for nothing but board. One leader quoted a white woman who announced, "At last I've found a woman who will come in and clean up my house for her dinner!"

This was familiar territory for Hick, who once protested to Eleanor that she had "been a slavey" and didn't wish it on anyone else. She suggested to the black leaders that there should be a training course for the housewives—instead of the maids.

Hick's travels through Georgia, Florida, and North and South Carolina led her to conclude that the rural South had never progressed beyond slave labor. "When their slaves were taken away, they proceeded to establish a system of peonage that was as close to slavery as it possibly could be and included Whites as well as Blacks. That's all the tenant farmer is . . . a slave."

The complaint of Governor Talmadge, that federal funds were luring workers away from the fields and causing a labor shortage, was false, Hick concluded. There was still plenty of surplus labor almost everywhere. What really riled the establishment, as Hick wrote in southern parlance, was that the federal government should "take all that trouble for 'jest pore white trash an' Niggers.'"

Hick herself had become increasingly unhappy with the federal relief program because of the way it played out in the racist South. For blacks who earned fifty cents a day or less as farm laborers, federal relief was welcome. But white growers liked it too, because it provided meager sustenance to their workers in the off-season, perpetuating an invidious system. Deeply ingrained racism meant that working- and middle-class whites were ashamed to "stand in line with niggers" and ask for relief. Furthermore, even if they got desperate and joined the relief rolls, these workers were unable to sustain their higher living costs with what relief provided. The result was that the relief rolls all over the South were disproportionately black.

This became Hick's mantra wherever she went in the South and the Southwest: there were "two classes of people"—people of color and working and middle-class whites. This was a fact on the ground that the federal government wasn't going to change. The relief program merely perpetuated the entrenched class and racial divides. But even though Hick tempered her language about race after the Warm Springs reunion, her bias continued to show in a more subtle way as she traveled to Texas, Arizona, and New Mexico. "We are carrying on relief," she wrote, "thousands of Mexican and Negro families, to whom relief, however low, is more attractive than the jobs they can get," while whites over forty-five, who would "*never* get their jobs back," aren't taking advantage of it. "They're our babies. And what are we going to do with them?" Whites were more "ours" in Hick's mind than people of color. Despite her bias, she proved correct in her conclusion that the federal government should get out of "this business of relief." Real work—not relief—was the answer. But things didn't look promising in the spring and summer of 1934. Under pressure from his conservative budget director, Lewis Douglas, and worrying himself about overspending, FDR had decided to dismantle the one jobs program that was under way: the hastily put together CWA (Civil Works Administration), which put hundreds of thousands to work during the early days of the administration. The PWA (Public Works Administration), under Harold Ickes, was moving at a snail's pace on larger infrastructure projects. Outside of a few bright spots, most notably the massive Tennessee Valley dam project, PWA was having little or no impact. No wonder Hick's reports got bleaker and bleaker.

In Alabama, she met with three hundred displaced tenant farmers who begged her for tents. In Texas, she wrote of towns where you could immediately find the relief office because of the long line outside. In New Mexico, she saw small Mexican children working long hours in the sugar-beet fields under a blazing sun. She stood watching in the yard of one beet worker's shack as he and his family came home for lunch: there were a father and five children, two girls and three boys. "As he came trailing along across the field," Hick wrote, "the youngest child didn't look over 6 years old. But he told me he was 9. And on this sort of thing," she fumed, "is built up one of the most powerful industries in the country." The beet industry in 1933 had $78 million in assets.

One of Hick's lowest moments came at the scene of an execution in Cañon City, Colorado. Two boys had been convicted of killing a rancher in "a holdup which netted them only two cheap pistols." One of the boys put up $200 for an appeal, so he was still alive and able to stand trial. The other boy couldn't raise the $200. "And last night they killed him.

"The thing has nearly driven me crazy," Hick wrote Eleanor. "My first impulse was to hand over the $200 that night—I still had most of my paycheck. . . . And I still think I should have. I think the impulse was *right* and that I should have done it." The field representative she was with talked her out of putting up the money, arguing that her connection to the administration might make it into a story and embarrass the president. "I *loathe* myself for not having more courage and trying to stop it," she wrote Eleanor, "no matter what the consequences were. *You* would have *done* it. . . . I've become afraid of my impulses."

Eleanor made an unconvincing attempt to comfort Hick: "I would have felt as you did about the boy," she wrote, "but they were probably right or the Governor would have given him a stay so your giving the $200 would have been useless." But Hick was correct: Eleanor surely would have put up the $200.

Hick's life on the road was wildly different from Eleanor's back in Washington. Between January and July, she drove thousands of miles, crossing the country twice, enduring terrible food, spider bites, and long lonely nights pounding out her reports on her typewriter.

Eleanor, meanwhile, was attending symphony concerts, hosting balls, and receiving myriad visitors, including forty-nine thousand for the Easter egg roll on the White House lawn. For FDR's fifty-second birthday, Eleanor and Louis Howe dreamed up an elaborate skit in which FDR was cast as the great Caesar, a role he had already been assigned by his critics. The president, attired in royal purple and wearing a crown of laurels, was surrounded by his "vestal virgins": Missy, Tommy, daughter Anna, Nancy

Cook, and Marion Dickerman. The diminutive Louis Howe headed up the Praetorian Guard, wearing a plumed helmet. Eleanor, also keeping to her reputation, played the Delphic Oracle, dispensing wisdom from on high. "I evidently answered to their satisfaction," Eleanor reported to Hick afterward.

At the same time, Eleanor was doing serious work on the projects she shared with Hick. She met with Harry Hopkins to talk about the white-collar workers Hick worried about, with Clarence Pickett about Arthurdale, and with Walter White to draft the antilynching bill. She followed up on the recommendations she and Hick had made after their trip to Puerto Rico, which resulted in some important changes. Administration of the island was transferred from the War Department to the Interior Department, as Hick and Eleanor had suggested. Also a Puerto Rican Reconstruction Administration was created to expand and stabilize the economy. Their visit also led to the establishment of a minimum wage scale for women garment workers and to the building of new brick and stone schools and prisons, replacing rickety bamboo structures.

On April 21, Eleanor gave a daring and mischievous speech to the Daughters of the American Revolution. She talked to the ladies about the "mountain people" in Kentucky and Virginia who had "ancestry as good as any that we have in this country" but who lived in "deplorable" conditions. The ladies of the DAR were not pleased with the comparison between their lineage and that of the Hatfields and McCoys. Eleanor thought it was "rather fun." A few days later, an anonymous member sent a "stern reproof."

Everything went into Eleanor and Hick's daily letters: the weather, their schedules, their sleep, their dreams. "And now I'm going to bed—to try to dream about you," Hick wrote from Texas. "I never do, but I always have hopes."

"I thought about you in church," Eleanor wrote, "as I couldn't hear the sermon and . . . I imagined . . . you motoring along and wished I were with you."

At this stage of the relationship, Eleanor was the more effusive of the two. "What wouldn't I give to talk to you and hear you now, oh, dear one, it is all the little things, tones in your voice, the feel of your hair, gestures, these are the things I think about and long for."

She dreaded Hick's trip to the West Coast—partly because she would be so far away and partly because Hick planned to meet up with Ellie, her great love from Minneapolis days, in California. "I know I've got to fit in gradually to your past and with your friends so there won't be closed doors between us later on," Eleanor wrote. "Love is a queer thing, it hurts but it gives so much more in return!"

The worst happened even before Hick got to California, as she drove the hundreds of desert miles from Lordsburg, New Mexico, to Tucson, Arizona. On a rough gravel road near Bisbee, Arizona, where wrecks were common, her car rolled over and hurtled into a ditch. Eleanor's first reaction was to send a wire: "THANKFUL YOU ARE NOT BADLY HURT ANYTHING ELSE CAN BE QUICKLY REMEDIED." After a phone call, Eleanor worried more. "The 'what might have happened aspect' I can't face even now. Darling, I ought to drive you!"

Bluette was totaled, but Hick escaped with minor injuries and made light of the incident in her report to Hopkins. Apparently she had carried most of the weight of the car on the back of her neck for a split second during the rollover, so the doctor seemed to think it wise for her to spend a day in bed. "Incidentally, sir, you have to have a darned good neck to get away with anything like that. I think mine had no doubt got toughened up these last five or six weeks from carrying the weight of the world on it."

Hick found California infuriating. "This valley," she wrote Eleanor from El Centro, in Southern California, "is the damnedest place I ever saw . . . suspicion and bitterness all through the place." There was "an unreasoning blind fear of 'Communist agitators.'" Anyone who disagreed was labeled a Communist. "Oh, my dear," she wrote Eleanor, "I'm so sick of the whole miserable business!"

Only the prospect of her July holiday with Eleanor, planned to take place at the same time as FDR's voyage to the Caribbean, the Panama

Canal, and Hawaii, made Hick's life endurable. But even though they were soon to reunite, she felt remote: "You, Washington, the apartment in New York, Prinz—they all seem very far away this morning. I wonder if it will be like this when I die."

Eleanor, sensing that Hick was fearing disappointment, reassured her: "I can't understand why you are so worried dear, why can't you just be natural? Of course we are going to have a good time together and neither of us is going to be upset."

CHAPTER NINE

GETTING AWAY WITH IT

HICK AND ELEANOR had been exchanging letters for months about their West Coast trip, imagining quiet and seclusion in beautiful places. But when Hick walked into the lobby of the hotel in Sacramento where they were to meet, she encountered a swarm of reporters and photographers clamoring for a story about Eleanor. Thanks in part to Hick, Eleanor was now a darling of the press—celebrated for her astounding energy and ability to turn up here, there, and everywhere. Time alone together was going to be hard to come by. But Hick had a plan.

The next day, she picked Eleanor up at the Sacramento airport and shepherded her quickly through the crush of reporters in the hotel lobby, explaining that the First Lady needed to freshen up before any interviews. As a former reporter, Hick told them, she understood their situation. They agreed, for the moment.

Unbeknownst to the reporters, Hick had arranged for a state trooper to drive her newly acquired small convertible to the rear entrance of the hotel and wait for the two of them to emerge. They took the front elevator up, then another elevator down to the rear entrance, threw their bags in the rumble seat, jumped in, and started off, with the trooper at the wheel. The Secret Service, which Eleanor usually treated as the enemy, had helped out by changing Hick's D.C. plates for California ones.

It was no use. They hadn't even gotten out of the city before they discovered that they were being followed. The state trooper was game and stepped on the gas pedal. Another trooper swung around in front of their car and put on his flashing red lights. Hick was worried: her little Plymouth, an inexpensive replacement for Bluette, hadn't been broken in yet and the trooper was taking it up to higher and higher speeds.

It was Eleanor who finally called a halt to the chase. "It's no use. Let's stop." She thanked the state troopers and sent them on their way. "We'll have to find some other way out of this business."

The reporters who crowded around the two women had one main question: where were they going? Eleanor refused to answer. "This is my vacation," she told them, "and I expect to be treated as any other tourist would be treated." She pulled her knitting from the backseat and announced that she would sit there all day before she told them where she was going.

Finally, they all agreed to retreat to a nearby roadside restaurant, where the reporters got a story of sorts. Mrs. Franklin Roosevelt, said one account, was trying to "lose herself" and "get away from being the President's wife."

The two were characterized in a stereotyped way: Eleanor ladylike, Hick large and tough. Eleanor ordered only a toasted cheese sandwich and black coffee, while her companion, a "buxom businesslike individual," who was "presumably her secretary," ordered barbecue, beans, and buttermilk, "with utter disregard for the effect on the girth." Then both, as a goodwill gesture, finished off with a slice of the Windmill Restaurant's homemade apple pie à la mode. Mrs. Roosevelt's companion, according to the restaurant owner, "looked as though she might pack quite a wallop with either the tongue or the fist." Hick and Eleanor sped off, leaving the reporters guessing.

They were going to Colfax, California, a tiny town near the Nevada border where Ella Morse Dickinson now lived. It had been six years since Ella and Hick traveled together to California, and since Ella met and married Ray Dickinson. Even though she was devastated at the time, her friendship with "Ellie" had survived, and they still exchanged frequent letters.

Long before the visit, Eleanor had been nervous about Hick's reconnecting with Ellie. "I'll be glad when Ella can be with you," she had written Hick. "I'll dread that too just a little." The reunion with Ellie raised questions for Hick too. She wondered, in her letters to Eleanor, if she would have been more stable if she'd married, as Ellie had.

Eleanor had answered, "Yes, dear, I think you will remember that I once told you I wished you had been happy with a man or that it might still be, I rather think that the lack of that relationship does create emotional *in*stability but people do seem to weather it in time and who knows what the future holds. In the meantime Ellie and I will try to do a little stabilizing or at least help you to do it!"

Something like a marriage, a lifelong partnership, might have been possible with someone like Ellie. But Hick's relationship with Eleanor could never be that. Even if Eleanor had dared to leave FDR and live openly with a woman, she was not able or willing to devote herself to just one other person. She was always going to be tied not only to a husband but to bonds of duty and friendship with many others. This was a painful realization that had grown on Hick in the years since she had met and fallen in love with her. It made this time alone together especially precious.

Eleanor had been thinking about what might have been in her own marriage. Driving with Franklin on the small roads around the Hyde Park estate, she "kept thinking of the mess we had made of our young lives here and how strange it was that I return here as indifferent and uninterested as a stranger." She doubted that the children felt any differently, since nothing at Hyde Park had ever been their own. "It is a pity one cannot live one's life once again," she wrote Hick, "but at least we can try to keep one's children from making the same mistakes."

The children's marriages were very much on her mind that summer.

Everyone, including Hick, seemed to like Elliott's new wife, Ruth, and were hopeful this second marriage would last. Eleanor had great hopes too for Anna's second marriage to John Boettiger. At that moment Anna was in Reno, Nevada, fulfilling the residency requirements for a divorce from her first husband, Curtis Dall. The press had been in wild pursuit from the moment Anna arrived—to everyone's horror, one reporter had been killed, in fact, in a car chase. The whole thing was making Eleanor "boil."

For Eleanor, the visit with Ellie was a welcome respite from public life. For Ellie, it was a once-in-a-lifetime event—the First Lady and Hick, her former lover, stopping by for a few days on their romantic getaway out west. There were quiet dinners, picnics in the mountains, and evenings of reading aloud—things all three women loved. Eleanor read to them from Ellie's well-thumbed edition of *The Oxford Book of English Verse*.

Eleanor had insisted they would do a lot of "resting and reading" on their vacation. She had also mentioned, in passing, her idea of taking a little camping trip in the mountains. Now Hick discovered that there was an elaborate plan to explore Yosemite on horseback, riding up to a lakeside camp in the High Sierras, eleven thousand feet above sea level.

"How could you do this to me?" Hick protested.

"Oh, you'll manage," Eleanor replied casually.

Hick had no riding experience. In fact, her first published essay, for the Lawrence College literary magazine, had described her failed attempt to stay on a horse when she was thirteen. Nor was she in any shape for such a trip: she smoked too much, and she had gained weight during her months on the road. "Long busy days," she wrote Eleanor defensively at one point. "Lady, I get *hungry*."

Eleanor surely believed she was doing Hick a favor with her Yosemite plan. She worried about Hick's smoking and eating. She even suggested she take up knitting at one point, to cut down on cigarettes, and she wanted her to lose weight, because of her diabetes. Eleanor was following in the tradition of her uncle Theodore Roosevelt, who once threw her into the water to teach her to swim. Uncle Theodore advocated "the strenuous life" in which one "does not shrink from danger, from hardship or from bitter toil." A vigorous ride up the mountain would no doubt do Hick good.

For Eleanor, it was an exhilarating adventure. No longer was she the frightened little girl, reproached by her father for fearing to ride her donkey down a steep trail. Or the timid young bride on her honeymoon, left behind in the Dolomites while FDR took off up the mountain with a flirtatious rival. Now, at fifty, she was as fit and able as the rangers who guided them up the mountain. Later she would admit that the Yosemite plan might have been a wrong choice for Hick. "I learned that nobody who smokes a great deal and whose heart is not strong should try to camp above 10,000 feet. She more or less panted throughout the days we were there." It did not seem to occur to Eleanor at the time that Hick was now the one *she* used to be, struggling not to be left behind.

Nonetheless, both Eleanor and Hick had happy memories of the trip. Hick, who loved animals, developed an attachment to her little brown mare, who knew how to maintain her footing on the steep narrow trails. The camping was comfortable: a ranger cooked flapjacks and fresh-caught trout over a fire, and she and Eleanor slept on the ground outside their tent. "It's a wonderful experience to lie, warm and snug in a sleeping bag, high up in the mountains, and look at the stars," Hick wrote. Eleanor remembered that "the first rays of morning light over the mountain peaks were almost as lovely as the moon light."

Hick marveled at Eleanor's ability to plunge into the icy lake: she tried it once and thought she would never again catch her breath. When Eleanor decided to climb higher with one of the rangers, Hick stayed behind. "When they came down, I thought that Ranger was going to have a stroke. His face was purple." Eleanor, on the other hand, looked as though she had "come in from a stroll in Central Park."

But as long as they could be together, without the prying eyes of press and public, Hick was content. Even when her little mare decided to take a swim and dumped her in a creek, she was only embarrassed and amused. What infuriated her were the tourists who suddenly recognized Eleanor one day when the two of them came upon some tame chipmunks. They had just started to feed the animals when they noticed that people had surrounded them and were pointing their cameras at their rear ends. Hick exploded, employing some choice profanities. The two women left in a hurry, with Eleanor trying to shush her.

The rest of the vacation followed the same pattern. There were happy times in Hick's beloved San Francisco: a delicious evening at her favorite restaurant, Pierre New Frank's, followed by a cable car ride to the top of Russian Hill, where she had lived with Ellie. There was a quiet talk in the moonlight looking out over the bay. But the peace of that moment was followed by the shock of their return to a hotel lobby crowded with reporters and flashing cameras.

Over and over again, their private moments were interrupted. Finally they decided to get out of San Francisco ahead of schedule and head up the coast. When they got in Hick's Plymouth for the escape they discovered that it had been stripped bare by souvenir hunters. Even the Saint Christopher medal, which Eleanor had given Hick to protect her on her travels, was gone. On their final night together, at a hotel restaurant in Bend, Oregon, with a spectacular view of snowcapped mountains, they emerged to find yet another crowded lobby packed with curious townspeople, including the mayor.

Eleanor silently handed Hick the keys—she knew by now that Hick was likely to behave badly under such circumstances. Hick went up to their room, leaving Eleanor to deal with the crowd.

Eleanor arrived a half hour later, slamming the door behind her. "Franklin was right," she declared. "He said I'd never get away with it, and I can't.

"From now on I shall travel as I'm supposed to travel, as the President's wife, and try to do what is expected of me."

When they got back to Portland, where Eleanor was scheduled to meet FDR's ship, returning from Hawaii, the sitting room was filled with flowers sent by the First Lady's admirers—more flowers than either of them had ever seen in one place. To Hick, the flowers represented the future; the intimate life she and Eleanor had hoped for was simply impossible. "All you need," she declared, looking around at the extravagant display, "is a corpse."

Eleanor stayed on in Portland to greet FDR and her two youngest sons, Franklin Jr. and John, after their monthlong vacation on the tropical seas. "Elaborate preparations for welcoming the chief executive were receiving final approval," the AP reported the day before his arrival. There would be bands, large crowds, dignitaries, naval officers, and several cabinet members, along with Mrs. Roosevelt and her oldest son, James.

As she prepared to resume her official role, Eleanor told the *Berkeley Daily Gazette* that she should have a right to privacy when on vacation. Then she added a piece of ironic advice about catching the gangster John Dillinger, who was currently on the lam. "If I had charge of the Dillinger case," Eleanor told the reporter, "I would call off the police and send reporters after him. They would find him."

"DARLING, HOW I HATED to have you go," Eleanor wrote Hick after they parted in Portland. "It is still a pretty bad ache and I've thought of you all day, especially as we drove along the road we had covered yesterday."

Hick had gone on to San Francisco, where she met with the mayor to discuss the longshoremen's strike. "There have been times," she wrote Eleanor, "when I've missed you so much that it has been like a physical pain, and at those times I've hated San Francisco because you were not there."

What made it harder was the realization that there was no easy solution to their longing. "I'm afraid," Eleanor observed, "you and I are always going to have times when we ache for each other and yet we are not always going to be happy when we are together."

After she arrived at Campobello, Eleanor received an apologetic note from Hick. "I hope you are having a happy, restful time at camp—a happier, more peaceful time than you had with me. Oh, I'm bad, my dear, but I love you so. At times it becomes just one long, dreary ache for you. But I'm trying to be happy and contented."

Eleanor acknowledged that she was partly to blame for the tensions in the relationship. Hick might have been too demanding, but she was too restrained, too unable to express her needs. She admitted to giving everyone the feeling that "I don't need anything from them." Then, when they resented it, she wondered why. "I can't help it," she explained, "something locked me up and I can't unlock!" It was easier for Eleanor to express her concern for the other person than her own needs. She fretted when Hick developed a stomach illness, brought on by bad water. "Oh dear one," she wrote, "what wouldn't I give to have you here with me to-night & know just how you are & be able to take care of you." She worried too about "Stepchild," the unreliable Plymouth that had replaced the wrecked Bluette.

The truth was, however, that Eleanor was more carefree at Campobello than she had been with Hick. "Yes, I am happy here," she wrote her. Partly it was because she felt "needed and wanted." Her adoring friend Earl Miller was there, as was Nan Cook. Eleanor's German shepherd, Major, who had been exiled from the White House, was there too. But partly it was also "the place" that made her happy—a place that must have seemed even more precious now that privacy was so hard to come by. Campobello, a rocky island covered with pointed firs, was accessible only by boat in those days. The year-round population of sardine fishermen lived in small houses with picket fences and well-tended flower gardens. In the summer, wealthy families, including the Roosevelts, arrived to escape the summer heat on the mainland.

Eleanor and Franklin had spent a happy August in the Roosevelts' thirty-four-room "cottage" on the island in 1904, before their marriage. In 1908 they had moved into a house of their own, thanks to a neighbor who offered it for sale to the family in her will. The furniture and dishes came with the house, but Eleanor spent many pleasure-filled hours rearranging things the way *she* wanted them. She loved the place, even in the fog, and Franklin did too.

"Franklin was always on vacation when he came to Campobello," she remembered, "and many of the children's happiest times were with him there." Even after the terrifying days in August 1921, when FDR lay paralyzed and marooned on the island with an undiagnosed illness, Eleanor continued to love Campobello.

She described a happy moment there to Hick: "The sun is out, and the fog is rolling out to sea, and I'm sitting in the bottom of the boat, sniffing salt air and every now and then looking over the water to my green islands and grey rocky shores."

Hick had visited Campobello once, during the car trip she and Eleanor took together into Canada. That was one of the rare occasions when the place was unpopulated. But for Eleanor, Campobello had always been somewhere to welcome and entertain friends—not just one special friend. Campo was never going to be the quiet cottage for two that Hick dreamed of.

At times, Eleanor had gone along with Hick's fantasy. Earlier that year, at an exhibit of furniture made at the Val-Kill factory, she had written her about "one corner cupboard I long to have for our camp or cottage or house, which is it to be? I've always thought of it as in the country but I don't think we ever decided on the variety of abode nor the furniture." She added that "we probably won't agree."

By the fall of 1934, both Eleanor and Hick knew that dream had died. Hick was learning to accept, with varying degrees of success, that she wasn't going to get all of Eleanor, as she had somehow imagined when she left the AP, but was going to have to share her with a whole host of others. There were her husband and children, of course—that went without saying. But there was also Earl, whose attentions were important and flattering, and Nan Cook, and also Louis Howe, whose support had been so critical at difficult times in the past. Louis was living at the White House, slowly dying of emphysema. When she was in town, Eleanor took him out for a drive almost every day. Most of all, there was Eleanor's work. At night she worked on her mail until the wee hours. During the day, Tommy was constantly by her side taking dictation. Hick was still fond of Tommy, but she had learned never to hope for Eleanor's attention when she was around: the two of them never stopped. "My real trouble is not that I don't care enough," Eleanor once acknowledged to Hick, "but that for so many years I've let my work engulf me . . . it has become my master!"

Hick understood that she was either going to have to share Eleanor Roosevelt with her work and with the rest of the world or lose her altogether. She acknowledged that she was "the worst of the lot" in asking and expecting too much from her beloved Eleanor. But she insisted she was trying not to be that way anymore. She added and underlined, "I'm going to succeed."

CHAPTER TEN

NOW OR NEVER

THE MIDTERM ELECTIONS that fall of 1934 were going to be the first real test of the Roosevelt presidency. FDR's election in 1932 was more of a referendum on Hoover's failures than on FDR's promises. But now, after two years of activism and some signs of progress, the New Deal was on the line. To move forward with the "bold, persistent experimentation" he promised when he took office, FDR needed an unprecedented midterm triumph: a net gain of seats in House and Senate that would allow him to be even bolder, to complete what many, including Eleanor Roosevelt, considered half-measures that "only bought time."

As the election drew near, Eleanor reluctantly resumed her role as "Mrs. R." She was pleased, as she wrote to Hick, that FDR was in a "militant" mood after the resignation of his budget director, Lewis Douglas, a man who opposed public works measures. She was also enthusiastic about participating not just in FDR's campaign but also in the campaign of her friend Caroline O'Day, who had worked on Democratic campaigns with her in the past. O'Day was running for "congressman-at-large," a position that was created to reflect a population increase without the reapportionment of districts. She would be representing all of New York State.

Both the Roosevelts were eager to have O'Day in Washington. Eleanor in particular saw O'Day's candidacy as an opportunity to influence decisions on the issues she cared most about: peace, women's rights, Negro rights, and the exciting new idea of Social Security.

Eleanor Roosevelt was breaking new ground: never before had a president's wife participated in a congressional campaign. As usual, she insisted that her work as finance chair for O'Day had nothing to do with the White House or being First Lady. "I believe in certain things," she told the *New York Times*, "and I think a person who does believe in certain things has a right to support them."

Campaigning for O'Day brought back happy memories of the 1920s, when the two were part of a lively political quartet, along with Nancy Cook and Marion Dickerman, barnstorming around New York State. O'Day, who devoted herself to politics after her wealthy husband died in 1916, even played a small part in the original Val-Kill partnership. "When politics is through with us," she wrote in the *Women's Democratic News* in 1925, "we are retiring to this charming retreat that is now rearing its stone walls against the beautiful cedars of a Dutchess County hillside."

Eleanor liked to point out in her stump speeches around the state that O'Day represented "the real reason most women enter politics"—not to win elections but to change the social order. Eleanor criticized the Republicans for their short memories. In 1933, they were willing to accept regulation. They said, "'Take our business. Do anything to make it run.'" Now "the sick man is better and doesn't like 'regulation.'" Nothing matters but profit. Nor was it right for Republicans to call for a "balanced budget" when so many people were still suffering. "Are you going to stop feeding the hungry?" she asked.

Hick too was caught up in the partisan fight. Her reports, as she made her way east from California through Nevada, Wyoming, Utah, and finally Kansas, devoted more time to taking the temperature of the electorate. California, she reported, was on a hunt for Communists, orchestrated by the right-wing, "violently anti-administration" metropolitan newspapers. The list of "reds" included Secretary of Labor Frances Perkins and, down in the Imperial Valley, Harry Hopkins and the president himself. But Hick had the impression that the majority of Californians, while they hated and feared Communists, "do not believe quite all the newspapers have to say on the subject."

Farther east, in places like Winnemucca, Nevada, she found ordinary people—garage men, filling station people, restaurant keepers, storekeepers—believing that business was a little better than it had been the year before. "Sometime, somewhere, somehow, they feel the President will find a way out."

There was even some good news in a couple of places. Virginia City was prospering, thanks to a new gold and silver mining technique. And the construction of the monumental Boulder Dam (later Hoover Dam) now employed about forty-eight hundred men, many of whom would have otherwise been wandering the country in search of work and shelter.

What people didn't like, however, was the intrusive "social working" by the federal government, especially when it meant that pay was sporadic and inadequate. "This ain't a job," a worker on a high school stadium in Casper, Wyoming, told her. "I don't know exactly what you'd call it, but it ain't no job—not when some case worker comes and tells you how much you need to live on, decides for you, and you only work two or three days a week, and then maybe you don't even get all the case worker says you should have. A man doesn't feel he's getting anywhere, somehow."

People asked when the federal government would bring back the Civil Works Administration, a program that had employed hundreds of thousands building roads and bridges for a brief period before being discontinued out of political caution. It was a message that Hick's boss, Harry Hopkins, heard loud and clear.

In Kansas, where farmers had suffered years of drought, Hick saw miles of burnt brown pastures and Russian thistle piled up to feed the very thin cattle. Yet farmers who were offered a chance under a federal relocation program to move to better land refused. "All we need is a little rain!" one protested.

"Human patience," Hick wrote Hopkins, "is a beautiful—and terrible—thing!"

It was funny in a way. Here she was, bringing hope for the future, and they were telling her they didn't need her government welfare. Just a little bit of rain. "They don't want to be 'rehabilitated,'" Hick wrote Eleanor in September. "Tonight the humor of it hit me right in the stomach. I laughed and laughed. . . . I wonder if we aren't rather losing our perspective."

ON NOVEMBER 6, 1934, Caroline O'Day and the entire Democratic ticket scored a huge and unprecedented victory in the midterm elections. For the first time in history, the party of a sitting president gained seats in both houses of Congress: nine in the House and nine in the Senate.

A few days later, Harry Hopkins was driving with his assistant Aubrey Williams and a few other political pals to the racetrack in Laurel, Maryland, when he suddenly announced, "Boys, this is our hour. We've got to get everything we want—a works program, social security, wages and hours, everything—now or never. Get your minds to work on developing a complete ticket to provide security for all the folks of this country up and down and across the board."

Very soon Hopkins had a proposal to take to FDR, who was spending his traditional Thanksgiving break in Warm Springs. By the end of the vacation, Hopkins and FDR, with the help of Rex Tugwell and others who were on hand, had worked out a plan for the most ambitious program ever undertaken by any federal government anywhere in the world. At that point, the new plan did not yet have a name.

It still didn't have a name on January 4, when FDR, giving his State of the Union speech to Congress, translated it into down-to-earth language. The heart of the plan would be work projects, using the skills and trades of the unemployed. The projects should be "useful," should spend a considerable portion on wages for labor, and should promise an ultimate return to the federal treasury. The government funds should be "actually and promptly spent" and must in all cases give employment to those on relief, in localities where need was greatest.

In April, when Congress finally approved and funded the new relief project, it was still a many-headed beast without a single leader; Harold

Ickes and Harry Hopkins were vying for dominance. FDR, trying to please everyone as usual, kept the two men guessing about who would head up what was finally taking shape as the Works Progress Administration (WPA). In the end, the risk-taking Hopkins won out over his more prudent rival Ickes, who was left to oversee larger projects as head of PWA.

Eleanor had her doubts about WPA. She feared it wasn't ambitious enough in a nation where unemployment was still at 20 percent. She and many others thought it a mistake to target only relief recipients for WPA assistance. In order to qualify, a person had to be reduced to destitution. Eleanor believed WPA should have been more inclusive.

But in the end, WPA would prove to be one of the New Deal's most important programs, providing more than eight million jobs to hungry and needy Americans, while enormously improving the country's infrastructure, transforming its public spaces, and inspiring a wave of creativity in the arts.

In the meantime, FDR's choice of Harry Hopkins to head WPA was good news for Hick. Hopkins trusted Hick's reports from the field; now he would need her to monitor implementation of the new program. Hick still had a job.

CHAPTER ELEVEN

BLOWING OFF

WHEN HICK AND ELEANOR went to the opera together, Hick, to the amazement of her companion, would sit frozen in a kind of trance after the curtain came down. She could be "torn to shreds" listening to a recording of Wagner's *Tristan and Isolde*. She rooted without reservation for *her* team—whether it was the Minnesota Gophers or the Brooklyn Dodgers—and she was amazed and amused that Eleanor cared not a jot one way or the other. In October 1932, in the middle of FDR's first campaign for president, Hick got to attend the World Series with the Roosevelt family at Yankee Stadium. It was game three of the Series, between the New York Yankees and the Chicago Cubs—a thrilling game in which Babe Ruth and Lou Gehrig each hit two home runs. But what made the game a baseball legend for all time was Babe Ruth's "calling" his second home run—pointing out the spot in the bleachers where he planned to land it—before he swung the bat. Eleanor, comfortably wedged between FDR and her son Jimmy, slept through the entire thing.

There were many times when Eleanor grew impatient with Hick's lack of control over her feelings. "Why do you have to *feel* in a way which makes you have bad times?" she protested to Hick, after Hick had stormed off in one of her fits of jealousy. Yet Hick's ability to "feel" was one of the things Eleanor loved about her. Though Eleanor kept her own feelings under control, she gravitated to people who were capable of strong emotion and rebellion. At Allenswood, she passionately defended the girl who was expelled for throwing an inkstand at a teacher. As First Lady, she took her cue from people who were zealous about their causes. Even though she often wished Hick could be calmer about their relationship, Eleanor admired Hick's ability to write and live with such passion. She once praised one of Hick's reports for being "explosive."

Even after the satisfaction of the midterm victory, there was still plenty for Hick to rage about back in the field. After the passage of WPA legislation, in April 1935, things got worse instead of better for people relying on the New Deal. With the mindlessness of a huge bureaucracy, the federal government cut off funding for existing programs in many places before the WPA funding made its way through the pipeline to actual human beings. It led Hick to file some of her most outraged reports. In Toledo, Ohio, she wrote, seventy-two crossing guards had their pay cut off yet continued to guard children crossing the street, working only for groceries while they waited for the WPA to kick in. Two months went by, and there were still no paychecks.

"People keep asking them, 'Got your pay yet?' When they answer no, the President loses another friend."

"We're getting a bad reputation," Hick warned, "for not living up to promises."

Even more shocking was the situation in the Upper Peninsula of Michigan, where Hick arrived that December in biting cold and deep snow. The district WPA director, one Mr. Sweet, met her at the train station and drove her, slithering and slipping, up to the worksite on top of a small mountain. In wind that cut to the bone, two hundred men were at work clearing underbrush and digging out stumps to make a roadway and build a ski jump. The road they were building was to be named Franklin D. Roosevelt Parkway. It was a magnificent site, with forty-mile views on a clear day. From one spot, Hick counted eleven lakes. Beautiful pines ran down the steep slopes. It was indeed a perfect spot for a park and a ski jump.

But the men, Hick learned, had been taken off relief just as soon as they went to work for the WPA, and had been waiting for a whole month for the first paycheck from the new agency. Some of them had been coming to work with "nothing but onions" (Hick underlined for emphasis) in their dinner pails. Thirty of them, she realized, "hadn't brought dinner pails because there was nothing to bring in them." Some of them were threatening to walk off the job. But so far they were "still plodding along, patient, dumb. . . . Ye Gods," Hick fumed, "doesn't anyone in Washington realize what it means to run into debt when you are trying to support a family?" She returned to the office and "landed with both feet" on the disbursing officer, who promised to get some of the checks out there that afternoon, and the rest the next day.

But Hick couldn't get the workers out of her mind, "out there in the bitter wind, working on the 'Franklin D. Roosevelt Parkway.'" Mr. Sweet couldn't either. Finally, he said, "Aw, hell, let's send some food out there." Hick responded, "You bet," and offered to pay for it.

"No, you won't," was his answer.

Sweet gave an assistant a ten-dollar bill and told him to load up the car with sandwiches and hot coffee and get it out to the job. "And God help him if he ever told where it came from." Hick and Sweet agreed to go fifty-fifty on whatever it cost.

Hick considered writing a report to Harry Hopkins that would be "anything but pretty." But she decided to wait, believing that the payroll business would work itself out. "We're in this mess," she wrote Eleanor. "It should have been prevented, but wasn't. . . . And in the meantime I blow off to you. Because you are *safe*."

Hick knew that she was sometimes viewed back in Washington as a Cassandra who saw only the "dark side." But what she was witnessing, day in and day out, would make anyone feel gloomy. "And God help us if Congress ever really *does* start an investigation of relief and WPA. . . . The thing's too big. It's got out of hand. And much of it is so ridiculous. . . . Objective? HELL—I can't be objective."

As outspoken as she was, Hick was temperate in comparison with a seventeen-year-old colleague and friend named Martha Gellhorn. Hick had encouraged Harry Hopkins to hire Gellhorn to report from the field. But she sensed early on that Gellhorn was likely to be even less able than she to keep the emotional distance required for the job. After two months in the field, Gellhorn was so outraged by the poverty and bureaucracy that she stormed into Hopkins's office and threatened to quit and write an exposé. Hopkins convinced her to go meet with Mrs. Roosevelt instead.

Gellhorn took an immediate liking to Eleanor; she later described her blue eyes as "attendrissantes"—enveloping their object in tenderness. Eleanor managed to get past Gellhorn's indignation about relief programs and discover that she was unhappy as well about the winding down of her affair with Bertrand de Jouvenal. Eleanor convinced her to stay on the job, promising to make sure her reports got read and to try to turn them into action.

Gellhorn now became Hick and Eleanor's shared project. "Poor Marty!" Eleanor wrote Hick. "I guess you've got to take her on and be her 'tower of strength.' Don't let her get sorry for herself and become just another useless, pretty, broken butterfly. She has too much charm and real ability for that."

Hick promised to do her best. "Since I backed her originally," she wrote Hopkins, "I'm prepared to take any rap there is." There were two things to be done, Hick believed. First, she had to get "a broader, saner viewpoint on this thing." Second, she had to learn to "keep her mouth shut." She has "plenty of ability," Hick told Hopkins. "I'll manage her somehow, or wring her neck."

But Gellhorn refused to be managed. She stayed on the job for another ten months. Then one day, on a visit to the little town of Coeur d'Alene, Idaho, she discovered a group of farmers and ranchers toiling away for a dishonest contractor. "They told me about how awful it was—these big strong westerners just shoveling mud around." She took the workers out for beers and suggested to them that the way to get attention was to throw some bricks though the windows of the Federal Emergency Relief Administration offices. After she left town, some of the men did just that, triggering an FBI investigation of possible Communist activity. Gellhorn wrote gleefully to her parents that she was now considered a "dangerous Communist." Hopkins was forced to fire her.

It says a lot about Eleanor's attraction to dissent that she remained Gellhorn's friend and admirer. She invited her to dinner with FDR and encouraged her to speak her mind to him. Knowing that Martha had no place to go when she lost her job, Eleanor even invited her to live and write at the White House. It was there that Gellhorn began work for which she was much better suited, using her experience in the field to create a masterful collection of fiction, *The Trouble I've Seen.*

What set Hick apart from someone like Martha Gellhorn was her ability to be a team player. Unlike Eleanor, Hick had a fan's temperament: just as she had cheered on the Gophers back in Minnesota, she now rooted wholeheartedly for FDR, Hopkins, and the WPA. When there was good news, she was just as capable of celebrating as she had been of crying foul. There was, increasingly, more to celebrate. Back in 1933, Hick had written a vivid description of sixty-three families blacklisted by a mining company for union activity, and living for the two years since in tents about forty miles from Charleston, West Virginia.

"Gosh," she had written Eleanor, "I wish I could make you see that place as I saw it!" The tents, damp and black with coal dust, were huddled together near a river, with "those beautiful, and rather terrible hills" in the background.

A little group of men were sitting silently on a big rock: "Ragged, discouraged, bitter." There were women around, doing a little washing and cleaning up, and there were a few pathetic gardens. "And those terrible looking children." Dysentery was so common it was ignored, and the children had skin diseases. She saw a small baby covered with sores, a woman wearing nothing but a ragged dress and no shoes, and a man whose trousers were so patched you couldn't see the original cloth. There were thirty-four able-bodied men in the tent colony.

"What they ought to do with that mine is to put a few sticks of dynamite under it and blow it up," one of them had told Hick, "and I'd certainly like to be the guy to do it." Hick watched as several of the men came up to the investigator and begged her, "almost with tears in their eyes," to get them out of there before winter.

"These tents won't last another winter," one of them said.

When FDR heard about the tents from Eleanor, he told her, "Get those families out of those tents before Christmas." With the help of Hopkins and the Quakers, it was done.

Now, two years later, Hick revisited the scene of the tent colony that had "got the President all worked up." The tents were gone, "every last, horrible one of them!" The families that remained were living in wooden houses they had built for themselves with the help of relief workers. There were gardens around them, and even flowers.

Hick drew double lines under the next piece of news: "<u>And all but 15</u> <u>of those blacklisted coal miners are back at work—and in the mine that</u> <u>blacklisted them!</u> Isn't that simply swell?" The Wagner Act, passed in July 1935, prohibited the mine company from discriminating against miners affiliated with a union. The law changed everything for the tent families.

There was good news in Indiana too: farmers, with a boost from federal programs, were beginning to prosper again. Knowing that Harry Hopkins's father had sold harness for a living back in Grinnell, Iowa, Hick sought out a harness salesman in the little town of Bluffton, Indiana, to see how things were going. It turned out the man had gone from selling twenty-five sets of harness in a full year to selling fifty-four in ten months. And the farmers were coming in with cash, not asking for credit. "A set of harness (in case you've forgotten) costs about $65," Hick wrote Hopkins. There was no way, she predicted, that FDR could lose Indiana in the coming election.

One of Hick's happiest moments on the job came in January 1936 on a visit to Newark airport, where some eighteen hundred men were at work enlarging the field and installing drainage. It was a hard assignment: dig down three feet and there was trouble with water, muck, and quicksand. Some of the men were working in water up to their knees.

It was payday. Hick stood by the paymaster's window for an hour, watching the men as they lined up to get their checks. In her letter to Eleanor, she added the exhilaration she left out of her official report. "That WAS an experience. A seemingly endless procession of eyes—gleaming, anxious, expectant. The smile of relief when the check was handed over. . . . On the whole, I feel encouraged. These men have had a couple of pay days. They look better fed and, certainly, better clothed than those out in Michigan. Things have settled down." This kind of progress made Hick increasingly confident that FDR would win a second term. The only person in FDR's circle who wasn't excited about the growing possibility of a second term was Eleanor. In April 1935, she made the mistake of telling her mother-in-law that "it would not break my heart if Franklin were not re-elected." Sara Roosevelt reacted by asking her grandson James, after Eleanor left the room, "Is that why she stays in politics, just to hurt his chances of re-election?"

Eleanor was wounded and angry that her mother-in-law didn't trust her to support FDR. "Now I ask you," she wrote Hick, "after all these years?" Hick was the only one she could safely confide in about her hurt.

What her mother-in-law couldn't understand was how much she hated all the hoopla, all the scheming, all the infighting, and all the adulation. "And they say one day I might run for office," she once wrote Hick. "I'd have to be chloroformed first!"

Most of all, Eleanor hated the press scrutiny of her family. All the prurient interest in Anna's divorce and remarriage had been especially painful, and the younger boys had gotten into minor scrapes that attracted the attention of reporters, who were always ready to think they were wild or spoiled. The incident that upset her most, however, had to do with FDR's decision to bring the Roosevelts' eldest son, James, on board as an adviser. Eleanor had been against it from the start, knowing that it was going to provoke accusations of nepotism. But FDR went ahead anyway, encouraging James to leave his business in New York (a decision that entailed some expense) and join him in the White House. Then, once he was criticized,

FDR reversed course under false pretenses, claiming that the doctor had advised that the D.C. climate would be bad for James and he should return to his previous job.

"I've been ready to chew everyone's heads off!" Eleanor wrote Hick. "James looking upset and bewildered meets me outside and says his health has nothing to do with it but he thinks FDR is afraid if he gives up his work it will bring more stories so having spent $1000 on legally getting out of business he's been told by Pa to go back on a 3-day a week basis. . . . He's going back to N.Y. tomorrow. . . . He's hurt and I'm so mad with F.D.R. I'm so on edge it is all I can do to hold myself together just now."

Even Hick was alarmed, fearing Eleanor might actually leave her marriage for good. Whatever her personal wishes, Hick understood that a break would destroy FDR's political future and undermine the still-fragile national recovery. Eleanor reassured her: "Hick darling, I'm sorry I worried you so much. I know I've got to stick. I know I'll never make an open break and I never tell F.D.R. how I feel. I blow off to you but never to F!"

EVEN AS HICK DID HER BEST to keep Eleanor on an even keel, the intensity Eleanor admired in Hick's work was becoming a growing problem in their relationship. Hick resented being sandwiched in among Eleanor's many obligations. She resented even more being sandwiched in among Eleanor's friends.

"It's sometimes rather tough to be the most recent of the people who have any claim on you!" Hick wrote. "I have no seniority rating at all!" She promised that it would be easier "when the time comes when I don't care so much—or at least not in the *way* I care now."

In the meantime, however, Hick failed miserably at sharing and wound up lonely and angry as a result. She strongly disliked some of Eleanor's closest friends. She considered Nan Cook and Marion Dickerman snobs, and they in return thought she was coarse and common. That eliminated many possibilities for Hick to be with Eleanor, who almost never said no to one friend because she wanted to be with another. Nan had come with her often to Campobello and helped her redecorate the White House, on top of working with her as a partner in the Val-Kill furniture business. Nan had seniority, as Hick pointed out. Nan was a given.

Hick's behavior toward Earl Miller touched off a rare moment of anger from Eleanor. "I think you can scarcely realize how you made me feel to-night," she wrote Hick after an encounter during one of Eleanor's radio broadcasts. "You went right by me at the studio without speaking. You told me you would entertain yourself in Washington before I had time to tell you whether I was busy or not, you barely spoke to Earl and Jane [Earl's companion] at the play who were my guests and certainly did noth-ing rude to you and when I asked you to go in so you could sit by me you deliberately changed and sat as far away as possible. . . . I'm so deeply hurt tonight that I almost wish I had no friends. . . . For Saturday and Sunday at least let's try to be cheerful and polite and not make everyone uncom-fortable."

Hick's jealousy wasn't directed so much at any one person, however. It was about the impossibility of being *the* person. Hick was even jealous of people she liked. A fundamental shift was occurring in the relationship. Hick's intense craving for intimacy was beginning to feel suffocating to Eleanor. Her reaction was to distance herself. She began making a distinc-tion between the way she felt and the way Hick felt. "You have a feeling for me which I may not return in kind," she wrote. She loved other people "in the same way or differently but each one has their place and one cannot compare them."

Even more pointed was her suggestion that Hick might want to look elsewhere for affection. "If I know someone I love is unhappy I can't be happy and I would be happier . . . to know they were happy even if it meant giving up my own relationship to them in whole or in part."

Alarm bells must have gone off when Hick received that letter. She wanted to be with Eleanor and no one else. But if she couldn't moderate her jealousy and passion, she risked losing any relationship with the one she cared most about.

Hick seems to have decided then that the only way to hold on to Elea-

nor was to need her less. The next spring, in an effort to change herself—
and to change Eleanor's feelings about her—she announced that she was
going to stay on the road, doing her job for Harry Hopkins, for the next
four months without a break.

"Are you taking the absent treatment because it helps?" Eleanor asked.
"If so I won't say a word." But her hurt feelings showed beneath her pretended indifference: "Well, dear it is for you to decide, for you are the one
who suffers and I just enjoy what I can have and learned long ago to accept
what had to be."

Perhaps in response to Eleanor's suggestion that she find someone else,
Hick got back in touch with Alicent Holt, an inspiring Latin teacher who
had been not much older than she when she went to Battle Creek High
School. Over several visits during her trips to Michigan, Hick and Alicent
renewed the connection of twenty-five years earlier, with open expressions
of affection. Alicent's letters to "Rena" began "Carissima" and "my very
own dear" and talked of how happy and energetic she felt anticipating
Hick's letters and visits. "I suppose I shall love you as long as you do me,
at least, and perhaps a little bit longer," Alicent wrote Hick.

In South Dakota, too, Hick sought a loving figure from her past: Lottie McCafferty, the childhood friend who had rescued her by finding a
place for her to live when her father and woman friend kicked her out of
the house in Bowdle. Lottie was "a swell person," Hick reported to Eleanor. "Warm, generous, *fine.*" She'd never finished high school, and her
husband was working as a machinist's helper on the railroad, happy to
have a job after being laid off for three years. Hick planned to take Lottie
with her as she traveled across Dakota and into Iowa.

"What I've tried to do this summer," Hick wrote, sounding very much
like she was emulating Eleanor, "has been to give a few people as much
fun as I could, as I went along. Lord knows when I'll ever be able to
again—if ever. Anyway, it's been fun. Alicent was the biggest success."

In June, she and Alicent spent several days together, sharing "a lovely
room" at the Lake Breeze Resort Hotel on Lake Superior. "This is it," Hick
wrote Eleanor. "The perfect place—in all the world—to spend a week

end." She added the usual "wish you were here" at the end of the letter, but this time it was more polite than desperate.

Hick was actually sounding happy much of the time as the summer wore on. "I realize what a fascinating job this has been," she wrote Eleanor. She dreaded going back to Washington and New York. No matter what she was doing a year hence, she thought she would look on this as "one grand Summer."

Meanwhile, Eleanor was enduring a July 4 celebration with FDR and his political and Harvard friends. "Dearest, how I wish you were here tonight. . . . I envy you off with one person when the day's work is done." Most of the time, she conceded, she'd rather be in a crowd than with one person. "But I'd like a few hours with you now and then."

Two weeks later, Eleanor sounded even sadder: "It is a strange world, so few of us free enough to do what we want to do, all of us trying to be happy in spots and make the best of what we can have." She had decided not to join FDR on the campaign trail in August, but to stay in New York. Ironically, it was now Eleanor who didn't want to share Hick, in the midst of a political campaign, surrounded by so many people. "It wouldn't be satisfactory after not seeing you for so long," she wrote, "to see you that way."

Eleanor was pessimistic about the campaign. FDR was losing support, she told Hick, but there was time to turn it around. "I feel, as usual, completely objective and oh! Lord so *indifferent*!"

Hick pushed back, forcefully. "I'm wondering if you or I—or any other enlightened person—really has any right to be as *indifferent* about the outcome of this election as you are. Oh, I know—you hate it all. The 'position.' And so do I when I'm with you. I can't even be polite about it. . . . A daily dose of Missy, along with all the fuss and pomp and adulation the man receives, will distort anyone's view. And you, personally, would like to be free. . . . And, so far as evaluating the president and his administration go—you 'can't see the woods for the trees.'"

She continued, "With all the faults—and the faults of some of the people around him—I still think he is a very great man. His defeat . . . will be a terrible calamity for millions of people in this country, the kind of people *you*, of all people, are supposed to care about. The poor and the lowly."

Despite her adoration, Hick wasn't afraid to speak her mind to Eleanor when it mattered. She *could* see the forest for the trees: the country's future depended on FDR's reelection. She was an essential counterforce.

Eleanor's reply was defensive: she was doing all she could. "One can be personally indifferent and yet do one's duty." She even argued that her unhappiness made her more effective. It was "only when one is oneself unhappy that one ever thinks about the individual right to the pursuit of happiness."

It wasn't easy, though, for Eleanor to keep her unhappiness out of her public appearances. "I'm back at my worst verge of tears condition which I hoped I could eliminate this summer," she wrote Hick in August. "I only hope no one else realizes it and I don't think they do for I look well."

Whatever the reasons for Hick's "absent treatment," it did create a new equilibrium in the relationship. After they reunited in New York in late September, Eleanor wrote her a joyous note: "All your fight has been worth while. It was grand being with you, feeling no strain and I take my hat off to you. . . . Bless you for one grand person."

Yet something had shifted, away from the initial intimacy toward a deep friendship at a lower temperature. Hick was going to have to accept being "one grand person"—not the one and only.

In the weeks leading up to the election, Eleanor's private annoyance with FDR made it easier for her to follow the advice of his campaign managers and keep a low profile. Her opposite number, Alf Landon's wife, Theo, had vowed to stay out of politics entirely and devote herself to her family, so the advisers wanted Eleanor to do the same. In her "My Day" column, which she had begun writing in December 1935, she was a model of neutrality on the day before the election: "What happens tomorrow is entirely out of our hands, the record of the past four years, the campaign that has been waged, all are over and whatever the decision may be one accepts it and builds as useful and pleasant a life as one can under whatever circumstances one has to live. You can not get unduly excited about the inevitable!"

Other people did get excited, though, when the returns started to come in. The electoral results were unprecedented. Roosevelt's 523-to-8 victory over Alf Landon was the most lopsided in a hundred years and marked the beginning of a new Democratic coalition that would change American politics for decades to come. On election night, several thousand neighbors, bearing torches and accompanied by a band playing "Happy Days Are Here Again," walked over to Hyde Park to cheer their hero. Back in Washington the next day, thousands gathered on the White House lawn to celebrate.

The victory freed both Roosevelts to speak their minds. On January 6, before a joint session of Congress, FDR went after the Supreme Court for consistently ruling New Deal Programs unconstitutional. He gave the National Recovery Act (NRA) as an example. "The statute has been outlawed," he told Congress. "The problems have not." According to the *New York Times*, "riotous cheering" greeted every one of his references to the recalcitrant Supreme Court.

The next day, Eleanor gave a feisty address to one hundred members of the New York Junior League, defending WPA workers who were being accused by New Deal critics of "leaning on their shovels." She urged the Junior Leaguers to go out and talk to the WPA workers and "get a cross section of their thoughts and needs." Or, Eleanor suggested, the Junior Leaguers could just try shoveling snow for a little while to see how it feels. "I know," she told the ladies, "because I've done it myself."

CHAPTER TWELVE

LOOKING FOR A HOME

ELEANOR ROOSEVELT HAD SPENT her entire life adjusting to houses that didn't feel like home. As a young child, she had moved with her family from place to place as her parents sought a cure for her father's ailments. After her mother died, she had been a lonely inhabitant of her grandmother's house, with only servants and much older aunts for company. In marriage, of course, she had lived in grand houses, in Hyde Park and Manhattan, but they were decorated entirely by her mother-in-law. Nor had she felt particularly attached to the governor's mansion in Albany. Once, when Frances Perkins visited there and expressed admiration for Eleanor's flexibility in sleeping in one room or another, Eleanor told her, "This isn't my house. It belongs to the State of New York. It's furnished by the State of New York . . . in the official taste of the State of New York. . . . I've never bought so much as a teacup for myself. . . . I've never had anything." The White House wasn't home any more than the governor's mansion had been. But she worked to make it comfortable.

The Roosevelts had a more casual attitude toward the White House than many of its previous inhabitants. "There was a sense of cluttered, natural comfort and democratic hospitality," Marion Dickerman remembered. Since they were aristocrats themselves, Martha Gellhorn noted, both of the Roosevelts were quite used to big houses. "It was one of the most pleasing and easy-going, amusing places you could possibly be in." The White House was also an ancestral home of sorts, familiar to Eleanor and Franklin from the presidential term of their uncle/cousin Theodore.

Eleanor rearranged the second-floor living space in a way that helped humanize the oversized rooms, with their tall ceilings and grand windows. At one end of the vast central hall, she replaced Mrs. Hoover's palms, bamboo furniture, and canary cages with big sofas and chairs slip-covered in cotton—not unlike those in the library at the big house in Hyde Park—and closed it off with folding screens. That space became the West Hall breakfast nook, where Eleanor launched the day—with Hick if she was in town between field trips. Breakfast was a more bountiful meal than most at the Roosevelt White House: juice, eggs, muffins, popovers, bacon. The president's little dog Fala was always on hand, ready to do his tricks in exchange for a few bites of toast from Eleanor. After that, the First Lady would retreat behind the *New York Times*.

Eleanor ate sparingly, Hick remembered. "Fala and I did not." Fala would come around to her side of the table and beg every crumb of bacon he could get. "I think he always thought of me as 'the bacon woman.'"

Eleanor would pour café au lait—a drink she had learned to love as a schoolgirl in England—out of two pots, one in either hand. It was a "remarkably deft performance." Hick always drank hers in a big blue-and-white willow ware cup.

Mrs. Hoover had carefully redone the Monroe Room, with Monroe-era replicas of fine French furniture. But this too Eleanor undid, turning it into another sitting room, furnished with her own blue velvet chairs and sofas. It was there that she passed out candied fruit and useful information to the "news gals," comfortably ensconced on chairs, sofas, and, when necessary, the floor. The replica chairs were dispersed to other parts of the house.

The Oval Room, which sat like a large button right in the middle of the classic rectangular layout, had served as a sitting room with a grand piano in the Hoover era. Now it became FDR's study—stuffed with the objects of an inveterate collector. A British visitor who kept a diary described it as "a delightful oval room . . . and one of the most untidy rooms I have ever seen. It is full of junk. Half-opened parcels, souvenirs, books, papers, knick-knacks, and all kinds of miscellaneous articles lie about every-where, on tables, on chairs, and on the floor."

Nautical prints and ship models covered the walls, along with portraits of FDR's mother and wife. A herd of ceramic pigs, and at least one donkey, were part of the crowd on his large desk. Conveniently, the Oval Room adjoined FDR's bedroom and bath. From his bed, he had a fine view of the Washington Monument out the south-facing window.

There were sliding doors connecting FDR's bedroom to Eleanor's suite of rooms next door, but at some point he had them blocked with a large seven-drawer highboy. Nonetheless, Eleanor visited FDR most mornings as he breakfasted and planned out his day.

Eleanor also enjoyed a view of the Washington Monument from her southwest corner suite, and wrote in "My Day" that she always looked at it first thing in the morning and just before she went to bed at night. "It would be impossible to live in the White House and forget the Father of our country, for his monument is the one thing you never lose sight of if you look out of any of the south windows."

Eleanor used the large room as an office, and the small adjoining room (probably designed originally for a valet) as her bedroom. This too resembled the arrangement at the big house in Hyde Park, where FDR had the big bedroom and Eleanor occupied a spartan cot in a room next door. Eleanor's overnight guests usually stayed in the bedroom at the northwest corner of the building, which contained Lincoln's bed.

Hick, who lived in the White House off and on throughout the Roosevelt presidency, stayed in the little room adjoining the one with the Lincoln bed. Her budget was tight, and it cost nothing to stay at the White House when she was in Washington. "But that wasn't the only reason I stayed on at the White House, although I never told Mrs. Roosevelt," Hick confessed in her unpublished autobiography. "I couldn't bear the idea of being in Washington and hardly ever seeing her. And with her schedule as heavy as it was, I was certain that that was the way it would be. Even staying in the house I used to think I did not see very much of her—but at that I think I fared better than most of her friends."

Often when she was in town, Hick would get in at 10:30 or 11:00 at night and stop by Eleanor's sitting room, where Eleanor was usually buried in mail. If Eleanor was out for the evening, she would sometimes come into Hick's room when she got home and sit on the end of the bed to talk.

Hick's little room at the White House wasn't fancy. The furniture—a bed, a dressing table, a desk that jiggled, a rocking chair—was painted gray. A commode served as a night table, and there was a reading lamp on it that had a tendency to blink on and off. There was a dangerously small ashtray. Hick replaced it with a larger one from the dime store after a cigarette rolled off and burned a hole in the lace cover. There was also a comfortable green-and-brown overstuffed chair.

What made the room special, however, was the fireplace. "It was so placed that I could look into the fire only while in bed. But I never knew any greater comfort or luxury than lying in the bed with the flu . . . looking into that fire." What's more, someone came in twice a day with logs, poked up the fire, and swept the ashes.

Once, when the exiled king of the Serbs visited, Hick moved to the third floor so that his valet could stay next to him. It was one of the rare occasions on which the bedroom plan fulfilled the eighteenth-century architect's intentions. After the king left, Hick found one of his collar buttons in the corner of a dresser drawer and kept it as a souvenir.

There were some things Eleanor especially appreciated about the White House. She and FDR made good use of the swimming pool, which was added during their time. Eleanor was also, as she wrote in her "My Day" column, grateful to Mrs. Coolidge for installing a sun parlor on the third floor where the grandchildren could play and guests could recuperate. She loved having her family occupying the third floor, which was really "a little household with a kitchen of its own." It was "very amusing to go up at noon into the sun parlor and see the babies in their carriages and the older ones sitting at the table with their nurses, each one trying to show how proficient they are in table manners."

Missy's room was on the third floor, as were the servants' rooms and the room the Roosevelts called the "Chamber of Horrors," repository of all the many peculiar and unusable gifts that arrived at the Roosevelt doorstep. There too was Eleanor's Christmas closet: a room she filled with gifts throughout the year, and kept well supplied with wrapping paper and ribbon. Eleanor managed to give thoughtful presents to an astoundingly long list of acquaintances; she kept a record of each year's gifts in a thick alphabetized notebook. In her letters to Hick, she often mentioned that she'd been working on her Christmas list or in her Christmas closet.

Holidays were the times when Eleanor seemed to enjoy the White House most. She avoided the nightly "children's hour," where FDR poured drinks and joked with his entourage. That kind of gathering, which required everyone to laugh at FDR's stories and put up with his teasing, made her uncomfortable. But she was an entirely different person on special occasions like FDR's birthday and the annual Gridiron roastings, when parody and outrageous costumes were the order of the day. When there was a big inclusive celebration, with a planned program, she lost her usual inhibitions and took part with something close to abandon.

Even though Hick lived in the White House whenever she was in Washington, she retreated to her New York life when friends and family of the Roosevelts descended for special occasions. She was happy to have her private Christmas celebration with Eleanor, usually in New York, and hear about the White House festivities from Eleanor after it was over.

Christmas was the biggest White House occasion by far during the Roosevelt years. That was when FDR read Dickens's *Christmas Carol* aloud, doing all the voices, to the family. That was when all those presents piling up in the locked Christmas closet on the third floor finally came tumbling out and into the hands of friends and relatives. That was when, as Eleanor's grandson Curtis Roosevelt recalled so touchingly in his memoir *Too Close to the Sun*, his grandmother's "normal reserve" broke down. "All the preparations and festive merrymaking were permeated with a feeling of gaiety, and everyone, especially my grandmother, embraced the old-fashioned yuletide spirit." Along with everyone else in the family, she spent hours decorating the private, twenty-foot tall Christmas tree in the East Hall, placing real candles on all the branches to add to the excitement. The six-foot tall Roosevelt sons had the job of climbing up to light the highest ones.

Christmas morning, the stockings were hung in FDR's bedroom, and the children waited impatiently for the adults to appear. "While waiting, we would have identified our particular stocking, overstuffed with presents—truly overflowing because my grandmother always liked to add just one more small item to an already full stocking." Later in the day, there would be a few bigger presents to open under the tree.

Often when the Roosevelt children got together, the discussions were so heated that outsiders were alarmed. "What I loved about this Christmas ritual," Curtis wrote many years later, "was the sense of our family gathered together—a rare occasion when the usual conflicts and tensions were subdued and less competitiveness was on display."

Being together at Christmastime meant a lot to Eleanor too. In 1935, when Anna and her family stayed on the West Coast, she wrote that she and the dogs "felt very sad every time we passed your door it was hard to decorate the tree or get things distributed at the afternoon party without you and I dread dinner tomorrow night . . . and if anyone says much I shall weep for I've had a queer feeling in my throat whenever I thought of you. Kiss Sis and Buzz and tell them . . . we miss them very much."

Despite her efforts, however, the White House was never going to be the home Eleanor had sought for much of her life. Val-Kill had been her first attempt to create a home of her own. For ten years, starting in 1926, it was indeed a simple and pleasing retreat, away from the big house. But Val-Kill was shared with Marion Dickerman and Nan Cook. It would become entirely her own in the end, but only after a prolonged and difficult negotiation.

The very first place Eleanor could truly call her own was her apartment at 20 East 11th Street, in Greenwich Village. She began renting it in October 1935, just as she was turning fifty-one, midway through FDR's first term in the White House. Everything about her "little apartment," as she always called it, was liberating—beginning with the midnight train ride she usually took to get there from D.C.

"I really feel quite at home in the little room on that train," Eleanor confided in "My Day." The porter didn't even have to ask her what time she wanted to be awakened. Once in New York, the days were never long enough: there was Christmas shopping always, there were fittings for clothes at Arnold Constable or Milgrim, lunches and teas out with friends, and many, many evenings at the theater.

The apartment was a floor-through third-floor walk-up in an elegant brick town house owned by Esther Lape and her partner, Elizabeth Read. Eleanor had visited Esther and Lizzie there often in the 1920s, and her friendship with them was an important part of what she later called "the intensive education of Eleanor." In fact, the very first entry in the FBI's large file on Eleanor Roosevelt, accumulated over her years of activism, concerns the work she did with Lape and Read, along with Narcissa Cox Vanderlip, in 1924, on the effort to establish a World Court.

Nan Cook and Marian Dickerman had an apartment only a few blocks away from Eleanor's, on West 12th Street. Just across the hall from them lived Molly Dewson, a key player in the Democratic Party who became a great friend, along with her partner, Polly Porter. The books on their shelves were stamped "Porter-Dewson."

None of these women used the word "lesbian," but those in their circle, including Eleanor, understood that they were lovers and partners for life. In the Village, they could live without constant fear of disapproval.

"The easy unconventionality," observed the writer of *The WPA Guide to New York City*, "the charming old houses, comfortable as an old shoe, still invite the Villager, emerging from the subway after a visit to more formal neighborhoods, to drag off his or her hat and swing along home."

The freer atmosphere of the Village attracted some of New York's most important writers and thinkers. Willa Cather, whose work both Hick and Eleanor admired, lived there for twenty-one years with her companion, Edith Lewis, and hosted a salon on Fridays, with delicacies prepared by her French cook. Ida Tarbell, who brought down Standard Oil with her two-volume exposé, lived on 9th Street. Mabel Dodge, who inspired a prose poem by Gertrude Stein and a sculpture by Jo Davidson, attracted those in the know to her stunning all-white living room on the second floor at 23 Fifth Avenue. The Provincetown Players made MacDougal Street their winter home, and from there launched the career of one of America's most important playwrights, Eugene O'Neill.

Many of these inhabitants of the Village were quite conventional. Marianne Moore and Willa Cather were, as critic Alfred Kazin noted, "about as rakish as Calvin Coolidge." But a much wilder world existed a few blocks away, around Sheridan Square, where there were tearooms and restaurants owned and openly enjoyed by a more daring gay crowd. Such places no doubt inspired the 1936 article in *Current Psychology and Psychoanalysis* entitled "Degenerates of Greenwich Village," which described the Village as a "mecca for exhibitionists and perverts of all kinds." More benign stereotypes surfaced in the 1932 Clara Bow film *Call Her Savage*, in which the actress visits a dive where male couples and female couples sit with their arms around each other, and young men wait tables wearing frilly white aprons and maid's caps.

Eleanor's apartment was in the elegant part of the Village, just a few blocks from Washington Square, at an address even her mother-in-law would approve of. Yet when she came there, the Secret Service, the press, and the general public left her, miraculously, alone. For Eleanor, who hated being watched and followed, this was a great gift. It meant she could walk the streets and interact with other people, unencumbered by the distancing barrier of fame.

In her letters and in her column, Eleanor always describes the apartment as a happy place. "Now I am here and I am unpacked and feeling very content," she wrote Hick. Eleanor had a copy made of Hick's photo, to keep at West 11th Street. "This is a haven." It was a "hideaway," she told her "My Day" readers, a place where she could wake up after a good night's sleep and enjoy "a cheerful breakfast by the open fire." It was a place where she could stretch summer into October, lunching on her porch when "the sun was shining in so brightly it was almost too warm." It was a place she loved to come to and hated to leave.

The greatest advantage of the apartment was that it allowed Eleanor to dictate who would come when, without having to contend with all the competing demands and jealousies that surrounded her at Hyde Park and the White House. When Hick was in New York, she and Eleanor often met for dinner and the theater. When that happened, Eleanor would invite Hick to bring a robe and stay with her at the place that felt most like home.

FOR HICK, who had been kicked out of her own home at fourteen and spent many of her subsequent years trying to belong in an unwelcoming world, the idea of being allowed to stay at the White House was thrilling and intimidating all at once. The first night she stayed there, and was urged by Eleanor to "go say goodnight to the President," she was suddenly "scared stiff" of FDR, "a man with whom I had joked and laughed with complete ease when he was governor of New York."

Hick was deeply embarrassed one summer night after she unknowingly opened the windows and caused the room humidifier to overflow, soaking the rug and even seeping into the president's bedroom. No permanent damage was done, but for several days afterward she snuck into the state dining room immediately below to make sure there were no water stains on the ceiling.

FDR teased Hick about the incident for some time afterward. "It seems to me, Hick," he would say at lunch or dinner, "that Washington is a little less humid than it was." Then he would turn his gaze toward her. "What do you think, Hick?"

"I think you are right, Mr. President," she would answer meekly.

Hick worked hard to make herself inconspicuous when she stayed at the White House. If she heard the bell sound announcing that FDR was about to use the clumsy elevator, she would slip back into the adjoining room and wait until he had passed by in his wheelchair. The president even remarked once to Eleanor that he never knew when Hick was around.

Awed though she was, Hick took advantage of many of the perks the White House offered. When she was on the road working for Harry Hopkins, she sent her laundry back to the place she and Eleanor both referred to as her home. When she was in town, the White House seamstress, Frankie, refitted Eleanor's hand-me-down dresses so Hick could wear them. "The dresses are going to be *perfect*," Hick reported to Eleanor. "The black one really needs very little alteration—just moving some fasteners and shortening the skirt and sleeves! And the evening gown can be fixed quite easily, too. Thank you—and I shall love wearing them."

One of Hick's favorites among the staff was Elizabeth MacDuffie, known to everyone as "Mrs. Mac." Mrs. Mac's mother had been born into slavery in Georgia. She herself, however, was a graduate of Morris Brown College in Atlanta, had taught school, and knew a vast trove of poems by heart. One she recited for Hick, with great passion, was "Hagar's Farewell" by Augusta Moore, a retelling of the biblical story of the slave Hagar, ordered by the childless Sarah to become a second wife to Abraham:

> *I never asked his love; I wished it not;*
> *I feared ye both, for was I not your slave?*
> *I was an orphan, friendless and forlorn,*
> *A stranger among strangers and a slave.*

"My God," Hick wrote Eleanor, "what feeling she puts into those lines!"

Once, when Hick was in bed with the flu, Mrs. Mac said, "Didn't anybody ever iron you?" She directed Hick to lie on her stomach, spread a towel over her back, and passed a warm iron back and forth over her back and shoulders, "quietly talking to me of her girlhood days in the old South, until I felt completely relaxed and drowsy."

Several of Eleanor's guests who stayed in the room adjoining Hick's became Hick's lifelong friends. One was Belle Roosevelt, wife of Teddy

Roosevelt's son Kermit, who defied her Republican relatives to become an eloquent speaker for Democratic women. Another was Helen Gahagan Douglas, the actress who served as California's first Democratic congress-woman. Hick remembered one night when she and Douglas discovered that they had been standing facing each other for nearly two hours, lean-ing on the mantel and staring at themselves in a huge, gilt-framed mirror that hung above it, completely absorbed in their conversation. "You two haven't any more sense than a couple of school girls," Eleanor told them.

Some of Hick's most memorable times at the White House, however, came when the Roosevelts were out of town and there were no guests to be found. Not long after FDR's victory in the 1936 elections, the Roo-sevelts took off in different directions. Eleanor was the first to leave, set-ting out by train on a speaking tour. Not long after, FDR boarded the USS *Indianapolis* for a cruise to Buenos Aires, where he was to attend the Inter-American Conference for the Maintenance of Peace.

For several weeks, the only guest at the White House was Lorena Hickok. Hick was there because Eleanor insisted she should write a book based on her reports to Harry Hopkins from the field. Hick needed to dig into the files at the White House, then read through and edit the reports, as well as some of the letters she had written to Eleanor.

Despite her fear that she would be viewed by others in the administra-tion as one of Eleanor's charity cases, Hick had won the respect of a discern-ing audience. Harry Hopkins predicted that her reports would be published one day as one of the best histories of the Depression. FDR, too, read the reports and made use of them in clever ways: not only did he pass them on to the foot-dragging Harold Ickes, head of the PWA, as an argument for quicker action, but he also used them to impress people in conversation. According to Assistant Secretary of Agriculture Rex Tugwell, "her reports on conditions throughout the country . . . were responsible in large part for the fund of information with which the President often astounded visitors."

Publishing a book would give Hick a chance—perhaps her only chance—to hold on to her identity as a writer. She would have gladly re-turned to her old job at the AP in New York, but she knew it wasn't possible, despite Eleanor's arguments to the contrary. "Now if you could just stop talking about your friendship for me and ignore it I think you would find it is practically forgotten," Eleanor wrote her at one point. "If you get a job in N. Y. I don't think you need fear their demands for I think they don't need you now to get any story they want."

Hick was "amused at your idea that I could get a newspaper job, telling them I never saw you and didn't know what was going on. They'd NEVER believe it, dear—unless I actually did quit seeing you. And that would be expecting a good deal of me. Gosh I'm not prepared to give you up *entirely*! (And I don't believe you would want that, either)."

But Hick was tempted, as the Spanish Civil War heated up, by the possibility of following her friend Marty Gellhorn to Europe. In several ways, Gellhorn represented the path not taken. Her reporting style would never have gone over at the AP: while far away in England, she had managed to write a piece about lynching in the South, purporting to be an eyewitness account but drawn entirely from her imagination, that prompted a congressional committee to call her in to testify. But her fictionalized portraits of life during the Depression, published that year under the title *The Trouble I've Seen*, received well-deserved praise. Now she was off on the *Île de France* with $250, most of which she'd earned from an unsigned article for *Harper's Bazaar* called "Beauty Hints for Middle-Aged Women."

"I don't worry about Marty," Hick wrote Eleanor after a luncheon send-off. "If she has to, she can always cable her mother for help. And if she gets into a jam—which she probably won't, being very courageous, clever and good looking—she'll probably land on her feet. As a matter of fact, if she should get shot, she'd probably die happy. She's that kind." Hick added that "the adventure of the thing" would appeal to her too, if she "had a mother I could cable for funds."

Hick might have been a great war reporter. After it was all over, a friend of hers inscribed his book on World War II, "To Hick, who could have covered this story better than any of us." But Eleanor gave only half-hearted support to Hick's idea of reporting from Europe. "I'd hate you to go to Europe and see a war," she wrote Hick in September 1936, "but if you really want it I'll speak to Roy Howard [of Scripps-Howard newspapers] if you think it would help."

But then she sent Hick a clipping about a correspondent covering the Italian invasion of Ethiopia, lying in his bed and gasping for breath in the extreme heat. The headline on the story was "War Correspondent Finds Many Troubles." The truth was, Eleanor didn't even like having Hick on the West Coast, let alone across the ocean. And Hick didn't want to be so far away either. If she was to have a future as a writer, she was going to have to publish a book. And that was why she found herself all alone at the White House.

"The White House, when the family are all away," she noted, "is about as cozy as Grant's tomb after midnight. Even the dogs get low in their minds." It was during this period that she formed a bond with Anna's Irish setter, Jack. She found him waiting for her when she arrived home in the evening and was so flattered by his enthusiasm that she took him for a run on the South Lawn. After that, Jack slept on her bed and followed her into the bathroom to lie beside the tub while she took a bath.

With Jack at her side, Hick made her way through the reports and letters, reliving the highs and lows of the last four years. Sometimes she was encouraged by what she found. "Really some of it reads rather well," she wrote Eleanor. "I'm surprised!"

On one day Hick came across a lot of early letters written to Eleanor while she was still at the AP. "Dear, whatever may have happened since whatever may happen in the future—I was certainly happy those days, much happier, I believe, than many people ever are in all their lives. You gave me that, and I'm deeply grateful."

The next day she was in despair about her wordiness. The letters, she wrote, "depress me horribly, and I wonder if sometimes in the last four years you haven't been as tired of looking at my handwriting as I am now!"

Hick's turbulent emotions about her writing were interrupted by tragic news: the young son of Mabel Webster, Eleanor's personal maid, had died after an illness. Marshall Webster had been an athlete, president of his class in high school, and was planning to be a minister. He had turned twenty just two days before he died.

Hick decided to attend the funeral. It was a cold day in December, so she borrowed Eleanor's fur-lined coat. "I hope you don't mind," she wrote Eleanor, who was in New York, "and don't think you will because you have let me wear it before." Accompanied by Mrs. Mac, she drove down to Catlett, Virginia, a "typical little Southern town, probably hot and dusty in Summertime—pretty cold and bleak today in the pale winter light."

The service was held in "a chilly, shabby little church down near the railroad station," with hard benches and "pieces of cardboard replacing the glass" in some doors, "a wheezy old organ," and fans with "colored pictures of Jesus preaching beside the Sea of Galilee." The place was filled. The eleven people who came from the White House were seated prominently up front. Except for several ladies in the balcony, Hick was the only white person in attendance.

There were many flowers, Hick reported, including a very large set piece, a floral wheel with a spoke and part of a rim missing. Across it on white ribbon, in letters of gold, were the words "My Darling."

Mabel, Hick reported, "simply sat, perfectly quiet, looking down. At times her lips would move. She looked as though she had wept until she could weep no more.

"Poor, poor Mabel," Hick wrote. "But she was splendid today. You know, in a way she reminded me of that statue in Rock Creek cemetery. There wasn't the beautiful face, of course, or form. It was just fat, pudgy, black Mabel—who has trouble with her arches and keeps saying she must cut down on starches. But, oh, my dear, the dignity of her! She was quiet, spent, relaxed, like that woman in the statue. And in it, somehow, she was beautiful!"

PART III

TOGETHER
AND APART

CHAPTER THIRTEEN

TRADING JOBS

IN THE END, Hick didn't succeed in finding a publisher for her book about the Great Depression. Only one editor nibbled, and his letter to her wasn't encouraging. Eleanor cheered Hick on to "tell him with a little fire such as you are capable of what you did . . . and he will be interested. Go after him!"

But even though Hick could generate plenty of fire when she was going after a scoop, she was terrible at selling herself. When she first met George Bye, the agent she shared with Eleanor, he said, "Good Lord, are you always so humble and so unsure of yourself in anything you do?" To which Hick replied, "No, I was a darn good reporter and knew I was."

The underlying problem, once again, was that Hick was now linked in everyone's minds to Eleanor, for better and for worse. People were much more interested in Eleanor Roosevelt than they were in stories of the Great Depression, which they were living through at that very moment. And those Roosevelt stories were the ones Hick wouldn't tell.

But the same connection that undermined her writing career became an asset in hunting for work. It was probably Eleanor's idea, and it was certainly her political influence, that helped Hick get a new job working for the dapper and politically connected Grover Whalen, who was in charge of the 1939 New York World's Fair. Hick was hired to work in promotion at $5,400 for the first year. It would mean living most of the time at her New York apartment, which she had kept during her years on the road with Hopkins. She would have to take a pay cut (she had been paid $6,000 a year by the government). Also, doing PR was a step down for a self-respecting newspaper person. But Hick told Eleanor she was "pleased to have it settled." Nor did Hick seem to mind that the *Ladies' Home Journal* had offered Eleanor $50,000, on the basis of one installment, for her memoir about her early life. Hick read and critiqued all the installments. When they came out in book form, with the title *This Is My Story*, Hick exulted in the reviews: "I read the notice in the *Times* today," she wrote, "and it is marvelous. I'm so pleased and proud. . . . I think the review is very sincere—an honest tribute to a *real job*."

The sheer volume of Eleanor Roosevelt's writing over a lifetime is astonishing. In addition to three lengthy memoirs, she wrote a half dozen other books and scores of magazine articles. But her most astounding accomplishment by far was her newspaper column, "My Day," which she began writing late in 1935. From then until the month before she died, in November 1962, Eleanor filed her column. Most of that time she filed it six days a week. At its height, "My Day" reached over four million readers and placed her in the redoubtable company of Heywood Broun and Dorothy Thompson.

Eleanor was proud of the writing identity she had developed, with Hick's encouragement. She joined the Newspaper Guild and referred on several occasions in "My Day" to her "fellow columnists." For the most part, as she acknowledged, she was "a painter of pictures and a chronicler of unimportant events," rather than a deep thinker. Especially during the early years, "My Day" was really the same diary of daily life that she had been sending to Hick in letter form since 1932—supposedly with the idea that Hick would one day write her biography. Now it was dictated to Tommy in the same casual fashion, but without the private emotions. The voice was friendly and smiling, and the style was conversational. Phrases like "you would like," "I wonder how many of you," and "I must tell you" were common. Small things, like a tickle in the throat at a concert, or feeding her horse Dot sugar cubes after a ride, were the usual fare.

To her credit, she listened to and even published the words of her critics, including a letter from a woman "very much in earnest" who complained about her filling up her column "with inane chatter about your family affairs—words, words, words, which are . . . only once in a blue moon of any value whatsoever. Why do you consider those things interesting to intelligent people just because you happen to be the President's wife? Why waste your valuable time and the space in the paper . . . when you could so easily write something which might have marvelous results for the betterment of the world?"

The day after she published this critique, Eleanor returned to tried-and-true cataloging of the day's events: tea with a bishop who was an old family friend, a press conference, a meeting about the national folk festival, followed by the largest dinner of the year—for the Diplomatic Corps. It turned out, as Eleanor also learned from her mail, that a lot of people enjoyed entering vicariously into the First Lady's daily routine. It was also true that, as the wife of the president, she couldn't ever say what she really felt.

In the early years, some of Eleanor's more outspoken "My Day" columns concerned the role of women in the world. When the critic John Golden claimed that women could never become great playwrights because they "do not know as much as men," she responded that "as a rule women know not only what men know but much that men will never know. For how many men really know the heart and soul of a woman?"

As if to prove her point, many male readers wrote to Eleanor complaining about women who were taking paid jobs and did not need them. Some women, she argued, get jobs because they are not entirely satisfied with work in the home. "This does not mean that they are not good mothers and good housekeepers, but they need some other stimulus in life." Regular readers of "My Day" would have understood that Eleanor was one of those women who longed for more.

The enormous victory in the 1936 presidential election gave Eleanor more freedom to participate in public life. In January, she delighted her friend and ally, the civil rights activist Mary McLeod Bethune, by speaking at a national gathering on the future of the Negro. She spoke in support of a low-income housing bill, sponsored by Senator Robert Wagner of New York, even before FDR endorsed it.

She also spoke out on the single most controversial issue of FDR's second term, and perhaps of his entire presidency: the attempt to remake the Supreme Court. On February 5, 1937, just a few weeks after his inauguration, FDR sent a special message to Congress proposing the transformation of the Court. Under his plan, the president would have the power to appoint an additional member to the Court whenever a justice reached age seventy. Since six of the nine members were already over seventy, FDR's proposal would have increased the number on the Court by six, all of them allies of the president.

FDR had good reason to be frustrated with the Supreme Court: the justices had overruled every major New Deal measure that came before them—the National Recovery Act (NRA), the Agricultural Adjustment Act (AAA), and even a minimum wage law. But the president handled his effort at court reform badly: he consulted no one ahead of time, telling congressional leaders about his plan at the very last minute. He made disparaging remarks about "horse-and-buggy" justice handed out by "elderly judges living in cloistered seclusion and thinking in terms of a by-gone day."

FDR's proposal was viewed by friend and foe alike as an unwise power grab and a sign of dangerous dictatorial tendencies. His allies in Congress deserted in droves. Even Governor Herbert Lehman, the Roosevelts' old friend, became a critic.

Eleanor had qualms too. But she always cared more about helping people in need than about strict adherence to the rules. She rose to FDR's defense in "My Day." Opposition to the plan came from "the same group which opposed much of the social legislation of the present administration." The will of the people, expressed in the November election, should "determine our government," not "a minority group" of critics.

"Lord, I love it when you get your back up," Hick wrote Eleanor after reading the column. But Hick wasn't entirely convinced herself, even after FDR delivered one of his most persuasive fireside chats, assuring his audience that "you who know me can have no fear that I would tolerate the destruction by any branch of government or any part of our heritage of freedom."

Eleanor, however, praised Franklin's "calm, dispassionate delivery" and dismissed fears of dictatorship. "That isn't my worry," she told Hick. "I wonder if in the long run it will accomplish the desired results!"

ELEANOR'S SPEAKING TOUR of the Midwest after the election was followed several months later by a longer tour of the South and West. Huge crowds greeted her wherever she went: ordinary citizens, Girl Scouts, Boy Scouts, marching bands, and, of course, reporters. After she visited a college in Oklahoma, the students who saw her off at the train station brought fifty-four boxes of flowers with them in tribute.

Eleanor was uncomfortable as usual with all the attention and attributed it, in her "My Day" column, to the president's popularity. But she was not very convincing. She had to know by this time that she was an attraction in her own right.

Hick watched it all—sometimes anxiously, sometimes longingly—from her new perch in the Empire State Building, where she was now working in public relations for the World's Fair. Hick worried about Eleanor's bruising schedule: "Really this trip of yours sounds rather appalling," she wrote. "Why *so many* speeches every day?"

When Eleanor visited Milwaukee and Minneapolis, Hick's old stomping grounds, Hick agonized about Eleanor meeting her old friends. She wanted it to happen, but she worried about burdening Eleanor. On the other hand, she worried that her friends would be deeply hurt and blame her if they didn't have the chance to meet the First Lady. "Why must I be such a damned fool!" she lamented to Eleanor, when she realized all her obsessing was for naught. Of course Eleanor looked up Hick's friends, pleasing all parties.

In "My Day," Eleanor wrote only the good news about the New Deal out in the country. In Kansas City, one WPA sewing room employed nineteen hundred women and occupied six floors of an office building. In Chicago, she watched out-of-work artisans, subsidized by the government, honing new skills at the Field Museum, restoring ancient vases and meticulously reconstructing animal skeletons. The museum director told her that the WPA workers had become indispensable, and in some cases gone from relief work to jobs on the staff. "There isn't any useless boondoggling at the Field Museum," he told her.

Eleanor's reports in her column provided good publicity for the New Deal at a time when the administration needed friends. Her private reports to FDR undoubtedly gave him more balanced information. She couldn't go behind the scenes in the same way that Hick had, but she was now doing a version of the same job Hick had done during FDR's first term. The multiple ironies of the situation could not have been lost on Hick. *She* had been the professional writer, earning a good living with a top job at the AP. Now it was Eleanor who was earning a much better living from her writing than Hick ever could have. Moreover, it was now Eleanor who was, as Hick noted, leading the adventurous life, traveling around the country and reporting back to Washington. Hick, on the other hand, was stuck behind a desk, trying to get the public excited about a manufactured event, the 1939 World's Fair. What's more, she was now working at a job that involved tact, something Eleanor excelled at but that she herself achieved only with great difficulty.

The contentment Hick and Eleanor had achieved some months earlier seemed to evaporate as Hick took on the World's Fair job. She wrote Eleanor frequently about how little she cared about anything, about how old she felt, though she was only forty-four. She was completely unfit to be an executive, she told Eleanor. "All day I 'sit on myself,' so to speak, disciplining myself, trying to control my impatience, my natural irascibility, my loathing of friction and disorder. By night I'm exhausted."

Hick was sounding like a more strident version of Eleanor, who was herself feeling more trapped than ever in the wrong job. "Why can't someone have this job who'd like it & do something worth while with it?" she had complained to Hick after FDR was reelected.

Despite her still-frequent letters, Hick was trying not to rely so much on her relationship with Eleanor. She invited old lovers to visit her in New York: Alicent Holt came from Michigan, but Hick found she couldn't "give Alicent what she wants—which is a lot of affection and consideration." She felt "all dried up inside." When she learned in February that Ellie, her first love, was having difficulty in her marriage, she told her she should come back "whenever she wants." But when Ellie did come, four months later, for an extended visit, Hick was miserable much of the time. Ellie was a dear, Hick reported to Eleanor, and the "most painless house guest imaginable." Yet Hick often wanted to be alone, got low and disagreeable, and then couldn't explain why. Still, she thought she'd done "fairly well" hosting Ellie, "with one or two notable and pretty tragic exceptions."

At work, Hick disliked the innuendo she detected from people about her friendship with Eleanor—the "sidelong glances" and the comments about her "connections." But the deeper reason for her despair surfaced when she and Eleanor had a talk about their relationship one evening in September at the Village apartment. "It's this drifting—or seeming to drift—apart that bothers me so," Hick wrote afterward. What got her down and discouraged was "the thought of seeing you—or trying to see you—when you didn't want to see me."

Eleanor wrote back, "I didn't realize you thought we were drifting apart. I just take it for granted that *can't* happen."

After that, Hick and Eleanor managed some very happy New York encounters. Eleanor was pleased that they could have such a good time doing the things she did with other friends—going out to dinner and the theater. "Yes, I had a good time too, last night—a heavenly time," Hick replied.

They made plans to exchange presents at the Village apartment a few days before Christmas. "Don't dress," Eleanor instructed. "Just bring your wrapper and pyjamas and be comfortable for the evening." The next day,

Hick wrote Eleanor that it was "a lovely 'Christmas' last night—one of the nicest I can remember. . . . Dearest one—still, and always, dearest one— you made me very, very happy, and I thank you."

What did happen between Hick and Eleanor on these intimate occasions? It is possible, as Eleanor's grandson Curtis Roosevelt has claimed, that his grandmother's "visceral dislike of physical contact" confined the bodily expression of their love to kissing, cuddling, and tickling. It's also possible that Eleanor's wish to please allowed Hick to lead her further into sensual pleasures that she avoided at other times. There is no answer. But Hick's gratitude suggests that she, at least, continued to derive a deep and important satisfaction from these intimate times together.

As long as Eleanor was present in her life, Hick could maintain her equilibrium. But the problem, as both she and Eleanor now knew well, was that Eleanor was spread too thin to satisfy her longings. And when Eleanor wasn't available, Hick could quickly go into a tailspin. "I'm being perfectly honest," she wrote Eleanor on one of these occasions, "when I say I'll be relieved when it's over. . . . You are always horrified when I say that I wish it had happened when I had that automobile accident out in Arizona. . . . I'd have died happy, as happy as I've ever been in my life."

Characteristically, Eleanor blamed herself for Hick's unhappiness, believing that their relationship had forced Hick to give up the old life and work she loved. "It won't help you any but I'll never do to anyone else what I did to you. I'm pulling myself back in all my contacts now. I've always done it with the children and why I didn't know I couldn't give you (or anyone else who wanted and needed what you did) any real food I can't now understand. Such cruelty and stupidity is unpardonable when you reach my age."

Hick assured her that "never in your life have you deliberately done anything to hurt me or hinder me professionally." On the contrary, Eleanor had given her help "many, many times." "As I look back on these last five years—I don't think anyone ever tried harder to make another human being happy and contented than you have tried with me."

It must have been difficult at times for Eleanor to gauge just how unhappy Hick was. Within a single letter, she was capable of going from suicidal to matter-of-fact with astonishing ease.

Just a week after she and Eleanor spent a blissful time together, Hick was so unhappy at work that she was ready to end it all. "WHY can't I be better adjusted to life?" she lamented. "God knows, I try. But about 90 per cent of the time I'm out of step with life and miserable. I'll not try to step out of it. . . . But it's been a miserably uncomfortable business, most of it, and I'm tired of it all and bored with past, present, and future."

This long paragraph of lament was followed by two brief ones:

"There, there, Hickok!"

And then: "I must powder my nose and get going. Much love, dear."

CHAPTER FOURTEEN

THIS PLACE!

STARTING IN 1937, Hick counted on a country place on Long Island she named the Little House to help her recover in difficult times. She would often say in ensuing years that there were only three things she cared about in the world: Eleanor Roosevelt, her dog Prinz, and the Little House.

It was Hick's alternative to Val-Kill, a place teeming with rivals for Eleanor's attention. Although she accepted, on most days, that she would never have Eleanor to herself in a little cottage for two, she was excited when Eleanor agreed to join her at the Little House for a few days that first year of Roosevelt's second term. "If you like it one-tenth as much as I do, I'll be satisfied," she wrote.

What Hick loved about the Little House was not just the house itself, with its fireplace and cozy rooms and sunny porches, or the setting in the woods, not far from the ocean, but also the atmosphere of casual friendliness created by owners Bill and Ella Dana. The Danas were a wealthy couple whom Hick had first met at their Nevada ranch, during the California trip she had taken with Eleanor several years before. They lived in the grand house on the Long Island property. But there were several farmhouses and outbuildings around the place, occupied by people of modest means, all of whom were to become Hick's friends. Ella Dana, once she understood how much Hick loved the place, offered to fix up yet another house for her and rent it to her for $35 a month.

Hick was thrilled. But in order to afford it she needed a partner. She invited Howard Haycraft, a friend from Minnesota twelve years her junior, to come for a trial visit. Haycraft shared Hick's passion for opera, politics, good food and drink, and Minnesota football. They liked being together.

When they weren't listening to music, Howard and Hick loved to argue. They had a "perfectly joyous argument" one night about FDR's proposal for enlarging the Supreme Court. Howard argued for changing the Court through a constitutional amendment.

Hick stood up in the middle of the apartment and declaimed, "Here and now, Howard Haycraft, I say to Hell with the Constitution! And I warn you that, if you have your state conventions, that may very likely be the attitude of your delegates, and you don't know *what* kind of goofy amendment you'll get!"

Howard grinned and promised to use her argument the next day against every Tory he ran into.

"He's such fun," Hick wrote Eleanor, "but in an argument so damnably logical."

Like Hick, Howard was a wordsmith with a job to match: he spent his workdays editing literary anthologies of various kinds for H.W. Wilson Co. His great love, however, was the detective story, which he described as "the one dependable and unfailing anodyne in a world so realistically murderous that fictive murder becomes refuge and retreat." Haycraft was the first to write critically and in depth about the detective story. When he died at age eighty in 1991, an aficionado told the *New York Times* that Haycraft's 1941 book *Murder for Pleasure* was the "most insightful, perceptive and fair-minded book ever written on the subject."

Hick's partnership with Haycraft in the Little House was a satisfying variant of traditional homemaking. Hick and Howard seemed to enjoy cooking for each other when they were there together. Hick fed Howard what she called "gruel" when his stomach took a bad turn, and made the

The Roosevelt family in July 1932. Seated from left: FDR; Eleanor with granddaughter "Sistie" (Eleanor); Anna with son "Buzzie" (Curtis); Sara. Standing from left: Franklin, Jr.; James; John; Curtis Dall (Anna's first husband). Elliott is absent.

Eleanor and her friends during a summer visit to Campobello in 1926. From left: Marion's sister, Peggy Levenson; Nancy Cook; Eleanor; and Marion Dickerman.

Lorena Hickok during her time at the *Minneapolis Tribune*.

ABOVE: Hick on assignment for the *Tribune*. Dressed in engineer's overalls, she climbed aboard the legendary locomotive *Old Lady 501* for its regular run out of St. Paul.

RIGHT: Hick on a visit to her aunt Ella, who had rescued her from life as a hired girl in South Dakota.

Hick on the road for Harry Hopkins in 1936 with the car she and Eleanor named Stepchild.

Hick and Eleanor at the Pan American Day concert, April 16, 1935.

[March 7(?), 1933]

THE WHITE HOUSE
WASHINGTON

Hick darling, All day I've thought of you & another big day I will be with you, & yet to-night you sounded so far away & formal, oh! I want to put my arms around you, I ache to hold you close. Your ring is a great comfort, I look at it & think she does love me, or I wouldn't be wearing it!

Well here goes for the diary (let me know when you get bored!) Breakfast downstairs Elan & I joined, very late by James. Then E.R. interviews her & he & I at the top of the house meets all the domestics & talks over work, then with Tommy I must see.

Eleanor and Hick exchanged well over three thousand letters. Both women wrote that they "ached" for each other, but Eleanor was more open in her expression of longing to touch and hold Hick. In this letter, Eleanor finds confirmation of Hick's love in the ring Hick has given her (a ring presented to Hick by her friend the contralto Ernestine Schumann-Heink). In the second paragraph, Eleanor begins the "diary" the two have agreed upon—a daily report of the life of a First Lady that will eventually become her column, "My Day."

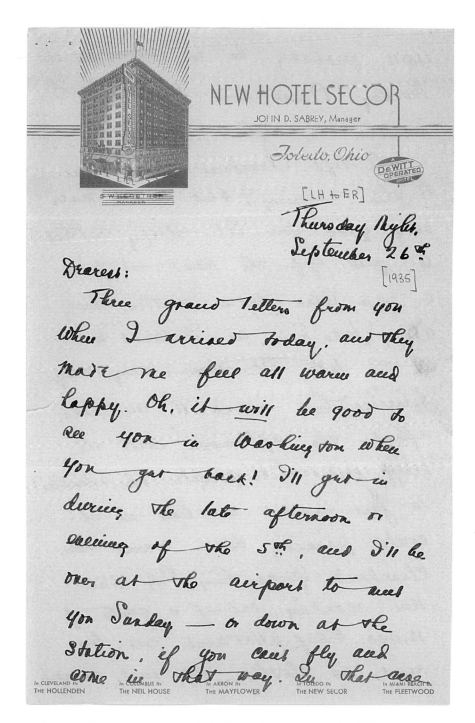

NEW HOTEL SECOR

JOHN D. SABREY, Manager

Toledo, Ohio

[LH to ER]

Thursday Night,
September 26th

[1935]

Dearest:

Three grand letters from you
when I arrived today, and they
made me feel all warm and
happy. Oh, it _will_ be good to
see you in Washington when
you get back! I'll get in
during the late afternoon or
evening of the 5th, and I'll be
over at the airport to meet
you Sunday — or down at the
station, if you can't fly and
come in that way. In that case

In CLEVELAND its
THE HOLLENDEN   In COLUMBUS its
THE NEIL HOUSE   In AKRON its
THE MAYFLOWER   In TOLEDO its
THE NEW SECOR   In MIAMI BEACH its
THE FLEETWOOD

Hick's letter from the road, two and a half years later, in September 1935, suggests how important Eleanor's letters were to her mood and well-being.

Eleanor and Hick on their inspection tour of Puerto Rico, March 1934.

An injured miner
and his family
in Pursglove,
Scotts Run,
West Virginia,
September 1938.

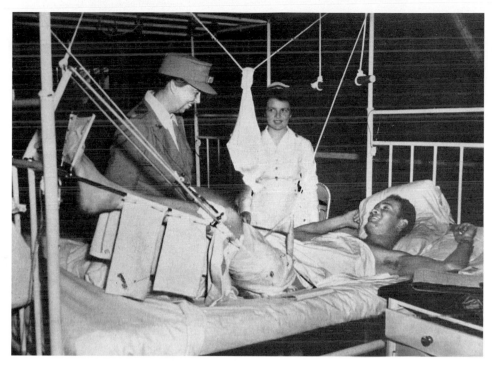

Eleanor visiting a wounded soldier in the Pacific during World War II.

Eleanor and David Gurewitsch in India in 1952.

Hick in 1932, the year she and Eleanor met. Eleanor once
told Hick that this was her favorite photo of her.

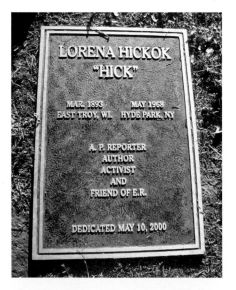

The plaque at the Rhinebeck
Cemetery pays belated
tribute to Hick.

beds—just as Eleanor did at Campobello—in anticipation of his arrival. It turned out that Howard loved the place as much as Hick did, waking up early to go hawk shooting with Bill Dana or spending days sailing with him in the bay.

Bill Dana was the other person who made the Little House special for Hick. Both he and Ella lived on inherited wealth. Ella, who was a Floyd by birth, still traveled in privileged circles: she was one of the elite group of women who lent their names to the World's Fair Women's Committee, headed up by Mrs. Vincent Astor. But it was Bill, a World War I vet who loved to hang out with the local fishermen, who became Hick's boon companion. They would walk and talk together in the woods by the hour, their dogs bounding about them.

Hick didn't herself hunt, but admired Bill's prowess. When he presented her with two fox skins, she had them made into a stole and proudly told admirers that her friend "Daniel Boone" Dana had bagged them. When she was at the Little House, though, her favorite attire resembled Bill's: corduroy riding breeches, plaid shirts, and boots from L.L. Bean.

The Little House in spring with the apple trees in bloom was especially wonderful. There were lilacs and tulips around the Dana house and wisteria embracing it. Hick delighted in the birdsong and the whistling of the quail. "Golly—*this place!*" she wrote Eleanor.

Eleanor visited during Hick's first fall at the Little House, and wrote with genuine enthusiasm in her column about her "brief visit with a friend." The house was "far away from the world," at the end of a drive through untouched woods. There were game birds, occasional deer, and very few strangers. There was also an unforgettable sunset at the end of an evening boat ride. "When we started back in the little motor boat the sky was red, but gradually sky and water seemed to merge in color until the water looked iridescent as it reflected every shade of green, purple, blue and scarlet, streaming across the sky."

Sunsets were special to Hick and Eleanor. They wrote often of missing each other as they watched a beautiful sunset, and they remembered the ones they shared on their trips in New England and California. Hick, reading about the sunset in "My Day," would have recognized the description as a private note in a public place.

The next August, Eleanor kept a promise to Hick and returned to the Little House. Hick wrote excitedly to her about this—maybe it would be an alternative to the trips they used to take together! It could also provide Eleanor with a much-needed rest away from the relentless demands of the mail—Eleanor tried to answer every letter—and the schedule. But Eleanor's second visit didn't work out nearly as well as the first. Eleanor assured Hick that she had had "a grand week." But then she added, "I wish the mosquitoes had let us walk in the woods."

Eleanor confided to others that the visit was more duty than pleasure. "I wouldn't live on Long Island for all the world!" she wrote Franklin, who was on the USS *Houston* in the Galápagos. "Everything sticks and I don't want to move!"

In "My Day," Eleanor wrote of a "personal triumph" she achieved on the visit: producing a readable version of her column on her portable typewriter. But the truth was that she missed Tommy's secretarial skills. Nor did she care much for the isolation. "There is no telephone in this house to disturb us," she wrote, "and I know that I should be taking advantage of such unusual peace to think out some really important problem." She resolved to "vegetate" and "knit" instead, and "take part in some of the daily tasks which form the pattern of most women's lives." In the end, she explained to her readers, she needed to find a telephone. "A kind friend spent all day yesterday trying to get me to a telephone and I finally went to a neighboring house this morning and called in answer to several urgent messages." The best part of her visit was seeing that kind friend, Hick, in a place where she was so content. But the Little House was not for her.

When she returned from Long Island to Val-Kill, Eleanor was greeted with Nan Cook's reproaches about being unavailable, no doubt heightened by jealousy about Eleanor's spending a whole week with Hick. The confrontation made Eleanor realize that Val-Kill was no longer a happy place for her either.

For several years, tensions had been growing between Nan and Marion on one side and Eleanor on the other. It began with the decision in 1936 to move Val-Kill Industries off the property. Eleanor seemed to believe it was a mutual and uncomplicated decision. She wrote in "My Day" that "we have turned over our various industries at Hyde Park to the workers," since they are now able to run them themselves. She claimed it was "a pleasant experience."

Nan must have found Eleanor's blasé attitude maddening. For her, the move was devastating: the shop had been a creative touchstone and the source of her connection to many Roosevelt projects, including Arthurdale and Warm Springs.

The new arrangement had allowed Eleanor, along with Tommy and their many guests, to use the factory building as their place, leaving the original cottage to Nan and Marion. Eleanor was clearly pleased to have her own house at last. A window placed over her desk was a great joy, looking out over the swamp, still bright with purple loosestrife. She looked forward to autumn, when she could sit and work and look out at the trees as they turned red, gold, and brown.

Tommy, who kept Anna Roosevelt apprised of events at Val-Kill, reported that Nan was defiantly spending money on the cottage "like a drunken sailor," but still hadn't entirely accepted Eleanor's claim to the factory building. When Tommy moved in with her boss, and referred to her part of the factory building as "my house," Nan "turned on me in a real fury and said it didn't belong to me, that she and Marion had much more money in this building than Mrs. R and Mrs. R could not give me any of it so I could say 'mine.'" Tommy told Nan that she would refer to it from then on as "the place where I live and sleep." Eleanor was sitting next to Tommy and witnessed the entire exchange.

On another occasion, according to Tommy, Nan reproached Eleanor for being slow to greet one of her guests, pointing out that she and Marion had entertained all of Eleanor's guests at great expense for years.

The truth was that Eleanor's world had expanded out of all proportion to Nan and Marion's, and now included a lot of guests they didn't approve of. Nan and Marion, despite their liberal politics and unconventional living arrangement, came from upper-class Protestant backgrounds. They had made it clear that they considered Hick unrefined. They thought Earl Miller too forward with Eleanor and were offended by his tendency to put his hands on her. Marion remembered the days when Earl was one of the state police assigned to FDR. "When Earl first came to the Big House with the Troopers," Marion noted, "he would eat out with the servants. That changed and he was later eating with the family." Another friend of Eleanor's, Mayris Chaney, a music hall dancer, certainly wasn't their sort of person either. And those were just a few of the unusual assortment of friends who wound up visiting Val-Kill.

But Eleanor felt a genuine connection to all kinds of people. One time, when she was coming back from a vacation in the Adirondacks with Nan, a young tramp approached her at a gas station and asked for money. He explained that he had tried to join the Civilian Conservation Corps, the New Deal work program for young men, but couldn't because he had no home address. She handed him $10 and her New York City card and told him to call on her at five that Monday. Nan bet she would never see him again.

But on Monday when she arrived at her 65th Street town house, Eleanor learned from the guard that a bum had been hanging around asking to see her. Somehow he had gotten her card. Eleanor invited him in for dinner, called a friend to arrange a CCC job for him, and suggested he stay the night.

Even Hick, who was with Eleanor at the time, was shocked. Sistie and Buzzie, Eleanor's oldest grandchildren, were staying in the house with them. "How do you know he won't kidnap the children?"

Eleanor had thought of that and locked the elevators. But she trusted her new acquaintance, Al Kresse. And her trust turned out to be well placed: he thrived in the CCC and became a supervisor. He and his parents visited her at the White House, and she became godmother to his daughter.

Once you became Eleanor's friend, you were her friend forever. The one great exception to the rule was her friendship with Nan and Marion, which came to a painful end that summer of 1938.

It was "a little thing," according to Eleanor, that made her decide to confront Nan about the Val-Kill partnership. Perhaps it was Nan's complaint about the silt kicked up by the dredging of the swamp, or perhaps Eleanor raised doubts about some of Nan's selling tactics in connection with Val-Kill Industries. Whatever the reason for the confrontation, it came at a time when Nan was feeling particularly vulnerable. Earlier that summer, Marion had gone to a conference in Europe. "It leaves Nan high and dry and very lonesome and a little forlorn looking," Tommy reported to Anna. Then Eleanor went off to visit Hick. Even though Eleanor invited Nan over for one meal every day, she remained "so listless that I begin to wonder if she is ill."

Eleanor's description of the conversation in her letter to Anna made it sound sensible and measured. It was "a calm talk" in which she explained that her feeling had changed toward them both and that from then on they must have "a business like arrangement." She added that it could be "friendly" and "agreeable," but that her "old trust and respect was gone and could not be recovered." She thought they probably felt the same way and were as justified as she was. "I am glad to have been honest at last!" she told Anna.

Nan Cook, however, was devastated by the same "calm talk." Five days afterward, she met Marion's boat at the dock looking drawn and pale, her eyelids red and swollen from weeping. There had been a conversation with Eleanor, she told Marion, a "long and tragic talk" in which each of them "had said things that ought not to have been said."

Nan could never, in all the searching conversations that followed, explain to Marion just what had transpired. But the subsequent legal wrangling, as Eleanor attempted to extricate herself from the partnership, gave some clues.

Over and over, in increasingly bitter exchanges, Eleanor referred to Nan's claim that the entire partnership had been a charitable act—an attempt to help the unhappy Eleanor find fulfillment. "[Nan] told me . . . that while we were working in the committee, in the school, and in the industries together, you had both always felt that whatever was done, was done for the sole purpose of building me up."

This wounded Eleanor deeply, not only because it was a grossly unfair characterization of the partnership, but also because she could not bear to be the object of charity. Her entire life was devoted to helping, not to being helped!

It was true, in the early years, that Eleanor sometimes presented herself as the grateful recipient of Nan and Marion's know-how. "You are dears," she had written them, "to let me join in it all for I'd never have had the initiative or the ability in any one line to have done anything interesting alone!" But that had been 1926. In subsequent years, Eleanor had proved the essential spark behind all their undertakings: she turned out to be a much-loved teacher at Todhunter, a key salesman for Val-Kill Industries, and an important partner in the Democratic Party in New York. When the cottage became too small for Val-Kill Industries, the three of them shared the costs of tools, but she alone put up the money for a second building. Eleanor was also hurt by the implication, which emerged during these conversations, that her name on Todhunter School literature might scare off wealthy conservative contributors who disliked the Roosevelt administration.

There was to be one more painful incident before the final breach. On August 27, Eleanor was hosting a picnic for about a hundred people at Val-Kill. Her brother Hall was there, sharing "a choice few cocktails" in Nan's garden, and got "very tight." In his drunken state, he got into a playful wrestling match with his son Danny and broke the boy's collarbone. Marion Dickerman, without telling Eleanor, insisted on taking Danny to the emergency room with the drunken Hall at the wheel. Very soon there were shouts for help from across the pond, and Eleanor got the news that Hall's car had turned over in a ditch.

"I left the tables," Eleanor wrote Hick, "and 'managed' Hall and the situation for nigh on an hour and a half! I'll tell you the details when we meet but I was mad for two days!"

In fact, Eleanor was angry for much longer than two days. She was angry with Nan for plying Hall with drinks, and she was angry with Marion for taking off with him to the emergency room without telling her.

"I realize," she wrote Marion months after the incident, "that probably not being familiar with gentlemen under those conditions . . . you did not realize what was happening. It might have been possible for me to prevent Hall taking the car had I known in time. That would at least have obviated the danger that the situation in the ditch caused, or anything else which might have occurred had you got beyond the ditch."

What made the incident especially painful for Eleanor was that it confronted her, in such a public way, with the fact that Hall's alcoholism was reaching the tragic extreme so familiar to her from her family history. Eleanor was deeply attached to her tall and handsome brother and clung to great hopes for him. Hall had shown such promise, graduating at the top of his class from Groton and with a master's degree in engineering from Harvard. Recently he had kept an apartment in Eleanor's building in Greenwich Village and seen his big sister often, meeting her at the airport when she came to town and chauffeuring her around town on numerous occasions. She made a point of mentioning his attentions in her column. Privately, in letters to Hick, she would write hopefully when he showed up at her apartment and didn't smell of alcohol. But she also confided, to Hick only, about how loud and wild he often was, driving her from place to place at eighty miles an hour and showing up late at her apartment with rowdy friends. The rage she visited on Marion and Nan might better have been directed at Hall.

After that incident, Eleanor's communications turned formal and distant. Instead of writing to Nan and Marion by hand, as she always did to her friends, she began dictating letters to Tommy, typed catalogs of several pages evoking the history of who had contributed what to the partnership, referring to the "long and illuminating talk with Nan," and suggesting various ways to break up and distribute the Val-Kill properties. In her hurt and anger, she went to extremes—at one point vowing to give up Val-Kill altogether. "I shall only come to Hyde Park when the President is at the big house and I will stay at the big house."

Nan and Marion, in turn, made exaggerated claims for their part of the assets. "Nancy has made up the accounts," Tommy reported indignantly to Anna. "The furniture in your mother's house and in mine amounts to over $4000. The furniture in the cottage is worth only $850.00!" To add insult to injury, Nan and Marion asked for support from Missy, who was inevitably viewed by Eleanor as FDR's agent. "I can't imagine why those two dames are holding out and I can't imagine how they could have been so stupid as to enlist Missy on their side," Tommy wrote Anna.

Marion tried in vain to break through the wall that Eleanor had erected. "CANNOT OUR YEARS OF CLOSE ASSOCIATION HELP US AT SUCH A TIME?" she telegraphed. But her efforts were rebuffed; a return telegram from Eleanor said, "VERY SORRY EVERY MINUTE TODAY IS FILLED. IF YOU WILL ASK NAN TO TELL YOU OF CONVERSATION WITH HER LAST SUMMER THAT SHOULD MAKE EVERYTHING CLEAR." She told them she was leaving everything in her lawyer's hands.

"My cottage difficulties did not smooth out till I actually ordered the water off," Eleanor wrote Anna that November. "Then the agreement was signed."

In subsequent years, there were polite exchanges back and forth, and Nan and Marion were invited to major events, like the famous hot dog picnic at Val-Kill for the king and queen of England the following summer. But there would be no more camping together in the Adirondacks or idyllic summer days at Campobello. Eleanor would no longer take an active part in the Todhunter School nor work with Nan on the homestead projects. Instead they would coexist uneasily side by side, Nan and Marion in the stone cottage, where they continued to live for the next seven years, and Eleanor in the redesigned factory building with Tommy, who was now her closest companion, and with the constant stream of visitors of all kinds who filled her eventful life to overflowing.

Marion and Nan were devastated by the breakup and never fully understood it. Eleanor was deeply wounded as well. "It has done something to me inside," she wrote Anna, "and I never want any intimacy again." "She has been so completely disillusioned about those two," Tommy wrote

Anna, "and realizes she cloaked them with many virtues . . . which they never had."

For an entire week, Eleanor refused to see anybody. Tommy was alarmed. Never before had she seen her boss so silent and closed off to everyone and everything, lying in bed with her face turned to the wall. Finally one evening, at the 11th Street apartment, Eleanor dropped in on Esther Lape and Elizabeth Read to announce that she had "recovered from my disappointment. . . . I simply had to let you know that all is now well. I am unable to lead a life based on an illusion."

On Eleanor's birthday, in October 1938, FDR presented his wife with a good-sized check to defray the costs of the dredging of the swamp at Val-Kill, a project that had angered Nan and Marion. "This is TOWARD the new 'Lake Eleanor' at Val-kill," FDR wrote. "I will take you cruising on it." Since Eleanor had suspected FDR of siding, through Missy, with Nan and Marion, the check was a peace offering of sorts.

In November, Eleanor and Hick spent an evening together at 11th Street, talking about the breakup with Nan and Marion. Hick sympathized with Eleanor, writing that she "couldn't understand how they could be such damned fools!" At least it was settled for Eleanor, if not for Nan and Marion. Hick hoped Eleanor could now get some fun out of Val-Kill. "For yourself."

WHEN ELEANOR TOLD HER FRIENDS that she refused "to live a life based on illusion," she was referring in particular to her relationship with Nan and Marion. But it could have described her feelings about her life in general. She no longer was willing to go along with Hick's fantasies either.

When Hick wrote that it would be fun "if some day we could just go off bumming, looking at things, visiting all sorts of funny little towns," Eleanor replied, coolly, that she would only be able to travel "on a money-making basis . . . and I cannot imagine that you would enjoy it even if I were not the president's wife."

Eleanor was rebelling that summer against her role as the president's wife as well. FDR had written her twice from the Galápagos, asking her to join him on a ceremonial mission to Canada. She wrote back that "I don't want to go anywhere I don't have to go until my lecture trip which starts October 12."

Ironically, FDR's trip to Canada was for the purpose of dedicating the International Bridge between the two countries and extending the Good Neighbor Policy to Canada, something Eleanor had long wanted him to do. "This bridge stands as an open door," FDR announced in an historic speech. "There will be no challenge at the border and no guard to ask a countersign. Where the boundary is crossed the only word must be Pass, friend."

Then FDR pledged that "the people of the United States will not stand idly by if domination of Canadian soil is threatened by any other empire." It was an important first step toward FDR's effort to build quietly a hemispheric defense against the threat that was increasingly the central concern of his presidency: the growing menace of Hitler's Germany.

The real reason Eleanor refused to play "Mrs R." in Canada was that she was deeply involved in an event in her own backyard—one whose aims ran counter to FDR's. While he was in Canada laying the groundwork for a military alliance, Eleanor was attending the World Youth Congress at Vassar College in Poughkeepsie, a gathering of some five hundred young delegates from fifty-five countries around the world whose final resolution called for an end to the drift toward armed conflict.

The Youth Congress, held in August 1938, was an exuberant affair, kicked off with a welcoming ceremony at Randall's Island in New York City. American students performed the "collegiate shag," the "Polish Falcons" gave a gymnastic display, and a Chinese choir sang, before an audience of twenty-three thousand. Then, after a boat ride up the Hudson, the delegates assembled at Vassar, just down the road from Hyde Park and Val-Kill. The president of Vassar, Henry MacCracken, set the tone: peace, he told the youths, was "the most radical, the most revolutionary idea in the world." Eleanor echoed his welcome, hailing world youth as the "best agents for peace." Then she settled in to listen attentively, as her knitting needles flew, to reports from youth movements around the globe.

Afterward, she submitted to an hour and a half of tough questions from the delegates, replying thoughtfully and without condescension. Some of Hick's reporter friends thought the students' questions had been disrespectful and even rude, but Eleanor didn't seem to mind. She had often complained to Hick that her own sons didn't take her views seriously: at least these young people did.

"I felt what they *said* was young and impulsive," she explained to Hick, "but their faces and their earnestness and the good manners and restraint of the audience was remarkable." She was impressed with their tolerance when they heard their countries criticized. It was "a lesson to their elders."

That evening, Eleanor returned and sat in the front row for an international variety show. Delegates from Czechoslovakia and Indonesia danced, a Negro chorus sang spirituals, and the Canadians presented a parody of themselves. The master of ceremonies, Seumas O'Heavy of Ireland, interrupted the proceedings to lead a chorus, in Eleanor's honor, of "For She's a Jolly Good Fellow."

The repercussions from the Vassar conference would continue for many months. Eleanor would be the target of sharp criticism from the Catholic bishops, who feared godless communism; from right-wing politicians like Martin Dies, of the House Un-American Activities Committee; and also from some thoughtful critics who found her naïve. The whole experience would force her to become increasingly articulate in her own defense, and in defense of the young people she had come to like and admire.

CHAPTER FIFTEEN

TIME TEARS ON

THERE WERE A LOT of ways to get around the 1939 New York World's Fair. You could walk, of course, but the fair, whose slogan was "Time Tears On," covered more than twelve hundred acres on sixty miles of paths, so that would require many visits. You could take a bus with a musical horn, or jump on one of the little trackless trains that snaked along to the tune of "Sidewalks of New York." You could hire a bicycle rickshaw. You might even, if you were a person of importance, ride around in a long black open car, as did the king and queen of England on their visit in June. But on May 1, 1939, two days after the fair opened, Eleanor wired Hick requesting an unofficial night out there with her brother, niece, and nephew. "NOT TELLING ANYONE LOVE ER." Hick suggested that their little group travel about in sightseeing "chairs," open three-wheeled chariots with upholstered seats, steered from behind by a smartly uniformed driver. "Bring warm wraps," she counseled.

Hick had been promoting the fair for two years already by that time. Eleanor had been involved almost as long, because of Hick. She had lunched with Hick at her first office, high up in the Empire State Building. She had visited her several times more after her office moved to the fairgrounds at Flushing Meadows in Queens. To help out the fair, and

Hick as well, Eleanor had made mention in "My Day" of various attention-grabbing events during the long buildup to opening day.

She had even participated in the promotion of the ubiquitous symbols of the fair, the Trylon and Perisphere, two gigantic geometric shapes that rose high into the air at the fairground's hub. The Trylon was a slender three-sided spire seven hundred feet high. The Perisphere was the largest globe ever constructed by man. Their bright white shapes were visible for miles around.

The Trylon and the Perisphere were embroidered on the uniforms of the Yankees, the New York Giants, and the Brooklyn Dodgers. Medallions of the structures decorated New York license plates. Even Hick's stationery was topped by an image of the two icons. On opening day, Eleanor wore a brown silk dress printed with Trylons and Perispheres, along with matching hat and bag. Eleanor explained in "My Day" that the dress was designed by "my young niece" (Hall's daughter Eleanor) and had been "bought by a department store that makes many of my clothes."

Despite the mind-numbing promotion, the objects themselves elicited near-universal admiration. Even Hick, a selective admirer of the fair, was moved by the sight of the Perisphere at night. "It is very, very beautiful dear," she wrote Eleanor a few days before the opening. "The big white globe looks like a giant, transparent, iridescent soap bubble. It actually seems to float on the fountains underneath it! And the colors and the reflections in the pools—gorgeous."

On that cool May night, Eleanor returned with Hall and his daughter to see for herself. A sad event hovered over the visit: two weeks before, Hall's son Danny—the same one involved in the wrestling match at Val-Kill—had been killed when he flew his small plane into the side of a mountain in Mexico. But tragedy was no reason, in the Roosevelt family, not to carry on. The little group, all bundled up in their car chairs, succeeded in remaining anonymous as they took in the spectacle. They returned home not long before midnight, after an evening Eleanor deemed "delightful."

"I have seen the fireworks and fountains in action at Versailles and am familiar with other displays of this kind," Eleanor wrote in her column, "but, for the first time, they have found a way here to keep the color in the water right to the top of the spray." It was "breathtakingly lovely."

Eleanor continued to visit and promote the fair in "My Day" throughout the summer. She marveled at Futurama, General Motors' ambitious three-dimensional car trip through the city and country of the future, savored the smorgasbord at the Danish Pavilion, and took special pleasure in the little houses in Tomorrow Town. She noted that "no one should go to this Fair with the idea that one or two visits will satisfy their curiosity."

The fair was largely a corporate event, with the grandest buildings sponsored by railways, automobile and appliance manufacturers, and food producers like Heinz, which handed out one of the fair's most coveted prizes, a green pickle pin. After all was said and done, such fairs inevitably offered, as one astute critic noted, "material comfort for those who can afford it; vulgar recreation for those who can't."

Yet there was good reason to root for the fair. With the Depression still deep and getting deeper again, the fair created tens of thousands of jobs, first for construction workers, who replaced an ugly and malodorous dump with a park and a temporary city. It also employed an impressive array of promising artists, including Jo Davidson, Arshile Gorky, Salvador Dalí, Alexander Calder, Philip Guston, and Rockwell Kent, who covered building façades with murals and punctuated pathways with sculpture. The artists might not have done their best work for the fair—a lot of it was in a style one critic called "modernoid"—but it at least tided them over. Finally, the fair gave jobs to all manner of guides and greeters and cleaners and gardeners, not to mention a large team of publicists, including Hick.

The pretext for the fair was the 150th anniversary of George Washington's inauguration as the first president of the United States, which took place in New York City in 1789. But despite the sixty-five-foot statue of Washington that towered over the promenade, the GW who dominated the fair was without a doubt not George Washington but the fair president, Grover Whalen.

Whalen, aka "Mr. New York," was the ultimate promoter: he had been the city's "official greeter" in the 1920s, organizing parades and receptions for such celebrities as Charles Lindbergh and Queen Marie of Romania. After a flashy stint as New York police chief, during which he installed a statue of Napoleon in his office, Whalen had moved on to the World's Fair, where he could give full rein to his grandiosity. He convinced Joseph Stalin, through an emissary, to build a $4 million pavilion by promising him the most desirable location on the fairgrounds. Then he used Stalin's commitment to convince rivals and enemies to come on board. He traveled to Italy for a personal interview with Il Duce, persuading him that he could promote Italy's vision of the future for a mere $5 million. By the time he was finished, Grover Whalen had promises from sixty-two nations—all the nations that, to quote the *New York Times*, "were not too busy with war or persecution to participate." Germany and Spain were absent.

The World of Tomorrow, as envisioned by Whalen and the fair's planners, was meant as a grand expression of a prosperous future after years of bleak deprivation and struggle. War was not part of the picture because Whalen didn't believe in it. "My personal investigation in Europe has conclusively proved to me that there'll be no war," he told the *New Yorker*. "A wave of enthusiasm for the World's Fair is sweeping Europe. That's what Europe is thinking of now—not war."

Only a few ventured to disagree. When asked to speak at the dedication of the Palestine Pavilion, Albert Einstein, a recent refugee from Hitler's Germany, told the thousands listening attentively in the Court of Peace that "the World's Fair . . . projects the world of men like a wishful dream. Only the creative forces are on show, none of the sinister and destructive ones which today more than ever jeopardize the happiness, the very existence of civilized harmony."

Most Americans were too concerned about their own struggles, and too disillusioned by the last war, to take in such grave warnings. One hundred sixteen thousand Americans had lost their lives in the Great War, a war many believed had been fruitless. Isolationism ran deep, in both the general population and in the political leadership. "Let us turn our eyes inward," Pennsylvania's Democratic governor George Earle declared in 1935, "and preserve our own oasis of liberty."

For different reasons, Franklin and Eleanor were inclined to share the general public's desire to keep a distance from the violence in Europe. FDR, as a former undersecretary of the Navy and student of history, understood early that the United States would eventually be drawn into the conflict. He also knew, however, that the country was woefully unprepared and needed time to develop its armed forces and weaponry. What's more, he was going to have to move slowly and carefully in persuading a resistant American public.

The middle years of FDR's second term had been close to disastrous on several fronts. His Supreme Court initiative had failed miserably, and his attempt to balance the budget by cutting back on relief programs had proved to be a serious mistake. In the autumn of 1938, stock prices plunged and unemployment spiked, signaling the beginning of a second, "Roosevelt" depression. Roosevelt's decision to campaign against conservative Democrats in the South also backfired: Republicans added many seats in Congress and eleven governorships in the midterm elections of 1938.

It wasn't going to be easy for FDR, with all these domestic woes, to persuade the public to prepare for war. Yet in the fall of 1937 he had begun laying the groundwork, telling a Chicago audience that "the epidemic of world lawlessness is spreading."

Eleanor had been an advocate of world peace since her earliest days in politics. At a League of Nations convention in 1921, she had watched Carrie Chapman Catt argue passionately for the league. "Let us consecrate ourselves to put war out of the world," Catt told the women that day. "It seems to me God is giving a call to the women of the world to come forward, to stay the hand of men, to say: 'No, you shall no longer kill your fellow men!'"

Eleanor was "positively disgusted" by the bombing and destruction she watched on newsreels from Europe. "How can we be such fools as to go on senselessly taking human life in this way?" she asked rhetorically. "Why the women in every nation do not rise up and refuse to bring children into a world of this kind is beyond my understanding."

And yet it was she, not FDR, who wanted to send military aid to the Loyalist side in the Spanish Civil War. Just months after the electoral victory of a left-leaning government in Spain, a Fascist army under General Francisco Franco sought to bring it down, with the blessing of the Catholic Church. Franco appealed for help to his natural allies, Mussolini and Hitler, who responded readily with infantry and air support. The elected government got almost no help from the countries that should have been allies, Russia and then-socialist France. As a result, Spain became a testing ground for Italian and German firepower, resulting in the devastating bombing of civilian populations—vividly depicted in Picasso's painting of the obliteration of Guernica. Congress reacted to the war by updating the Neutrality Act so that no arms could be shipped to the defenders of the democratically elected Republic.

Eleanor was both frustrated and helpless. She believed in the Spanish Republican cause but couldn't convince FDR to take a stand and risk alienating both the Catholics and the isolationists.

Thanks to the impassioned letters of their friend Martha Gellhorn, who was reporting from there, the war in Spain was vivid in the minds of both Eleanor and Hick. "I think of those people in Bilbao strafed by low-flying aeroplanes with machine guns," Gellhorn wrote Eleanor in July 1937, "and think of thirty shells a minute landing in the streets of Madrid, it makes me sick with anger. Anger against two men whom I firmly believe to be dangerous criminals, Hitler and Mussolini, and against the international diplomacy which humbly begs for the continued 'co-operation' of the Fascists."

Soon after, Martha Gellhorn paid a visit to Hyde Park at Eleanor's invitation, accompanied by her "two trench buddies," Ernest Hemingway and Joris Ivens, to screen the film the three had made about the war, *The Spanish Earth*. The film employs stark, lovingly edited black-and-white footage of a small Spanish village to tell a story of peasants working with their mules to irrigate their dry land and soldiers fighting to defend Madrid, using hopelessly antiquated armaments. The fight was still ongoing when *The Spanish Earth* was made. But no one watching it could doubt that these humble country people, fighting on their own, were doomed to fail. Gellhorn was pleased when FDR urged her to make the film even more forceful and Harry Hopkins seemed "very moved by it." It didn't change FDR's position on the embargo, however.

In January 1938, more terrible news of the Spanish Civil War came to Hick from another quarter: Eddie Neil, a friend and fellow AP correspondent, died of shrapnel wounds, along with two other reporters, while covering the Franco forces on the front lines in Teruel. Neil was best known for his lively writing about boxing. There was a famous story about the first time he met Jack Dempsey: the boxer shook Neil's hand, then punched him hard in the ribs. Neil punched back. The two clinched, fell to the ground, and rolled over and over. It was the beginning of a beautiful friendship.

In the hospital after the explosion, Neil seemed to be responding to blood transfusions. "So long until tomorrow," he told his visitor from the *Times*. "Tell my office I'm going to Paris as soon as I can and I'll soon be all right again." He died not long after from gangrene poisoning. He was thirty-seven years old, and left behind a wife and a small son he called "Champ."

Hick and two of her newspaper friends mourned Eddie Neil's death in a New York pub a few days later, drinking and talking until three in the morning. Eleanor, who had met Neil through Hick, celebrated him in her column. "I remember him as a charming, very much alive, human being."

It was "a waste," she wrote, ". . . for the sake of getting more colorful news, to send these men . . . into such positions of danger." Hick appreciated Eleanor's column, and so apparently did some of her friends at the AP, who pinned it to the board, with underlining. But Eddie Neil would not have agreed with the sentiment: he was willing to risk everything to get the news. Some days earlier, after he had sent a story over the wire to the AP, a bullet had whizzed by within inches of his head and lodged in the stone wall behind him. His only reaction was to say he was glad it happened *after* he had filed.

"It seems to me the world is almost too black to behold," Gellhorn wrote Eleanor in February 1938. "Half of it is bullied and terrorized and debased by dictators and half of it is soppy with cowardice and sloth and selfishness."

In March, Austria fell to Hitler. Only Dorothy Thompson, among American commentators, sounded a loud alarm, calling the annexation "the most cataclysmic event of modern history." She predicted that "one of two things will happen: Germany will dominate the continent of Europe, or millions of lives will be spent in another war."

By summer, Gellhorn was in Czechoslovakia, waiting for Hitler to make his next move. It felt, she wrote Eleanor, like "waiting in an operating room for the surgeon, who will come to work with a blunt knife and no anesthetic."

September and November proved to be the cruelest months yet. In September, twelve thousand Jews with Polish passports living in Germany were forced to leave their homes without warning. Then, on September 29, 1938, British prime minister Neville Chamberlain and French prime minister Édouard Daladier conceded the German-speaking part of Czechoslovakia to Hitler in Munich, hoping to appease his monstrous appetite. Ten days later, on Kristallnacht, the "Night of the Broken Glass," rioters in Berlin and Vienna destroyed Jewish shops and homes and torched fifteen hundred synagogues.

"War itself," Gellhorn wrote Eleanor in December 1938, "war in the trenches between armed men, is of course bad enough, but it is a circus compared to the helpless Jews living in ditches between Czecho and Germany, and the helpless solitary man caught up in the ghastly machinery of the concentration camp, and the seven months old babies with rickets or TB in Barcelona."

On March 15, 1939, Hitler took over the rest of Czechoslovakia. Frustrated with the inaction of Britain, France, and the United States, Gellhorn wrote Eleanor, "I do not believe that Fascism can destroy democracy, I think democracy can only destroy itself."

On April 15, FDR made one last attempt at diplomacy. His message to Hitler listed thirty-one countries by name and asked for an assurance that neither Germany nor Italy would attack them for at least ten years.

Hitler responded by delivering what journalist William L. Shirer described as the most brilliant oration of his career, before a wildly enthusiastic crowd at the Reichstag. "For sheer eloquence, craftiness, irony, sarcasm and hypocrisy, it reached a new level that he was never to approach again," Shirer wrote. Hitler heaped scorn on Roosevelt, pointing out that he himself had conquered chaos, created great new roads and built factories, and employed seven million, while Roosevelt was still struggling to overcome the Depression.

"Roosevelt put his chin out," Republican senator and leading isolationist Hiram Johnson of California noted, "and he got a resounding whack on it."

Three days later, on April 30, FDR opened the New York World's Fair, declaring the country "united in a common purpose to work for the greatest good for the greatest number . . . and united in its desires to encourage peace and goodwill among all the nations of the world."

It was not to be. Over the summer, as millions streamed through the gates of the World's Fair and marveled at its wonders, the hope for peace and goodwill among nations faded away. In August, Hitler and Stalin signed a nonaggression pact. Poland, it was generally agreed, would be the next to fall. If that happened, the British and French would be forced to declare war.

On September 1, 1939, FDR was awakened at 3 a.m. by the U.S. ambassador in Paris, William Bullitt, with the news that "several German divisions are deep in Polish territory."

"Well, Bill," FDR replied, "it has come at last. God help us all."

PART IV

THE WORLD

AT WAR

CHAPTER SIXTEEN

AFRAID NO MORE

Sunday, September 3, 1939, was one of those precious sunny days at the Little House—the kind of day that Hick would usually spend reading on her porch and walking with Prinz in the woods. Instead, she stayed inside, close to the radio, listening with Howard to the news from England.

At 12:45, King George VI addressed "every household of my peoples, both here and overseas" in a halting and gentle voice.

"For the second time in the lives of most of us," he began, "we are at war.

"Over and over again," he continued, "we have tried to find a peaceful way out of the differences between ourselves and those who are now our enemies, but it has been in vain."

Hick and Howard "wept openly and without embarrassment."

"What can one say?" she wrote Eleanor. "Nothing. I can't even think very clearly. Just now one can only feel." In a postscript, she added, "I find being an isolationist rather hard going today! And so does Howard!"

Eleanor was listening too, at Val-Kill, where only two and a half months earlier she had played hostess to the king and queen and reported her impressions to Hick. She had found the queen self-conscious, but "who wouldn't be? Turning on graciousness like water is bound to affect one in time!" She had warmed to the king, though. "He is very nice and doesn't stutter *badly* when speaking aloud and not at all in quiet conversation."

On September 3, the king's stuttering hesitations, coming at odd moments, seemed to add to the power of his address. Every word was hard-earned, just as the decision to go to war was hard-earned, and the quietness of his delivery was a welcome contrast to Hitler's screaming invective. "There may be dark days ahead," the king warned, "and war can no longer be confined to the battlefield, but we can only do the right as we see the right, and reverently commit our cause to God."

FDR's speech that evening was careful for a different reason: he didn't want to stir up isolationist and antiwar sentiment. "This nation," he told his radio audience, "will remain a neutral nation, but I cannot ask that every American remain neutral in thought as well. Even a neutral has a right to take account of facts. Even a neutral cannot be asked to close his mind or close his conscience." He ended with the promise that there would be "no blackout of peace in the United States."

Eleanor, who was often critical of FDR's speeches, found this one "restrained and wise." Despite her sympathy for the Spanish Republican cause, she still hoped the United States could keep out of the war in Europe.

Increasingly, she focused on fear as the source of discord, at home and abroad. Fear became the subject of the most probing essays she was now providing for various journals—essays through which she defended her own alliance with putatively "Communist" youth groups and went on to argue for greater tolerance of differences of every kind.

The battle between those who feared Communism and those who feared Fascism was a misguided, negative battle, she argued. "We must not fight <u>against</u> something, but <u>for</u> something. We need not fear any 'isms' if our democracy is achieving the ends for which it was established."

In the best of several essays on fear, Eleanor began with the painful childhood memory of the time she disappointed her father by refusing to ride down a steep trail in Italy on her donkey. It was then, she wrote, that she realized fear was something to be overcome. She was a timid child, "afraid of many things—afraid of the dark . . . afraid of being scolded, afraid that people would not like me." It took time to realize that such fears "paralyzed growth."

She argued that a "complex of national fears" had developed since 1929—fear of the CIO's power, of Negroes "getting too ambitious," of Jews whose "interests lie with international bankers," of Communism, of Fascism. Fears of Communism and Fascism were "nothing more than lack of confidence in ourselves." Fear underlay hyperpatriotism as well, and the "hysteria" about aliens and immigrants. Taken together, Eleanor's essays became an extended elaboration of the great phrase from FDR's first inaugural: "the only thing we have to fear is fear itself."

"My dear," Hick wrote Eleanor, "I've just read your article on 'Fear' and it is *magnificent*! Bravo! Again and again." She went on, "I wonder if you realize how much better your stuff is . . . than it was three or four years ago. They are so much more interesting . . . they sound as though you had given them so much more careful thought."

Hick suggested Eleanor go back, "just for the fun of it," and look at some of her early writing, in 1932 and 1933, to compare it with her recent pieces. "You'll be amazed, I think. And you'll understand, too, I think, why I never used to be really satisfied with what you wrote those days— and why I am so darned pleased and so proud of you now."

Perhaps the source of Eleanor's new confidence and force of argument on the page was the showdown over Val-Kill, or the need to defend her alliance with the American Youth Congress, or her growing alarm over the rearmament that FDR was already undertaking. Whatever the reason, the "slight stiffening of the backbone" that Tommy had observed at the time of the Val-Kill affair seemed to be carrying over into not only her writing but also her actions.

That November, Eleanor attended the Southern Conference on Human Welfare, a mixed-race gathering in the segregated city of Birmingham, Alabama. On the first day of the meeting, blacks and whites intermingled freely in the audience. But the next morning the church was surrounded with Black Marias and police, who warned that anyone who broke segregation laws would go to jail. The delegates complied to avoid trouble: blacks sat on one side and whites on the other.

Eleanor arrived late that day with the WPA's Aubrey Williams and AYC's Mary McLeod Bethune (who was black) and slipped into the first seats they could find—on the "colored" side. Very quickly, Eleanor was reminded by a policeman that she would have to move. Eleanor's reaction was to pick up her chair and place it in the aisle between the white and black sections. The weekly *Afro-American* took note of her gesture, commenting that "sometimes actions speak louder than words."

Five months later, Eleanor was faced with yet another chance to act against racism, when the Daughters of the American Revolution barred Marian Anderson from Constitution Hall. One night in 1936, Anderson had sung for the Roosevelts, accompanied by her longtime partner, the Finnish pianist Kosti Vehanen. Vehanen, who had traveled the world with Anderson, noticed that she sang "with a special fire that night," as she tended to do when she especially admired her audience. Anderson may not have known, and probably would not have cared, that she was the first African American singer to perform at the White House. She always insisted that she was not meant to be a fearless fighter, "just as I was not meant to be a soprano instead of a contralto."

But in 1939, forces beyond her control swept Anderson up in a historic confrontation when the board of the DAR voted to deny her access to the only performance space in Washington suitable for an artist of her stature, Constitution Hall. The ladies of the DAR cited their "white artists only" policy as justification. NAACP president Walter White, already an ally of Eleanor's on antilynching legislation, wrote to newspapers, rallied other musicians to protest, and announced that Eleanor Roosevelt would present the NAACP's prestigious Spingarn Medal to Marian Anderson— all in an effort to shame the DAR into reversing its position.

Eleanor hoped for weeks that public pressure would bring the DAR around without her having to resign. But on February 27, 1939, she announced her decision in "My Day." In the past, she explained, she might have "stayed and made a fight." But this time, since she could "do no active work," she had decided to submit her resignation.

The resignation letter, addressed to the DAR president, was written in Eleanor's typical self-effacing style: "I am afraid I have never been a very useful member of the Daughters of the American Revolution, so I know it will make very little difference to you whether I resign," she began. ". . . However I am in complete disagreement with the attitude taken in refusing Constitution Hall to a great artist."

Of course, Eleanor's resignation made *all* the difference. Hundreds of other DAR members followed her lead and resigned as well.

Walter White, along with Anderson's manager, Sol Hurok, and other supporters of the cause, began to consider the possibility of defying the ban with an outdoor concert. Somehow the idea emerged—no one is sure who thought of it first—of a performance at the Lincoln Memorial, a novel venue at the time.

Anderson, meanwhile, watched from the sidelines with alarm. The "weight of the Washington affair bore in on me," she later wrote. "I had become, whether I liked it or not, a symbol, representing my people."

On Easter Sunday 1939, an audience of seventy-five thousand gathered on the National Mall, and many thousands more gathered by their radios all around the country, to hear Anderson sing. Harold Ickes made the introductory remarks. "In this great auditorium under the sky," he began, "all of us are free. When God gave us this wonderful outdoors . . . he made no distinction of race, or creed or color." Cheers cascaded back through the huge crowd, extending all the way to the towering Washington Monument at the other end of the Mall. The vast seated figure of Lincoln, "the great emancipator," floated above the proceedings.

Anderson looked small, huddled in her caped fur coat under the great pillars of the memorial. She stood for an unusually long time in the expectant silence before she nodded to her pianist to play the introductory six bars of "My Country 'Tis of Thee." Later she would write that she "felt for a moment as though I were choking. For a desperate second I thought that the words, well as I know them, would not come."

But the words did come. Surprisingly, and fittingly, she changed the usual "of thee I sing" to "of thee *we* sing." Her luscious contralto voice gained conviction and volume with each phrase. Anderson's beautiful smooth face, which had looked worried when she began, broke out in a radiant smile as the crowd cheered and cheered.

Eleanor chose not to attend the event, probably because she did not want to draw attention away from Anderson. But the crowd in attendance knew the story: an aristocratic woman had dared to speak up against racism to her own kind, the ladies of the DAR. Some months later, Eleanor readily took a public stand once again, this time against Martin Dies and the House Committee on Un-American Activities—later called HUAC. For over a year, the committee had been using outrageously unfair tactics to go after organizations it considered Communist. The Federal Theatre Project, one of the worthiest of the WPA arts projects, had been virtually destroyed by accusations of Communism brought by the committee the previous year. Now, after the committee heard unreliable testimony from witnesses hostile to the American Youth Congress, it summoned on short notice the leaders themselves to defend their activities, including the World Youth Congress at Vassar the previous summer.

Eleanor happened to be in New York on November 30, 1939, when the leaders got the call. She agreed to meet them at Penn Station so that they could ride "the midnight" down to Washington together. For an hour, as the train made its way south, Eleanor and the excited young leaders huddled in one compartment and talked strategy. She advised them to be helpful, to volunteer information, to keep their hostile feelings under wraps. She suggested using her tried-and-true technique: get cooler as you get angrier. She promised, if she could get FDR's approval, to come with them to the hearing. After that she left for her berth in the sleeper; her coconspirators sat up in coach, working on their statements for the committee.

The next morning, Eleanor appeared in the hearing room along with the young leaders. The committee was taken aback. Joe Starnes, an Alabaman with southern manners, asked her if she would like to sit up at the table with the congressmen.

Eleanor replied, "I came only to listen. I can hear very well from here."

Not surprisingly, the proceedings remained bland and polite in her presence. "I think the Youth Congress people made a grand impression," she wrote Hick proudly. "Their testimony was clear and carried conviction. The Committee oozed encouragement and confidence in them!"

At noon, Eleanor invited several of the congress's leaders to ride over to the White House in her car for lunch. And that evening, she invited them back to stay overnight. She relished having "a house full of young people."

On the second day, the committee heard testimony from an intense young activist named Joe Lash. Until then, Eleanor hadn't taken particular notice of Lash. It was his slightly unsteady testimony that day that piqued her curiosity. When asked why the Student Union, which he represented, didn't ban Communists, he didn't deny that there were Communists in the organization, but said instead that "we have found it a good thing to discuss things with people you disagree with." It wasn't clear from his response whether he might be a Communist or former Communist himself.

"I had a feeling that your political opinions were not completely clarified," Eleanor wrote Lash after the hearing. "If you ever feel that you would like to see me and talk things over, either in New York or here, I shall be glad to have you come either alone or bring anyone you want with you."

Eleanor's instincts were correct: Lash was struggling with several moral dilemmas, both political and personal. He had been sympathetic to Communism until Stalin made a deal with Hitler the previous summer; now he was disenchanted. But others in the student movement were secretly sticking to the party line. He had been unwilling to reveal this truth and betray his friends in front of the hateful Martin Dies. Lash was also unhappy in his marriage. It was in the process of trying to figure all this out, with Eleanor as concerned listener and faithful correspondent, that the friendship blossomed. Before long, Eleanor had not only learned Joe's life story—he was the oldest of five born in New York to Russian Jewish immigrants—but also paid a visit to his mother at her grocery store. At thirty, Joe was young enough to be Eleanor's son, and he was in many ways the son she wished she'd had. In a letter to Hick, she noted that Joe's idealism, though admirable, was going to make it hard for him to earn a living. "My children could better afford the ideals and they are not touched by them."

Eleanor never worked out her own views alone. There were always individuals she was strongly attracted to and learned from at the same time. Hick was one of the most important ones. After that fateful day at the Dies hearing, Joe Lash became another.

Hick, for whatever reasons, didn't seem envious of Eleanor's new relationship with young Joe. Perhaps it was because he *was* young, or because Eleanor's relationships with men were not a direct threat. Or perhaps it was because she was deeply immersed in her own eventful life, which at that moment was careening even more than usual between great satisfaction and panic about the future.

Ever since she had met Eleanor and left the AP, Hick worried that her employers viewed her as the First Lady's charity case—someone they had to hire because she was Eleanor's friend. She worked harder, fearing this, and succeeded in winning the genuine admiration of her bosses—Harry Hopkins at WPA, and now Grover Whalen, the temperamental president of the World's Fair.

There was a period, early on in her stint at the fair, when Hick headed off a clash of egos between Whalen and the highly vocal congressman from New York, Sol Bloom, who felt his proposals for the fair had been ignored. The resulting alliance produced a bill to fund the World's Fair and word that "the whole World's Fair organization [had] fallen in love" with her. Then came a time when Hick was so out of favor with Grover Whalen, for unknown reasons, that she expected to be fired.

By the time the fair opened, in the spring of 1939, Hick was back in favor in a big way: she had three secretaries working for her and a reputation in some quarters as a "human dynamo." She credited Eleanor with teaching her how to be efficient on the job. "It amuses me, sometimes, how much I've copied from you." She added, "If I'm a 'human dynamo,' my dear, how would one describe you?"

Hick had wooed thousands of New York City teachers and children to the fair. "Nickel Day," overseen by Hick, attracted great crowds of fairgoers with its promise of five-cent admission. A poster contest for high school students—her idea—drew lots of media attention as well. For a time, she headed her department at the fair, and she was given a raise when others were being let go.

The ultimate proof that Hick's status had changed came two weeks before the opening of the fair, when she got a summons from the boss. Whalen was in bed and seriously ill with pneumonia. For some reason, he wanted to see Hick, and his wife and nurse couldn't talk him out of it. So Hick drove from Queens to his house in Greenwich Village to hear what he had to say. Whalen, in his feverish state, was worrying about opening day, and the possibility it might not be as outrageously over the top as he wanted it to be. Word was out that the U.S. naval fleet had been sent to the West Coast and wouldn't be around for opening ceremonies.

"Obviously," Hick wrote Eleanor, "there's nothing I can do about the fleet, and I hope he understands that!" Mrs. Whalen was impressed nonetheless. "Grover has a great deal of confidence in you," she told Hick. In the end, the Atlantic Fleet showed up. The hundreds of thousands in attendance were treated to the sight of twenty-eight men-of-war steaming into the harbor "with the white of the bow waves curling beneath their cutwaters." Whalen rose from his sickbed and took part in the ceremonies, along with the president, the First Lady, the mayor of New York, the justices of the Supreme Court, the cabinet, governors from many states, and ministers and ambassadors from all over the globe.

The World's Fair, like so many such extravaganzas, didn't come close to making money and paying back investors. Whalen's grand dream of peace among nations also faded quickly from view during that summer of 1939. Nonetheless, the World's Fair board decided to keep the fair open for a second season. Hick could have stayed on: her boss—and friend— Howard A. Flanigan, a World War I Navy commander who was now a fair executive, told her there was a job for her at the fair as long as she wanted one.

The friendship of the man Hick called "the Commander" may have been the best thing that happened to her at the World's Fair. The two of them consoled each other when they were in Grover's "black book" and celebrated together when things were going well. The Commander once paid Hick an unlikely compliment: "You are a true aristocrat," he told her, "in the best sense.

"You'd rather be the sort of person you are—even if you have to take it on the chin sometimes—than to be a rat."

"It made me feel *good*," Hick wrote Eleanor.

True friend that he was, the Commander called Hick into his office for a lecture as 1939 came to a close. He knew she was eager to find a new job and leave the fair, and also that she was doing almost nothing to make it happen.

First he wished her happy New Year. Then he proceeded to lecture her about her reclusive and counterproductive ways. First of all, she had skipped his Christmas cocktail party and had been unreachable, out at the Little House, when he tried to call her on Christmas Eve. Now he reproached her "at length" for "drawing into a hole" and "never seeing anyone."

"You never do anything except sit around that apartment evenings and go off to the country to be with that damned dog of yours," he said. This made Hick smile, but she knew he was right.

Hick was hoping to get a job, with Eleanor's help, working for the Democratic National Committee, but the Commander pointed out that she would be wise to develop other connections. "How the hell do you think you're ever going to get another job if you don't make contacts and use the connections you have?" he asked. Then he accused her of once again letting Eleanor find a job for her, instead of going out to meet people and putting on cocktail parties.

"It was *bad*," she wrote Eleanor, "because it brought to the surface things that I've been secretly worrying about for weeks and weeks. He's right, of course, and he obviously *did* mean well—I do think he's really fond of me and worried about me."

Eleanor thought the Commander was too hard on Hick, but Hick defended him as only telling the truth. In fact, she did get her next job, once again, through Eleanor's connections. But this one, unlike the World's Fair stint, proved to be a perfect fit—for Hick and, it turned out, for her boss, Democratic Party publicity director and former newsman Charlie Michelson. Michelson hired Hick to go out into the country, particularly the Midwest, and sample popular sentiment about FDR and the Democratic Party. Hick, even though she was stuck for long hours on buses and trains going from one town to the next, had never enjoyed herself more.

"This job is such fun, dear," she wrote as she got ready for a three-week trip to Ohio and Indiana. It was the "nearest thing to newspaper work I've found since I left AP," she wrote from Cincinnati. Her three and a half years on the road for Harry Hopkins, along with her old newspaper contacts, were "standing me in good stead."

Two conclusions emerged from Hick's investigations. First, the women of the country, like Eleanor, were dead set against going to war. Second, the American attitude toward a Roosevelt third term had shifted overnight with the European declaration of war in September 1939. "Darling, I'm sorry, but it's all Third Term!" Hick wrote to Eleanor from Indianapolis. If the country was going to go to war—as seemed more and more likely—then people wanted Roosevelt to lead the way. Eleanor summed up her reaction to this news in two words: "I groan."

A showdown of sorts between Eleanor's point of view and her husband's took place on February 11, 1940, when thousands of left-leaning young people brought their message to the president in a gathering called the Citizenship Institute on the White House lawn. Their message, as delivered to the president by American Youth Congress chairman Jack McMichael, was that "America's twenty-one million youth are ready to fight, but determined to do their fighting at home—against indifference, intolerance and greed, for jobs, civil liberties and peace."

FDR welcomed them from the White House porch, then proceeded to deliver what columnists would later describe as a "spanking." He started with a defense of the New Deal, stressing all that had been done to improve youths' prospects, including the American Youth Act. But he added, "Don't seek or expect a panacea . . . a guarantee of permanent re-munerative occupation of your own choosing."

FDR was just getting warmed up. He moved on to foreign policy, criticizing the AYC for passing "resolutions on subjects which you have not thought through and on which you cannot possibly have complete knowledge." He zeroed in on their criticism of loans to Finland, which was at that moment engaged in a "winter war" to fight off Soviet aggression. Their criticism was, he told them, "unadulterated twaddle, based on . . . 90 percent ignorance." It was at about this point that some in the audience began to hiss—quickly silenced by others.

The lecture continued: "The Soviet Union, as everybody who has the courage to face the fact knows, is run by a dictatorship as absolute as any other dictatorship in the world. It has allied itself with another dictator-ship, and it has invaded a neighbor . . . infinitesimally small."

Eleanor, as usual, stayed cool and calm, answering questions for over an hour afterward in a "kindly, sincere and considerate" manner. She told the youths they shouldn't pass any resolutions they didn't believe in. "In all fairness, I think, however, it should be said that there is no excuse for a big nation invading a little nation that has not been attacked by that little nation."

Tommy was furious with the young people's rudeness toward the president. When some of them came to tea afterward, she upbraided them: "How dare you insult the President of the United States?" The pres-ident, when he heard about it, called her in to his office and said, "Thank you, Tommy."

But some weeks later, Tommy reluctantly typed yet one more essay by Eleanor about "Why I Still Believe in the Youth Congress." All the attacks on the Congress, Eleanor argued, had "only consolidated the feeling of 'youth against the world.'" She didn't "condone bad manners" or "disrespect for high office," but after all, only a few of the young people had been rude. And they had been standing in the cold rain after spending the night in buses with very little sleep. "I wish we could look at this whole question of the activities of youth-led organizations, from the point of view of the wisest way for old people to help youth."

Hick was inclined to sympathize with Tommy and FDR at this point. "I *don't* believe in baiting Communists," she wrote Eleanor, ". . . and I think making martyrs of them is silly. It's alright with me if they want to be Communists, and I know, as well as you do, what *makes* Communists. I think that's why I liked 'Grapes of Wrath' so much. It shows so clearly and, to my mind, convincingly what *makes* Communists. But Communists I do not like."

At the same time, Hick admired Eleanor's ability to be "sane and dispassionate" while others "get annoyed with a few brash young leaders and lose sight of the real picture. . . . I do get so irritated at times with what one might call 'professional Youth.'" She admitted that she might have behaved "just as they do—probably worse." Back in 1917, she had been such a vocal opponent of the war that she was briefly investigated by the Department of Justice.

Hick had engaged in passionate debates with her newspaper colleague "Hi" Austin Simons about his decision to resist the draft and go to jail in 1917. When he wound up in federal prison, she wrote him sustaining letters. "I am sitting on my bench, grinning the grin that your letter has evoked every time I have read it," Simons wrote Hick from Fort Leavenworth in Kansas. "It lies beside me, its pages margined with memory—pictures of old days, its lines interwritten with swatches of old conversations, old discussions and old projects, its 'sincere affection' saluting all the warm greetings and comradely emotions I have wished for many months to give you." The memories that Hick, like so many others, carried of the First World War made it hard to accept the inevitability of the Second.

But events were slowly forcing even Eleanor to change her mind. Her April defense of the Youth Congress was to be her last. That same month, Germany occupied Denmark and took over Norway by sea; in May it invaded neutral Belgium and Holland. It looked as though France would fall too. On May 20, after reading the morning papers, Eleanor wrote to the Youth Congress leaders, warning them that she was willing to speak at their next meeting but that her speech "could not be to the liking of the group."

Five days later, she told the closing Youth Congress session that even though "you don't want to go to war" and "I don't want to go to war," "war may come to us." It was not what the crowd wanted to hear. "Her scolding did no good," the *New York Times* noted the next day. "They refused to reconsider their resolution against preparedness."

Eleanor went through an unusually discouraged period that spring. No doubt it saddened her to part ways with her young friends after so enjoying their company. Tommy wrote Anna that her mother was frustrated because she didn't yet have a job to do in the war effort. But Eleanor's mood was surely most affected by the realization that everything was moving inexorably toward a third term. She not only hated the idea of carrying the First Lady's ceremonial burden for four more years, but also dreaded the effect of the goldfish bowl on her children, who were easy prey for scandal-loving journalists. Even Franklin, she believed, would have liked to retire to the "role of elder statesman."

But retiring was not an option. By the time the Democratic convention opened in Chicago on July 15, France had surrendered and Hitler had driven the British forces back to Dunkirk, where they were forced to abandon all their weaponry and flee home. Hitler had announced his plan, called Operation Sea Lion, to invade Great Britain.

"Do you think Hitler really will send 3000 planes to bomb England?" Hick asked Eleanor on July 6, 1940. "The very thought makes me feel sick at my stomach."

A few weeks earlier, the Republicans had chosen Wendell Willkie, a likable utilities magnate with no government experience of any kind, to be their presidential candidate. By the time Hick left Washington to attend the convention, there could be very little doubt in the minds of most people that Roosevelt would have to stay on for a third term. Ironically, it was going to be Eleanor Roosevelt who would smooth the way to his nomination.

CHAPTER SEVENTEEN

A BETTER POLITICIAN
THAN HER HUSBAND

TO L A HICKOK, STEVENS HOTEL CHICAGO

WILL ARRIVE ABOUT 6:40 CHICAGO DAYLIGHT

SPECIAL PLANE, WILL NOT NEED A ROOM AS

RETURNING AS SOON AS POSSIBLE

LOVE ELEANOR

ELEANOR'S TELEGRAM TO HICK said it all. Disagreement about FDR's vice presidential choice at the Democratic convention in Chicago was threatening to derail his nomination for a third term. Eleanor had reluctantly agreed to fly to Chicago and give a speech, in hope of smoothing ruffled feathers. But she was determined to do it with as little disruption of her life as possible. She would fly in, do her duty, and fly out again on the same day. No need to stay over at the Stevens Hotel, which would be swarming with reporters and Democratic operatives. She had always disliked all the hoopla of political conventions, much preferring to follow events from Val-Kill with Tommy and Joe Lash.

Hick, of course, was the opposite. She savored every minute of the Democratic convention of 1940, where she was privy to the plots and counterplots, resentments and surprises. One surprise, right from the start, was that Democratic Party chairman Jim Farley, who had so successfully operated FDR's previous campaigns, was only nominally in charge. "I'm the only one around here who doesn't know anything," Farley peevishly told a *New York Times* reporter on the first day of the convention. Did he have his usual direct line to FDR at the White House? Farley was asked. "Apparently," he replied, "there is a different situation now."

It didn't take reporters long to discover that if there was a "smoke-filled room" in Chicago, it was located on the third floor of the Blackstone Hotel, in Harry Hopkins's suite. Hopkins had a direct line to the White House in the bathroom, where he could discuss tactics with FDR in private. One convention delegate, using a rustic metaphor, explained that "the boys knew they had rings in their noses, but they did not know who held the leading strings."

Hick knew, of course. Although she was fond of the man she called "the boss," she understood how party regulars—including her current boss, Charlie Michelson, as well as Jim Farley—would resent the intrusion of Harry Hopkins, a social worker and political amateur, into the quadrennial party rite.

Nor was Hick surprised that the delegates were less than enthusiastic in the early going, given FDR's refusal to state his own position on running for a third term. "I have thought for some time that he was overplaying his role of indifference and was displaying too much coyness," Harold Ickes wrote in his diary. FDR didn't want to *ask* for a third term, he wanted to *be* asked, unanimously if possible.

The mood of the convention intensified on the second day, when veteran orator Alben Barkley took the podium, starting off with a few jabs at Wendell Willkie, then moving on to shout the magic name of Roosevelt. For the next twenty-five minutes, the thirty-five hundred delegates turned into a "wild, shifting mass of screaming, standard-waving humanity."

When Barkley finally restored order, conveyed FDR's calculated message that he had no wish to run for a third term, and released the delegates to vote as they pleased, the crowd erupted once again in a "draft Roosevelt" demonstration. "We want Roosevelt," an amplified voice roared.

"Florida Wants Roosevelt," came another voice. "The whole world wants Roosevelt!" "Willkie wants Roosevelt!" The shouting, interspersed with marching tunes, went on for an hour.

But Hick, watching from the sidelines, observed that grassroots Democrats from around the country weren't joining in the cheering. What's more, a *New York Times* reporter soon discovered that the loudest Roosevelt chants were coming not from the convention floor but from the basement, where the Chicago superintendent of sewers, a man with a powerful booming voice named Thomas F. Garry, had his own microphone.

Whether Harry Hopkins knew in advance about the "voice from the sewer" or not, the demonstration highlighted a deep division at the convention. From his perch at the Blackstone Hotel, Hopkins had rallied the support of power brokers like Mayor Ed Kelly, but he had alienated the party regulars across the street at the Stevens Hotel. In particular, he had ignored and infuriated Farley, a man whose long years as party boss had won him many friends. Farley had packed the balcony with his supporters, and had sentimental support among the delegates on the convention floor as well. Eventually that discontent would take the form of opposition to FDR's vice presidential choice. The ensuing quarrel threatened to reverse the Roosevelt juggernaut.

FDR was nominated with relative ease. The trouble came when he sent word of his choice for vice president: Agriculture Secretary Henry Wallace. It was a surprising choice. FDR had never been close to Wallace, but he now decided that he was "the kind of man I like to have around," someone who "is good to work with" and "knows a lot."

Wallace, however, was exactly the kind of New Dealer the party regulars disliked: a former Republican and an impractical left-leaning utopian. There were actually boos from the convention floor when his name was proposed.

Back at the White House, FDR was digging in his heels. Either he got Wallace, he told his advisers, or he retired to Hyde Park. He even wrote out a brief speech to that effect and sent his speechwriter Sam Rosenman off to polish it up for delivery.

Meanwhile, at Val-Kill, Eleanor was becoming more and more indignant about Hopkins's treatment of Jim Farley. "Harry has been running things," she told Frances Perkins, and has not been "very tactful."

Even before the convention, Eleanor had felt abandoned by Hopkins. In the past, he had always been her ally in her mission to address societal wrongs. Now, as Tommy wrote Anna, he had "gone completely over to the other side of the house." Not only had he moved permanently into the White House that spring, but he had become FDR's regular companion at lunch, dinner, and in between—and before long his most important deputy, using all his connections in business, industry, and politics to mobilize for national defense. Now he had also usurped Farley's role in the nominating process, without any consideration of the loyal old friend's feelings.

Eleanor was genuinely fond of Farley, a bighearted Irish Catholic from upstate New York who had been Roosevelt's political right-hand man since he had run for governor in 1928. Farley had played a critical role in FDR's two previous presidential victories. He had worked closely, too, with Molly Dewson and Eleanor to provide jobs for women in the Roosevelt administration.

Farley had angered FDR by arguing against a third term, considered by many to be a dangerous, undemocratic precedent. Farley also had suggested himself in Democratic circles as a potential presidential candidate. Nonetheless, Eleanor didn't think he deserved the rude treatment he had gotten thus far at the 1940 convention.

As news of FDR's choice for vice president got around the convention, a revolt looked very possible. First Franklin had shunned Farley for Hopkins, and now he was overlooking Democratic regulars for a maverick. Labor Secretary Frances Perkins was extremely worried. She wanted FDR to come to the convention and calm everyone down. When FDR refused, Perkins called Eleanor and suggested that she come instead.

When Eleanor called the president to ask if he wanted her to break precedent and speak to the convention, he asked, "Well, would you like to go?"

Her answer was, "No, I wouldn't *like* to go! I'm very busy and I wouldn't like to go at all."

Then she asked, "Do you really want me to go?" It was the game the two played: neither liked to acknowledge their need for the other.

FDR managed to admit that "perhaps it would be a good idea."

Eleanor agreed to go, provided Farley agreed.

When Farley heard that Eleanor was calling, he was so moved he could barely speak. He told her it was all right for her to come, and that he would delay the vice presidential nomination until after she made her speech. Then Farley, who knew Hick had influence with Eleanor, got in touch with Hick and told her to call Eleanor back and "tell her I mean it. Things are bad."

That was when Eleanor figured out a way to enter and exit the Chicago convention with record speed. She arranged for a small plane to pick her up at Wappingers Falls airport, just fifteen miles from Val-Kill. On the trip south to New York City, the pilot allowed Eleanor to steer the plane, following the Hudson River. It gave her, she wrote years later, "a real sense of exhilaration." It was probably the most carefree moment she would have that day, or for days to come.

When she landed in Chicago, Farley was waiting for her, along with the women of the press. They wanted to know if she was happy about the nomination.

"Happy!" she replied. "I don't know how any one could be particularly happy about the nomination in the present state of the world."

It wasn't what they wanted to hear. Did the president want you to come? they asked. "Did he wish you well?"

"I don't remember that he wished me well," she answered. "I suppose, of course, that he was willing for me to come—or I would not have come."

Once out of the public eye, Eleanor went to work patching things up. She called FDR and insisted he talk to Farley and affirm Wallace as his choice. Farley, after arguing to no avail, agreed to try to make it happen. But by that time mutiny was in the air.

At 10:30 p.m., when Eleanor slipped quietly into a seat on the crowded platform, the delegates were a screaming multitude. "Mention of Wallace started a roar of boos and catcalls," Hick recalled, "in which even the magic word 'Roosevelt' was so drowned that it gave the impression that he was being booed too." Hick and Frances Perkins stood in the wings and "watched with horror as [Eleanor] moved forward through the haze of dust and tobacco smoke under the glaring lights to the speaker's stand— tall and proudly erect, her head held high." The boos and the catcalls stopped. In dead silence, without written notes, she spoke "as calmly as though she were talking directly to each man and woman in that crowd."

She began by thanking "our National Chairman," Jim Farley. "Nobody could appreciate more what he has done for the party."

Then, instead of endorsing Henry Wallace by name and setting off more protests, she stayed on higher ground, emphasizing "responsibility," a word she used six times in her brief speech. The man who would become president (no mention of FDR either) would be faced with "a heavier re-sponsibility than any man has ever faced before in this country." This man would have to stay "on the job," leaving the "grave responsibility" of cam-paigning to the delegates. They would have to rise above "narrow and partisan" considerations. And they would have to understand that "no man who is a candidate or who is President can carry this situation alone." Without saying it, she was suggesting that the nominee, at such a critical moment in history, had the right to choose his replacement. "This is a time when it is the United States we fight for." As she returned to her seat, the organist softly played "God Bless America."

Noise and confusion returned as the delegates rallied behind their vice presidential nominees. Mrs. Wallace, sitting next to Eleanor on the plat-form, looked very unhappy, commenting to Eleanor, "I don't know why they don't seem to like Henry." But eventually Eleanor's argument that her husband deserved to choose his possible successor in such perilous times saved the day. Wallace won—by a mere seventy votes—over House Speaker William Bankhead of Alabama.

As soon as Wallace's nomination was assured, Eleanor said a quick goodbye to Mrs. Wallace, left for her chartered plane, which was waiting for her on the tarmac, flew back to LaGuardia, picked up her car, and drove on to Val-Kill, arriving in time for nine o'clock breakfast.

FDR had managed to reach Eleanor at the airport just before she left Chicago and tell her she had done a good job. Afterward, he told several people that her speech had been "just right." Others were more effusive. According to the *New York Daily News*, Mrs. Roosevelt's remarks did "more to soothe the convention bruises than all the efforts of astute Senators." Hick's boss Charlie Michelson observed that "on that occasion, at least, she was a better politician then her husband."

Tommy wrote Hick from Val-Kill that they were "swamped" with letters and wires of approval, including a "beautiful letter" from the grand old man of progressive Republican politics, Senator George Norris, which especially pleased Eleanor.

"When it seemed to me all of the good work President Roosevelt had done . . . all of his ability to continue his work in the future," Norris wrote Eleanor, "were about to be cast aside . . . when it seemed the battle for righteousness was about to be lost, you came on the scene, and what you said in that short speech caused men of sense and honor to stop and think before they plunged. . . . You turned a rout into victory. . . . This country owes you a debt of gratitude it can never repay and which it does not now fully comprehend."

Tommy had worried that Eleanor's unprecedented speech at the convention might resurrect the old antisuffrage cry of "petticoat rule." But after seeing her "quiet that bunch of wild kids at the Youth Congress," she never had any doubts that she could handle any crowd.

"She is truly a magnificent person," she wrote Hick, "and while you and I have always known that . . . it takes a dramatic thing once in a while to recharge us."

Eleanor herself may have been the only one with mixed feelings about her appearance. "I felt," she remembered later, "as though it had all been a dream with a somewhat nightmarish tinge."

FOR THE FIRST TWO MONTHS after the convention, FDR left the campaigning to others, as Eleanor said he must. Willkie, on the other hand, campaigned vigorously, even frantically, laying great emphasis on the dangers of an unprecedented third term. In a world menaced by dictatorship, he argued, Roosevelt was nearly as dangerous as Hitler or Mussolini.

Willkie was prone to making wild accusations: at one point, he accused FDR of telephoning Hitler and Mussolini and urging them to "sell Czechoslovakia down the river at Munich."

"Golly he must be tough to cover," Hick wrote Eleanor. "So much extemporaneous speaking—and always a chance to deny he said a thing, or to say that he was misinterpreted. Bet the correspondents will get plenty sick of him."

"The more he hollers," H. L. Mencken wrote, "the plainer it will become that he is really saying nothing. He will be lucky if his laryngitis returns, and his friendly doctors lock him up for the duration."

But Willkie was, in Harold Ickes's estimation, "an attractive, colorful character" who wasn't going to be easy to defeat. There were other major threats to FDR's reelection as well. One was a venomous speech by John L. Lewis, powerful leader of the CIO, saying that the reelection of FDR would be "a national evil of the first magnitude."

Lewis's attack backfired: telegrams of support poured in to the White House afterward. But FDR's determination to put the nation on a war footing was controversial. Just weeks before the election, FDR announced that he had reached an agreement to supply Great Britain with World War I destroyers in exchange for British-controlled bases in the Caribbean. At just the same time, Congress was considering a bill that would establish the first peacetime draft in U.S. history. Add to that the near-unanimous endorsement of Willkie by major newspapers—including the *New York Times* and the *Washington Post*—and by October, FDR's supporters were urging him to shed his presidential detachment and go on the offensive.

FDR did so with relish. "I am an old campaigner," he began telling crowds, "and I love a good fight." He accused Willkie of using totalitarian techniques: repeating falsehoods over and over until people believed them. "The overwhelming majority of Americans will not be scared by this blitzkrieg of verbal incendiary bombs."

FDR paired stern rhetoric with a playful mocking of the house's three die-hard isolationists: Congressman Joseph Martin, Congressman Bruce Barton, and Congressman Hamilton Fish. He told a crowd of twenty-two thousand at Madison Square Garden that Great Britain would never have gotten any help at all had it been up to "now wait, a perfectly beautiful rhythm—Congressmen Martin, Barton, and Fish." By the end of the speech, the audience had turned "Martin, Barton, and Fish" into a chant. For the rest of the campaign, audiences waited for "Martin, Barton, and Fish." FDR happily obliged. He also kept his listeners happy by promising not to go to war "except in case of attack." On one important occasion, late in the campaign, FDR neglected to add that qualifying phrase, causing his advisers to worry that he was making a promise never to go to war.

Hick spent election night at the party's press headquarters in New York, wearing a path in the carpet between the "tabulator" and Charlie Michelson's desk. The earliest returns, trickling in from New England towns, didn't look good. But then came Boston, which turned the Massachusetts tide. Then Connecticut began to look good. When the president swung into the lead in Ohio, confidence swelled. And when the *Cleveland Plain Dealer* conceded Ohio, it was all but over.

"Along about 1 am," Hick wrote Eleanor, "the drunks began to pile in." By 2 a.m., "it was just a question of how many states we would carry."

The final tally in electoral votes was 449 to 82. FDR lost Maine and Vermont, as in the past, but he also lost in the heartland for the first time. Thanks to the hard work of political operatives like Hick, however, the Democrats maintained their majorities in both the House and Senate, which were going to be critical in the president's efforts to lead the country in the dangerous days ahead.

On the other side of the Atlantic, Winston Churchill was watching anxiously. By that time, more than ten thousand Londoners had perished in the Blitz, and Churchill grumbled in private that the Americans were "very good in applauding the valiant deeds of others" while keeping out of the war themselves. His message to FDR, however, was restrained and gracious: "I did not think it right for me as a foreigner to express any opinion upon American politics while the election was on but now I feel that you will not mind my saying that I prayed for your success and that I am truly thankful for it. . . . I must avow my sure faith that the lights by which we steer will bring us all safely to anchor."

CHAPTER EIGHTEEN

IN RESIDENCE

AS USUAL, ELEANOR AND HICK observed the Christmas holiday together in New York in 1940, a few days early. "One of my friends," Eleanor
noted in "My Day," "with whom I always make it a point to have a reunion
before Christmas, came to dinner and we spent a happy evening together."

Hick gave Eleanor special logs for her fire, a basket of jellies, and something Eleanor described in her thank-you note as a "lunch set." But Hick,
like all of Eleanor's friends, had long since given up competing in the gift
department. "Madame," she protested to Eleanor, "am I never to stop receiving Christmas presents from you? Oh, damn it—what have I ever
done to deserve a friend like you! Well, anyway, I thank you—for a very
great deal of pleasure."

According to Eleanor's Christmas notebook, Hick received oranges,
raisins, and a fur coat for Christmas. But then there was also a surprise
fruitcake for dessert. And of course there was a toy for Prinz, which he had
to wait to open. "He'd lie on the floor and look at it long minutes at a
time!" Hick reported. "You *should* have seen him open it!"

Hick had an extra reason to celebrate. The November election had
brought an end to her publicist's job. Then, two weeks before Christmas,
she learned that she would be hired as executive secretary of the Democratic Party's Women's Division.

It hadn't been easy to get the job. Both Eleanor and Molly Dewson, who had made the Women's Division into a Democratic powerhouse, worried that Hick wouldn't have the patience "to answer endless letters constructively and help endless 'little' women to move up one step at a time in organization."

Eleanor and Molly felt proprietary about the Women's Division. Some of Eleanor's happiest times in earlier days had been spent raising money and awareness for it. With Louis Howe's encouragement, she had taken charge of what became the *Democratic Digest*, a "serious but gay and friendly messenger," first in New York and then in Washington. After FDR won in 1932, Eleanor was the one who convinced him to establish the Women's Division as a permanent part of the Democratic National Committee.

As director, Molly Dewson conferred almost daily with the First Lady on placing women in patronage jobs and had more success than any previous administration. She also worked energetically to educate women, America's newest voters, at the grassroots level. It was her idea to introduce a character called "Mrs. County Leader," a perky little woman with a big can-do smile, wearing a small felt hat with a single feather. Handouts showed Mrs. County Leader bent double in front of her car, rear end in the air, turning a crank. "Be a self-cranker," read the caption, because the Party "has no automatic starter." Elsewhere, Mrs. County Leader is fishing in "rock-ribbed Republican" waters, to "catch voters not lucky enough to be born Democrats."

The Women's Division under Dewson turned out information flyers in rainbow colors, addressing succinctly every issue from farming to taxes to nutrition to rural electrification. Metal banks in the shape of donkeys were distributed for the purpose of raising gas money so that women could travel around knocking on doors. The women, under Dewson, were one of the reasons the 1936 election was the most lopsided Democratic victory in American history.

Charlie Michelson described Molly Dewson as "the greatest she-politician of my term." To Jim Farley, she was simply "the General." Even though "the General" had retired in 1938, both she and Eleanor remained influential. There was no doubt in Eleanor's mind, or Molly Dewson's, that Hick was carrying on *their* tradition. They sensed that Hick's rough edges might be a problem on the job.

Dewson was hardly a conventional lady herself. She and her life partner, Polly Porter, went from cow farming in western Massachusetts to working for the Red Cross in the south of France during World War I. She wasn't afraid to use her elbows in fighting for progressive causes: "I am oblivious to a few digs in the ribs and cracks on the head," she told a colleague. "I just pull my hat on straight and prepare for the next objective, while all the time continuing [to be] the perfect Yankee with a complete sense of humor."

Dewson wore homespun suits—the jacket pockets sagging a little because of her habit of thrusting her hands into them—comfortable shoes, no makeup, and small wire-rimmed spectacles. But she was a Wellesley graduate from a respectable New England family, while Hick had neither college degree nor pedigree. Hick had acquired her style, and the unladylike nickname, in the tough world of daily journalism. But, perhaps hearing "the Commander's" lecture in her ear, she argued passionately for herself.

"I honestly don't think you and Molly have any real cause for worry about my getting bored or impatient with the ladies," she wrote Eleanor. "What neither of you seems to realize is just how desperate my plight is—and how little I can afford to be choosy!" She was forty-seven—an age when it is "very, very difficult" for a woman to get a job. "This particular job appeals to me more than any other I might get." She suggested there could be a "front woman" to make most of the speeches and pose for photographers. "And whatever else I have to do I *can* do."

In the end, Charlie Michelson, her boss during the campaign, may have won the day for Hick. Michelson had hired Hick because Eleanor recommended her, but whatever doubts he had were dispelled on the first day, when she did exactly what he asked her to. Like Michelson, Hick could turn out copy in a hurry: over two days at one point she wrote seven speeches for Democratic candidates on a wide range of issues. It didn't hurt that she listened with rapt attention to Michelson's stories about his early days in journalism, going back to the McKinley assassination. "What a newspaper career that man had!" Hick wrote Eleanor. Michelson told Hick she was the only woman qualified to take over the Women's Division; he came back early from his vacation to lobby on her behalf.

In the end, Eleanor and Dewson decided to act on Hick's suggestion about hiring a "front woman." Mrs. Gladys Tillett would be given the title of director of the Women's Division. Hick would have the title of executive secretary and work behind the scenes. "You are under her," Eleanor wrote pointedly, "and work out plans with her." Hick would have a one-year contract. "But," Eleanor added, "I'm sure you can count on four years if you get on with the gals coming in." Mrs. Tillett, according to Eleanor, was "delighted to have you."

Gladys Avery Tillett was the daughter of a North Carolina Supreme Court justice and a graduate of the Women's College of the University of North Carolina. She had been an early leader of the League of Women Voters in her state and a delegate to three Democratic conventions. She was also married to a lawyer, had three children, and was, according to one society page profile, "one of the most eloquent and 'to the point' speakers on the American scene."

This story was accompanied by a photograph of Tillett's long, delicate face in profile. Her hat, made of some gauzy material stretched over wire, resembled a large exotic flower. It was tilted forward at a becoming angle. Clearly, Mrs. Tillett had the style required of a "front woman."

No matter how serious the occasion, the press still paid a remarkable amount of attention to the dress and appearance of women in politics. When Eleanor arrived at the 1940 Democratic convention to make her historic speech, the *New York Times* spent two whole paragraphs on what she was wearing. "Her traveling suit was a tailored ensemble of navy cloth coat with long lapels of Eleanor blue, with the soft crepe dress beneath in the same shade. Her hat was a small one of navy straw in a modified beret type with Eleanor blue flowers topping the low crown. She carried a large navy calf purse, and later . . . added a shoulder spray of white orchids to her costume."

Hick was an old pro at this kind of fussy writing: she had done plenty of it in her early days in Milwaukee and Minneapolis. In truth, she was better at describing the style than living it. Still, "front woman" or no, she was going to have to meet certain sartorial expectations.

One of them was a hat. In the *Democratic Digest*, there is hardly a woman, in all the hundreds of photographs of women at meetings, who is pictured without a hat—often an outlandish one. In one of the pictures Eleanor wears a hat that has an off-kilter twisting tornado shooting out of the top. Others wore tiny flying saucers precariously perched on top of their hairdos, or more daring styles, including a fat roll wrapped around the head suitable for an imam. A lady Democrat needed a hat.

So one day in March, when a milliner visited her on Mitchell Place, Hick brought out her black straw hat with silver quill. It was a Lilly Daché, Hick noted proudly. Eleanor had given it to her just seven years earlier.

"I want a hat just like this one," she told the milliner firmly.

"No," said the milliner, just as firmly.

For the next ten minutes they argued back and forth. But in the end the milliner won. Even though Hick thought it impractical, and likely to break on her travels, the milliner insisted on giving her a feather quill instead of a silver one, not to mention an updated hat. At the end of the interview, the milliner gingerly picked up Hick's old Lilly Daché model and asked, "Did you wear this hat last Spring?"

Hick answered defiantly, "Yes, I did, and nobody said a word, either!"

"You should have seen the expression on her face!" Hick wrote Eleanor.

Fortunately, Hick was going to remain hatless and inconspicuous much of the time. In the introductory profile in the *Democratic Digest*, she spoke of "Tillett and Company" and explained that she, Lorena Hickok, was the "and company." She would be "behind the scenes," the position she had come to prefer. But there can be little doubt that she was the reason that the Women's Division and the *Democratic Digest* became energetic and intelligent advocates for progressive Democratic candidates over the next four years.

Since the new job would require Hick to live in Washington, D.C., for a good part of the time, Eleanor suggested that she find a country place near the District and give up the Little House. But Hick refused—the Little House was too important to her. She figured out that her $6,000 a year would allow her to sublease her Manhattan apartment and continue to spend time at the Little House, while renting a single, furnished room in D.C.

"Well, if that is the way you are going to live, you might just as well stay on here," Eleanor told her. And so for the next five years Hick went from being an occasional to a regular resident of the White House.

Hick vowed that this stay at the White House was going to be different from the early ones, when she was so jealous of rivals for Eleanor's attention. "That business of moping about the White House," she wrote Eleanor. "Never again." She planned to come and go in businesslike fashion, enjoying "glimpses of you" whenever they happened.

Her trouble had always been that when it came to Eleanor, she was "more interested in the *person* than the *personage*. I resented the personage and fought for years an anguished and losing fight against the development of the *person* into the *personage*. I still prefer the *person*, but I admire and respect the *personage* with all my heart!"

Eleanor was uncomfortable with this suggestion. "The personage is an accident and I only like the part of life in which I am a person!" Yet Eleanor's life in the public arena left little time for anything else. Her speaking engagements, her radio talks, the constant barrage of letters, all of which she insisted on answering, kept her going through long days and longer nights.

Eleanor might have explained that she needed the money her public appearances brought. Or that she was merely doing her duty, responding to other people's requests. But being the center of attention, as she had so wished to be as a little girl, must have been gratifying some of the time.

There was also the crucial fact, which she admitted more than once, that being a whirlwind of activity staved off sad feelings that lurked beneath the surface. There were some days, she confessed to Joe Lash, when her life was so overwhelming that "I try to be a machine or I would break into tears or run away."

Joe Lash was the one she made time for now. "No other engagement can't be given up, if there is a chance to see you!" she wrote. She kept a large photo of him on her desk, wrote him affectionate letters daily, sometimes twice daily. "I've grown to love you so much that your moods and anxieties and joys and sorrows seem very close to my own heart and you are very constantly in my thoughts." She was vicariously involved, in an intense way, in Lash's struggle to woo Trude Pratt away from her unhappy marriage.

As her affection grew for Lash, whom she sometimes thought of as another son, her worries over her own sons continued. Not long after the election, she wrote Hick that she dreaded "getting accustomed to four more years of easy living" in the White House. Hick was quick to protest that Eleanor worked harder than anyone she knew. But perhaps Eleanor was thinking about the effect of "easy living" on her sons, who had been surrounded much of their lives by special privileges and harsh public scrutiny. It wasn't easy to grow into adulthood in such an atmosphere.

Franklin Jr. seemed to have inherited the family drinking problem. After he got a job working in Hick's office during the 1940 campaign, Eleanor asked Hick to keep an eye out. "If you hear of F Jr drinking too much let me know," she wrote her. "I think I should talk to him but it is like talking to a feather pillow." There had been several car accidents. After one of them, he angrily tripped a photographer and broke his camera.

Elliott, whom others in the family considered to be Eleanor's favorite, had given her constant cause for worry, including a first marriage that lasted only a year and left a son behind. Now a second marriage to Ruth Googins, a woman Hick and everyone in the family liked, was in trouble. He too had been in a car accident that landed him in the hospital and knocked out his two front teeth—an event that Eleanor mentioned in her column. "I must say that the loss of two front teeth does cause rather a change in his appearance." The reference was unusual: for the most part, Eleanor wrote only to Hick and her daughter, Anna, about such events. Hostile members of the press, especially a venomous columnist named Westbrook Pegler, were always eager to pounce on such family embarrassments.

The situation with her oldest son, James, over the last several years may have been the most distressing to Eleanor, because FDR was involved. In September 1938, James landed at the Mayo Clinic with what seemed to be an ulcer, but which everyone feared might be something worse. Eleanor spent two weeks there with him, and even FDR, for whom travel was a major undertaking, paid a visit. Exploratory surgery found nothing fatal, and James slowly recovered. But the background of his illness was troubling. James had married Betsey Cushing, one of a trio of sisters who had dazzled Boston society. While James was working at the White House as FDR's aide, Betsey proved to be a lively and attractive presence who sometimes played hostess in Eleanor's place. FDR, as James later wrote, was a ladies' man by temperament and "at his sparkling best when his audience included a few admiring and attractive ladies." He engaged in a flirtation with Betsey that deeply wounded his son. By the time James was hospitalized, the marriage was in serious jeopardy. FDR's highly unusual visit may have been an attempt to make amends. Eleanor was used to Franklin's flirtations, but this one must have bothered her more than others. She wrote Anna from the Mayo Clinic that "this situation seems to me incredibly unreal but Pa and Betsey refuse to acknowledge it." While at the clinic, James became involved in a new romance with one of his nurses, much to both FDR's and Eleanor's dismay. Finally, at Eleanor's suggestion, Harry Hopkins called the nurse's boss, an action that infuriated James. Betsey sued for divorce, asking an enormous alimony. James ultimately married the nurse.

No wonder Eleanor wrote Joe Lash that she wouldn't mind seeing her boys going into the armed services. Of course the public and the press would expect them to enlist, since others of their age were making the sacrifice. One by one, the four sons did sign up for military duty. In September 1940, Elliott joined the Army Air Corps. By October James was in California, drilling with the Marines. In 1941, the two younger boys reported to the Navy.

Increasingly the entire nation was consumed with war preparation. Even those who opposed a foreign war now feared an attack on the homeland. The regional conferences Hick put on for the Women's Division now focused on "hemispheric defense." Eleanor was traveling as much as ever, but her visits now included airplane factories and ballooning military installations. Fort Bragg, North Carolina, she told her "My Day" readers, was now home to sixty-five thousand recruits; a new building was going up there every thirty-five minutes. Her speeches now defended the all-out military buildup against the attacks of strident isolationists who accused FDR of warmongering. "It is stupid," she told a Women's Division conference in St. Paul that Hick organized, "to say . . . that safeguard[ing] the integrity of our hemisphere puts us in the category of those who desire world domination."

Hick may have been at the White House more than Eleanor in 1941. But she worked hard at keeping that a secret from almost everyone, fearing that the women she worked with around the country would want favors if they knew she lived in such proximity to the Roosevelts.

Sometimes Eleanor would invite visiting Democratic women to the White House for tea or lunch—an especially helpful gesture whenever there were squabbles in the organization. "Many a ruffled feather she smoothed that way for us," Hick noted. On those occasions the doormen and ushers colluded with Hick. "They would greet me formally, along with the rest, take our names, and escort us to the Red Room."

Mrs. Roosevelt would play along too, greeting Hick as though she hadn't seen her for a month, even though they had breakfasted together. Once, an usher, helping Hick out of her coat, asked, "In residence today? Or just a visitor?"

One hot Sunday afternoon in August 1941, Hick nearly had her cover blown in a most embarrassing way. The Roosevelts, she knew, were out of town, so the house was empty except for the servants. She went up to the

White House roof after breakfast in her bathing suit to bask in the sun. Then, as she was about to return to her room, she heard a lot of male voices on the second floor. Looking down through the skylight, she recognized Secretary of State Cordell Hull, Undersecretary Sumner Welles, several generals, and a whole lot of Navy men dripping gold braid. There was no way to get to her room without passing them, and she didn't have even a towel. She beat a quick retreat. It took a long while, but finally she managed to get a servant to bring her some clothes so she could slip by to her room inconspicuously.

The next day, she discovered the reason why all those brass were at the White House: FDR had pulled off a deception on a grand scale. While all the world believed he was on an innocent fishing trip, he had boarded a thousand-man warship for a rendezvous off the coast of Newfoundland with the man code-named "former naval person": Prime Minister Winston Churchill.

CHAPTER NINETEEN

IN IT, UP TO THE NECK

FDR PLANNED HIS ESCAPE from the White House with glee: first, a train to New London, Connecticut, where he would board the presidential yacht, the *Potomac*, head out toward Martha's Vineyard, and weigh anchor for the night. Then at dawn the next day, with the Secret Service left behind to impersonate a president at leisure with guests on the deck of the *Potomac*, he would transfer to the flagship USS *Augusta*, a heavy cruiser armed with an arsenal of guns and torpedoes. Accompanied by another heavy cruiser and four destroyers, the *Augusta* would speed north into Canadian waters off Newfoundland to meet with its opposite number, the HMS *Prince of Wales*, carrying Prime Minister Winston Churchill, the man who, in Harry Hopkins's estimation, was "the one and only person . . . with whom you need to have a full meeting of minds."

A full meeting of minds didn't take place: Churchill was hoping for a declaration of war from Roosevelt—a declaration the president could not give without setting off a rebellion back home. FDR proposed something quite different: a declaration of principles for a postwar, and postcolonial, world. Since Roosevelt held most of the cards, Churchill reluctantly agreed to go along especially after FDR asked him, as wordsmith extraordinaire, to draw up the first draft. The result was the Atlantic Charter, a historic agreement granting self-determination to all nations once the war was over. It was a very optimistic undertaking, since at that moment the Germans were intent on obliterating the British nation. There was no guarantee that the Atlantic Charter had a future.

Still, FDR was pleased with the meeting. The conference produced a document that echoed the American Bill of Rights and disassociated the United States from the British colonial tradition to which Churchill clung with a passion. At the same time, it allowed FDR to take Churchill's measure without making promises that would alarm the American people. Churchill, though he had hoped for more, announced that he had established "warm and deep personal relations with our great friend."

As it happened, both Franklin Jr. and Elliott were able to join FDR on the *Augusta*—Franklin Jr. from his accompanying destroyer and Elliott from a nearby base. Roosevelt had not only the pleasure of his sons' company, but also the added support of their strong arms and handsome uniformed presences. For FDR, there was also the sheer delight, for a man forever confined to his wheelchair, of carrying off a daring escapade, undetected by the American press. "The fact that he had pulled the trip off without being discovered," Eleanor wrote, "gave him a deep sense of satisfaction."

Eleanor knew nothing about the Atlantic Conference before it happened. But there can be no doubt that her influence had a lot to do with the document it produced. For years she had been speaking and writing about the importance of fighting for the core beliefs of a strong democracy rather than simply against the evils of Fascism and Communism. That was the idea underlying one of the most important speeches of FDR's presidency, delivered to Congress that January, laying out the "Four Freedoms" worth fighting for: freedom of speech, freedom of worship, freedom from want, and freedom from fear. The Atlantic Charter drew on the same principles; it became the template for postwar peace agreements and the charter of the United Nations and the Universal Declaration of Human Rights, in all of which Eleanor played a critical role. When the agreement was announced on the radio on August 14, Eleanor wrote in "My Day" that "it was an important moment in the history of world progress."

Three weeks later, the excitement in Eleanor and Franklin's public life was suddenly overshadowed by private sorrow. Sara Roosevelt had been ailing since the spring. "I found Mama in bed with high blood pressure," Eleanor had reported to Hick in May. "I think she just missed having a stroke and I fear it means I must be a bit more considerate of her, instead of running away. You know that won't be to my liking."

Sara Roosevelt died on September 7 at Hyde Park, not long after returning from Campobello. Eleanor had come up to help her move back in for the winter. They were eating breakfast together when she noticed that her mother-in-law was very pale and short of breath. Sensing that the end was near, she called Franklin in Washington. He came as quickly as he could—in time to spend the day of September 6 with his mother, recounting the details of his historic meeting with Winston Churchill at sea. His mother, who lived for his visits, seemed to revive at dinner. She died the next day, two weeks before her eighty-seventh birthday.

For Franklin, the loss was enormous. For several days, the *New York Times* reported, he "shut himself off from the world" more completely than at any time since he became president.

"That big house without his mother seems awfully big and bare," his cousin and frequent companion Daisy Suckley wrote. "She gave him that personal affection which his friends and secretaries cannot do, in the same way—He was always 'my boy,' and he seemed to me often rather pathetic, and hungry for just that kind of thing."

Eleanor, as usual, sprang into action, informing family members and arranging for the simple burial her mother-in-law had requested, in the graveyard at nearby St. James Episcopal Church. But her efforts were complicated by a much more troubling event: on the same night her mother-in-law was dying, her brother Hall Roosevelt, then living nearby in Hyde Park, became seriously ill and had to be hospitalized in Poughkeepsie.

"Hick dearest," she wrote from Hyde Park on the day of Sara Roosevelt's death, "I am so weary I cannot write." She had been up most of the night, dealing not with Sara's peaceful death but with putting Hall in the hospital and trying to keep him there. "I've got to be at the hospital at 9:30 am and try to use moral suasion."

But moral suasion was no longer enough. Eleanor spent Hall's last days by his hospital bed, along with his companion, Zena Raset. It was, she wrote Joe Lash, "my idea of hell . . . to sit or stand and watch someone breathing hard, struggling for words when a gleam of consciousness returns and thinking 'this was once the little boy I played with and scolded, he could have been so much and this is what he is.'"

Hall Roosevelt had been only one year old when his mother died, and he had barely known his father. "Take care of Brudie," Eleanor's father had charged in one of his letters. Eleanor mothered "Brudie" and felt responsible for him all his life. Hall had lived with Franklin and Eleanor early in their marriage and came to them often with his problems.

"He had great energy, great physical strength and great brilliance of mind," Eleanor wrote, "but he never learned complete self-discipline." Hall was twice divorced and the father of six. He had tried many things— always with flair but never for long. For a time, he worked in the relief administration in Detroit and lived on the same allowance as his relief clients. In 1938, in the midst of the Spanish Civil War, he located 150 planes that could be flown across the French border to fight Franco. He flew to Paris, with a wink from FDR, to carry out the scheme, only to find that changed conditions on the ground made it impossible. Not long before he died, he was working on a book about his experiences as a young man in Alaska. "I think you will all enjoy the vivid pictures of the development of this northwestern corner of our country," Eleanor wrote hopefully in "My Day."

Early in the morning on September 25, 1941, Hall died at Walter Reed Hospital, with his older sister by his side. As soon as she returned to the White House, Eleanor walked into FDR's study to tell him the news. "Hall has died," she said. James, who happened to be with his father at the time, vividly remembered the tender scene that followed: "Father struggled to her side and put his arms around her. 'Sit down,' he said, so tenderly I can still hear it. And he sank down beside her and hugged her and kissed her and held her head on his chest. I do not think she cried. I think

Mother had forgotten how to cry. But there were times she needed to be held, and this certainly was one. . . . And she spent her hurt in Father's embrace."

Hall was buried in the family vault in Tivoli, alongside the mother and father he barely knew. "I know he would want all of us to remember," Eleanor wrote in "My Day," "but to remember happily." There were things about Hall, Eleanor wrote his daughter, also named Eleanor, that made him irresistible. "He enjoyed life in spots so spontaneously that certain moments with him stand out as the gayest moments in my whole life!" Sometimes at White House parties the Marine Band would strike up a waltz. Then Eleanor would flip her long train over her arm and take to the floor with her brother, who was even taller than she. They both waltzed beautifully. Everyone else would leave the floor to watch them.

Eleanor tried to put Hall's death behind her quickly, numbing herself with activity. But she confessed to Hick that she was "in a horrid frame of mind" and felt "indifferent inside." Hick wrote her back, "I think Hall's illness and death undoubtedly took more out of you than you realize or would ever admit, even to yourself." This was followed by a pep talk: "I know of no other woman who could learn to do so many things after 50 and to do them so well as you have."

Eleanor was by then pouring herself into her new job at the Office of Civilian Defense (OCD). It was the first real job she had taken on since becoming First Lady, and she took it very seriously, walking the half hour from the White House to her ninth-floor office in Dupont Circle every morning and working there with her assistant and friend, Elinor Morgenthau. Her goal, as she understood it, was to heighten preparedness by encouraging people to get involved as volunteers.

It was during these months, when she was working during the day at the OCD office, and attending to everything else when she got home, that a night guard noticed that her light had stayed on all night. FDR had asked her the next day, "What's this I hear? You didn't go to bed at all last night?"

Franklin himself almost always managed a good night's sleep. But in 1941, his waking hours might have seemed like a bad dream. He had persuaded Congress to approve a draft and to dramatically step up weapons production so that the country might become, in his words, the "arsenal of democracy." He had managed to convince Churchill of America's commitment to his cause. But he couldn't find a way to convince the wary American public to go to war. "He had no more tricks left," writer Robert Sherwood observed. "The bag from which he had pulled so many rabbits was empty."

Meanwhile, on October 31, a German torpedo sank the destroyer *Reuben James*, killing over a hundred American sailors. What's more, those who knew most about the atrocities Hitler was committing on the ground in Europe were crying out for action. Dorothy Thompson was one of the first American journalists to truly understand that Hitler was hell-bent on carrying out the annihilation of European Jewry.

Thompson spent Thanksgiving of 1941 typing out a long memo to Eleanor Roosevelt, urging her to convince FDR to act immediately. "TAKE ACTION!" she typed in capital letters. "The action should be sudden and of complete audacity." Her suggestion: send the Marines to seize Martinique, now a territory of Nazi-controlled Vichy France. "America will become excited with the first American coup," she predicted.

Of course FDR could do nothing of the kind: he still had the isolationists accusing him of provoking encounters. All he could do was wait for an attack large enough to justify a declaration of war. It wasn't long in coming.

Harry Hopkins and FDR were having lunch together as usual on December 7, 1941, when a call came in from Secretary of the Navy Frank Knox: his staff had picked up a radio signal from Honolulu about an air raid—and it wasn't a drill. Hopkins didn't believe it at first: no one had suspected that the Japanese would target Hawaii. Roosevelt believed it right away.

Eleanor, who was at the White House that day, knew from a glance into FDR's study that "finally the blow had fallen and we had been attacked."

All the secretaries were there, two telephones were in use, and senior military were on their way to the White House. She noticed that FDR remained "deadly calm" as activity swirled around him and news from Hawaii continued to come in, "each report more terrible than the last."

The attack on Pearl Harbor lasted less than two hours but exacted a horrible price. Twenty-one ships of the Pacific Fleet, including eight battleships, were damaged or sunk. FDR, a naval man and lover of ships, must have felt the losses as body blows. More devastating was the loss of more than twenty-four hundred lives.

It so happened that Eleanor's weekly radio broadcast on NBC took place on Sunday, December 7. So it was she, not FDR, who spoke first to the American people about the event. Her style, as usual, was homey and undramatic. "For months now the knowledge that something of this kind might happen has been hanging over our heads and yet it seemed impossible to believe, impossible to drop the everyday things of life and feel that there was only one thing which was important." Now that was over. There was no more uncertainty.

"We know what we have to face and we know that we are ready to face it. Whatever is asked of us I am sure we can accomplish it. We are the free and unconquerable people of the United States of America."

Horrible as the attack was, Pearl Harbor freed FDR at last to do what he had wanted to do for some time. "Hostilities exist," he told Congress and the American people the next day. "There is no blinking at the fact that our people, our territory, and our interests are in grave danger. With confidence in our armed forces—with the unbounding determination of our people—we will gain the inevitable triumph, so help us God."

Eleanor accompanied FDR to the Capitol for his speech, but joined her superior at the Office of Civilian Defense, Mayor Fiorello LaGuardia, soon after to fly to the West Coast, where there were fears of a coming Japanese attack. The time had come to finalize and implement the plans of the OCD.

Hick, who heard the news of Pearl Harbor over the radio from the

Little House, returned soon after to a chill and silent White House, "as though it had died." Even the president's little dog Fala didn't bark. Outside, all day long and into the night, she heard the sound of a steam shovel digging a trench across the front lawn toward the Treasury building. Workers were creating a tunnel from the White House to a presidential bomb shelter, in a vault deep underneath the Treasury Department. FDR, ever the joker, claimed he would only go there if he could play poker with the gold bricks.

To Winston Churchill, the news of Pearl Harbor came as a great relief: the attack meant the Americans were finally "in the war, up to the neck." Now it was a matter of coordinating a strategy for future victory. Right away, Churchill began planning a trip to visit his "great friend" at the White House. And so while Eleanor was still on the West Coast, he and FDR agreed on an extended visit, to begin on December 22 and last through Christmas and beyond. FDR had issued the invitation three days after Pearl Harbor, and Churchill embarked from England soon after for the eight-day voyage. No one had thought to inform Eleanor of this "top secret" plan, however, until the very day of Churchill's arrival.

Eleanor was furious. Not only had she been left out of the loop, but she was going to have to completely revise her complicated arrangements of who slept where and who came to dinner. What's more, Churchill's visit was going to interfere with the annual Christmas rendezvous that she and Hick had planned for that very night.

Hick and Eleanor usually celebrated together in New York; it was an intimate and quiet time that both looked forward to. But in 1941 Eleanor's schedule made that impossible. So the plan was to dine and exchange gifts in Eleanor's sitting room at the White House. In midafternoon, Hick got a call from Tommy: could she come early? Something had come up that was going to occupy Eleanor later that evening.

At a few minutes before six, Hick walked through the West Hall to her room, observing to her surprise that there were highball glasses, liquor bottles, and ice on the tea table. She had only been in her room a few minutes when Eleanor appeared, looking quite annoyed.

"'Hick, I'm afraid our party is ruined,' she announced. "Winston Churchill is arriving. Franklin has gone to meet him—they'll be here any minute."

Hick stared at her friend for a minute, then threw back her head and howled with laughter. Eleanor, she remembered, "didn't see anything funny about it, at the moment."

CHAPTER TWENTY

RISKING EVERYTHING

Never had Eleanor Roosevelt felt more alone in the White House than she did during the Christmas season of 1941. It had begun badly, when her special time with Hick was spoiled by Churchill's visit. Then, on Christmas morning, there were only two Christmas stockings for her to stuff: one for Harry Hopkins's daughter Diana and one for FDR's little dog Fala. "It just didn't seem as though anywhere around there was much personal feeling," she wrote Anna in Seattle. But she added that "I think Pa enjoyed all the officialdom."

The "officialdom" in this case was Winston Churchill and his retinue. Though Eleanor had expressed admiration in the past for Churchill's eloquence, there was very little she enjoyed about the prime minister in the flesh. To begin with, there was his drinking: early on in his visit he had made arrangements with the president's butler to have a tumbler of sherry before breakfast, scotch and soda before lunch, and champagne and ninety-year-old brandy at bedtime.

Bedtime, as it turned out, was very late: Churchill liked to stay up until 2 or 3 a.m., smoking cigars and brainstorming with his new ally. FDR, who usually went to bed at a reasonable hour, found Churchill's company irresistible, even in the wee hours. "There is no question," Eleanor noted, "when you are deeply interested it is possible to go on working 'til all hours of the night. But for the people who have to wait up 'til you are through it is a deadly performance."

Underlying Eleanor's unhappiness was the realization that Churchill and FDR were engaged in an elaborate courtship that excluded her and everyone else. When they moved from room to room, Churchill gallantly insisted on wheeling FDR's chair himself, imagining, as he later wrote, that he was like Sir Walter Raleigh throwing down his cloak for Queen Elizabeth. FDR, for his part, opened up as never before—confessing at dinner that he had been unhappy at Harvard when he was rejected from the Porcellian Club. To which Churchill gave the perfect riposte: "When I hear a man say that his childhood was the happiest time of his life, I think, my friend, you have had a pretty poor life."

There was plenty of competitive sparring as well, with each head of state trying to top the other's stories and arguments. But all of it took place in an atmosphere of great camaraderie. Indeed, the two men seemed to relish the terrible task they were now undertaking together—something Eleanor especially disliked. She "saw in Churchill a male tendency to romanticize war," her grandson Curtis observed, and she distrusted Churchill's attachment to the colonial past. It troubled her to walk by the map room, hastily assembled in what had been the ladies' coatroom, and glimpse FDR and Churchill engaged in animated conversation before a map with pins highlighting battlefields around the world. "They looked like two little boys playing soldier," she observed.

For Eleanor, it was impossible to forget for even a moment that there were real soldiers all around the world risking their lives. Her four sons were now among them. In another few months, Joe Lash, the new friend who occupied a special place in her heart, would join them. She was alternately saddened and enraged at the situation.

"I grow deeply resentful inside when I look at these boys," she wrote Hick from a plane filled with soldiers, "that now we spend so much on, that they may go out and die for a way of life that a few years ago we didn't want to tax ourselves to try to give them. . . . Will we do it all over again when those that live through it come back with the McKellars and Byrds [conservative southern Democrats] in power?"

This was her theme, over and over again, in her speeches and her writing. "At the end of this war," she wrote in "My Day," "that other war has to be fought."

Eleanor had hoped to use her job at the Office of Civilian Defense to lay the groundwork for nothing less than a new social order. Defense, as she defined it, included "better nutrition, better housing, better day-by-day medical care, better education, better recreation for every age."

But after Pearl Harbor, people were understandably more concerned about the distribution of gas masks and the hiring of air raid wardens than they were about what Eleanor liked to call "winning the peace."

When it was discovered that several of Eleanor's good friends, including the actor Melvyn Douglas and the dancer Mayris Chaney, were on the OCD payroll, her position became untenable. The venomous syndicated columnist Westbrook Pegler, who made a career of attacking Eleanor, accused her of political scheming for her own ends and reducing OCD to "absurdity and contempt." Enemies in Congress had a field day—railing against "fan dancers" on the federal payroll and pointing out that Chaney was making more money than a heroic soldier killed in action, and Douglas was making as much as General Douglas MacArthur, who was fighting a life-and-death struggle in the Philippines.

By February 1942, Eleanor realized she was going to have to resign. "I still believe in all the things we started out to do," she wrote WPA leader Florence Kerr, "but I know if I stayed longer, I would bring more harm than good to the program."

The truth was that the New Deal was being put on hold. Eleanor was going to have to find a way to fight for her values in a nation obsessed with war—a war that, so far, was going badly for the United States and its allies.

Under the circumstances, Democratic Party politics also seemed unimportant. It looked for a while as though the entire party apparatus might lose its budget—leaving Hick without the job she was starting to enjoy. In the past, Hick had sometimes displayed conventional biases toward strong women. Eleanor had once taken her to task for describing a woman she met who was practical, good at business, yet "very attractive," as having "the mind of a man." She had clashed with the previous boss of the Women's Division, Dorothy McCallister. Hick's attitude was one reason why Eleanor and Molly Dewson worried about whether she would fit in at the Women's Division.

But at the Women's Division, for the first time, Hick found herself in the company of women who were as politically savvy and passionate about making a difference as she was. On her fiftieth birthday that March, she thanked the diminutive and feisty Gladys Tillett for being "the best boss I ever had," and promised to "try to live up to the kind things you said." As usual, she apologized for her outbursts: "I fancy the thing I should try hardest to do is control my impetuosity and irritability." She promised to do this "even if I explode inside in the attempt."

Hick's annual celebration with Eleanor changed that year. It turned out that Democratic congresswoman Mary Norton had the same birthday. Starting that year, and for many years to come, Eleanor put on a joint birthday party for Norton and Hick. It made the party less intimate, but more festive.

Congresswoman Norton, a warm and buxom Irish Catholic from New Jersey, was an unlikely trailblazer. She was handpicked to run for Congress in 1920 by Jersey City mayor Frank Hague, a man whose political machine was well known to be one of the most powerful and corrupt in the nation. According to Dewson, Mayor Hague picked Norton because he didn't want a rival in Congress and felt "safer" with a woman.

Throughout her long career, Norton always had to battle suspicions that she was in Hague's pocket. But it didn't keep her from rising to a leadership position in the House and championing the New Deal. She was the first woman from the Democratic Party to be elected to Congress. As chairwoman of the Labor Committee, she fought hard for the groundbreaking Fair Labor Standards Act of 1938, which outlawed discrimination, mandated a minimum wage and forty-hour workweek, and outlawed child labor. Norton told Hick that she was prouder of getting that bill through the House than anything else she had ever done in her life.

Hick and Norton had a lot in common. Mary had lost her mother when she was quite young and had been left to run the house. She had never finished high school—she stepped aside so that one of her brothers could become a priest—and kept that fact a secret throughout her career in Congress. She married a widower and had one child, who died tragically. After that, she consoled herself by becoming involved in a local nursery school—an early experience that would translate later into advocacy for childcare during the first world war. Norton might have followed her sisters into a modest career as a secretary had it not been for Mayor Hague, who was looking for an agreeable woman to represent his district.

Norton was agreeable. Some called her "Aunt Mary." But she was also known as "fighting Mary Norton." Her black eyes flashed and her eyebrows went into action when she was angry. When southern Democrats tried to block Fair Employment legislation, she delivered "an intelligent tongue-lashing."

Hick and Mary Norton were coconspirators by that time, talking by phone almost every day and meeting frequently for business and pleasure. They spoke the same blunt language. Norton was pleased, she wrote Hick, when a speech she gave "made the boys mad. . . . It's nice to get 'under their skin.'" One of her colleagues was "a smooth son of a ___" who "loves the Pres. about as much as he does the devil."

Mary Norton was a good Catholic who would never put a swear word to paper. But she could be forceful. When the Republicans later gained a majority in the House, she resigned from the Labor Committee in protest. She looked the new chairman of the committee, New Jersey congressman F. A. Hartley, coldly and calmly in the eye, and announced that she would not serve under him. Hartley, she said, "talks as if he knew something about labor." But "in the 10 years I was chairman of the committee, [he] attended exactly six meetings." Serving under Hartley, she declared, would be dangerous for her blood pressure.

One Thursday evening in February 1942, Hick was with Mary Norton when it looked as though an important part of her signature legislation, the Fair Labor Standards Act, might be undone by an amendment from the conservatives. "I don't think I've ever seen Mary more tired and discouraged," Hick wrote Eleanor.

But the next day, when Mary called up, she was jubilant. The Smith Amendment, "which would have cancelled practically all decent labor legislation enacted in the last 50 years," was overwhelmingly defeated. "It certainly is a nice surprise, for last night we all thought it would be passed like a shot."

The triumph in Congress added to the upbeat feeling at Hick and Mary's first joint birthday party a week later at the White House. So did the presence of Marion Harron, a friend of Mary's who was becoming more than a friend to Hick. Her gift to Hick was a Kachina doll, sacred to the Hopi people, and a wish that "the best will come to you in great abundance."

Harron was the most serious contender as a replacement for Eleanor in Hick's life. A Phi Beta Kappa graduate of the University of California Law School, she was another of the women reformers who now surrounded Hick. Harron had fought for the minimum wage for women even before she graduated from law school. After coming east, she worked on a New York state commission aimed at improving workers' lives. In 1932 she joined the Roosevelt administration, probably through the good offices of the Women's Division under Molly Dewson. She worked for two New Deal agencies—first the National Recovery Administration (NRA), and then, after NRA was vitiated by the Supreme Court, the Resettlement Administration (RA), the agency that oversaw the development of newly built communities like Arthurdale. After the RA too was attacked and weakened, the Women's Division managed to get Harron appointed to a twelve-year term on the U.S. Board of Tax Appeals, replacing the court's first and only female member.

Judge Marion Harron was ten years younger than Hick, and a physical opposite. Her face was slender and delicate, her hair carefully parted and pulled back to the nape of her neck in a bun. Her eyes looked resolute, as did the set of her mouth. She in fact proved to be forceful in the courtroom—so forceful that some male lawyers felt intimidated. But she was a complete pushover when it came to Hick.

"You don't even have the faintest notion of how magnificent you are," Harron wrote Hick later that March. "I shall try to introduce you to yourself." In May, after a trip together in the Shenandoah Valley, she wrote to Hick about "how good the week end was" and "how grateful I am to you for it. . . . It seems as though the time was not hoarded enough."

Hick now started doing for Marion what Eleanor had done for her: giving her gifts that would change her life for the better. She sent Judge Marion off to get a new suit from Nardi, the tailor Eleanor had sent her to, and encouraged her to outfit herself with new shoes. Marion added a new marcelled hairdo.

Hick also urged the overserious Marion to "take my eyes off the fine print." Marion, for her part, wrote amusingly of how absurd her job was at times. "How in God's name did I ever fall into this morass?" she wrote Hick as she studied a case. Sitting in a tax court in Columbus, Ohio, she told Hick that she could draw an exact diagram of the pattern of decorations on the courtroom ceiling—"where my eyes travel while slow attorneys and slow witnesses travel along trails of questions and answers which are very familiar to me."

Hick and Marion became a couple. Marion visited often enough at the White House to be waved through by the guards. She and Hick were frequently together as well at the Little House, where they took moonlight walks and spent many hours adding new varieties of flowers to Hick's garden. Increasingly, Hick divided her time in Washington between the White House and Marion's place in nearby Chevy Chase, Maryland.

Eleanor seems to have taken Hick's new love interest in stride. Probably she was relieved that Hick had found someone else and needed her less. Her own attentions at that moment were focused on Joe Lash, whom she cared for in a way that was intense, yet motherly. Lash had long since given up his antiwar activities and joined the Army. In April, when he left for training, Eleanor gave a party for him in New York, complete with catered food and music. While he was away, she traveled with Trude Pratt to Nevada to keep her company while Pratt filed for divorce in order to marry Joe, just as she had when Anna sought a divorce years before.

Tommy, who watched at close range, was appalled by Eleanor's involvement with Lash and Pratt, whom she referred to, in an indignant letter to Esther Lape, who had become her confidante, as "the Lash" and "the Pratt." But then Tommy was indignant about all the "satellites" who circled around Eleanor, taking up her time and energy with their demands. Earl Miller was noisy and had a girlfriend who called at all hours, and Mayris Chaney was two-faced. But some of her sharpest complaints in her ongoing rant to Lape were reserved for Hick.

"Hickok is still here," Tommy wrote Lape in 1941, "she can't pay rent and her income tax and her dentist bill—so she has cut out paying rent! The Treasury isn't as cooperative as the White House." And then, two years later, "Our friend, Hick, is still . . . here and I imagine it will take dynamite to blast her out."

Hick's little room at the White House had changed dramatically since Pearl Harbor. The heavy blackout curtains, which were everywhere, made it very dark and gloomy in winter and hot in summer. After a while the edges of the curtains began to curl and stretch, so they had to be pinned together. Twice Hick was called because guards reported light escaping from her windows.

Along with the black curtains came garbage cans painted bright red and filled with sand. No fires were allowed in the fireplaces—a winter hardship in the big, tall-ceilinged rooms—so the cans of sand must have been provided in case a bomb dropped. Two large mirrors covering the east and west walls of the lobby were crated now, so that they wouldn't shatter if the White House were hit.

Even when everyone was there, the White House was more somber than it used to be. In the early days, FDR's laugh could be heard all over the house. It was "a great, ringing, musical laugh," Hick remembered, "so joyous and so infectious that you involuntarily laughed too." After the war began, the laugh was heard less and less frequently.

Partly it was because the war wasn't going very well: news of setbacks in the Pacific came in relentlessly over the wire in the White House press office. But partly it was because FDR's small inner circle was sadly diminished. Louis Howe was long gone. Then, in July 1942, the man FDR had chosen to take his place, Harry Hopkins, married a lively young editor from *Harper's Bazaar*, Louise Macy. After that, even though he continued to live in the White House with his wife, Hopkins was no longer available morning, noon, and night.

The greatest blow by far, however, was the loss of Missy LeHand. Missy had been at FDR's side for most of his waking hours for twenty years—as his immensely capable secretary who needed only a yes or no to answer most of his correspondence, but also as his adoring companion.

In June 1941, when she was only forty-three years old, Missy suffered the first of two strokes that would leave her without the ability to speak. After attempting to recuperate at Warm Springs, she returned to her room on the third floor of the White House. She felt helpless and deeply unhappy there, where the reminders of her old life by FDR's side were all around her. Eventually she moved back home to her family in Somerville, Massachusetts.

FDR had made only brief, uncomfortable visits to Missy's third-floor room when she was at the White House. But he did quietly change his will so that half of his estate could go to pay for her care. "I owed her that much," he told James. "She served me so well for so long and asked so little in return."

At the same time, FDR began to look elsewhere for companionship. One day after Missy suffered her first stroke, the name "Mrs. Johnson" appeared on the president's calendar. "Mrs. Johnson" was in fact Lucy Mercer, whose affair with FDR in 1918 had shattered the Roosevelt marriage. Lucy had married the much older Winthrop Rutherfurd, who was now incapacitated. Over the next few years, FDR would see more and more of his old flame.

FDR also invited Crown Princess Martha of Norway, who was living in exile nearby, to join him on numerous occasions. The princess was a stylish and flattering companion, and her husband, Prince Olav, was in England. It was obvious to everyone in FDR's circle that he was involved in a flirtation with her, at the very least.

According to son James, FDR may have also been hoping for renewed closeness with Eleanor. Even though it was hard for him to ask, Franklin seems to have wanted Eleanor to travel with him, in September 1942, on his eight-thousand-plus-mile cross-country inspection tour of munitions factories.

In the push and pull that characterized their relationship, Eleanor agreed to join him—but only for part of the trip. Still, Franklin made sure there was backup: his quiet and attentive distant cousin Daisy Suckley went along too.

Daisy was often by FDR's side now, listening and admiring. She was a seemingly uncomplicated person, a lover of dogs who had raised and presented him with Fala. FDR could tell Daisy when he felt "a bit 'cast down'"—something he couldn't admit to others. He complained to her, as he never would to Eleanor, about the pain his braces caused. Daisy seemed to have an intuitive understanding of what might please FDR. In the spring of 1942 she had arranged for him to go out bird watching with her at Hyde Park in the early morning hours: drawing on his boyhood skills, Franklin identified 108 species that morning, including 22 from their songs alone. With Daisy, FDR exchanged design ideas for Top Cottage, the stone house he was building on a hillcrest at Hyde Park.

FDR's first cousin Laura Delano, a flamboyant contrast to Daisy with her lavender hair and jangling bracelets, came along on the cross-country trip too. Laura, who was called Polly in the family, provided the gossip. FDR liked having them around because he did not have to make any effort with either of them. That, of course, was not true of Eleanor, who always brought along problems she had learned of from her many correspondents—problems she believed FDR needed to do something about. The cross-country journey did little or nothing to bring Franklin and Eleanor closer. But it did everything to bolster FDR's confidence in ultimate victory. Everywhere he went, he saw evidence of the astonishingly swift buildup in production. In Detroit, he inspected a factory that would soon be turning out thirty tanks a day. At Ford, in Willow Run, a B-24 airplane was coming off the line every sixty-three minutes. And in Seattle, an entire ship was being turned out every fourteen days. By the end of the year, the United States would produce more war materiel than Japan, Germany, and Italy combined. FDR also witnessed the transformation of U.S. military forces. America's army and air force, which had once been smaller than Romania's, would number 7.5 million by the end of 1942.

Perhaps even more important, FDR witnessed a kind of defiant fervor everywhere he went. "Bring the Germans and Japs to see it," boasted Ford's production chief at Willow Run, "hell, they'll blow their brains out." A woman worker at Kaiser shipyard, where 576 ships were built in eighteen months, talked about her pride in finishing "one of those beautiful ships. . . . Once it . . . withstood the test of water your whole body thrilled because you'd done something worthwhile."

More and more women were now part of the defense industry, a fact that Eleanor celebrated often in her column. Women at home were being called on to do their part as well.

DID YOU EVER SAY ANY OF THESE THINGS? the *Democratic Digest* asked its female readers in May. A list of false statements followed: "Our real enemy is the Japanese, we should unite with Germany against the yellow peril"; "Stalin and Bolshevism will sweep Europe"; "The cost of war will bankrupt the nation"; "We are lost in the Pacific"; "The British are telling our government what to do."

DID IT OCCUR TO YOU, asked the *Digest*, THAT YOU MIGHT BE SAYING EXACTLY WHAT HITLER WANTED YOU TO SAY?

"Be a lie swatter," urged Gladys Tillett in her editorial.

The *Digest* energetically promoted salvage of every kind. "Buy carefully," Tillett instructed readers in the month after Pearl Harbor, "use carefully what you have, waste nothing." March brought recipes for sugarless cookies. April called for women to "Take the Offensive in Your own Home" with a Victory Garden. Save fabric, save rubber, save paper, urged the *Digest*. To strengthen the argument, the *Digest* provided detailed conversion lists: a newspaper could make three twenty-six-pounder shell cups, and old letters could make a box for rifle cartridges.

The drive for scrap aluminum was an obsession: reports came in from all over the country on how many pounds various Democratic women's clubs had collected. "Metals over Miami," read one headline. The story described a contest involving hats made out of scrap aluminum: large utensils were trimmed with smaller ones like cookie cutters and spoons, "perhaps a cake turner," perhaps "pom-pom partitions" made from ice cube trays. In the end, all that aluminum wasn't pure enough to use for fighter planes. But it almost didn't matter, as long as the aluminum drive stirred up enthusiasm for the war effort.

FDR returned from his inspection tour convinced that the war could and would be won. The Axis powers, he explained in a fireside chat in October 1942, had already reached their full potential, and "their steadily mounting losses in men and materiel cannot be fully replaced." He assured Americans that the "worst times are now over."

But the American public wasn't convinced. So far, they had made enormous sacrifices and seen very little in the way of results. That meant, as FDR well knew, that the midterm elections of 1942 were going to be an uphill fight for Democrats—especially New Deal Democrats.

No one understood this better than Hick and Tillett. They organized speaking tours, described in the *Digest* as "Mrs. Charles W. Tillett's flying squadron of wisdom and eloquence," to meet with Democratic women's groups and urge them to get out into the precincts, where the battle would be won or lost. The *Digest* claimed that these women provided "that rare experience, much light without heat. Don't miss them." One of the "flying squadron" was Hick's partner, Marion Harron.

Hick organized ambitious regional conferences as well, with prominent speakers. Eleanor spoke at the midwestern one in St. Paul, Minnesota, in the spring. In September, as midterm elections drew near, a star-studded event in Los Angeles featured Melvyn Douglas and his wife, Helen, Edward G. Robinson, Bette Davis, and Douglas Fairbanks Jr.—

good Democrats all. It ended, as the *Digest* reported, with one thousand on their feet, "singing America as they had never sung it before."

The *Digest* carried a full page of quotes from leading Republican isolationists who had inveighed against the war. "Where Would We Be Today If These Philosophies Had Prevailed?" asked the headline.

The last issue of the *Digest* before the vote included a letter from a war worker who reported proudly that the men at his plant had been working at top speed, had taken no time off on strike, and had even worked New Year's Day, July Fourth, and Labor Day. He had had "quite an argument" at the plant about whether it was "patriotic" or not to take time off to go vote. The *Digest* put the question to Donald Nelson, chairman of the War Production Board.

Nelson gave the obvious answer: the worker should vote. "The right to vote is what this war is all about." Nelson added that he didn't care *who* the worker voted for. Then he added, "When you vote, vote fast and get back on 'the machine.'"

Despite the *Digest*'s message, only 35 percent of eligible voters turned up at the polls, and more of them were Republicans than Democrats. The GOP picked up nine seats in the Senate and forty-four in the House. Afterward, Gladys Tillett declared that "our heads were unbowed, but pretty bloody."

Mary Norton retained her seat, but that was not a surprise. The real worry was the survival of the New Deal. Although the Democrats were still in the majority in both houses, Congress was now composed, as Hick wrote Eleanor, of "Republicans and the worst Democrats." She didn't think Norton would be able to "hold the line any longer in that House."

The one good piece of news, Hick reported, was that California had bucked the national trend and gotten most of its Democratic congressmen elected, in large part due to the work of Helen Gahagan Douglas and the Women's Division. It was, Hick wrote Douglas, "the one bright spot in our lives last week." The California success was an important step in Douglas's own political career. Two years later, she would become the first woman elected to Congress from California. Through the experience of working together, Hick and Douglas cemented a partnership and friendship that would last for life.

Still, for Hick, the overall election results were "awful" for the president and "what he stands for." Surprisingly enough, FDR seemed untroubled by the election losses. In a phone call soon after with Canadian prime minister Mackenzie King, he pointed out that, "everything considered," it wasn't too bad to still have control of both houses of Congress in a third term.

The reason for the president's upbeat mood, in the face of political defeat, was hinted at by Daisy Suckley in her diary. "For weeks," she wrote, "the P. has had something exciting up his sleeve." A few days later, the world would find out just what that was.

AFTER PEARL HARBOR, FDR and Churchill had agreed that Americans must initiate a major action sometime within the next year. The question was where to strike. Initially, military advisers in both countries toyed with the idea of a cross-Channel invasion of the European mainland. FDR was one of the first to realize that that was too big an undertaking for year one of U.S. engagement. Churchill and the British soon came to the same conclusion.

That was when FDR began to nurse what everyone called his "great secret baby," the idea of an invasion of Vichy-held northwest Africa, with American troops in the lead and British forces following along behind. Roosevelt believed that this would be an effective way to take the Germans, who were better prepared for a mainland assault, by surprise. It would also buy time for a later assault on the mainland, perhaps in 1943 but ultimately, as it happened, in the spring of 1944.

Stalin, whose troops were holding off the Germans at Stalingrad at an enormous human cost, was desperate for an invasion that would draw the Nazis into battle on a second front. Churchill and U.S. ambassador Averell Harriman went to Moscow to present FDR's plan to the surly dictator, who listened warily. Churchill used a vivid analogy to explain the strategy to Stalin. Rather than attacking the head of the crocodile, with all its teeth and armor, the Allies would go after the "soft underbelly" of the beast in North Africa.

Stalin had been furious and rude to the messengers at first, when he learned that the cross-Channel invasion was off. But once he understood that the decision had been made, he reluctantly gave his blessing to their new proposal. "May God help this enterprise to succeed," the Communist leader told Churchill and Harriman as they went on their way.

FDR's own generals and secretary of war were adamantly opposed to his plan, which was given the name Operation Torch, and tried desperately up to the last minute to talk him out of it. Secretary of War Henry Stimson feared that American troops would be mired in a stalemate in Africa. "We are all very blue about it," he wrote in his diary. The generals wanted to pour all their planning and energy into a cross-Channel invasion. They even proposed that the plans for a first major strike shift to the Pacific. General George C. Marshall called the plan "a dreadful thing." General Dwight D. Eisenhower declared that the day Operation Torch was chosen was the "blackest day in history," especially given the distinct possibility of a Russian defeat.

Eventually, FDR got his way. He had hoped Operation Torch could take place before the midterm elections, but weather considerations made that impossible: there were only a few days in November when the seas were calm enough to allow an invasion. So in the end, the largest amphibious landing in American history—involving over a hundred ships and one hundred thousand men—took place five days *after* the election, on November 8, 1942.

FDR was at Shangri-La, the rustic camp on Catoctin Mountain that had become his retreat, hiding out from curious reporters who might sense that something was up. There were constant phone calls all through the day. But the call FDR had been waiting for, from his chief of staff, Admiral Bill Leahy, came to him in his bedroom that evening. FDR's secretary, Grace Tully, was on hand when Admiral Leahy called with the news.

Never in his entire presidency had Franklin Roosevelt's judgment, and his legacy, been put to a greater test than at that moment. Would he be vindicated in his decision to pursue his "secret baby"? Or would his military advisers, who had fought his decision every step of the way, turn out to be right that Torch was a tragic mistake?

FDR's hand was shaking, Grace Tully noticed, as he picked up the phone. He listened in silence for several minutes. "Thank God. Thank God," was his first response. Smiling broadly, he put the phone down and announced, "We have landed in North Africa. Casualties are below expectations. We are striking back."

IT TOOK ELEANOR A WHILE to find her role in the changed landscape of the nation at war. In the beginning, her efforts to set an example for the country sometimes backfired. When she learned that sugar might be rationed, for instance, she announced that she was cutting back on sugar at the White House, substituting corn syrup and other sweeteners. But since official rationing hadn't occurred, this prompted the hoarding of sugar all around the country.

Eleanor was indignant about such behavior. "It never crossed my mind that you couldn't tell the American people the truth and count on them to behave themselves accordingly." It was this sort of comment that made her seem out of touch.

If you were an admirer of Eleanor, you might applaud her willingness to make sacrifices—to substitute cotton stockings for nylon and to ride her bicycle to save on fuel. But if you weren't already in her camp, you might resent her high-mindedness. When coffee rationing was proposed, Eleanor said she didn't mind drinking tea or even hot water instead. But other people weren't so casual about cutting back on their morning coffee.

Eleanor could be surprisingly insensitive in her "My Day" column as well. She began one column by quoting a letter from a father whose son had been killed, and who was convinced from reading the death lists that only "inconspicuous people" were dying in the war. Prominent people, he wrote, were being given special protection. Eleanor assured the grieving father that this was untrue, and that many high officials in Washington had also lost sons. Her column ended with the news that Elliott had just been "invalided home" from the South Pacific and would be with his family for a few days. "These are days in which one grasps every joyous moment and savors it to the full," she wrote. She may have intended this as evidence that her sons too were engaged in the fight. It was true: the Roosevelt sons were exposed to danger and served with distinction in the war. But to this bereft father, it must have looked like proof of his thesis. The First Lady was able to have a "joyous moment" with her son. He wasn't.

There was a difference, however, between the Eleanor Roosevelt of public pronouncements and Eleanor Roosevelt in person—in Hick's words the "personage" and the "person." And the "person" had a unique ability to connect with people one-on-one. Her physical presence made an enormous difference to people: they saw real interest in the way she listened and in the expression on her face, especially in her eyes. Her tirelessness, a frequent subject of press coverage, bore witness to her genuine sympathy. Nowhere was that more true than during her wartime inspection tours— in England in 1942 and the Pacific in 1943.

The London of Eleanor's happy girlhood years, when she was a student at Allenswood, had undergone an unspeakable ordeal in the two years before her visit. Hitler's bombing operation had destroyed grand historic buildings and modest neighborhoods alike. Night after night, Londoners had hurried into bomb shelters and underground rail stations, carrying their bedding and hoping to survive the Blitz. Over forty thousand British citizens had died while America watched from the sidelines. Now, at last, the United States had joined the fight; Eleanor's visit signaled that Great Britain was no longer alone. Columnist Raymond Clapper wrote that "because of . . . her own personal warmth and genuine qualities of frankness and sympathy, Mrs. Roosevelt can if anybody can, convince the people of England that they are not isolated from us in spirit."

For nearly a month, while FDR and his generals were working out plans for the landing in North Africa, Eleanor staged an invasion of her own, visiting with both the ruling class and the ordinary men and women who were carrying on the fight. The Secret Service gave her the highly appropriate code name "Rover."

She had to begin properly, of course, with a visit to the king and queen at Buckingham Palace. She wrote Hick on palace stationery: "This is to impress you." Her room was so vast, she wrote, that she felt "lost in space," and she wondered what the maid must have thought, unpacking her modest wardrobe: one evening dress, two day dresses, one suit and a few blouses, one pair of day and one pair of evening shoes.

The royal couple took her first to meet the "faithful watchers," who slept at St. Paul's Cathedral so they could immediately battle the fires that the nightly bombings set off. With the king and queen, she got her first real look at the devastation: blocks upon blocks of rubble. In a neighborhood called Stepney, where people lived in close quarters over their shops, the death toll was especially high. "Each empty building speaks of personal tragedy," she wrote in "My Day."

Eleanor seemed to enjoy her visit with the king and queen, whom she thought "a young and charming couple." Not surprisingly, she felt less at home at Chequers, the official country residence of Prime Minister Churchill. Americans in general found Chequers uncomfortable in winter: Harry Hopkins used to hole up in the bathroom when he visited because it was the warmest room in a very cold house. But Eleanor and the PM simply rubbed each other the wrong way.

At dinner one evening, Eleanor raised the topic of the Spanish Civil War. Why couldn't something have been done to help the Loyalists? she asked. Churchill told her that she and he would have been the first to lose their heads if the Loyalists had won. To which Eleanor replied that she didn't care whether she lost her head or not. "I don't want you to lose your head and neither do I want to lose mine," answered Churchill. Mrs. Churchill, hoping to make peace, suggested that Mrs. Roosevelt might be right. But the PM declared, "I've held certain beliefs for sixty years and I'm not going to change them now."

The other anecdote about Churchill Eleanor included in her diary involved his grandson, who was "a sweet baby" and looked "exactly like the PM" when the two of them were playing together on the floor. Churchill reported to FDR that "Mrs. Roosevelt is winning golden opinions here for all her kindness and her unfailing interest in everything we are doing." He had advised a "reduction in her programme" to no avail. She "proceeds indefatigably." He added, "I only wish you were here yourself."

Eleanor was happiest when she could mingle with ordinary soldiers and war workers. At the Red Cross club in London she watched "boys" at leisure—"a boy playing the piano and many boys sitting around talking, lounging, reading the papers. . . . Boys were in the snack bar; boys were upstairs in the library." Eleanor's manner put them at ease. There were shouts of "Hi, Eleanor" from various parts of the crowded room. One GI yelled out, "How's Poughkeepsie?"

The boys felt comfortable enough to register several complaints—among other things, they were getting blisters because their socks were too thin. Eleanor promised to take action. The next day, she spoke with General Eisenhower, who checked with his quartermasters and discovered that there were a half million pairs of woolen socks in warehouses that could be distributed at once.

Nothing pleased Eleanor more than producing such concrete results. But she understood as well that her mere presence made a difference. "Every soldier I see is a friend from home," she wrote in "My Day," "and I want to stop and talk with him whether I know him or not. When I find we really have some point of contact, it gives me a warm feeling around the heart." Within weeks, many of these "boys" would be fighting a life-and-death battle in North Africa.

Women warriors and workers were Eleanor's special focus throughout her trip. A frustrated pilot herself, she especially admired the women who flew planes from one airstrip to another around the country, to outsmart the German bombers. She visited model nurseries run by women as well as clinics and hostels for women workers. She asked hard questions about the frequency of venereal disease and—intriguingly—what she called "abnormal sex cases." Clearly she was referring to lesbians among the women soldiers. "They take refuge in subterfuge," she wrote in her diary, "and do not discharge for this reason if it is necessary to do so [i.e., discharge]."

Eleanor visited women of the "land army": former hairdressers, typists, and housewives who were learning to drive tractors, tend cows, and thatch houses while the men were off at war. One night toward the end of her stay she talked, as midnight approached, with eight hundred women workers on the night shift at a Rolls factory.

"Darling," Hick wrote Eleanor from Washington, "I am thrilled about you—and worried." Hick fretted when she learned that the Germans had bombed Canterbury Cathedral just after Eleanor was there. But Hick was delighted to read all the positive commentary about the trip being published in American newspapers, especially after Eleanor's humiliating experience at the Office of Civilian Defense. "Your press over here is wonderful," she wrote. Two of the most admired commentators, Edward R. Murrow and Drew Pearson, had weighed in with enthusiasm. "You *are* doing a good job, dear," Hick wrote. "The kind of job you can do better than anyone else I know."

Before her tour was over, Eleanor had walked so many miles on her inspection tour that she had worn holes in her day shoes. The head usher at the White House sent her a replacement pair by diplomatic pouch. On the Sunday before she left, church bells rang out all over England, celebrating initial victories in North Africa. It would take seven months, and cost many lives, to finally defeat the Axis powers in Africa. But as Eleanor wrote in "My Day," there was now a feeling everywhere in Great Britain that "we are fighting together."

Eleanor was pleasantly surprised to find Franklin's car and entourage waiting to greet her at the airport in Washington. "I really think Franklin was glad to see me back," she scratched in pencil in her diary. At lunch, and again at dinner, she recounted to him all that she had seen and done, and she was pleased to discover that he had read her day-by-day account of the trip as well. It was an affirmation that he valued the work she was doing.

Before the trip, Secretary of War Stimson had worried that Eleanor might stir up race issues during her visits to the troops in England, where Negro units were segregated from white ones. Already, some white southerners were uncomfortable with the mixed dating that went on more easily among blacks and whites in England. Stimson urged FDR to tell his wife to go easy. Eleanor seems to have heeded the warning: although she visited a Negro unit, she made only positive comments about their accommodations. That didn't mean, however, that she was going to let the subject drop. Both before and after the trip to England, she waged a persistent battle against racism in the military.

In March 1941, a photographer captured a special visit. Eleanor is seated in the cockpit of a tiny plane, behind a black pilot named Charles "Chief" Anderson. Much to the chagrin of the Secret Service, she is about to take off on an hour's flight over the airfield at Tuskegee University, where black pilots were training in preparation for war. She is wearing a little saucer hat with flowers on it, a ruffled blouse, and pearls, and she is grinning from ear to ear.

The visit and the airplane ride were just a first step. Long after the Tuskegee Airmen were ready to fly combat missions, the war department kept them out of action. Air Force general Henry "Hap" Arnold claimed that he couldn't use Negro pilots because they would be placed above white enlisted men, "creating an impossible social situation." Eleanor joined other voices in protest. Finally, in April 1943, the Tuskegee Airmen were deployed as bomber escorts and went on to serve with great distinction.

Around that same time, a black soldier named Henry Jones wrote Eleanor a letter describing segregation at recreational facilities at military bases. Negroes were often confined to a few seats in the last row at lectures and concerts, he wrote, and were never certain of access to post exchanges and other privileges. The letter, with 121 signatures attached, sent Eleanor into action. The numerous letters of protest to General Marshall forced him to reassign clerical staff, and eventually to make a change. On March 10, 1943, a directive was issued prohibiting all segregation in recreational facilities. It was not a complete victory, but it was a beginning.

"Never get into an argument with the Missus," FDR had once told Hick, only half in jest, when they shared a rare dinner for three. "You can't win. You think you have her pinned down here (thumping the table with his forefinger) but she bobs right up away over there somewhere! No use—you can't win." Several generals would have heartily agreed.

FOR THE FIRST TIME in ten years, Eleanor and Hick made no effort to get together at Christmas in 1942. Hick spent the holiday at the Little House, sharing a "kind of Community Christmas dinner" with her neighbors. The two exchanged gifts, of course—Eleanor sent a box of "lovely handkerchiefs," along with a turkey. Eleanor always sent a turkey from Val-Kill at Thanksgiving and Christmas, and Hick always raved about how delicious it was. But even this ritual was complicated by the war: trips to the post office from the Little House had to be drastically reduced because of gas rationing, so the turkey sat in wait for some time.

For Eleanor, at the White House, the Christmas celebration was much better than it had been in 1941, when she had been blindsided by the arrival of Winston Churchill and his entourage. Also, there had been no grandchildren around the previous year. So 1942 was an improvement. "It is a pleasant thing to have some children around who can be completely joyous over this Christmas season," Eleanor wrote in "My Day."

Still, it was difficult to be joyous in December 1942. While American soldiers were dying in combat in the Pacific and in North Africa, it became clearer than ever that atrocities were occurring on a massive scale in Europe. Early in December, Stephen Wise, eminent Reform rabbi and president of the American Jewish Congress, wrote his "old friend" FDR requesting a meeting to discuss "the most overwhelming disaster of Jewish history [which] has befallen the Jews in the form of the Hitler mass-massacres." It was "indisputable," Wise wrote, that "as many as two million Jews had been slain." A few days later, Eleanor wrote of her "horror" in learning that two-thirds of the Jews living in Poland had been slaughtered. On December 13, Edward R. Murrow described "a horror beyond what imagination can grasp" and concluded that "concentration camps" had become "extermination camps."

After the grandchildren opened their stocking gifts, Eleanor went off to visit soldiers at Walter Reed Hospital who had been wounded in the African campaign. She encountered one young man on the ward that day whose severe burns made it difficult for him to speak. He had been a pianist, Eleanor learned, but his hands were so damaged that he feared he would never play again.

After the visit, Eleanor wrote the soldier's commanding officer to say that the young man was welcome to practice on the White House piano when he got better. After seventeen months of recovery, Hardie Robbins took up the invitation, practicing on the White House Steinway for an entire year, working to get the suppleness back in his hands so that he could again earn his living as a pianist. Naturally, he was invited to join the Roosevelts for dinner. He became yet another of Eleanor Roosevelt's friends for life.

A FIGHT FOR
LOVE AND GLORY

ONE NIGHT IN 1942, Hick returned home to the White House while the Roosevelts and their dinner guests were watching a movie in the West Hall. The film, *In Which We Serve*, starred Noël Coward and was based on the true story of a British destroyer sunk by German warplanes. "The screen was so placed that one could get an oblique view by standing squeezed in a corner just outside the elevator door," Hick remembered. She stood transfixed, undetected by the dinner guests, through the rest of the movie, watching at an angle that left her eyes hurting and her legs cramped.

Movies about the war were a welcome distraction from the war itself. But sometimes movies and real life overlapped. On New Year's Day 1943, FDR and his guests watched the movie *Casablanca* with old friends. The Casablanca they saw on the screen was peopled by French and German soldiers, shady opportunists, a beautiful girl, and a couple of suave gents who stood up to the Nazis. Everybody in that Casablanca was trying to escape to America. Nine days later, FDR headed in the opposite direction, toward the real Casablanca, to meet up with Churchill and work out plans for the real war.

Like the movie version, the real Casablanca was swarming with Vichy and Axis agents, and Roosevelt's advisers worried that Berlin would find out about the meeting. So FDR traveled once again by a circuitous route—first heading north by train as though going to Hyde Park, then turning around in Baltimore and heading south on another line to Miami, and finally taking off by plane for North Africa. As it turned out, the deception didn't work: the Germans discovered that Churchill and Roosevelt were meeting in Casablanca. But they translated "Casablanca" as "white house," and assumed the meeting was at the White House in Washington.

Despite the grave circumstances surrounding the meeting, Roosevelt and Churchill thoroughly enjoyed themselves. As one of Churchill's aides noted, neither man had ever completely grown up, and they welcomed this chance for an adventure. They also welcomed the chance to put distance between themselves and the relentless demands back home.

Both delegations were housed in sumptuous villas: FDR's had a sunken bath and a view of lush orange groves. Roosevelt and Churchill dined with a sultan in white silk robes who presented a beautiful golden tiara to Mrs. Roosevelt in absentia, and they took the time to travel together to Marrakech, an ancient city of mosques and gardens. Churchill insisted that his friend be carried up six hundred narrow steps to the top of a tower so he could take in the spectacular view of the magical city and snowcapped mountains beyond. The two men sat for half an hour, watching the changing light.

The final farewell was in comic contrast to Rick and Ilsa's rain- and tear-soaked farewell on the tarmac. Churchill had planned to get up in time to see Roosevelt off early the next morning. But he overslept and had no time to get dressed. At the last possible moment, he rushed out to wave goodbye, attired in his red-dragon dressing gown and black velvet slippers.

As the plane disappeared into the blue yonder, Churchill grew solemn: "If anything happened to that man," he told an aide, "I couldn't stand it. He is the truest friend; he has the farthest vision; he is the greatest man I have ever known."

HICK COULD ALWAYS TELL, during the war years, when the president left town. She just had to peek out the tall window in her room and take a look at the machine gun on the roof of the swimming pool. When he was out of town, the gun was covered and unattended. It may have been during that January trip to Casablanca that Howard Crim, the head usher, informed Hick that she was "the sole occupant of the White House tonight—with forty-seven men to guard you."

Both Roosevelts were frequently away from the White House in 1943. FDR traveled abroad that year more than at any other time in his presidency: to Casablanca at the beginning of the year, then in August to Quebec, to meet once again with Churchill and develop plans for the European offensive. Then in November he embarked on a long and exhausting trip to Tehran, where he met, at last, with Stalin.

Casablanca, though beautiful, turned out to be the least satisfactory of the gatherings, from the American point of view. Churchill and FDR did agree that they would join forces on a bombing campaign over Germany and that the Allies would settle for nothing less than "unconditional surrender." But the Americans, who had not yet assumed control of the alliance, wound up going along, reluctantly, with Churchill's strong preference for a continuation of the war in Sicily. That decision meant further delaying a cross-Channel invasion. Stalin, whose forces were still fighting the bloodiest battle of the war in Stalingrad, was enraged by the news that the second front had been put off once again.

Soon after Casablanca, however, the war began to turn decisively in favor of the Allies. In February, at long last, the Russians turned back the German offensive at Stalingrad. Around the same time, the Allies began to win the Battle of the Atlantic, sinking German U-boats at a crippling pace. The continuation of the war in Sicily and then in Italy was costly and slow. But in July, Benito Mussolini's reign ended.

"The plans we made for the knocking out of Mussolini and his gang have largely succeeded," FDR announced. "But we still have to knock out

Hitler and his gang, and Tojo and his gang. No one pretends that this will be an easy matter." By August 1943, when FDR went off to Quebec, Americans were making headway against the Japanese in the Solomon Islands, including, most important, Guadalcanal.

The battle for control of Guadalcanal, a two-thousand-square-mile island of great strategic importance to both sides, was one of the longest of the war in the Pacific. American Marines began landing on the island in August 1942 and slowly overwhelmed the Japanese with superior arms and sheer numbers. Finally, late in the year, the Japanese abandoned their fight for the island. For the Allies, Guadalcanal became essentially an unsinkable aircraft carrier, critical to bringing in men and supplies for the war in the Pacific.

Guadalcanal had a particular importance in the mind, and heart, of Eleanor Roosevelt: Joe Lash was sent there in May 1943 with his unit of weather forecasters. Even before that, Eleanor had been making tentative plans to visit the troops in the Pacific theater. After that, her plans took on a new urgency. She was determined, she wrote Joe, to visit "your island."

Publicly, her reason for touring the Pacific was to bring a message of support and gratitude from the commander in chief to American troops stationed in Hawaii, New Zealand, and Australia, as well as numerous Pacific islands. But she wrote Lash that the thing she cared most about was the chance to have a few hours with him. It was, she wrote him, "the one happy and personal thing." There were only very few people who mattered to her, and Joe was one of them.

After her successful tour of England, Eleanor traveled and spoke around the country more than ever. Most of the time she traveled with Tommy, fitting in visits to Anna or her sons when they landed somewhere between military assignments. Because Hick was another of the few people who mattered, she paid a visit to her that June at her Little House. It was, she wrote Lash, "a journey undertaken for friendship's sake," adding, "I enjoyed . . . seeing Hick in the one place she really enjoys."

But the main focus of her attention and concern in 1943 was Lash. Because of Lash's earlier radicalism, the FBI was keeping an eye on him, and seems to have bugged a hotel room in Chicago where he and Eleanor met. In his extensive writings about the relationship, Lash insists, convincingly, that he and Eleanor were simply good friends, not lovers; Lash was in love with Trude Pratt, as Eleanor well knew. But Lash believed the FBI used the hotel recording, no doubt filled with expressions of affection, to threaten exposure and embarrassment to him and to Eleanor. That may well have been the reason why orders came from above (the source was never clear) to dispatch Lash and his unit off to Guadalcanal abruptly, without explanation. For Eleanor, Joe's sudden departure added another layer of concern, especially when reports came of continued Japanese bombing of the island.

In July, for Joe's sake, Eleanor traveled with Trude Pratt to Reno, keeping her company while she filed for divorce so that she could marry Joe. She wrote Hick while she was there, remembering the time they had accompanied Anna Roosevelt on a similar errand ten years earlier, and also "what fun we had" at Yosemite. When her muscles grew stiff from horseback riding, it made her realize that she had been "brutal" in expecting Hick to keep up with her on the steep trails.

In mid-August, right around the time that FDR left for the Quebec meeting, Eleanor finally embarked on her visit to the Pacific theater. She was traveling in her official capacity as First Lady, of course, but with a private plan to see Joe as well. "I wish so that you could be in my pocket," she wrote Trude Pratt shortly before she left. The crew for the trip named her plane *Love, Eleanor.*

It was the first time in years that Eleanor had embarked on a long trip without Tommy, and it gave her loyal secretary a "queer feeling." Tommy wondered what it meant that Eleanor had left all her jewelry behind. She hadn't done that when they went together to England. Eleanor was uneasy too, especially since she didn't know what kind of reception she would get from the military authorities.

The initial encounters weren't promising. In Samoa, a Marine general kept her away from the troops entirely. And at headquarters for the South Pacific, in Nouméa, New Caledonia, Admiral William "Bull" Halsey seemed annoyed that he was going to have to shuttle this do-gooder from island to island, taking time and energy away from the war effort. Halsey became a convert, however, when he saw Eleanor in action, going into every ward and paying real attention to every soldier. What was his name? How did he feel? What did he need? "I marveled most," Admiral Halsey said, "at their expressions as she leaned over them. It was a sight I will never forget."

Eleanor had decided to go on the trip as a representative of the Red Cross, and so she wore the official uniform: a summery blue-gray three-button jacket over a flared skirt. Standing tall and straight in her officer's billed cap, with white gloves, black purse, and clipboard in hand, she looked both sympathetic and eager to learn. In a hospital in Wellington, New Zealand, she met a soldier from Poughkeepsie who had lost an arm. He assured Eleanor that he was going to be okay—he could already tie his tie with one arm. "When you get home tell the boys at the toll booth on the Midhudson Bridge that you saw Nick," he said. Of course she took down Nick's address, along with many others, so she could report to his family when she got back.

"These boys break your heart," she wrote Hick, "they're so young and so tired. Malaria is almost as bad as bullets." And yet they were hardly out of the hospital before they were back at the Red Cross clubs, dancing and enjoying themselves.

Eleanor's view of the trip swung wildly between optimism and despair. She felt best when she was able to talk with the men. Some of them told her what it was like moving forward through swamp water up to your waist, balancing on slippery mango roots and knowing that if you stumbled and fell you would drown. At the same time, you had to hold your machine gun up high to keep it dry and try to shoot a Jap up ahead, well camouflaged in a tree.

"I do camps, hospitals, Red Cross services day and evening," she wrote Hick. She saw men "who have either been into New Guinea and come out with a shadow on their faces . . . or new men going in to something they know nothing about and are ill prepared for." Their hatred of "the Japs," although alien to her, seemed to help them fight.

What frustrated her most was being insulated from the troops by official greeters and protectors. "I'm surrounded by Generals and Admirals and M.P.'s wherever I go," she complained to Hick, "and you know how that would please me. . . . I'll need a long dose of the cottage and N.Y. City to forget this pomp and ceremony!" In her letters to Franklin she was even more indignant: "I have all the pomp and restriction and none of the power! I'm coming home this time and go [sic] into a factory!"

Nothing pleased her—or the troops—more than a chance to defy protocol. She arrived at a Red Cross Club unannounced and encountered two young privates standing in their underwear near a radiator, waiting for their trousers to be repaired. Without blinking, she "coolly and graciously chatted with the two boys," a soldier reported in a letter sent back home, "both paralyzed with amazement and chagrin but thrilled thru and thru." After she left, the two "grasped their scorched legs and burst into all sorts of excited exclamations. . . . One of the kids, eyes big as pool-balls, said 'She—the wife of the President—talked to me!'"

"It's sumpin'," the correspondent concluded, "when half a dozen general officers wait gasping for someone to complete a casual talk with two privates! It's sumpin' and it's Eleanor."

This writer was convinced that Eleanor's trip made a difference. "I keep thinking of those two boys without any pants and how they'll remember that morning perhaps when they're in a nasty fox hole trying not to do anything foolish or panicky." He maintained that "Eleanor created two damn good Marines in a few minutes that morning and I don't know an officer in the battalion who could do the same."

But as Eleanor suspected, there was plenty of grumbling about her visit behind her back. "They caricature her speech," the letter writer reported, "estimate the cost of the trip and . . . ask what the hell she's doing tearing around; why doesn't she stay home."

Eleanor still hoped most of all that she would get to Guadalcanal to see Lash. The ostensible reason for going to the island was that it was a powerful symbol of the war in the southwest Pacific. But the problem with Guadalcanal was that it remained vulnerable to Japanese bombing. Admiral Halsey didn't want to do anything that would draw unwelcome attention to the island, with its vital airstrip and major hospitals. FDR, it turned out later, had given orders that she must not go. Finally, however, at the very end of her trip, Admiral Halsey gave her permission. "Happy tonight for we are going to Guadalcanal," she wrote Tommy.

She left in the belly of a huge bomber at two in the morning, because there had been air raids on previous nights, and sat shivering in the dark. One of the boys, "a baby it seemed to me," brought her coffee and a blanket.

Eleanor spent one long hectic day on the island, touring the hospitals and the strategic airstrip. When she saw Lash, she gave him a public kiss, in defiance of the gossips. She spent several hours with Joe, paying a visit to his tent and meeting the other members of his weather forecasting group.

Eleanor's visit with Lash provided fodder for her archenemy Westbrook Pegler's column: he condemned the entire trip as a waste of taxpayers' money and an excuse for her rendezvous. But Eleanor also wrote her own column, including a touching account of a visit to the Guadalcanal cemetery. "The little white crosses climb up the hill, on the summit of which stands a high flagpole from which floats our flag. . . . I thought of the women at home whose hearts are partly buried here, too, with the men they loved. I think they would feel not only peace on this spot, but pride in the cause for which so many made the greatest possible sacrifice."

Seven thousand Americans died in the battle to take Guadalcanal, and perhaps three times that number of Japanese. It was the kind of statistic that made Eleanor insist, as she so often did both publicly and privately, that there should never be another war like this one.

By the time she left for home, Eleanor had visited New Zealand, Australia, and seventeen islands, and seen about four hundred thousand men in camps and hospitals. She had lost weight, and she was exhausted. But she came to the conclusion, despite criticism from some quarters, that the trip to the Pacific theater had been worthwhile. Over time, it became one of the most storied and important trips of her public life.

Back at the White House, Eleanor spent two hours with FDR over lunch, telling him of her experiences. She invited Hick to join them that night and continued her account. They likely also talked about Hick's pressing issue at the Women's Division: women were being completely ignored on postwar planning commissions. Very soon after Eleanor's return, that began to turn around.

Within a month of Eleanor's return from the Pacific, FDR was off again—this time to the most important Allied gatherings yet, first at Cairo, and then Tehran. In the past, these conferences had been top secret, with minimal coverage afterward. But the meeting of the Big Three in Tehran was different. The *Democratic Digest*, along with every other news outlet, published results of the proceedings not long after the conference adjourned.

Hick never signed her name to any of the *Democratic Digest* articles when she worked at the Women's Division. But the report on the Tehran meeting sounds like it went through her typewriter: "At the foot of snow-capped Damavend, in Iran, the three leaders met on a spot which had played a role in the lives of empire builders of ancient times—Alexander, Darius, Xerxes and Genghis Khan, and there mapped out destruction for those who dreamed of world empire in our time."

The big news from the Tehran Conference was that the Allied leaders planned to launch a second front in the spring of 1944, to be called Overlord. "We have reached a complete agreement as to the scope and timing of operations," the Tehran document declared. "The common understanding which we have here reached guarantees that victory will be ours." The fact of the invasion was out there for all to know, including the enemy; the time and place were not.

Hick celebrated two pre Christmases in 1943—one with Eleanor as in the past, and one with Marion Harron at the Hay-Adams Hotel. Afterward, Marion sent Hick a postcard of the Hay-Adams with an arrow pointing to a sixth-floor window. "X marks the spot," she wrote on the front of the card, adding, "I will always remember the pleasant and happy hours of last evening."

The Roosevelt family celebrated Christmas at Hyde Park, with seven grandchildren in attendance, for the first time since FDR became president. Joe Lash and his messmates on Guadalcanal spent Christmas surrounded with lighted bayberry candles Eleanor had sent. Each one of them had a stocking of his own, also courtesy of the First Lady.

The greatest gift of all that Christmas came in FDR's fireside chat on Christmas Eve. "At last," he told Americans at home and around the globe, "we may look forward into the future with real, substantial confidence that, however great the cost, 'peace on earth, goodwill toward men' can be and will be realized and ensured. . . . Last year I could not do more than express a hope. Today I express—a certainty."

WINNING WITH
THE WOMEN

AFTER SHE RETURNED from the South Pacific, Eleanor became listless for a time—worrying Hick, Tommy, and others who knew her well. The horror of war had come home to her in a new way on her travels. She was also distressed by congressional criticism of her junkets as costly and unnecessary, criticism which grew so strident that FDR told her she shouldn't take any big trips for a while. Her frustration was compounded when FDR refused to take her along on his trip to Tehran to meet with Stalin. Anna had petitioned to go as well. "No women," FDR ruled, even though she would later discover that Churchill had invited his daughter, Sara. Nothing bothered Eleanor more than feeling hemmed in and "useless."

Finally, in March, she was set free to travel once more—this time to visit troops in the Caribbean and to continue on to South America. "Have a good trip dear," Hick wrote. "I'm sure you will do a grand job."

Eleanor wrote Hick from Puerto Rico on the tenth anniversary of their visit there together, remembering the birthday picnic they had shared on top of a mountain.

"I too have thought a lot about you starting out over the route we covered ten years ago this Spring," Hick replied. So much had happened since then. It was "a beautiful trip," she wrote, but she wished she had been "more mature, more stable."

Both Eleanor and Hick had fond memories of their times together, but they couldn't find their way back to them. Hick's jealousy in Puerto Rico a decade earlier had been both personal and professional: she had resented the fact that what was to be her field trip turned into a distracting media event. And she had resented, as always, the public life that made intimacy with Eleanor nearly impossible. Eleanor had moved on: if she had any romantic longings at that point, they were for Joe Lash, who was in love with someone else. Eleanor seems to have preferred these three-way attachments, where she could love without being expected to risk all of herself, to unlock that something that was "locked up inside." Her relationship with Hick had been the one exception.

For Hick, there were no such restraints. She would surely have dropped everything to give herself entirely to Eleanor, even then, if that were possible. But she had found substitutes. At fifty-two, she was enjoying the warm and caring company of other women more than ever before, both in and out of work. Because rationing made it impossible for Democratic women to travel to large meetings, Gladys Tillett traveled around the country making serial speeches to small groups, sometimes with Hick at her side. From Michigan they wrote a mischievous joint letter back to the office: the adventures of "Heecock" and "Tilletts"—names one of their hostesses gave them.

Many speeches were required at every stop—in Lansing, in Detroit, in Chicago, where the duo entered the Stevens Hotel with Tilletts "dripping with corsages down to her knee-cap." The hotel clerk asked the two of them if they were there for the DAR convention. "Heecock almost drops typewriter," says the letter. In Iron Mountain, Tilletts was relieved that the band concert, given in her honor, would give her time to "think up the three or four more speeches which will no doubt be needed."

The question, concluded the letter to the office, was whether Tilletts and Heecock could "get out of Iron Mountain without thinking they're God Almighty or Franklin D. Roosevelt."

If there was more laughter in Hick's life, it was partly because of Marion Harron, who was wholeheartedly in love with her. Unlike Eleanor, Marion held nothing back. "Do you know," Marion wrote Hick after a four-day interlude together, "that your mirth is as light and bright as sunshine, and as warm."

Harron was a serious thinker who had written her J.D. thesis on the dissenting opinions of Justice Louis Brandeis. But she loved the borscht belt humor of George Jessel and frequently made her friends laugh. When Hick had to go to an obligatory event—one of "those huge God-awful affairs" where you stand around "on tired feet" and "shout inanities at the top of your lungs"—she recovered at dinner with Marion, "who was very, very funny about Washington society!" Hick and Marion both liked good food and drink.

Hick's side of the correspondence with Marion hasn't survived, but some comments suggest her letters were less fulsome than Marion's. "Your letters are short," Marion wrote, "but they mean so much." Marion was clearly the pursuer, longing for more than Hick was giving. Marion's intensity seems to have caused Hick to back off and shut down, just as Hick's passion had with Eleanor.

Once, after a happy time together, Marion wrote that she was a "little dog," but one "going along on two feet. . . . My name is Butch—or Bo— and I always come when you whistle—lie flat when you say 'flat'—and lick your cheek as well and as much as . . . those four-footed-furry dogs." Right now, she wrote, she had her "chin on one paw and my ears are drooping."

The letter was signed, "All my love dear—today and all through the year. Marion. Butch." She drew a paw print after the signature and added, "And I lick your cheek—madame! Good night and sweet sleep." Marion delivered this letter to Hick at the White House

BY THE TIME ELEANOR RETURNED to Washington from South America that spring, there was one thing on nearly everyone's mind: the cross-Channel invasion called Overlord, announced by the Big Three in Tehran the previous November. "We don't know when an invasion of Europe will begin," Eleanor wrote in "My Day" on Easter 1944, "but we do know that when it does begin it will be the great test."

At first military planners hoped for a May landing, but in the end, despite worries about rough weather, D-Day was finally launched on June 6, 1944. "You are about to embark on a great crusade," General Dwight D. Eisenhower told his assembled troops, "toward which we have striven these many months. . . . The eyes of the world are upon you. The hopes and prayers of liberty-loving people everywhere march with you."

At midnight Washington time, twenty-four thousand British, Canadian, and U.S troops began to wade through the rough waters of the North Atlantic onto the beaches of Normandy. The largest amphibious operation in history was under way.

Eleanor had been too nervous to sleep, knowing the invasion was starting. So when word came in of the landing, the switchboard called her first. She woke Franklin, who had somehow managed to sleep. He sat up in bed, put on his sweater, and began to take phone calls.

"Some of our landings were desperate adventures," FDR reported to the American people, "but from advices received so far, the losses were lower than our commanders had estimated would occur." The worst loss of life was at Omaha Beach, where twenty-four hundred died. But by the end of the first day, thirty-four thousand troops had landed on the beaches of northern France. Within three weeks of D-Day, one million had been put ashore. It would be another two and a half months before the Allies liberated Paris from the Nazis, and another seven months of brutal warfare before the war ended in Europe. But the end was now in sight.

Under the circumstances, there seemed little doubt that FDR was going to have to run for a fourth term in 1944, so that he could, as the campaign posters put it, "stay and finish the job." It was not what Eleanor wanted, of course, although she understood that it was probably necessary for the good of the nation. A fourth term was not even what Franklin wanted. "All that is within me," he wrote the chairman of the Democratic Party, "cries out to go back to my home on the Hudson River." But he had "as little right to withdraw as the soldier has to leave his post." His nomination, at the 1944 Democratic convention in Chicago, had to be.

Anyone who saw photographs of FDR in this period—gaunt and slack-jawed, with dark circles under his eyes—suspected he was ill. Under the circumstances, the vice presidency assumed new importance. Eleanor wanted Franklin to stick with Henry Wallace as vice president, both as a matter of loyalty and also because Wallace shared her liberal views. But Hick, as early as March, was convinced the Democrats were going to opt for a more centrist candidate. "There's quite a boom on for Senator Truman for vice president," she reported to Eleanor. "Personally, I very much prefer Truman to [Speaker of the House] Sam Rayburn, who, I think is one of the weakest men in politics."

FDR played his old games, promising Wallace he would support him but insisting at the same time he didn't want to dictate the outcome. "Hard position when you don't want to be a dictator but you want your own way," Eleanor wrote Hick. FDR let it be known that he would accept either William O. Douglas or Harry Truman.

In the end, the convention nominated Truman, a Democrat who began his political career as a creature of Tom Pendergast's Democratic machine in Kansas City but established a reputation for independence as a senator investigating irregularities in the World War II defense industry. Truman had grown up on a farm, served in World War I, and run a clothing store for a time in Kansas City before going into politics; he didn't have a college degree. He was, in short, a man with whom Roosevelt had very little in common. But FDR accepted the will of the convention, for the same reason he accepted the nomination. Political squabbling would distract from winning the war.

In 1944, for the first time in American history, the majority of voters in a presidential election would be women. The Women's Division, under the leadership of Hick and Gladys Tillett, worked hard to press that advantage by dramatically increasing the participation of women at the convention. Campaign schools for women were held for the first time and attracted overflow audiences. According to the *New York Times*, "every possible method of communication with a war-harried public was discussed briefly by Mrs. Charles W. Tillett and other Democratic women." Tillett told her students that this was "not like any other school you will ever attend." There would be no grades and no diploma. The only thing that mattered in this school was the "final exam." And that exam took place on election day, November 7, 1944.

The female star of the convention was Helen Gahagan Douglas, who gave a rousing speech to the delegates in which she declared that the Democrats were the "true conservative" party because they had "conserved hope and ambition in the hearts of our people" and "saved millions of homes and farms from foreclosure." The Republicans, who had chosen New York governor Thomas E. Dewey as their standard-bearer, had "no contact with the people or with the realities of their wants and needs." Their program, Douglas told the true believers at the convention and Americans listening on the radio, was "a nightmare of muddle and confusion."

"Helen's speech was superb," Marion wrote Hick after hearing the broadcast from Chicago. "Her voice and delivery were excellent." In general, Marion noted, "the convention has done alright by the 'wimmin.'"

Post-convention, an exhausted Hick celebrated by spending two days with Marion, who was in the process of moving out of her mother's house into an apartment that she was painting and fixing up for two. She was "praying to the gods that you'll be here often and long," she wrote Hick. "You see, my dear, this is *your* apartment." In August, she and Marion spent two weeks together at the Little House. "A perfect vacation," Marion wrote.

Back in D.C., Marion found Hick's letters from the Little House a "great comfort and joy," and added that writing helped ease the pain of separation. "I miss you more than I can tell you dear," she wrote.

But a strain in the relationship was obvious by the end of summer, when Hick wrote offering to pay for some peonies Marion had contributed to the Little House garden. "You see," Marion wrote poignantly, "a day will come, I feel all too certain, when I may not be in your garden myself—and I will be pleased if a peony or two is there in my place. . . . I know, better than you think, the wisdom of cherishing the present."

Hick was beginning a process of withdrawal: from Marion and from her work at the Women's Division. When Eleanor wrote in September asking if she would need a skirt and coat, she wrote back that "I'll be spending a good share of next year down in the country." While she knew she would have to work for the rest of her life, she explained to Eleanor, she was tired. It was "a kind of cumulative fatigue that has been building up for a couple of years." She believed her working life would be prolonged by a good, long rest. "So I'm going to take it. Six months any-way. Longer if I can swing it financially." She planned to stay only through the inauguration.

Eleanor was wary of this plan for good reason, since she knew of Hick's tendency to retreat to solitude at the Little House. "I think I would resign Jan. 1st if you really feel completely exhausted," she wrote. "I doubt how-ever whether you will need or want more than 3 months rest and I'd try to get the future job lined up before you leave." It was good advice, which Hick unfortunately didn't take.

NEITHER ELEANOR NOR FRANKLIN gave in easily to physical ail-ments. FDR, after all, had spent half of his adult life proving that his handicap didn't get in the way of his career. At Warm Springs, he called himself "Old Doctor Roosevelt" and invented new exercises for the other "polios." When asked by reporters in late 1943 if the New Deal programs were over, he spun out an elaborate analogy in which he was again the doctor, coming to the rescue of a sick patient, the United States. When he first came into office, FDR explained, the country was suffering from a "grave internal disorder." So they sent for the doctor, Dr. New Deal, who prescribed numerous remedies: the SEC, PWA, WPA, CCC, NYA, among others. It took several years for the remedies to take hold. But in time, the patient got better.

Then on December 7, 1941, the patient had a bad "smashup": broken hip, legs, arms. "Some people didn't even think he would live." Dr. New Deal didn't know how to fix broken bones, so he called in a specialist: Dr. Win the War. "And the result is that the patient is back on his feet. He has given up his crutches. He has begun to strike back." FDR, and the entire nation, needed to believe that Dr. Win the War was strong, healthy, and in charge—at least until the war was won.

"The President," Eleanor reported in "My Day," "has had bronchitis and he has been weary, but I think it is probably as much the weariness that assails everyone who grasps the full meaning of war, as it is a physical ailment." When it came to illness, Eleanor and Franklin thought alike: just ignore it and it will go away.

Fortunately, another member of the family thought differently. Early in 1944, Anna Roosevelt moved back to Washington and into the White House along with her husband, John Boettiger, and family. It wasn't planned that way: Anna had come for a brief visit at Christmas. But now that Harry Hopkins had moved out with his wife, Louise, his bedroom was available. John was working nearby at the Pentagon.

It soon became obvious that FDR loved having his daughter around. She was vivacious and capable. A friend recalled being in the president's study when Anna walked in wearing her riding boots: "His whole face lighted up. . . . He just adored her." She laughed at her father's stories and had some stories of her own to tell. Eleanor, who had felt usurped in the past by some of Franklin's companions, gave her blessing to Anna's role as assistant to her father. Soon, FDR was saying "ask Anna to do it" on a regular basis.

Anna, unlike her parents, sensed that something more was wrong with her father than bronchitis. She also suspected that Dr. Ross McIntyre, the ear, nose, and throat man who served as family doctor, didn't know what he was talking about. At her urging, McIntyre reluctantly agreed to recommend a thorough going-over. On March 28, 1944, Roosevelt was wheeled into the office of a young cardiologist named Howard Bruenn at Bethesda Naval Hospital.

Bruenn suspected something was terribly wrong as soon as he saw him. "His face was pallid and there was a bluish discoloration of his skin, lips and nail beds. He was also having difficulty breathing." Bruenn concluded that FDR was suffering from congestive heart failure, but did not share his diagnosis with his patient.

True to the Roosevelt style, FDR chatted genially throughout the exam and ended it with a smile and a handshake. "Thanks, Doc," he said. He asked no questions. Later that day, he told reporters that he was on the mend. A week later, Dr. McIntyre backed him up: he told the press that "for a man of 62 we had very little to complain about." McIntyre was of the school that believed it was better for patients not to know the extent of their illness—a view that dovetailed nicely with the Roosevelts' own propensity for denial. At McIntyre's insistence, FDR was told nothing of his serious heart condition.

Fortunately, FDR's ignorance didn't keep him from changing his diet, limiting his smoking and drinking, and taking digitalis. He also went off, on doctors' orders, to spend a month at Hobcaw, the plantation of Bernard Baruch in South Carolina. There he had plenty of time to rest in beautiful surroundings. Also, while he was there, Lucy Mercer Rutherfurd came to visit. Lucy's situation had changed that March, when her husband died after a long illness. She was now a widow, free to spend time with the man she admired and adored. FDR returned to Washington in May, looking and feeling better.

Despite painful attacks of what may have been angina, FDR pulled off several campaign marathons in the fall of 1944, touring four of the five boroughs of New York City in an open car in pouring rain and traveling through seven states in three days, stopping to make major addresses in Philadelphia and Chicago.

Had he made no other speech, FDR might have been able to win the election on the strength of an address he delivered to the Teamsters Union on September 23, 1944, in which he defended his irresistible little black Scottie, Fala. "Well, of course, I don't resent attacks, and my family don't resent attacks," he told the union members, "but Fala does resent them. You know, Fala is Scotch, and being a Scottie, as soon as he learned that the Republican fiction writers in Congress and out had concocted a story that I'd left him behind on an Aleutian island and had sent a destroyer back to find him—at a cost to the taxpayers of two or three, or eight or twenty million dollars—his Scotch soul was furious. He has not been the same dog since." FDR hadn't forgotten how to deliver a story: the union audience loved him.

After that, some observers claimed the contest was between New York governor Dewey, stiffly handsome with his mustache and neatly parted black hair, and Fala, who was all black hair, and more endearing.

On election night, Hick escaped the noise and excitement at Democratic headquarters to listen to the results on the radio at the home of Belle Roosevelt, daughter-in-law of Teddy Roosevelt and one of the most popular speakers for the Democratic Women's Division. After Dewey finally conceded, at 3:13 a.m., she left for home and bed, only to be awakened by Helen Gahagan Douglas, who was thrilled to report that FDR was going to carry California by 250,000 votes. Much later that day, Hick learned that Helen herself had been elected for the first time to the U.S. Congress. "*Was I happy!*" Hick wrote Eleanor.

The popular vote in the presidential election was closer than ever, but FDR won big in the electoral college: 432 to Thomas Dewey's 99.

"Darling," Hick wrote Eleanor after the results came in, "I don't like to think about the next four years for you. Rotten luck—but, my God, we couldn't let that little man with the mustache be president! Not *now*."

THERE IS ONLY
ONE PRESIDENT

"THERE ARE A LOT OF THINGS I don't like to think about just now," Eleanor wrote Hick shortly after Franklin was reelected, "but perhaps the answers will come as we go along." She had been troubled by FDR's abandoning Henry Wallace, and she was lobbying now to make Wallace secretary of commerce. But Franklin was tired and not in the mood to listen to Eleanor's unending demands. "I have a feeling," Wallace wrote Henry Morgenthau, "that at the present time he fights everything she is for."

There were obvious signs by now that Franklin was seriously ill, but Eleanor resisted the idea, even complaining about his need for a special diet. At the same time, she wondered, as she wrote Esther Lape, if she would be most "useful" if she became a "good wife" and waited on FDR, as Daisy Suckley had done and as Anna was now doing. "I'd hate it but I'd soon get accustomed to it," she wrote. But she added, in another letter four days later, that Lape was wrong to think her caring would be motivated by love. "There is no fundamental love to draw on, just respect and affection. . . . On my part there is often a great weariness and a sense of futility."

Eleanor's letter to Hick around the same time made clear that she had no intention of becoming the good wife. Franklin, she wrote Hick, was going on to Warm Springs for Thanksgiving, taking along Daisy Suckley and Laura Delano, "so I won't have to go." Eleanor was hoping to spend Thanksgiving with Joe and Trude Lash instead. When that didn't work out, she substituted a maelstrom of activity involving a visit with veterans, an evening with a British war correspondent, a visit to her ailing friend Elinor Morgenthau, cocktails with Hick, and a dinner for nine guests on the South Portico.

She also fit in several phone calls to Franklin in Warm Springs to complain about conservative appointments in the State Department and pressure him about a new cause: Yugoslavia. A visit with two young Yugoslavs had convinced her that something needed to be done to support the Tito partisans in their desperate fight against the Nazis. Eleanor's persistence upset Dr. Bruenn, who was in Warm Springs watching over FDR's precarious health. The phone calls sent FDR's blood pressure through the roof, according to Bruenn. "He got more and more upset, as did I." He complained that Eleanor had "tunnel vision" when it came to lobbying for her causes.

It seems likely that Eleanor's "tunnel vision" at this point included refusal not only to accept the gravity of Franklin's illness but also to notice what was by now fairly widely known in the inner circle: Franklin was seeing Lucy Mercer Rutherfurd on a regular basis, and indeed was with her during this Thanksgiving visit to Warm Springs. In fact, Anna Roosevelt had been arranging the meetings, at her father's request, since July.

Anna was angry at first about her father's thoughtlessness in putting her in the middle. She knew that the Lucy Mercer affair had hurt her mother like nothing else in her life. But Anna also liked Lucy, and understood that she provided her father with the kind of intelligent and sympathetic company that might help keep him alive.

On one occasion that summer, FDR actually picked up Lucy Mercer in Georgetown and drove with her through the streets of Washington in his open car en route to the White House. There had been a dozen trysts since then, at the White House when Eleanor was out of town and now at Warm Springs.

Everyone in Warm Springs knew that FDR and Lucy were spending a fair amount of time together. Maids, cooks, and butlers knew, reporters who traveled with FDR knew, and of course secretaries and assistants to FDR knew. In September 1944, FDR's train to Hyde Park detoured onto a siding so that he could visit briefly with Lucy at her summer estate in northern New Jersey. Yet when he arrived at Highland Station in Hyde Park, Eleanor was there to greet him and they spent a quiet evening together at Val-Kill. Is it really possible that Eleanor knew nothing of what was going on with Lucy?

Eleanor had a knack for keeping painful realities at bay until she could deny them no longer. She had refused to acknowledge her father's errant ways until long after his death. She had ignored FDR's flirtation with Lucy Mercer until she was confronted with the irrefutable evidence of the love letters. Now, once again, she chose not to notice what was apparent to many around her. In the same way, she must have suspected, without really wanting to admit it, that FDR was fatally ill.

Eleanor had entirely different attitudes toward illness in the family and illness outside the family. When it came to the Roosevelt children, she tended to be shockingly indifferent. Once, when she was on a camping trip with the boys, Elliott, who was wearing corrective metal braces, got too close to the campfire and severely burned his legs. Her casual reaction may have led to the infection he got afterward. James recalled coming home from college with a high fever and being ignored for hours while his parents continued entertaining guests. Afterward, he developed double pneumonia.

When a friend was ill, on the other hand, Eleanor was quick to take action. Hick claimed that one of the best presents she ever got from her was a trip to the doctor shortly before Christmas in 1944. She had refused to go for months, insisting she didn't want to turn into a hypochondriac like her friend Mary Norton, who worried obsessively about her blood pressure. Finally, when Eleanor offered to take Hick to *her* doctor, she relented, only to discover that her diabetes was dangerously out of control.

"Were you ever right!" she wrote Eleanor just before Christmas. The doctor put her on a strict diet and told her she might need insulin in the future. He also told her that her heart sounded like "a tired old man," that she needed to sleep nine or ten hours a night, and that it would be a good idea for her to take a long rest at the Little House.

"Darling," she wrote Eleanor, "thanks for making me go to the doctor. He says you probably saved my life." The diagnosis explained Hick's complaints of "cumulative fatigue," and gave her a strong justification for leaving her job once FDR began his fourth term.

ON THE WEEKEND of the inauguration, in January 1945, the White House was full to bursting with the sounds of thirteen children, ranging in age from two to eighteen. FDR insisted that every grandchild be on hand for his fourth inaugural. It was, of course, a historic occasion. But perhaps the president also wanted an opportunity to be with all of them for what he sensed was the last time.

He looked pale as he gripped James's arm and pulled himself up to the lectern to deliver his speech from the South Portico of the White House. His smile, as he completed the oath of office, was faint. The speech itself was only five minutes long, and the entire ceremony lasted only a quarter hour. "Today, in this year of war, 1945," he told the crowd of seven thousand assembled on the snowy White House lawn, "we have learned lessons—at a fearful cost—and we shall profit by them. . . . We have learned to be citizens of the world, members of the human community. We have learned the simple truth, as Emerson said, that 'the only way to have a friend is to be one.'"

Even if FDR had been entirely healthy, an elaborate ceremony would have been inappropriate. It was no time, as his assistant Bill Hassett noted, for "fuss and feathers or peacock parades." On December 16, Hitler's troops had launched a surprise offensive on the Western Front. The monthlong Battle of the Bulge, in which nineteen thousand Americans would die, was going on as Roosevelt spoke. Victory in Europe was still a ways off; victory in the Pacific would take even longer.

Nonetheless, two days after the inauguration, FDR left Washington on a secret and lengthy journey to Soviet Crimea, to negotiate the future of Europe after Allied victory. Much to Eleanor's chagrin, Franklin invited Anna to go with him to Yalta. It made sense in several ways: Anna was now the caretaker, watching over his regimen. Anna was easier to be with. Eleanor, as she acknowledged in retrospect, hadn't yet accepted the fact "he could no longer bear to have a real discussion, such as we had always had." The tension between Franklin, who felt tired and burdened, and Eleanor, who could not stop pushing her agenda, was heightened by this choice. Eleanor received few letters from her husband during the conference, and was skeptical, when an underling delivered orchids, that the flowers had really been his idea. "Many thanks dear but I rather doubt his truth since you wouldn't order orchids and so I suggest you don't forget to pay him!"

The Yalta meeting itself ended in great optimism. At the final dinner, Stalin toasted the alliance, proposing that relations in peacetime should be as strong as they had been in war. Churchill said he felt they were all standing on the crest of a hill, with the glories of future possibility stretching out before them. FDR said he felt the atmosphere at the dinner was that of a family, and that was how he liked to characterize the relations among the three great nations.

Back home, the press hailed Yalta as a marvelous accomplishment—"a landmark in human history," in the words of veteran journalist William L. Shirer. Yalta turned out to be a landmark, but not of the kind so ardently celebrated at that final dinner. Some historians have blamed FDR's waning powers for the Soviet territorial gains agreed to at Yalta. But Eleanor pointed out that her husband rose to occasions when he needed to bargain. She was convinced that "the necessity of matching his wits against other people's stimulated him and kept him alert and interested," even at the Yalta Conference. FDR himself explained that Soviet occupation of much of Eastern Europe was a fait accompli that could not have been reversed without armed conflict. "At this stage of the war in Europe," historian David Kennedy has observed, "political decisions could do little more than ratify military realities."

Like the farewell dinner at Yalta, FDR's reception, when he addressed Congress on his return, was overwhelmingly positive. For the first time in his many years in office, Roosevelt spoke to the joint session sitting down. "I hope that you will pardon me for this unusual posture," he began, going on to explain that it was easier not to carry "ten pounds of steel" on each of his legs, and that he had also just completed a fourteen-thousand-mile journey. It was the first time FDR had made explicit public reference to his disability. Eleanor viewed it as a surrender, noting that he had "accepted a certain degree of invalidism." The applause from Congress was heartfelt.

The speech, however, was uncharacteristically long and rambling, replete with unfortunate ad-libbing. Those who knew FDR best were worried. Equally alarming was a new tendency to repeat the same stories to the same person in the same sitting. Sometimes he would greet one visitor with a cold, blank stare, only to return to his usual warm style for the next.

HICK LEFT HER JOB as executive secretary of the Democratic Women's Division that March, just as she celebrated her fifty-second birthday. Gladys Tillett organized a surprise farewell party for Hick at which her colleagues sang her praises. "I wish I could live up to the nice things that have been said to me," she wrote Eleanor. She faulted herself, as always, for her intolerance and lack of patience, and she felt "awkward and inadequate when people say nice things to me—even though I love to hear them."

The best praise came from those she most respected. "I guess I did not make any mistake in picking you either," Molly Dewson wrote her, pointing out that Eleanor had thought "it was not a job suited to you." In the *Democratic Digest*, Dewson wrote of "our friend 'Hick,'" who can write "battle pages during a campaign in which facts live." Hick's passion for anonymity meant that much of her work went unattributed. Yet, as the *Digest* noted in a final profile, Hick was "a gifted writer, a politically wise and realistic advisor, and one of the warmest and most penetrating personalities who has ever been with the National Committee.

"She knows how to present even the most complicated subjects with simplicity, and yet with drama and force. Much that has come out of the Women's Division in print these past few years came first out of Lorena Hickok's typewriter."

Hick would continue to ply her trade, using her typewriter. But after she left the Women's Division that March, she would never work in a salaried job again.

BY THE TIME FDR LEFT for Warm Springs at the end of March 1945, he was a man in desperate need of rest. Daisy Suckley and Laura Delano went along to keep him company, just as they had at Thanksgiving. Lucy Mercer joined them a week later, this time accompanied by her friend Elizabeth Shoumatoff, who planned to paint the president's portrait.

On April 11, FDR was in high spirits. He took all four women—Daisy, Laura, Lucy, and Elizabeth Shoumatoff—on a drive around the property in his customized '38 Ford. He also worked on his Jefferson Day speech with Grace Tully. "Let us move forward with strong and active faith," he wrote.

The next day, the president dealt with the mail pouch, as usual, signing and handing over documents to his aide Bill Hassett, who laid them out separately until the ink dried. FDR referred to this as "doing the laundry." At noon on April 12, he finished off a particularly large stack of mail by affixing his signature with a flourish to a piece of legislation. Daisy and Lucy were in the room with him. Elizabeth Shoumatoff was at her easel. "There," he told the women, "there is where I make a law."

An hour later, as lunch was about to be served, FDR's head drooped forward. Daisy hurried to his side, thinking he had dropped something. "He looked at me," Suckley remembered, "his forehead furrowed with pain, and tried to smile. He put his left hand up to the back of his head and said, 'I have a terrific pain in the back of my head.' And then he collapsed."

By the time Dr. Bruenn arrived, the president's valet and butler had carried the unconscious president into the bedroom and laid him down on the bed. Dr. Bruenn realized, as soon as he saw him, that Roosevelt had suffered a massive cerebral hemorrhage. Three and a half hours later, he was dead.

Back in Washington, Steve Early, who had served as FDR's press secretary throughout all his years in the White House, delivered the news by telephone to the three major news services. "Here is a flash," he began. "The President died suddenly early this afternoon."

There was a long silence on the line. Then one of the reporters asked, in disbelief, "Do you mean President Roosevelt?"

"Of course," Early answered. "There is only one President."

CHAPTER TWENTY-FOUR

THE GREATEST CATASTROPHE
FOR THE WORLD

EARLY ON THE FATEFUL DAY, Eleanor Roosevelt got a call from Laura
Delano reporting that FDR had fainted. She decided to carry on with her
afternoon engagements anyway, since any cancellation would arouse suspicion. She was at a thrift shop benefit when she was called to the phone by
Steve Early, who asked her to return to the White House at once. She rode
all the way there "with clenched hands," knowing in her heart what had
happened. Soon after she arrived at the White House and went to her
sitting room, Steve Early and Dr. McIntyre came in to tell her that FDR
had died.

Eleanor was at her best in such crisis situations. She immediately ca-
bled her four sons with the news: "Darlings. Pa slept away this afternoon.
He did his job to the end as he would want you to do. Bless you. All our
love. Mother."

Then she summoned Vice President Harry Truman to the White
House. "Harry," she told him when he arrived, "the President is dead."
Truman was too stunned to speak at first. Then he asked Eleanor if there
was anything he could do for her. Her reply was characteristic: "Is
there anything we can do for you? For you are the one in trouble now."

[303]

Truman would have agreed. "Boys," he told a group of reporters the day after he was sworn in, "if you ever pray, pray for me now. I don't know whether you fellows ever had a load of hay fall on you, but when they told me yesterday what had happened, I felt like the moon, the stars, and all the planets had fallen on me."

Eleanor flew down to Warm Springs soon after Truman's swearing in, accompanied by Early and McIntyre. It was almost midnight by the time they arrived. Lucy Mercer and Elizabeth Shoumatoff were long gone. It might have been possible for Lucy's visit to be kept secret, at least until after the funeral ceremonies. But Laura Delano, ever the gossip, soon revealed to Eleanor that her husband had been with Lucy at the time of his death. Eleanor also learned that Anna had arranged numerous meetings.

Once again, and more acutely than ever, Eleanor was forced to maintain a public façade that hid her private emotions. For days, weeks, and months to come, the entire nation would look upon Eleanor Roosevelt as the grieving widow of a great man. She would have to thank them all for their sympathy and agree with their hymns of praise. All the while, she would be unable to express her complicated feelings—feelings of loss, certainly, and regret for what might have been, but also of hurt and rage at Franklin's betrayal. Anna's recent involvement compounded the injury: it would take some time for mother and daughter to reconcile.

Eleanor wrote later, in her memoir *This I Remember*, of an "almost impersonal feeling about everything that was happening." She attributed it in part to having known for years that her husband might die at any time, and, more recently, that "some or all of my sons might be killed in the war." But then she added that "much further back I had had to face certain difficulties until I decided to accept the fact that a man must be what he is, life must be lived as it is. . . . You can not live at all if you do not learn to adapt yourself to your life as it happens to be." It was the closest she came to a public acknowledgment of the Lucy Mercer affair and its powerful effect on her life.

Eleanor rode north to Washington on the train that carried FDR's heavy brass casket. All night long, she lay in her berth with her shade up, watching the crowds that gathered in shock and grief along the route. Some sang, some knelt in prayer, many were in tears. All around the world, people mourned FDR and the hope he embodied.

"It seems sure," Dorothy Thompson told radio listeners, "that although his eyes are closed and although his golden voice is stilled, not only Roosevelt's war is won but Roosevelt's world will eventually triumph. . . . He saw a new world in which the labor of men and women, the resources of nature, must be organized for the general welfare."

"At midnight last night we heard the tragic news," a young soldier wrote home from France. "The greatest catastrophe that I can think of for the world, for the peace, and for humanity and for him—when it seemed that things were within his grasp." Letters poured into the White House for days and days, echoing those sentiments. Truman lent one of his secretaries to Eleanor and Tommy to help in merely opening them there were way too many to answer. It made Eleanor understand just how much people believed in her husband, and how frightened many were about having to carry on without him.

HICK WROTE A LETTER to Eleanor as soon as she got the news—a "dazed and incoherent letter" that she decided to tear up. "No use burdening you with _my_ bewilderment and terror." She realized she was only feeling like millions of other people in the world. "And they'll all be telling _you_."

Hick had planned to come to Washington and Hyde Park for the funeral ceremonies, but Eleanor talked her out of it. On the phone from Warm Springs, she told Hick, "You know what it will be like. And you, of all people, must realize what a load I am carrying now." Hick, with her serious diabetes, would "just be another worry" if she came.

If Hick felt rejected, she didn't admit it, perhaps even to herself. Instead, she chose to take Eleanor's request as a great honor. "I'll bet there are darned few people in this world to whom she would have felt that she could be so frank," she wrote Molly Dewson.

In the four days after FDR died, Eleanor and Hick were in close touch.

They not only talked on the phone, but they also exchanged letters each day. Since Eleanor always confided in Hick, it seems likely that she told her old friend about Lucy Mercer's presence in Warm Springs at the time of Franklin's death, and about Anna's betrayal. One comment of Hick's, the day after the event, suggests as much: "Darling," she wrote, "sometime I may get straightened out the mixed personal and—shall I say public—feelings I have about you and your family!"

ELEANOR HAD ONLY a few moments alone with her husband's body during the rush of events that followed his death. At Warm Springs, she sat in the bedroom for five minutes while his body lay on the bed. Then, again, after she walked on Elliott's arm into the East Room of the White House, she asked to be left alone, with the casket lid raised, so she could see his face for a last farewell.

Perhaps she thought then of the conversation she and Franklin had just three weeks before he died, about taking a trip together to celebrate the Allied victory in Europe. First they would visit the king and queen, then drive with the royals through the streets of London to the Houses of Parliament, where FDR would speak, then on to visit Churchill at Chequers. After that they would visit soldiers on the battlefields of Europe, pay a call on Queen Wilhelmina in Holland, and finish their tour in Paris. The trip would give them a chance to share in a great moment of victory and hope for the future.

Now instead there was this official ceremony in the East Room. Afterward, the president's casket was loaded onto a long funeral train, filled with mourners, for the journey north to his beloved Hyde Park, where the flag-draped casket was transferred onto a caisson and pulled by six horses up the steep dirt road from the railroad siding. It was a beautiful, sunny spring day; the lilacs were in bloom. "Taps" sounded as the casket was lowered into the ground in the rose garden. Fighter planes flew in formation overhead. Just twenty-three days later, the Allies would declare victory over Hitler's genocidal regime.

Eleanor went immediately from the Hyde Park ceremony to the White House to pack up. The accumulated possessions of the last twelve years filled a thousand boxes and twenty Army trucks. But by the weekend, she had turned the place over to the Trumans—with no regrets. "It is empty and without purpose to be here now," she wrote Hick.

"I have spent my last night in the White House," Eleanor wrote her "My Day" readers on April 19. "I have had my last breakfast on the sun porch."

Hick, reading those words, must have thought of the many pleasant White House breakfasts she had shared with Eleanor over the years—in the West Hall in wintertime, down on the south veranda in summer, and toward the end on the third-floor sun porch most easily accessible to the ailing FDR.

Eleanor thought of Hick, too, as she sorted through her thousands of belongings. Hick always drank her café au lait in a big blue-and-white willow ware cup. Eleanor kept the cup out of the boxes and gave it to her as a souvenir. Hick used it for the rest of her life.

PART V

STARTING

OVER

CHAPTER TWENTY-FIVE

SLIDING ON
MARBLE FLOORS

A FEW WEEKS AFTER THE FUNERAL, Hick wrote a piece entitled "Eleanor Roosevelt . . . First Lady" for the memorial edition of the *Democratic Digest*. "Wherever there are battles to be fought or injustices overcome," she predicted, "wherever there are people—individuals or masses of people—who need a friend, Eleanor Roosevelt will be there somewhere, very likely in the background . . . doing her job. And so, it's goodbye to Eleanor Roosevelt, First Lady, but *not* goodbye to Eleanor Roosevelt."

Hick's prophecy came true in spectacular fashion over the next seventeen years. It would take a little while, though, for Eleanor to shed the caution she had practiced for so long. "For the first time in my life," she told reporters, "I can say what I want. For your information, it is wonderful to feel free." Then she asked that this remark be kept off the record.

The greatest barrier to Eleanor's finding the "active and important place" Hick wished for her was her own habit of saying yes to everything and everybody. Now that she had left the White House, the Val-Kill house and the apartment in Greenwich Village became meccas for family, friends, and petitioners. On weekends, the house was so full that "arms and legs practically stick out the windows."

Tommy confided to Esther Lape that she was often in despair about the crowds at Val-Kill. "No matter who is here, Eleanor pays very little attention to them and that is the reason why they all gang up in my room." Tommy complained that children were "blowing soap bubbles all over my room and spilling soapy water on the rug." She had to hide her typewriter because two of the numerous grandchildren around the place thought it was "a wonderful toy." Some came for an overnight, and some, like Joe and Trude Lash, came for extended visits. Sometimes she had to kick everyone out in order to meet one of Eleanor's numerous writing deadlines.

Even before FDR died, Lape had urged Eleanor to be more selective about what she took on. She had a chance to use her power "for persuasion and enlightenment," Lape advised, but using it effectively required her to make choices.

"You spoke of a selective job," Eleanor wrote Lape, "and that is the hardest thing for me to do, since I've always done what came to hand." Saying no meant taking her position of power seriously, and that made her uncomfortable.

Even though she was busy during every waking hour, Eleanor couldn't block out worries about her family. "Somehow my family keep me stirred up," she wrote Hick. She had been heartbroken when Elliott left his wife, Ruth, whom she liked, for a movie star named Faye Emerson. Recently, Elliott had been in the papers again over some questionable business dealings. Now all the children were wrangling over what to do with the Val-Kill properties and the surrounding eight-hundred-plus acres. Elliott was planning to live in Top Cottage and try his hand at farming, much to the others' resentment. There were angry shouting matches between the brothers, with Elliott on one side and Franklin Jr. on the other. There was even talk of selling Val-Kill outright and dividing the proceeds. "I am quite shocked," Tommy confided to Lape, "at the acquisitiveness of the children."

Tommy accepted her boss's need to be in constant motion, but she wanted her to use her energy to higher purpose. "She has the heart and the courage to fight for what is good for the whole world," she wrote Hick. "These little people who waste her time and energy will be benefitted in the long run. The letters of introduction for jobs, the supporting of piddling organizations will not mean anything if the world is shaky."

The world was shaky in a whole new way when the Japanese surrendered, on August 15, 1945, in the wake of the atomic bombing of Hiroshima and Nagasaki. Many Americans took to the streets to celebrate. But Eleanor felt, as she told her "My Day" readers, that "the weight of suffering which has engulfed the world during so many years could not so quickly be wiped out." Also, as she confided to Anna, she missed "Pa's voice" and "the words he would have spoken." Increasingly, after his death, she came to appreciate how much she had relied on Franklin to shoulder the world's problems.

Other Americans felt the same way. Harry Truman's public pronouncements, delivered matter-of-factly in his flat Missouri rasp, were a poor substitute for FDR's engaging fireside chats. Critics on the right ridiculed Truman as a "model boy" thrust into a man's job. In more sophisticated circles, he was denigrated as a small-town pol who was out of his depth. According to Washington columnist Joseph Alsop, the White House now resembled "the lounge of the Lion's Club of Independence, Missouri," complete with an odor of "ten-cent cigars." Hick wondered, in a letter to Eleanor, if Truman was going to "get along with Congress by letting Congress run him." She hadn't fully appreciated before that "one never had to worry about the President letting anybody run him." FDR was still the president to Hick and many others.

Two months after she moved out of the White House, Eleanor returned there to lunch with the new president. It seemed, she wrote Hick, like an entirely different place, "bare and stiff." With his wife and daughter out of town, President Truman seemed "the loneliest man I ever saw. . . . He's not at ease and no one else is."

The contrast was striking, Hick agreed. "I've been sorry for them [Bess and Harry Truman] all along, both of them." She had heard through her journalist grapevine that they were "borrowing pictures from the Corcoran gallery to decorate their own living quarters!"

Truman might have been unsophisticated about art, but he was a clever politician. He knew he needed to form an alliance with Eleanor, the living link to the Roosevelt magic. It made sense too, given FDR's commitment to postwar plans for peace, that Truman should ask Eleanor to join the six-person delegation to the London meeting of the new UN organization.

As usual, Eleanor wasn't sure at first that she was up to the task. But in January 1946 she boarded the *Queen Elizabeth* and sailed to England for the conference. She gained confidence as she took the measure of her fellow delegates. "When I come home," she wrote Hick, "I'm going to give you thumbnail sketches of my playmates that I don't dare put on paper. The Russians are hard to work with, because everything has to be decided in Moscow, but I think a little frank firmness on our part would help."

Eleanor was assigned to the committee dealing with human rights because the others in the delegation, who had opposed her appointment, viewed that as the place where she could do the least damage. But it turned out that Committee Three, as it was called, was asked to confront one of the most critical of postwar issues: the status of refugees. The Russians and their allies wanted all war refugees in Germany to be required to go back to their countries of origin. Many were still living in camps because they didn't want to return to live under Communist rule. The United States and its partners argued against forced repatriation. Eleanor proved a formidable worker and speaker on the issue. When it came time for the decisive vote, she went head-to-head with the seasoned Russian diplomat Andrei Vyshinsky.

Eleanor was "tense and excited" as she approached the rostrum to make her case. She knew the Russian tactic was to delay the vote for hours, hoping the other side would tire and leave. Because she needed to keep the South Americans at the meeting, she evoked the memory of the great Simón Bolívar and his courageous fight for freedom in Latin America. The

South Americans stayed around to vote, and Eleanor won a significant victory.

On the final night of the meetings, she returned to the hotel around one o'clock, feeling very tired. As she walked up the stairs to her room, she encountered two of her fellow delegates, John Foster Dulles and Senator Arthur Vandenberg. They told her that they had thought her appointment a mistake, but had found her "good to work with" and would be "happy to do so again." Senator Vandenberg—an anti–New Deal Republican—was heard to say at dinner parties afterward, "I take back everything I ever said about her, and believe me it's been plenty."

HICK'S OWN TRANSITION into a new life was not going well. She worked hard to follow the doctor's orders and regulate her diet. But when she visited Val-Kill that summer of 1946, Tommy reported that she looked "ghastly." Her weight was down from 200 pounds to 138, which might have been a change for the better. But Tommy suspected she was "more sick than she knows."

Hick's friends, knowing how desperately she needed money, rallied around her. Mary Norton found a part-time salary for her in the congressional budget, and Helen Gahagan Douglas, now a congresswoman, asked for her help with research. Eleanor asked her to do background work for question-and-answer columns she was writing for the *Ladies' Home Journal*. Her former boss Gladys Tillett got into the act too, urging a moneyed Democrat to find a job for Hick, who had "good common sense," a "genius for writing," and "loyalty and devotion."

Hick expressed her gratitude repeatedly to everyone, but she was anxious, as she wrote Eleanor, to "get off your payroll and Mary's." She thought she'd found a solution when she was hired to write articles for a syndicate: the editor heaped on praise and promised the skies. He reacted to one of her pieces by telegram: "GAWD LADY YOU CAN WRITE." "God I'm favored by Providence!" she wrote Eleanor. "To have something to do that I know how to do—with a minimum of strain and effort. It's *wonderful*."

But her enthusiasm was premature. Hick wrote a number of articles, including one about the new president, but the syndicate didn't succeed in placing them. Before long, she was looking elsewhere for work.

Hick's relationship with Marion Harron was not going any better than her career. Marion was deeply attached to her mother, with whom she lived in Chevy Chase. Hick seems to have stayed with Marion only when her mother was out of town—a fact which suggests that Mother Harron didn't approve of the relationship. Mary Norton, who was a good friend to both Marion and Hick, predicted "that Mother dame will never let go of her."

Eventually Marion did leave for her own place in Washington, but she never convinced Hick to stay there for long. "I look at your slippers, dressing gown, typewriter, and there is even a razor here," Marion wrote, "but no you." She wished Hick good night. "I can dream of you anyhow." Marion spent two weeks with Hick that summer of 1945 at the Little House, but left in a huff after an argument with a neighbor—probably about politics.

"Marion has gone," Hick wrote Eleanor, "after a pretty stormy visit." Hick attributed Marion's flare-up to "change of life," which put her in a "nervous and emotional state very similar to mine at her age." It was what happened to "spinsters" when they were in their forties. "At least, that was my experience, and Marion seems to be going through the same thing. I feel terribly sorry for her, but there isn't much I can do except tell her that I probably understand a lot better than she thinks I do." She added that Marion was "a very dear, warm, generous person," of whom she was "terribly fond." Marion would not have been happy with that description of the relationship.

Although she saw Eleanor fairly often at Val-Kill and in New York, Hick was retreating more and more to the Little House and a life of solitude. The dietary requirements of her diabetes made it difficult, or so she claimed, to spend time in other people's houses. They didn't understand what she could and couldn't eat; one host bought her cheesecake because she told them she could eat cheese. She still saw her neighbors on occasion. Howard Haycraft, her former housemate, had his own house on the Dana property now, and he and his wife sometimes invited her to dinner. Hick's sister Ruby Claff and husband, Julian Claff, whom she had helped out when they were desperate for work during the Depression, now were prosperous enough to afford a weekend place near hers. Hick relied on Ruby, a trained nurse, to watch over her when she was trying to get her diabetes under control. But Ruby was an incessant talker and got on her nerves.

Hick's favorite companion was, as always, her dog. She had lost Prinz, after a long life, in the summer of 1943. She couldn't get back to Long Island in time to say a final goodbye, but her friends buried him, wrapped in one of her raincoats, in his favorite place, on a path they had often walked. Prinz was "an old, loyal and very dear friend," Hick wrote Eleanor, and she would miss him "all the rest of my life."

Very soon after Prinz died, an English setter puppy named "Mr. Choate" was delivered to the White House, thanks to Eleanor, to serve as a replacement. Mr. Choate was fluffy and caramel brown. Once he arrived in the country and got out of his box, he jumped up and down, Hick reported, like a bouncing cornflake.

While Eleanor couldn't seem to get enough of her friends, Hick's tolerance for company of any kind was increasingly limited. When the Haycrafts and the Claffs approached her porch one weekend to pay a courtesy call, they heard her muttering to someone else on the porch, "God damn it, here they come." Her refusal to go on a picnic with the Haycrafts because she had to "iron her dishtowels" became a shorthand explanation among friends for Hick's reclusive ways.

IN NOVEMBER 1947, Eleanor flew to Geneva to continue her human rights work, this time as chairman of the committee charged with drafting a Universal Declaration of Human Rights. It would turn out to be a yearlong project full of difficult, often tedious negotiation. But the tedium was offset by the pleasure of an unexpected new relationship with a tall, handsome forty-six-year-old physician named David Gurewitsch. Gurewitsch was an appealing combination of warmth and reserve, well educated and worldly without being a snob. Many women found him attractive. Eleanor, at age sixty-four, was one of them.

Gurewitsch was a specialist in rehabilitative medicine and had worked often with polio patients. He understood much better than most what FDR had overcome with his wife's help. But Eleanor first observed him in his role as general practitioner, treating Joe Lash's wife, Trude. Eleanor was so impressed that she asked him to be her physician too. There wouldn't be much to do, she assured him, since she was rarely ill.

In truth, Eleanor was no longer as invulnerable as she claimed—she had suffered several bouts of illness, including shingles. Gurewitsch first treated her in the summer of 1946, following a car accident. She had fallen asleep at the wheel, bruised her face badly, and broken her two front teeth. "Now I shall have two lovely porcelain ones," she wrote in "My Day" with her usual bravado, "which will look far better than the rather protruding ones most of the Roosevelts have."

Doctor and patient didn't become really close, however, until their roles were reversed. When Gurewitsch became ill with tuberculosis and needed to travel to Davos, Switzerland, for treatment, Eleanor arranged for him to travel there on the same plane she was taking to the Geneva conference. On their way, they were grounded by fog for three days at the airport in Shannon, Ireland. Eleanor became David's caregiver, bringing food to the barracks where they stayed during the layover, a mile away from the airport. The barracks were clean and the beds were comfortable, but there was no heat. "I was worried about his condition," Eleanor remembered.

In some ways, Eleanor's new interest in David Gurewitsch resembled her earlier attraction to the young radical Joe Lash. Like Lash, Gurewitsch was at an emotional turning point in his life—not just because of his illness, but also because he was in the process of ending a ten-year marriage to a beautiful professional singer named Nemone, whom he met around the time he first came to America. He and Nemone had a daughter, further complicating what had turned out to be an unfortunate marriage for both of them. Eleanor always liked to be needed. And David, like Joe, welcomed Eleanor's attention and warmth at a difficult time in his life.

There are only rare glimpses of David's feelings about Eleanor. But one letter suggests the great comfort he found in her company. After a rendezvous in Zurich some months later, he wrote, "It was so much more than I had anticipated. It was more intense and more intimate, it has brought you closer. I did not know that just accepting, taking, without another return except for gratitude and warmth could be as simple. You have done nothing but giving and I nothing but accepting, taking . . . and still I am not ashamed, not even shy about it, just grateful and much closer."

David Gurewitsch's childhood had been scarred by personal tragedy and war. He was born in Switzerland, the second child of Russian Jewish refugees. Three months before his birth, his father drowned in what may have been a suicide. When David was two, his mother deposited him, along with his three-year-old brother, at the home of his grandparents back in Russia and went off to England to study medicine, returning after five long years. When she did reenter his life, his mother was a commanding and judgmental presence. Eleanor, who expressed only love and admiration, was a welcome alternative.

It was natural for Eleanor, at a time when she was deeply engaged in international issues, to be attracted to a man whose life was profoundly shaped by the turmoil of the twentieth century. David had first studied medicine at Freiburg, in Germany. In 1927, fearing rising anti-Semitism, he left Germany for Switzerland, where he finished his medical training. Like many other young Jews in Europe at that time, he was enthralled by the Zionist idea of a Jewish homeland; after he graduated, he settled first in Palestine, before traveling to the United States to continue his training. Eleanor was drawn to David, as she had been to Joe Lash, at a time when his world gave deeper meaning to hers.

Yet in one important way, this relationship was different. Eleanor was now a widow—still full of energy and free to commit herself. She was well aware that David had other women in his life. But some of her letters suggest that she would have liked to have been his one and only. She was deeply hurt when he didn't show up for an evening date, and she scolded him for his tendency to passively go along with women who pursued him. "From all you tell me," she wrote him, "you have always been pursued and I think it is time for you to do the pursuing if any real good is to come to you." She noted that "happy marriages develop when the man shows his desire to the woman and she responds fully and happily." But then she added, "Tho' some physical satisfaction is essential, you must be even surer of mental interests and sympathetic understanding." It would be another ten years before David Gurewitsch decided to remarry. In the interim, and indeed for the rest of her life, Eleanor Roosevelt wrote or called him almost every single day. She kept his photograph on her bedside table, and she insisted that he was "the love of her life."

Eleanor's regular connection to David began at the time of the Geneva conference—a day didn't go by without a letter or a phone conversation. Despite her challenging schedule, Eleanor managed to send him thoughtful gifts: a radio, food, and parts of the manuscript of her new book, *This I Remember*, for his opinion.

The meetings of the Human Rights Commission were being held in the Palais des Nations, a very beautiful building in Geneva constructed after the First World War, when there was hope that a League of Nations could prevent a second conflagration. "At first," Eleanor wrote Gurewitsch, "it seemed sad to me to go into that beautiful building built with love and hope." But she came to feel that it was a good place to meet since it showed that "man's spirit, his striving, is indestructible." She added a question: "Do you think I'm being too optimistic?"

When she entered the historic building for the first time, Eleanor confessed to her State Department colleague, Jim Hendrick, that she would have loved to slide on the marble floors. When the commission, after many days of hard work, finally agreed, on December 10, 1947, on a declaration, Hendrick told her, "Now you can take your slide." Eleanor Roosevelt, chairman of the Commission on Human Rights, took a few running steps, followed by a satisfying slide along the marble floor of the Palais des Nations.

———

"IT REALLY ISN'T NECESSARY for me to go to the [Democratic] Convention" Eleanor told her "My Day" readers in July of 1948. "I can picture it in my mind's eye."

Eleanor was at Hyde Park, hosting her annual picnic for the boys of the Wiltwyck School, when the Democrats convened in Philadelphia to choose their nominee. The Wiltwyck School was just across the river from Val-Kill, and she felt a special bond with the boys there, most of whom were black and who had been sent to the school, a project of the Episcopal Church, because they had gotten in some sort of trouble back in the city. After they consumed hot dogs and prodigious amounts of milk, the boys gathered around her on the floor at Val-Kill to hear her read "Toomai of the Elephants" from Kipling's *Jungle Book*. The boys loved it, she reported, although they had probably never seen an elephant unless they had been lucky enough to go to a zoo.

Eleanor was staying away from the convention—partly, she claimed, because of her position on the Human Rights Commission, but also because she wasn't particularly enthusiastic about the interim president's becoming the likely Democratic nominee. Hick, on the other hand, rather liked Truman. He was familiar to her: a plainspoken midwesterner from the farm who had gone through hard times. Perhaps she also had sympathy for him because he was struggling to get out from under the shadow of the Roosevelts. Hick understood what that was like, after all.

Though she stuck close to home much of the time, Hick decided to join her many Democratic friends in Philadelphia for the convention. Unlike Eleanor, she enjoyed the political maneuvering, the horse trading, the last-minute surprises. And the Democratic convention, in the summer of 1948, had it all. It was the first party convention in American history to take place under the hot glare of television lights. The elite who owned a TV set could watch, in grainy black and white, as a historic civil rights battle played out on the convention floor. The majority civil rights plank made all the right promises, but vaguely. The minority plank laid out specifics: opposition to the poll tax, antilynching legislation, an end to segregation in the armed forces—in short, all the changes Eleanor had been advocating for years. When Hubert Humphrey, then mayor of Minneapolis, presented the minority plank to the convention, urging the Democratic Party to "get out of the shadow of states' rights and walk forthrightly into the bright sunshine of human rights," the great majority of delegates roared their approval. Only the southern Democrats sat on their hands. Later, as Truman was riding north to accept the nomination, delegates from Mississippi and Alabama walked out to protest the civil rights plank.

Though he was the presumptive nominee, Truman had had trouble finding a vice presidential candidate. Supreme Court Justice William O. Douglas turned him down, reportedly saying he didn't want to be the number-two man for a number-two man. Kentucky senator Alben Barkley made a rousing speech at the convention, but he mentioned Truman in it only once and never raised the possibility of a November victory. Both Truman and Eleanor, listening to the speech from different places, concluded that Barkley wanted to be president himself. In the end the Kentuckian agreed to take the vice presidential nomination, tilting the ticket to the South.

The final indignity occurred on the last night of the convention. Truman arrived in Philadelphia at 9:15, spotless in a white linen suit and ready to make his acceptance speech. But the seconding speeches and the balloting lasted for four hours, during which Truman and Barkley sat in stifling rooms waiting. It was nearly 2 a.m. when the pair finally stepped out onto the stage to accept their nominations.

Before they could begin, doves of peace, cooped up all evening in a floral Liberty Bell, were released into Convention Hall and flew all over in a panic, smashing into lights and furniture and people. Truman and Barkley, to their credit, stood on the stage laughing uproariously, especially when a bird landed on Speaker Sam Rayburn's bald head. Once the doves were corralled, Barkley made his acceptance speech. Then, at last, it was time for "the little man from Missouri," still looking fresh in his white suit, to step up to the podium.

Truman's hard-hitting speech delighted Hick and everyone else in the hall. "Senator Barkley and I will win this election," he told the crowd, "don't you forget that." He told farmers and laborers that if they didn't vote Democratic they were "the most ungrateful people in the world," and "don't let anybody tell you anything else." At one point he even lapsed into Missouri-speak: because of the Republican Congress, he said, the labor department "can't hardly function." Indeed, most of the speech was used to chastise the "do-nothing" Congress. "I wonder if they think they can fool the people of the United States with such poppycock!"

Truman had a surprise for Congress: "On the twenty-sixth of July, which out in Missouri we call 'Turnip Day,' I am going to call Congress back." He was going to ask them to pass laws to support the long list of promises in the platform—promises of better housing, aid to education, medical care, and civil rights that the Republican Congress had blocked in the past. "They can do this job in fifteen days, if they want to do it," he proclaimed.

"Gosh, my hat is off to the boy!" Hick wrote her journalist friend Bess Furman. "After all the throat-cutting, abuse, hysteria . . . for him to be able to make a speech like that. Wow!"

There had been many times, Hick told her friend, when she wished she were back in the newspaper business. "But never so badly as at the time of the Democratic convention in Philadelphia. What a story!" It surely occurred to her, watching the convention, that she could have covered this story. The Roosevelts were no longer in the White House, and she knew politics as well as or better than anyone else. But at this point her health wouldn't allow her to get back into daily newspaper work, even if she had the courage to start over again.

CHAPTER TWENTY-SIX

THE OPINION OF MANKIND

THAT SEPTEMBER, while Harry Truman was campaigning for the presidency, Eleanor Roosevelt delivered a speech in the grand amphitheater of the Sorbonne before a rapt audience of thousands. She spoke without a script, as usual, but this time in her excellent French, moving easily from the weighty subject of human rights to a light aside about her family. She thought she had reached the limits of human patience, she told them, in bringing up her children, but that was before she became chairman of the Commission on Human Rights!

Even more patience was required at the General Assembly over the coming months. Eleanor's committee insisted on debating the Universal Declaration of Human Rights "exactly as though it was all an entirely new idea," even though the same issues had been debated in Geneva. A grand total of eighty-five repetitive and tedious meetings were devoted to the subject, with the Soviets "telling us what dogs we are" before the document was finally forwarded to the larger Assembly.

Fortunately, David Gurewitsch had joined his new friend in Paris. "In spite of the fact that Mrs. Roosevelt had lots of things to do," he remembered, "there was still time for enjoying just Paris." There were strolls in the Tuileries, visits to the Louvre, and delicious dinners at Left Bank restaurants.

When David had to go back to his practice, Eleanor wrote him that she wanted him to "be on the same side of the ocean. . . . I'm glad you love me. I love you dearly and send you my most devoted thoughts."

Three months later, Eleanor returned to Paris for still more sessions before the final vote on the Universal Declaration of Human Rights. "The work is hard now and high tension," she wrote Hick, "but it is coming to an end." Finally, at 3 a.m. on December 10, 1948, the General Assembly of the United Nations adopted the Declaration. There were forty-eight yeas and eight abstentions, mostly from Soviet bloc countries. Afterward, the entire Assembly rose to give Eleanor a standing ovation.

The Universal Declaration of Human Rights is a carefully worded blueprint for a hoped-for world. The subtext, however, is the real-world experience of World War II, particularly the Holocaust. The Declaration begins by recognizing "the inherent dignity of all members of the human family" as "the foundation of freedom, justice and peace in the world," then goes on to note that "disregard and contempt for human rights have resulted in barbarous acts which have outraged the conscience of mankind." In thirty succinct articles, it addresses both what human rights should be universal—life, liberty, security, equality before the law, privacy, freedom of movement, freedom of expression—but also what is not acceptable to the community of nations: slavery, torture, cruel and inhuman treatment, denial of nationhood, political persecution.

Some doubters suggested that the Declaration meant little, since it was not legally binding on any country. But it has influenced the writing of laws and treaties all over the world since its passage, and is built into the founding documents of many nations. It also buttresses world opinion against those who violate its principles. It was an immensely meaningful accomplishment, and one that Eleanor had achieved using her own skills as a tireless and gifted negotiator. Hick's prediction, that she would find an "active and important" place after FDR died, was coming true.

BOOKS WERE POURING OUT by then about Franklin Roosevelt and the New Deal, and Eleanor's editor at the *Ladies' Home Journal* was eager for her to "get down to the business of writing your book as quickly and as definitively as you can." Bruce Gould, like others before him, suggested that Eleanor might need to "give up" some other activities to get it done. "Tell him I'm doing the best I can," Eleanor instructed Tommy.

It wasn't just a problem of time. It had been easier for Eleanor to write her first book, about her early years, than her second memoir, about her time as the wife of a governor and president; there was much she couldn't tell. For a while, she hired Hick to help her by going through some of the files at Hyde Park, pulling out stories and anecdotes and posing questions. But when she finally sent *This I Remember* off to Gould, he wasn't happy with it. "You have written this too hastily—as though you had written it on a bicycle while pedaling your way to a fire." He told her he wanted her to work on it for three more months, with a collaborator, and didn't promise to publish it even then. Eleanor balked. Gould told her to "sell her book elsewhere if she wouldn't improve it, and her column, too."

It was a parting of the ways he would live to regret. Otis Wiese, the publisher of *McCall's*, was willing to pay $150,000 for the book, sight unseen, along with the monthly question-and-answer column for $3,000 a month, $500 more than Eleanor had been getting from *Ladies' Home Journal*.

When *This I Remember* came out, in November 1949, it was praised for sounding like the Eleanor Roosevelt everyone knew. "It is almost shockingly delightful to read a book which could have been written by absolutely no one else in the world than the great and important figure whose name is signed to it," wrote Elizabeth Janeway in the *New York Times Book Review*. Eleanor Roosevelt was no stylist, Vincent Sheean noted, but what mattered was "the character of the author, and therefore it is from the character of the author that the pervading sense of great beauty arises."

If ever Hick had occasion to resent her dearest friend, this might have been it. Eleanor was being praised—not for writing well, but for writing in her own rather bland but highly recognizable style. Hick, who wrote far more vividly, couldn't manage to sell a thing.

Hick had shown some very justified resentment when she read what

Eleanor had written about her in an early draft. On her first day at the White House, Eleanor wrote, she was interviewed by Lorena Hickok. "Later, I came to realize that in the White House one must not play favorites."

This was an example of Eleanor at her most insensitive. The reference to the interview was one of the few mentions she made of Hick in the draft. What's more, it touched a nerve she should have been well aware of. Hick, the proud newspaperwoman, hated to be seen as only getting ahead because of Eleanor. Eleanor's mention of her reinforced that idea.

Perhaps because it was difficult for her to confront Eleanor, Hick protested in a three-page letter to Tommy. She didn't get the interview because she was "a nice, tame pet reporter." Rather, she got the story because "in those days (pardon an old lady her conceit) I was somebody in my own right. I was just about the top gal reporter in the country." She noted that "being a newspaper reporter was the only thing I ever was really good at.

"God knows," she added, "I've had the conceit taken out of me plenty in the years since."

Above all, Hick was a writer: she believed this about herself, and others believed it too. But she couldn't seem to sell her work. Part of the problem was her loyalty to the Roosevelts: all her pieces about them lacked critical distance. Even in other pieces, the habit of working for a partisan organization sometimes deprived her of her old edge.

A particularly cruel blow came in 1949, when she attempted several chapters of an autobiography. A publisher who read it concluded that it lacked "the breath of life." In fact the autobiography was full of life. But it was the life of an awkward girl who had crushes on other girls and who grew up to be a mannish woman, matching her male colleagues drink for drink. It was a world away from the sedate autobiographical writing of Eleanor, with whom she was linked in everyone's minds. At the very least, the book would have told a different story from Eleanor's. Hick's chapters retain their power even now. But she couldn't get them published in 1949.

Eleanor, responding to Hick's protest about her autobiography, revised her early draft to read, "Both my husband and Louis Howe agreed to this interview because [Lorena Hickok] was the outstanding Associated Press woman reporter and they both had known her and recognized her ability." She added that "we had become warm friends and I felt that she would always be fair and truthful." Then she ended the passage with a detail Hick had provided: the two of them were interrupted so often that they finally retreated to the bathroom.

The positive response to *This I Remember* was part of a general softening of the public attitude toward Eleanor Roosevelt. The *New Yorker* had already begun the process with a two-part profile entitled "The Years Alone," which emphasized her lifelong mantra: "Engagements must be kept." *New Yorker* writer E. J. Kahn told of a time the previous winter when she was supposed to travel to Poughkeepsie from Val-Kill for a radio broadcast and was snowed in. The radio producer offered to send a sleigh, but Eleanor insisted she didn't want to put him to so much trouble. She would find a way. She set out on foot through deep snow to reach the main road, two miles away, then hitched a ride from there to Poughkeepsie. After the broadcast, she was driven back to her jumping-off place. The return walk was easier, she explained, because she could follow the tracks she had made on the way out. She was sixty-three years old.

Increasingly, Eleanor showed her more relaxed and even playful side to the public. She engaged in conversations on ABC radio with Anna and hosted a Sunday afternoon television program, produced by Elliott, on which famous people came to tea. The programs were meant to help Anna get out of the debt she had built up in her failed attempt to start a newspaper, and to help Elliott develop his career. Unfortunately, neither of the programs succeeded in finding a permanent sponsor. Nor did a subsequent radio program, in which Elliott touted certain products, like soap and hairbrushes, as the ones "Mother uses." That show proved, according to *Billboard*, that "a boy's best friend is his mother." Eleanor made light of such criticism. She insisted she had enjoyed it.

Over the years, Eleanor would agree to go on both serious and frivolous TV shows—everything from *What's My Line?* to *Meet the Press* to Edward R. Murrow's *Person to Person.* She charmed a Tanglewood Music Festival audience with her reading of *Peter and the Wolf*. The critic Howard Taubman praised her "unaffected approach" and her "personal relish." "She sounded like a grandmother," he wrote, "reading a pleasant little story to her grandchildren."

Among those who were decidedly not charmed by Eleanor was Francis Joseph Cardinal Spellman. The cardinal was outraged by a "My Day" column Eleanor wrote in June 1949, responding to a request from the church for federal aid to Catholic schools. "The separation of church and state is extremely important to any of us who hold to the original traditions of our nation," she wrote. Catholic schools should not receive "tax funds of any kind."

Spellman's response astonished even good Catholics. "Your record of anti-Catholicism stands for all to see," he wrote in an open letter, "a record which you yourself wrote in the pages of history . . . documents of discrimination unworthy of an American mother!"

Eleanor suspected that there was a subtext. Her earlier alliance with the Communist-influenced youth movement, her sympathy for the Loyalists in Spain, her active opposition in the UN to the Franco regime—all no doubt contributed to the cardinal's outburst.

Her response to the cardinal was calm and masterful. She denied any anti-Catholic feeling, but insisted that spiritual and secular leadership should not intrude upon each other. "I assure you that I had no sense of being 'an unworthy American mother.' The final judgment, my dear Cardinal Spellman, of the worthiness of all human beings is in the hands of God."

Thousands of letters of support poured in to Val-Kill. Archibald MacLeish contributed a poem that began, "Have you forgotten, Prince of Rome / Delighted with your Roman title / Have you forgotten that at home / We have no princes?"

In the end, Cardinal Spellman was prevailed upon by others, probably including the Vatican, to backtrack. He called Eleanor and exchanged cordial words with her. Then a monsignor paid Eleanor a visit at Val-Kill to work out two conciliatory statements—one by the cardinal and one by

Eleanor. The cardinal's, while not mentioning Mrs. Roosevelt, referred to "the great confusion and regrettable misunderstandings."

It might have been the end of the story. But there was to be one last, rather astonishing chapter—described matter-of-factly in "My Day."

"The other afternoon," Eleanor wrote, "as I was signing my mail, with side glances out of my window . . . Miss Thompson came to my desk, looking somewhat breathless and said: 'Mrs. Roosevelt, Cardinal Spellman is on the porch and he wants to see you!'"

It turned out that the cardinal was in the neighborhood, dedicating a chapel in Peekskill, and stopped by for what turned out to be a "pleasant chat."

"I hope the country proved as much of a tonic for him as it always is for me," Eleanor wrote politely. Then she went on to discuss a letter she had received from a twelve-year-old.

At the height of the Spellman controversy, Eleanor told President Truman that she would willingly resign her UN post if he thought her reappointment would be divisive. Truman replied immediately that she was needed in the UN more than ever. With Truman's encouragement, Eleanor came to be what he called the "First Lady of the World." During the four years after he was elected, she traveled not only all over Europe but also, following the sixth UN General Assembly in Paris at the end of 1951, to Lebanon, Syria, Jordan, Palestine, Israel, Pakistan, and India. When she could, she brought David Gurewitsch along with her.

For David and Eleanor, the high point of their journeys may well have been the moment of their meeting in Israel. Eleanor visited the Arab countries on her itinerary without David: she was advised that as a Jew he would have been unwelcome. But he was waiting at the Mandelbaum Gate when she crossed over into Israel from Jordan. "It was an emotional moment for Mrs. Roosevelt," David wrote in his journal. "She had fought for Partition and was intensely and passionately pro-Israel." It had been seventeen years since David had lived in what was then Palestine. "It certainly was an emotional moment for me."

After Israel, Eleanor and Gurewitsch traveled on to Pakistan and then

India, where Eleanor used her experience with rebellious American youth to quell an angry crowd. She was in Allahabad, where she was to pay a visit to Prime Minister Jawaharlal Nehru and receive an honorary degree from Allahabad University. But then she discovered that the students had written an open letter of protest: Eleanor Roosevelt, an American imperialist, was not welcome! Timid officials wanted to cancel her appearance to prevent a scene. Eleanor would have none of it. She insisted on meeting with the protesters.

Madame Pandit, Nehru's sister and India's ambassador to the UN, had accompanied Eleanor to Allahabad. She was outraged. But Eleanor insisted that it didn't bother her. She had been through it all before with the Youth Congress back in the States, where she was sometimes "booed for five minutes." At her insistence, some of the students were allowed into the Nehru compound for a conversation. But many more were still shouting their protests from the other side of a tall fence surrounding the residence.

Madame Pandit, a courageous woman in her own right, went out and climbed first onto a table, and then onto a chair on top of the table, to speak to the angry crowd over the fence. To no avail. Finally, Eleanor came out herself and climbed up on the top of the table and chair. The students demanded she come back to meet with them at the student hall. She agreed, but would not let guards or even David accompany her. No one else should be endangered.

Back at the students' hall, Eleanor spoke briefly, then answered questions about America's treatment of Negroes, policy toward Red China, and attitude toward India's nonalignment. The meeting ended peacefully.

Eleanor's triumph in India was to be one of her last in an official role, representing the United States government. By 1952, Truman's popularity had plummeted—partly because of the bloody and unending war in Korea and partly because of congressional investigations that implicated some members of his administration. He decided not to run again. In his place, the Democrats nominated a very different kind of candidate: Adlai Stevenson. Stevenson was a Princeton-educated lawyer from a privileged Illinois family with deep Democratic roots—a family not unlike Franklin

Roosevelt's. He had been a delegate to the UN in 1946 and 1947, before he became governor of Illinois. Eleanor was an enthusiastic supporter. She believed he was a far better candidate than his Republican opponent, the popular World War II general Dwight David Eisenhower.

"I think on Election Day," she wrote in "My Day," "the votes will be cast for the man who really clarifies the issues and discusses them— Governor Stevenson—and not for the man who makes wild promises."

Republicans attacked the Truman administration's failures to address "Korea, Communism, and Corruption," including evidence that a large number of IRS employees had accepted bribes. But for the most part, the Eisenhower campaign relied on Eisenhower's popularity more than the issues. "I Like Ike" became the prevailing slogan.

Eisenhower won a landslide victory over Stevenson in 1952. Some hoped the new president might send Eleanor back to her position at the UN. But Eisenhower was not an admirer of Eleanor Roosevelt. There were perhaps too many substantive differences between them; it was also said that Eisenhower believed Eleanor had gossiped about his private life, though this would have been uncharacteristic. Whatever the reason, Eisenhower did not reappoint Eleanor to her post at the UN. At age sixty-eight, she was going to have to look for a new way to be "useful."

WHEN CONGRESSWOMAN MARY NORTON retired in 1950, at age seventy-five, she asked Hick to collaborate with her on her life story. Norton had served in Congress for twenty-six years—longer than any other woman to date. Nannine Joseph, who was Hick's literary agent as well as Eleanor's, predicted that her book would be a "big seller."

"Thanks for helping me write 'my baby,'" Norton wrote Hick after nearly a year of work on the book. "I know there were times when you felt like I did and wanted to throw it into the Potomac, but maybe when the baby grows up we will be proud of it."

When the "baby" went out into the world, however, there were no takers. Editors thought it was too heavy on issues and too light on personal anecdotes. Mary was disappointed but philosophical: she still had her health and sense of humor, she wrote Hick. "A big part of my disappointment has been on your account. I'm coming to believe that an author's life is a tough one. It's like a lottery."

Norton had been one of Hick's warmest supporters through all her personal and professional ups and downs. She told Hick she was one of the "grandest women" she had ever known. Hick, for her part, told friends she felt closer to Mary than she had to her own mother. When Hick was struggling, Mary prayed for her. As Hick's health deteriorated, she even asked the Benedictine Fathers to pray for her.

Hick had a part-time job working for the New York State Democratic Committee until 1950. After that, her occasional article sales were barely enough to keep food on the table, buy coal for heat, and pay her rent at the Little House. Eleanor's $100 checks, which arrived at Christmas, on her birthday, and even sometimes at Easter, were one of her few reliable sources of income.

In the summer of 1952, Eleanor threw out a lifeline. Harper Publishing wanted Eleanor to write a book about women in politics, but she didn't have the time. If Hick would do it, she would help, and "both our names can go on as co-authors." Eleanor would write some parts and go over all of it. "They'll give you an advance."

Hick jumped at the chance. It was a natural fit for her: she'd be writing about women she already knew and admired: Molly Dewson, Helen Gahagan Douglas, Mary Norton, Gladys Tillett, and, of course, Eleanor herself.

The advance on what would be called *Ladies of Courage* gave Hick a chance to stay a while longer at the Little House. She sent chapters to Eleanor as she wrote them, and Eleanor wrote back full of praise: they were "simply swell" and "much more interesting than I thought it could possibly be made."

But the book wasn't getting finished. Hick's health problems were slowing her down: she had dizzy spells and eye hemorrhages that temporarily impaired her vision. In July 1954, she had to ask Eleanor to send her $50 a month for the next three months. She had a second book project by then, thanks to another Eleanor connection: an immigrant Italian named Joseph Cucolo, whose company built the Tappan Zee Bridge, hired Hick to write the story of his life. "He seems happy . . . so don't tell him about your troubles," Eleanor advised. "Bless you and I'm sorry dear."

In May 1955, when *Ladies of Courage* was still not done, Eleanor asked delicately, "How nearly are you making the end of the book?" Eleanor was beginning to realize that Hick wasn't going to be able to earn a living from one or even two books, at the pace she was going. She suggested that Hick might want to "turn out lurid short stories for money to live on." She could "do them fast and write the books slowly."

The situation at the Little House had reached a crisis point. Hick was months behind on her rent, and Ella Dana was under financial pressure herself. So when a family Dana was fond of came to her looking for a place, she asked Hick to leave. Eleanor was in Colorado, visiting Elliott and his new wife on his ranch, when she got an SOS, probably from Ella, informing her that Hick was no longer welcome at the Little House. Eleanor immediately arranged for her chauffeur, Archy "Tubby" Curnan, to come for Hick. It had been almost twenty-five years since Hick had fallen in love with the beautiful woods, the nearby ocean, and the house itself. It was the only home she had ever cared deeply about. But in August 1955, she packed up her things and her little dog Muffin—Mr. Choate was no longer—climbed into Tubby's car, and left forever. "I will think of you," Eleanor wrote her from Colorado, "for I know it's a wrench."

ELEANOR SUFFERED painful losses of her own that year. Tommy, her beloved secretary and alter ego of twenty-nine years, died of a heart attack. She was one of the people, Eleanor wrote afterward, "who remain with you in your daily life, even though they are no longer physically present, who are frequently in your mind . . . part of your laughter, part of your joy. . . .

They are the people from whom you are never quite separated." Tommy, who was only sixty when she died, had been both an honest critic and unabashed admirer, always willing to work at Eleanor's consuming pace. There would soon be a new chief secretary, Maureen Corr, but no one was going to be able to take Tommy's place.

Tommy's death, sad as it was, was not nearly as difficult as the continuing problems Eleanor faced with her children. Anna's marriage to John Boettiger, which had seemed so strong for many years, fell apart after the two of them tried and failed in a newspaper endeavor, incurring worrisome debt. John succumbed to depression and committed suicide in 1950. Eleanor had been especially fond of John and had supported his courtship of Anna, even when she was married to Curtis Dall. She had encouraged the newspaper venture as well and watched in dismay as John retreated into a shell when it didn't work out. She blamed herself for not taking his depression more seriously.

There were painful family quarrels as well. In 1952, after his brother John and family moved into the original stone cottage at Val-Kill, Elliott sold Top Cottage without giving his mother any warning and left. Elliott was in his fourth marriage by then. (There would be a fifth.) Also, in 1954, James's marriage, to the woman who had nursed him at the Mayo Clinic, ended in a very public way, with California scandal sheets detailing his extramarital affairs.

Two of the four Roosevelt sons had some success in politics: Franklin Jr. became a congressman from New York City in 1949, and James, despite his marital woes, won a congressional seat from California in 1954 and served for the next ten years. But their public success didn't seem to carry over into contented private lives. Eleanor confided in Gurewitsch one day, after her sons turned on her in anger, that she sometimes wished she were dead. "My children would be much better off if I were not alive," she told him. "I'm overshadowing them."

Eleanor's greatest consolation and joy in these last years came from her continuing relationship with Gurewitsch. "I love you as . . . I have never loved anyone else," she wrote on his birthday in 1956. David was in ro-

mantic turmoil during those years—separated from his wife and pursuing, for a time, the mercurial Martha Gellhorn, whom he had met through
Eleanor. Disillusioned with the United States, Gellhorn had settled in
Mexico, where David visited her as often as possible over the two-year
period of the relationship. Eleanor had understood from the beginning
that he would eventually find a long-term partner closer to his own age.
"I'm going to cling to you very closely dear," she wrote, ". . . until you have
someone of your own to cling [to] even more closely."

CHAPTER TWENTY-SEVEN

A NEW WAY
TO BE USEFUL

AROUND THE TIME OF Eisenhower's inauguration, Eleanor Roosevelt walked into the offices of the American Association of the United Nations and asked the director, Clark Eichelberger, if he could use "an educational volunteer." Eichelberger was so surprised and delighted at the offer that he "practically fell on the floor."

The UN was under assault. Senators Joseph McCarthy and Pat McCarran regularly attacked it as a Communist hotbed. Ohio senator John Bricker was gaining support for an amendment aimed at limiting the role of the United States in international affairs, and "Get the U.S. out of the UN and the UN out of the U.S." was a popular slogan in right-wing circles. Eleanor's offer to work for the AAUN came at a critical moment.

She was soon installed in a modest office, where she applied strategies familiar from her work with Molly Dewson in the Women's Division of the Democratic Party, organizing chapters around the country to promote the goals of the United Nations. Before long, she set out on the first of several lengthy tours of the world—beginning with a visit to Japan, then making the long journey westward to Yugoslavia, with stops in Hong Kong, India, and Athens, where Gurewitsch joined her.

The trip ended with a visit to Marshal Tito at his vacation home on the island of Brioni in the Adriatic. Tito succeeded in captivating Eleanor. He was "youthful," but with "deep lines of experience in his strongly molded face." As he showed her around his private vineyard, she observed in him "the kind of buoyancy that comes from courage, the sort of courage I saw my husband and Winston Churchill show during the most trying times of World War II." It helped that Tito seemed to be a supporter of his young wife's efforts to go back to school and complete the education that had been interrupted by war. Not surprisingly, Eleanor came away from the encounter believing in Yugoslavia's independence and promise.

Even though she had spent many hours in negotiation with the Soviets in the UN, she had never before visited a Communist nation. Yugoslavia, she noted, was definitely a Communist country, but not a Soviet Communist country—or so its leader, Marshal Tito, convinced her.

Such sentiments were controversial in 1953, when anti-Communist hysteria reigned at home. But she insisted, in defiance of McCarthy and his witch hunts, that she should be able to "sit down with anyone who may have a new idea and not be afraid of contamination by association."

Westbrook Pegler, the columnist who had made a career of attacking Eleanor, wrote that "the time has come to snatch this wily old conspirator before Joe McCarthy's committee and chew her out." Eleanor noted that she had never been called to testify, but would be "very glad to do so." McCarthy knew better than to take her on.

HICK, WHO WAS USED to her quiet existence at the Little House on Long Island, was ill-prepared for life at Val-Kill when Eleanor's driver deposited her there in August 1955. When Eleanor was there, she received a steady stream of visitors, and some of them didn't welcome Hick's presence. Hick had a way of signaling her special relationship with Eleanor—calling her "darling" in front of strangers, and expressing her strong opinions on whatever subject was at hand. On one occasion, when Joe Lash came to dinner, Eleanor actually asked Hick to leave—an event Lash recorded triumphantly in his diary.

John Roosevelt's daughter Nina remembers Hick as "a massive presence," with a cigarette hanging out of her mouth in unladylike fashion. She sometimes wore sleeveless T-shirts and baggy pants, and she had rough hairs on her chin. But once you got past that, there was the possibility of a genuine connection. "She didn't talk down to you," Eleanor's oldest granddaughter, Eleanor Seagraves, remembered.

"You also saw kindness," Nina recalled, and a special tolerance for the grandchildren's rebelliousness. Nina worked at the Hyde Park Playhouse one summer when Gore Vidal was in charge. Her father, John, the Republican among the Roosevelt sons, heartily disapproved of her working with Vidal, who was known to be homosexual. But Nina, who was probably fifteen at the time, loved the whole scene—including her bit part as a prostitute in *The Matchmaker* and the socializing after shows at a local bar. Hick saw Nina at the bar ordering Brandy Alexanders on several occasions but told no one. "Hick covered for me," Nina remembered.

After the first year, Hick moved from Val-Kill to the Lakeview Motor Court up the road—a motel unit, in log cabin style, with a kitchenette and a porch looking over a small, reedy lake. Granddaughter Eleanor remembered driving up a steep hill, "like going up the side of a rock," to visit Hick there.

Since Hick had sold her car and relinquished her license when she left Long Island, a motel cabin perched on top of a rock seems like it would have been a dreadful choice. Yet she was happier there than she had been in years. She liked being near Eleanor, she confessed to an old friend. But even more important, she had figured out a way, at last, to make a living as a writer. It turned out that she had a knack for writing what Nannine Joseph called "juveniles," chapter books for grade school children. She had already turned out one about FDR's boyhood, and was starting on another about Helen Keller and her teacher Anne Sullivan. Hick had misgivings about the project at first, as she confided to Helen Douglas. "In my innocence I didn't think there was enough drama in Helen Keller's life to interest a child. . . . I'd thought of her vaguely as a combination of trained seal and do-gooder.

"Was I ever wrong!" She told Douglas she had never in her life met a human being who had quite the effect on her that Helen Keller did, and was enjoying the writing of the book "more than I've enjoyed any writing I've done in years—if ever." She hoped she could capture enough of "the real Helen Keller" to captivate "an eight-year-old who would much rather look at TV than read a book!"

The book couldn't have happened without Eleanor: it was she who persuaded a usually reluctant Keller to meet with Hick. But Hick brought her own storytelling talents and personal experience to bear: she understood something of Keller's girlhood rage and frustration. She used her skills as a reporter to help the reader grasp Sullivan's complex, ingenious methods for bringing young Helen out of her cocoon. The little book, first published in 1958 by Grosset & Dunlap, went into numerous printings and sold many thousands of copies.

IN 1956, the conservative Scripps-Howard chain of papers tired of Eleanor's liberal agenda and discontinued her "My Day" column. Her readership shrank, and her income from the column went from $28,000 to less than $10,000. But a new opportunity came along when the *New York Post* took over the column from the *World-Telegram*. The *Post*'s liberal publisher, Dorothy Schiff, offered to send Eleanor on an investigative trip to Russia. It was a trip Eleanor had been eager to make for years—all the more appealing now because she could travel there with her favorite companion, David, whose Russian would help to keep the interpreters honest. Ever since FDR had died, she had hoped to "write as a newspaper woman." The 1957 trip to the Soviet Union was the best opportunity she had to do that. Though she was now seventy-two years old, she was eager to take it on.

More than anything else, Eleanor wanted to meet with Premier Nikita Khrushchev, the survivor in the power struggle following the death of

Stalin. She knew from her UN experience with the Soviets that all power resided at the top. As soon as she arrived in Moscow, she requested an interview with Khrushchev. But the Russians kept her in suspense for almost the entire month of her visit. Finally, three days before she was to leave, she learned that Khrushchev was now willing to meet with her at his vacation home on the Black Sea. It meant a thousand-mile trip, by car and plane, to Yalta, and it might cause her to miss her flight home. But she took the chance.

There was a kind of poetic justice in the interview's taking place at Yalta. Eleanor had wanted to go there the first time around, when FDR, Churchill, and Stalin had met to map out Europe's future; she had felt hurt and left out when FDR had asked Anna to go with him instead. Now she had a chance to play an influential role of her own in a new postwar world—a world in which hope had been replaced by suspicion. The Soviets had acquired the atom bomb in 1949, changing forever the stakes of conflict.

Before the interview, Eleanor managed to tour briefly the palace where the Yalta Conference took place. Then she and David were chauffeured to Khrushchev's dacha. He greeted them in a white smocked peasant shirt and proudly escorted them around the place, which looked down over the city of Yalta. It was especially beautiful at night, he told Eleanor, when the lights came on. They settled down to conversation across a wide table on his porch.

Eleanor's questions to Khrushchev concerned the ways in which the Yalta agreement had been betrayed: the postwar arms buildup in particular, and Russia's refusal to allow arms inspections. She asked too about censorship and Soviet refusal to allow Jews to leave the country. David recorded the session and made sure the translation was accurate. They talked for two and a half hours. As Eleanor rushed off to catch her plane, Khrushchev asked her, "Can I tell our papers that we have had a friendly conversation?"

"You can say," Eleanor replied, "that we have had a friendly conversation but that we differ."

Eleanor saw Khrushchev twice more on his visits to the United States. The first time, he was in too much of a rush to do anything but place a wreath on FDR's grave at Hyde Park and grab a seed roll from the Val-Kill kitchen "for the road."

On his second visit, in 1960, he put on an outrageous show at the United Nations, insulting Secretary-General Dag Hammarskjöld and pounding his shoe on the desk. Afterward, much to the dismay of some critics, Eleanor invited him to her New York apartment for tea. She pointed out that "we have to face the fact that either all of us are going to die together or we are going to learn to live together and if we are to live together we have to talk." She also insisted that it was the correct thing to do. After all, he'd gotten nothing to eat when he last visited Hyde Park. It was simply good manners to ask him back for tea.

EVEN BEFORE THE TRIP to the Soviet Union, David Gurewitsch had begun the serious relationship with a younger woman that Eleanor both expected and feared. She was Edna Perkel, a petite and pretty young art dealer. According to Eleanor's secretary, Maureen Corr, Eleanor's face turned ashen when she learned that David was planning to marry Edna. She feared her relationship with him was over.

Not long after, Eleanor and Edna shared a strained lunch. As Edna left, Eleanor said, vehemently, "Don't worry. David will give you *everything* you want!" Edna made no response, "other than a strangled goodbye."

After that, Eleanor adjusted with astonishing speed to the new reality. In February 1958, Edna and David were married in Eleanor Roosevelt's apartment. A year after they married, the Gurewitsches bought a town house with Eleanor on the Upper East Side of Manhattan. The Gurewitsches and Eleanor kept separate apartments, but they often dined and did things together when Eleanor was in town. Eleanor and Edna came to love one another.

Thus Eleanor spent the last years of her life in a relationship that was, like so many before it, triangular. Though her parents were estranged, she

spent her childhood dreaming of a life with her father, even imagining
that she might play the role of mother to her siblings. She was often the
third wheel in her own marriage as well, since her mother-in-law held
sway over the household, and often over her son Franklin. Later, when she
teamed up with Nancy Cook and Marion Dickerman, she was once again
the outsider, even though the trio worked closely together. She had been
intensely involved in Joe Lash's search for happiness and embraced Trude,
just as she now welcomed Edna with increasing warmth. Hick may well
have been the only one of Eleanor's deep attachments who loved her above
all others.

"I WAS DELIGHTED to hear from Nannine," Eleanor wrote Hick in January 1957, "of a further payment for you. Keep going. You're doing well!"

She added a postscript: "I'm waiting for your outburst of fury."

Hick didn't like it when Eleanor condescended to her. But she *was*
doing well—so much better than she had been when Tubby had rescued
her from the Little House two years before. She had moved by now out of
the Lakeview Motor Court into a small apartment in town, in what had
been the Episcopal rectory but was now divided into four living units.
The apartment had a peculiar layout: the front entrance was through the
kitchen. But she had a very pleasing view from her front door, which
looked out on a green lawn sloping down toward the Hudson.

That October, after receiving a surprisingly large royalty check, Hick
wrote Nannine Joseph an exuberant letter. "Thanks for the check. It's
wonderful. I keep pinching myself!"

She had been "way over my head, in deep water," back in 1955. "In a
situation like that, you flail out with your arms and *try* to swim, or go
down for the third—and last—time. And I never could have done it anyway without you and Mrs. R. My successes may be modest, but—I'm still
afloat. And things are gradually getting better."

In 1960, in one of her last books, *You Learn by Living*, Eleanor surprised
Hick with unexpected praise for her tenacity, in the middle of a chapter

about dealing with adversity. "A case that comes most pressingly to my mind," she wrote, "is that of my friend, Miss Hickok." Eleanor described Hick's career as an AP reporter and investigator for Harry Hopkins. "Always she lived a dynamic life," Eleanor wrote, "surrounded by theatrical and political people, her friends among the celebrities in half a dozen fields, the news of the day a part of the very fabric of her life."

Then the "unexpected," the "unforeseen," forced her to adjust. She developed "crippling arthritis" and diabetes that affected her eyes. "How was she going to live in the future?"

Hick "moved to a little cabin of her own and plunged into the writing of children's books." She could work only an hour at a time because of her eyes. She couldn't read newspapers, which would have once seemed like "death itself."

Hick "took her limitations in stride," Eleanor wrote. By listening to the radio "she has become much better informed on the news . . . than most people. . . . She has taken what seemed to be a disaster, made her difficult adjustment, and created a new life, among new people, doing new work. . . . She had the courage to meet discouragement and turn defeat into a victory."

Hick was more worried about Eleanor than herself by then. Other people, who saw Eleanor traveling and speaking all over the world, insisted she was still "her old vigorous, alert, interested self." But Hick's long friendship and deep understanding of Eleanor made her believe differently. "She is by no means as well as she pretends to be, and her doctor worries about her all the time," Hick wrote Helen Douglas in December 1961. When Eleanor had been in the hospital in the fall for a checkup, she was much sicker than most people knew. "At this point I think she is going through the motions, on her nerve."

Six months later, Hick was sounding the same theme to Nannine. "It's as though she were walking away, disappearing over the brow of the hill." By that time, Hick was finally working on a book about her relationship with Eleanor, to be called *Reluctant First Lady.* "The contrast between the Mrs. R in my book and the Mrs. R today—hurts."

DESPITE HER DECLINING HEALTH, Eleanor continued to travel, returning to the Soviet Union and visiting Poland for the first time with David and Edna Gurewitsch. Her granddaughter Nina traveled with her to visit Anna and her third husband, a physician named James Halsted, who was helping to set up a medical school in Iran. Nina reported that her grandmother's fabled energy came and went. She was capable of falling asleep on her feet. "It can be awkward if she's in company," Nina reported. "I keep a very close watch. If I can catch her just as her head is nodding, one tap of the ankle is enough. But once her head reaches her chest, it takes a good old-fashioned shake."

In 1960 Eleanor campaigned hard for Adlai Stevenson to be nominated a third time for the presidency. She had serious doubts about his chief rival for the nomination, John F. Kennedy. She was alarmed that JFK's father, Joe Kennedy, was spending "oodles of money" on the campaign, and she also thought Kennedy had been less than wholehearted in his opposition to McCarthyism. Kennedy, in an effort to win her over, requested a meeting at Val-Kill. When Eleanor agreed, the young Kennedy was suddenly so nervous he insisted on bringing a friend. He told his friend that the meeting, planned for August 14, 1960, felt as momentous as the historic encounter between Czar Alexander and Napoleon on a raft at Tilsit.

Eleanor had suffered yet another personal blow the day before the interview, when John's daughter Sally, aged thirteen, died in a tragic riding accident at a girls' camp in the Adirondacks. Eleanor wrote in her column of "the slim young figure that was so graceful and so quick, such a good swimmer, such a good horsewoman." Kennedy offered to postpone the meeting, but Eleanor told him to come anyway.

Kennedy expected Eleanor to ask him to make Adlai Stevenson his secretary of state in exchange for her support. But she began by assuring him that she thought all presidents should be free to make their own choices. She went on, however, to tell him how much he was going to need Stevenson's support to win.

She concluded from their conversation that Kennedy had matured during the campaign and that he wanted to leave a good record for posterity. "I will be surer of this as time goes on," she reported to her Stevenson allies, "but I think I am not mistaken in feeling he would make a good President if elected."

Eleanor did everything she could from that time on to help John F. Kennedy win the presidency. William Walton, Kennedy's friend who had come along to provide moral support, reported after the lunch meeting that JFK was "absolutely smitten."

Eleanor continued to follow her rule that "engagements must be kept" until very near the end of her life. But starting in 1960, she suffered from persistent anemia, which made her prone to fatigue, frequent infections, and fevers. She kept going with the help of regular blood transfusions.

In January 1961, she attended Kennedy's inauguration in a snowstorm. "I thought the speech magnificent, didn't you?" she wrote Hick afterward. This was the speech in which JFK spoke the memorable line "Ask not what your country can do for you, but what you can do for your country." Eleanor told Hick she read the speech twice. Perhaps it reminded her of FDR's first inaugural, with its own memorable line about "fear itself."

In the summer of 1962, Eleanor kept one last important engagement: the dedication of the Franklin Delano Roosevelt Bridge, an international link between Campobello, in Canada, and Lubec, Maine, in the United States. At Campobello, a high fever made her realize, as she told Trude Lash, how easy it would be to die.

"I think she knew she was going, all summer," Hick wrote later.

On her way back from Campobello with Trude, Eleanor stopped to visit two of her oldest friends, Molly Dewson in Maine and Esther Lape in Connecticut. Then, when she got back to Val-Kill, she called Hick. "If you are going to be at home this afternoon," she said, "I might come over."

It was a beautiful late summer day, so they sat out in Hick's yard under a big maple tree. "That time she stayed more than an hour, and we had a long, quiet, relaxed, intimate talk that I shall always treasure," Hick recalled. It was the last time the two women would be together. But Hick

kept writing letters, reporting on her progress with a new book about Eleanor's friend, labor leader Walter Reuther, and sharing the good news
that her Helen Keller book was a Book of the Month Club selection. Most
of all, she urged Eleanor to listen to her doctors and work hard on her recovery. "Apparently that virus was even worse than you knew, and you'll
simply have to recognize that fact and take it easy for some time—which
you will hate, of course."

By October 1962, Eleanor was back in Columbia Presbyterian in New
York City, insisting to everyone who would listen that she was ready to
die. To a nurse who suggested that she must wait until God was ready
to take her, she muttered, "Utter nonsense." She resisted pills and food. At
one point, when she was semiconscious, she was heard to say, "Let the
ceremony begin."

Eleanor's one wish was to leave the hospital for home. "I am going to
ask David to let me rejoin the human race," she said on October 15. Two
days later, she did return home, accompanied by David, in an ambulette.
It was such a beautiful autumn day that she asked her driver to circle back
through Central Park a second time. She died three weeks later, following
a stroke. She was seventy-eight years old.

Gurewitsch had been the first to suspect the cause of Eleanor's illness—
a cause later confirmed on autopsy. Eleanor had died of complications of
tuberculosis she had been exposed to decades earlier, in 1919. Cortisone
treatments, which were given to counter internal bleeding, probably exac-
erbated old lesions and activated the TB in the bone marrow. The realization of what was happening came too late: tuberculosis had spread all over
her body by that time.

Eleanor Roosevelt's funeral was a grand and historic event. President
Kennedy and his wife flew into town on Air Force One, joining former
presidents Truman and Eisenhower in the Hyde Park rose garden, along
with the chief justice of the Supreme Court, the secretary of state, the
governor of New York, the ambassador to the United Nations, and repre-
sentatives of many countries of the world. Newsreels showed clips of the
"last rites for the First Lady of the World."

"In the death of Eleanor Roosevelt," St. James Episcopal rector Gordon Kidd said, "the world has suffered an irreparable loss. The entire world becomes one family orphaned by her passing."

Hick spent the morning with Ellie Seagraves. Then, because she knew how much Eleanor disliked such ceremonies, she drove to the Catskills to be with her friend Mary Margaret McBride, a popular radio broadcaster who had also loved her dearest friend.

Hick staged her own counter-ritual in the dark of night, with the help of Gordon Kidd. They drove onto the Hyde Park grounds and pulled up as close as possible to the rose garden. Hick, clutching a bouquet of wildflowers like the ones Eleanor loved to gather on her walks at Val-Kill, made her way toward the white marble slab marking the shared resting place of Eleanor and Franklin Roosevelt. But she couldn't walk well enough to make it all the way there, so the Reverend Kidd took her bouquet and added it to the mountain of flowers already piled on top of the grave.

Hick told her friend Helen Douglas she would want to die once Eleanor Roosevelt died. But she lived on for another five and a half years. Each year, on Eleanor Roosevelt's birthday, she visited the grave with her personal tribute to her dearest friend: a single yellow rose.

LIVING ON

"I'M GETTING OUT OF HERE over Christmas," Hick wrote Helen Douglas after Eleanor's death. "Coward. Can't take it." She wound up spending Christmas Eve with Helen and her husband, Melvyn, who were in New York preparing for a Broadway show, and Christmas Day at the home of Esther Lape.

"A year from now," Hick wrote the Douglases after the holiday, "it will be easier for me. These things do grow dim with time. Next year I think I shall be able to go along as usual—the lighted outdoor Christmas tree, the party for all the little [neighborhood] boys and so on. . . . Part of my trouble has been, I think, that I took Mrs. R too much for granted. All the thoughtful, personal, little things she used to do for me. For instance, on New Year's Day, which she usually spent in NY, she always called me, and so, involuntarily, I found myself listening for the telephone to ring that day."

Six months after Eleanor died, Hick told Jeannette Brice, a friend from Minneapolis days, that she was finally beginning to pull herself together. "Grief can be a very debilitating thing, and I haven't had much energy or interest in anything."

She went on to give a grim update on her health at age seventy: diabetes, controlled by insulin, badly crippled by arthritis, blind in one eye from a series of hemorrhages. "But I manage to keep going. And my books, bless 'em, provide me with a fairly good living." By 1963, she was getting as much as $4,000 every six months for the Helen Keller book and was swamped with fan mail from her readers.

Hick kept in touch with Anna Roosevelt (now Halsted) and was pleased that they had finally become friends. She had never had much to do with the Roosevelt sons, nor they with her. "I cannot forget or forgive them for the many, many hurts they inflicted upon her," she wrote Lape after Eleanor died. "It seemed to be my fate, since Tommy went, always to be with her when they hurt her."

Not long before Eleanor became seriously ill, two young families moved into Hick's neighborhood. There were the O'Learys, who had seven boys and one girl, and a Dutch refugee couple, who had six children, slightly older. "All of the boys in the neighborhood are on my payroll," she reported to Helen Douglas, "and they are in and out of the house all of the time. And do I love it?"

Three of the boys, age eleven and twelve, were dog walkers, taking turns a week at a time—"only one gets paid but frequently all three go along." Another was a dog groomer, "very gentle," and another a dogsitter. The smallest, "an adorable little Dutch boy named Tony," insisted on being Hick's leaf raker. "I didn't think he could do it," she wrote, "but I hated to humiliate him by telling him he was too small."

The appearance of the two young families in her life, just as she was losing her great love, seemed almost like a miracle. "I don't know," she wrote Douglas, "maybe there is a God—without the long white whiskers."

Yet Hick sometimes felt "as though I were trapped in a backwater of the Florida Everglades, without even a crocodile for company." Though she enjoyed the children, "I do long for adult conversation."

Hick's letters were her way of conversing. Because of her failing vision, she no longer wrote them in her bold hand. But she could type almost as fast as she thought, and she would often apologize for going on and on. "This letter is much too long," she once wrote. "I hope you haven't tried to read it in one sitting."

Even as she faced her own debilitating ailments, Hick had a habit of obsessing over other people's health problems and dispensing unwanted and dubious medical advice. But her better letters were full of stories and insights. To Helen, she lamented the terrible loss of JFK—"a fine mind, an open mind—what Mrs. R would have called a flexible mind—destroyed in one instant."

FDR, she told Melvyn Douglas, "was just an intelligent, well-informed conservative, aware that changes must be made, trying to keep as much as he could of 'the good old days.'" It was Eleanor, in her opinion, who was the true "small d" democrat.

She liked LBJ, because he had "remarkable political savvy," like FDR. "We never had a President who was worth a damn who did not have it. . . . Some people who worship the memory of Abraham Lincoln forget, if they ever knew—that he spent years and years in the rough-and-tumble of Illinois politics, right down at the dirt level, before he became President." The only problem LBJ had, she noted in November 1964, was "the stench of our foreign policy" in Vietnam.

It got harder for Hick to travel for research, but she kept at it until the very end. She told her editor, Allen Klots, that she was training herself "to work over an aching back as professional singers train themselves to sing over a heavy chest cold." Early in 1968, she hired a car to drive her to a New York City meeting with Walter Reuther.

Klots remembered watching her as she entered the hotel dining room. "Now almost blind, she nevertheless insisted upon making her way independently. It seemed forever, as she moved at a snail's pace with the aid of two canes, each step an expression of the agony she must have felt. . . . And then when she finally came to rest and began to talk through the cigarette smoke, one was reminded of the extraordinary vigor that made her the first-rate journalist she was."

That spring, Hick's doctor told her that circulatory problems in her legs were so severe that he was going to have to amputate at least one of them. After the surgery at Northern Dutchess Hospital in Rhinebeck, north of Hyde Park, her sister Ruby came from Long Island to be with her in what turned out to be her final days.

Lorena Hickok died there on May 1, 1968, from complications of diabetes. She was seventy-five. Hick made it clear in her will that she wanted to be cremated and "to avoid any sort of funeral ceremony." If the St. James rector, Gordon Kidd, who had officiated at Eleanor's huge, public funeral, was available, she would like him "to go to the crematory chapel and say a brief prayer before the cremation takes place." As for the disposal of her ashes, she wrote, "I should like to have them dug into the soil around growing trees, which may benefit from whatever chemicals the ashes contain."

Hick got the first part of her wish: the rector officiated, without anyone else present, at her cremation, not just saying a prayer but conducting the regular Episcopal service. But after that, Lorena Hickok's ashes sat on a shelf at the Dapson Funeral Home until they were buried, after twenty years, in the "unclaimed remains area" at the cemetery in Rhinebeck, ten miles north of the marble slab that marks Eleanor and Franklin's shared grave.

Hick left a three-page will in which she parceled out the things she loved, most of which were gifts from Eleanor. Almost all of her friends and their children got something—silver tea mugs, or pictures, or a poetry anthology she and Eleanor had enjoyed, or napkins and a runner embroidered by Eleanor with Hick's initials. Hick gave Eleanor's niece (Hall's daughter), who was also named Eleanor, the large blue cup she had used for café au lait during her years at the White House. Her most precious possessions, including her little sheepdog Jenny, went to Eleanor Seagraves (Sistie), the Roosevelt grandchild she had felt closest to in her last years. Eleanor Seagraves was a librarian and her husband, Van, a newspaperman, and they had three young children to educate, so Hick gave them the $700 she had left from the $1,000 Eleanor had given her when she died. She also gave Eleanor Seagraves several pieces of furniture, made in the Val-Kill workshop, including her treasured desk, and stipulated that she would receive the royalties from the Helen Keller book.

Many of the reports Hick had written for Harry Hopkins, turned down by publishers back in the 1930s, were finally edited by Richard

Lowitt and Maureen Beasley and published in 1980 under the title *One Third of a Nation: Lorena Hickok Reports on the Great Depression.*

"Unlike the convoluted government documents one is accustomed to," wrote Rhoda Lehrman in the *New Republic,* "Hickok's reports are really letters: persuasive, immediate, fiery, and memorable. The fear and hopelessness of the times are still palpable. The people are still vivid. What Hickok gave to her letters was passion."

Hick's book on Walter Reuther was completed by Jean Gould and published under the names of both Gould and Lorena Hickok in 1972 as *Walter Reuther: Labor's Rugged Individualist.* The *New York Times* called it "a fascinating book for the younger generation, as well as for labor historians."

Hick would have been pleased to know that Eleanor Seagraves has continued to receive royalties from the Helen Keller book, and that they have amounted over the years to $80,000. She would perhaps be even happier to know that Sistie, age eighty-seven at this writing, still sits at her Val-Kill desk.

POSTSCRIPT

PATSY COSTELLO HAS LIVED all of her seventy-five years in the same house on Main Street in Hyde Park, New York. The Roosevelt family saga has permeated her life. Her father served on the local Democratic Committee and her mother was president of the Roosevelt Home Club. As a girl, she was invited to Val-Kill, where Eleanor Roosevelt served her scoops of vanilla ice cream with fresh strawberries. Nowadays Patsy is president of the Hyde Park Historical Society, which mostly concerns itself with the Roosevelt legacy. Books about the Roosevelts and Roosevelt memorabilia fill the rooms of her 165-year-old house, which is also a bed-and-breakfast where the Roosevelt grandchildren sometimes stay.

From her screened-in porch, Patsy can see the apartment where Hick lived in her final years. Eleanor sometimes visited Hick there, and the two of them would sit out under the maple tree in the front yard and talk quietly. When Patsy worked in the local drugstore, Hick came in often to pick up a paper. By that time she had become kind of a town character—a cranky, heavy woman in baggy pants and men's T-shirts. Patsy thought she must be an embarrassment to Mrs. Roosevelt.

Then, thirty-one years after Hick died, a small theater company put on a play by Pat Bond called *Lorena Hickok and Eleanor Roosevelt: A Love Story*. Patsy, interested in all things Roosevelt, went to see it, and came away newly impressed with Hick. It didn't seem right that she had been so completely uncelebrated. Patsy was especially troubled when she learned that Hick's ashes had been dumped in the unclaimed remains area of the Rhinebeck cemetery. She got in touch with the feminist and activist Linda Kavars, whose company, Great Dames, had produced the play. Linda went to work, raising money for a memorial. On May 10, 2000, thirty-two years and nine days after Hick died, Linda Kavars and her partner, Dr. JoAnne Myers, along with Patsy Costello, Eleanor Roosevelt biographer Blanche Wiesen Cook, and a small group of others, staged a simple ceremony in a quiet corner of the Rhinebeck cemetery. Since Hick had wanted her ashes to fertilize a tree, the celebrants planted a dogwood and had a bluestone bench installed nearby. In the shade of the dogwood, there is a brass plaque that reads:

LORENA HICKOK
"Hick"
Mar. 1893   May 1968
East Troy, WI.   Hyde Park, NY
A.P. Reporter
Author
Activist
and
Friend of E.R.

ACKNOWLEDGMENTS

The Roosevelt Library became almost a second home during the years of this project: I always looked forward to my return, and to the warm and helpful staff—especially Virginia Lewick, Matt Hanson, Kirsten Carter, and Bob Clark. I am grateful also to Eleanor Roosevelt Seagraves, Curtis Roosevelt, and Nina Roosevelt Gibson, who provided memories of Hick and of their grandmother. Thanks also to Patsy Costello, Richard Peck, and Edna Gurewitsch, who filled out the story of Hick in her last years.

I am indebted to early readers, including Susan Ware, Michael Lipsky, Nigel Hamilton, Mark Schneider, Anna Wolff, Bob Erwin, and both Peg and Tom Simons. Thanks to fellow researcher Emily Wilson, who enriched my understanding of Val-Kill, to David Blumenthal for his expertise on presidential health, to Gillian Gill for thoughts on English girls' schools, and to Lucy Cleland for help with the book title. Hilary Maddux and Susan Heath's charming house was a haven during many visits to Hyde Park, and Mary Kruser made me feel at home in Minneapolis/St. Paul. I am especially grateful to Mary Jane Coulter and Patty Thomas, who welcomed me to the Scotts Run Museum in Osage, West Virginia, and shared their own memories of mining life. Thanks also to Jeanne Goodman, director of Arthurdale Heritage, Inc., and Vanessa Mulé, AmeriCorps worker and guide, for providing a window into life in the first New Deal homestead community at Arthurdale, West Virginia. My lunch group—Alison Cohen, Kathryn Kirshner, and Evy Megerman—have listened thoughtfully and given me excellent advice. And, once again, I am grateful for the wisdom of my biography group: Joyce Antler, Fran Malino, Megan Marshall, Lois Rudnick, Judith Tick, and Roberta Wollons. I have benefited over many years now from the warm companionship of other women writers at a retreat in Duxbury, Massachusetts—

ACKNOWLEDGMENTS

especially Kathi Aguero, Sally Brady, Ruth Butler, Judith Cohen, Christopher Corkery, Erica Funkhouser, Lydia Nettler, Marnie Mueller, and Judy Richardson. I am grateful as well to my children and their partners, Tom and Irina, Anna and Gretchen, all of whom have provided insights and support along the way. For joy, I thank my grandchildren: Alejandra, Daniel, David, Carolina, and Ecco.

I feel very lucky to have worked on this book with Emily Cunningham, an astute editor who has contributed mightily to improving the final product. Then there is Jill Kneerim. Jill is my agent, but that word doesn't begin to describe how much she means to me as a writer. She has sometimes been a critic, with tough words I didn't want to hear. But she has always also been a friend and a believer. Finally, I must once again thank my husband, Dan Jacobs, who has spent more hours listening, advising, reading, and rereading than anyone else, and whose love and support mean the world to me.

A NOTE ON SOURCES

I have relied most heavily on the archives of the Franklin D. Roosevelt Library in Hyde Park (abbreviated as FDRL in the notes), where I made extensive use of the Hickok papers as well as the papers of Eleanor Roosevelt, Harry Hopkins, Doris Faber, and Anna Roosevelt Halsted. I also used correspondence from the Mary Norton papers at Rutgers University, from the papers of Gladys Avery Tillett in the Southern History Collection of the University of North Carolina, the papers of Helen Gahagan Douglas in the Carl Albert Center at the University of Oklahoma, the Nannine Joseph papers in the University of Oregon archives, and the Dorothy Thompson papers in the Special Collections at Syracuse University. The Library of Congress was the source for Hick's correspondence with Bess Furman and also for the *Democratic Digest*. The Eleanor Roosevelt Papers Project at George Washington University has been invaluable. I am especially grateful for the digital access the project has provided to Eleanor Roosevelt's "My Day" columns.

In addition to the published writings of both Eleanor and Hick, I have depended most on a handful of major works: Blanche Wiesen Cook's two-volume biography of Eleanor Roosevelt has been an important source, as has Doris Kearns Goodwin's *No Ordinary Time*. I have also relied on Joe Lash's very inclusive biographies, especially *Love Eleanor*, *A World of Love*, and *The Years Alone*. I am grateful for the work of Roger Streitmatter, who edited and annotated many of the three-thousand-plus letters between Eleanor and Hick for *Empty Without You*, and for the work of Maurine Beasley and Richard Lowitt, who edited and provided context for Hick's reports in *One Third of a Nation: Lorena Hickok Reports on the Great Depression*.

NOTES

INTRODUCTION

2 "Oh! How I wanted": Eleanor Roosevelt (hereinafter ER) to Lorena Hickok (hereinafter Hick), March 10, 1933, Franklin Delano Roosevelt Library (hereinafter FDRL).

2 "There have been times": Hick to ER, August 8, 1934, FDRL.

3 She was also a reporter: Lorena Hickok, *Reluctant First Lady* (New York: Dodd, Mead & Co., 1962), 67.

3 "This valley is the": Hick to ER, July 3, 1934, in Lorena Hickok, *One Third of a Nation: Lorena Hickok Reports on the Great Depression*, ed. Richard Lowitt and Maurine Beasley (Urbana: University of Illinois Press, 1983), 304.

3 "run the Red Cross!": Hick to ER, October 31, 1933. *One Third*, 61.

3 "I'm back at my worst": ER to Hick, August 9, 1936, FDRL.

5 "How could any reasonably": From "How This Book Came to Be Written," a draft of the material that appeared in the preface, afterword, and "personal note" of Doris Faber, *The Life of Lorena Hickok: E.R.'s Friend* (New York: William Morrow, 1980).

5 "something like a classic state of shock": Ibid., 330-31.

5 "an uncontrollable craving": Ibid., 321.

5 "the Eleanor Roosevelt who emerges": Ibid., 6.

6 "akin to turning over Sappho's poems": "E.R. & Her 'Friend': A Timid Look Back," *Big Mama Rag*, vol. 8, #2, 1980.

6 "pink right down to her underwear": Colleen M. O'Connor, "'Pink Right Down to Her Underwear': Politics: The 1950 Senate Campaign of Richard Nixon Against Helen Douglas Reached an Unequaled Low. Comparison Is Unfair to John Van de Camp," *Los Angeles Times*, April 9, 1990, http://articles.latimes.com/1990-04-09/local/mc-664_1_helen-gahagan-douglas.

CHAPTER ONE: BEGINNING TO TRUST

11 "It's nice to be back": I have chosen not to annotate FDR's public speeches, because they are widely available from many sources.

12 "It seems undignified": ER to Hick, July 27, 1936, FDRL.

12 On her honeymoon: Eleanor Roosevelt, *This Is My Story* (New York: Garden City Publishing Co., 1939), 134.

13 Isabella had been a bridesmaid: Ibid., 124.

14 "Most women," fellow reporter: Walter B. Ragsdale to Hal Faber (Doris Faber's husband), December 13, 1978, Doris Faber papers, FDRL.

14 a red rash tended to develop: Jane Bancroft to Doris Faber, December 8, 1978, Doris Faber papers, FDRL.

15 **didn't trust her:** Hick, *Reluctant First Lady*, 14.

16 **stories of hardship:** Lorena Hickok, "Country Girl in Prison Cell Sobs Warning of City's Lure," October 2, 1921; "Job Hunt Futile, Man Crawls Under Bridge to Await Death," November 14, 1921; "Hurdy Gurdy Man, Already Deep in Despair, Told Wife Is Dying," January 22, 1922, all in *Minneapolis Morning Tribune.*

16 **"Many times, she came back":** Walter B. Ragsdale to Hal Faber, December 13, 1978, Doris Faber papers, FDRL.

17 **"deeply tanned, grim-faced farmers":** Hick, *Reluctant First Lady*, 36.

17 **family secrets she would keep:** Thirty years later, in *Reluctant First Lady*, Hick was still protective. John Boettiger was singled out because he "had become friendly with Anna and Jimmy," she wrote. *Reluctant First Lady*, 38.

17 **"Lorena was as excited":** Walter B. Ragsdale to Hal Faber, December 13, 1978, Doris Faber papers, FDRL.

17 **"I gave as little information":** ER, *This Is My Story*, 314.

19 **FDR's admirable efforts:** Lorena Hickok, "Roosevelt Makes His Farms Pay," AP, April 11, 1932.

19 **Yet it didn't show up:** Hick, *Reluctant First Lady*, 32–33.

19 **"the dame has enormous dignity":** Western Union telegram, n.d., Hickok papers, FDRL, box 14, 15.

19 **"She's all yours now":** Hick, *Reluctant First Lady*, 43.

20 **"good to be middle-aged":** Ibid., 44.

20 **"Most of the time":** Lorena Hickok, AP story datelined Potsdam, NY, sent by teletype, October 30, 1932.

20 **Eleanor operated by complicated rules:** Lorena Hickok, "Roosevelt's Wife Takes State Stump," AP, October 18, 1932.

20 **"If you and I":** Lorena Hickok, AP story datelined Potsdam, NY, sent by teletype, October 27, 1932.

22 **"may have many":** "Ten Rules for Success in Marriage," *Pictorial Review*, December 1931, quoted in Maureen H. Beasley, *Eleanor Roosevelt and the Media: A Public Quest for Self-Fulfillment* (Urbana: University of Illinois Press, 1987), 15.

23 **"I'm longer than you are":** Hick, *Reluctant First Lady*, 49.

23 **"May I write":** Ibid.

CHAPTER TWO: ELEANOR ACCORDING TO HICK

25 **the AP bureau:** The office was at 383 Madison Avenue.

25 **an orgy of baby talk:** Jane Bancroft to Doris Faber, December 8, 1978, Doris Faber papers, FDRL.

25 **The Turtle Bay neighborhood:** *The WPA Guide to New York City* (New York: Random House, 1939).

26 **"Hick batted out":** Gardner Bridge to Doris Faber, November 3 and 9, 1978, Doris Faber papers, FDRL.

27 **"neither Roosevelt nor any":** Gardner Bridge, AP series, November 8, 10, 11, 13, 15, 16, 1932.

27 **"He was grand":** Lorena Hickok, AP, November 18, 1932.

29 **"For the next ten years":** One child died in infancy.

29 **"Sometimes," she told Hick:** Lorena Hickok, AP series, "Never Wanted to Be 'First Lady,'" November 9, 1932; "War Gave Mrs. Roosevelt 'Emancipation and Education,'" November 10, 1932; "Mrs. Roosevelt Is Tireless," November 12, 1932.

30 "liked teaching better": Kenneth S. Davis, *Invincible Summer: An Intimate Portrait of the Roosevelts Based on the Recollections of Marion Dickerman* (New York: Atheneum, 1974), 87.
31 read periodicals instead of textbooks: Ibid., 78.
31 "something almost like a note of hope": Hick, *Reluctant First Lady*, 53–54.
31 "But I'm not the wife": Lorena Hickok, "Wife of Next President Arrives at School to Teach Current Events," AP, November 9, 1932.
32 "When I came in": Hick, *Reluctant First Lady*, 58.
32 "the first person": Lorena Hickok, unpublished autobiography, Hickok papers, FDRL.
32 "one of the most beautiful women": ER, *This Is My Story*, 1.
32 "Attention and admiration": Ibid., 22.
32 looked like a queen: Hick, *Reluctant First Lady*, 52.
33 "I was reminded of a fox": Ibid. 53.

CHAPTER THREE: JE T'AIME ET JE T'ADORE
35 That December, eight thousand: *New York Times*, December 3, 1932.
35 Over a thousand: Ibid., December 4, 1932.
35 When it snowed: Ibid., December 18, 1932.
35 "this Christmas belongs": Ibid., December 25, 1932.
36 "Roosevelt noncommittal in parley": Ibid., November 23, 24, December 21, 1932.
36 "too much respect for myself": Jonathan Alter, *The Defining Moment: FDR's Hundred Days and the Triumph of Hope* (New York: Simon & Schuster, 2006), 147.
36 "high time to begin": *New York Times*, December 17, 1932.
36 "a pleasant man": Alter, *Defining Moment*, 80–81.
37 "Some crackpot in Miami": Hick, *Reluctant First Lady*, 78.
38 "To a man": Alter, *Defining Moment*, 177.
38 "That drive to the hospital": Hick, *Reluctant First Lady*, 82.
38 "I'm not that important": Ibid., 83.
38 "very good friends": Ibid., 61.
38 "je t'aime et je t'adore": ER to Hick, March 6, 1933, FDRL. "Jimmy was near and I couldn't say 'je t'aime et je t'adore' as I longed to do but always remember I am saying it and that I go to sleep thinking of you and repeating our little saying."
39 "I do wish you were here": Blanche Wiesen Cook, *Eleanor Roosevelt*, vol. 1, *1884–1933* (New York: Penguin, 1992), 198.
40 make trouble when she could: Ibid., 220.
41 It may also have aroused: In fact, according to Cook, Lucy Mercer Rutherfurd came to the inauguration in an arranged car and spent some time on that day in the White House with FDR. Cook, *Eleanor Roosevelt*, 1:491–92.
41 Ellie was tiny: Faber, *Life of Lorena Hickok*, 62.
41 "Friends," Hick explained: Lorena Hickok, notes on Ellie for essay "The Most Unforgettable Character I've Met," ca. 1954.
42 gave parties together: Faber, *Life of Lorena Hickok*, 63. Hickok notes.
42 Hick was sent to Smith College: Faber, *Life of Lorena Hickok*, 69–71.
43 "never another word was said about it": Ibid., 79. Notes in Doris Faber papers, FDRL. In her book, Faber uses a pseudonym for Grace Beebe, "Barbara Hanson," but it is clear in the notes that the reporter was Beebe.
43 "A Very Merry Christmas": Christmas card, Hickok papers, FDRL.
43 In December 1932: Lorena Hickok, "Mrs. Roosevelt Borrows Fare to See 4th Grand-

child," AP, November 17, 1932; "Mrs. Roosevelt Walks to Inspect the White House," AP, January 28, 1933; "Roosevelt's Wife Selects Gowns for Inauguration," AP, February 10, 1933.

44 **"Accompanied by her two dogs":** Lorena Hickok, "Wife of Next President to Drive Alone to Capital," AP, February 13, 1933.

44 **Eleanor also brought:** Blanche Wiesen Cook, *Eleanor Roosevelt*, vol. 2, *The Defining Years, 1933–1938* (New York: Penguin, 1999), 13.

45 **"All the sorrow":** Hick, *Reluctant First Lady*, 90–92.

45 **Later that day:** Ibid., 94–96.

46 **"Stepping out of the elevator":** Teletype version of story, March 1933.

47 **Increasingly, however, her name:** *Lowell (MA) Sun*, May 20, 1933; *Gettysburg (PA) Times*, July 6, 1933; *Salamanca (NY) Republican Press*, July 8, 1933; *Olean (NY) Times Herald*, July 26, 1933.

47 **she had "achieved standing":** Ishbel Ross, *Ladies of the Press* (New York: Harper & Brothers, 1936), 204.

47 **"Hick, my dearest":** ER to Hick, March 5, 1933, FDRL.

CHAPTER FOUR: LORENA

49 **"I can still feel":** Amazingly, I found the want ad for this bindery job in the Aberdeen paper when I visited South Dakota. "WANTED—Girls to work in bindery," *Aberdeen (SD) Daily News*, March 14, 1907.

51 **Hick's puppy Mayno:** Hick believes the name derived from the French "mais non."

52 **"A very sad death":** "Sad Indeed," *Bowdle (SD) Pioneer*, September 20, 1906.

57 **"The hands she held out":** Lorena's story, including quotes (unless indicated otherwise), is taken from her incomplete autobiography, written in 1949 but never published. Her outline for the book contained summaries of twelve chapters. She wrote two chapters on her girlhood, a chapter on the Lindbergh baby kidnapping, a chapter on life in the White House, and a final one on the war years. Hickok papers, FDRL.

57 **"Now my dear girlie":** Aunt Ella to Lorena, June 1, 1913, Hickok papers, FDRL.

57 **Edna Ferber, whose novels:** For an insight into the life of a young reporter in Milwaukee, see Ferber's *Dawn O'Hara, the Girl Who Laughed* (New York: Grosset & Dunlap, 1911).

58 **"Being a big hearted":** Lorena Lawrence, "Girls! Here's Your Chance to Get a Husband! Cupid Points the Way, Provided You Qualify," *Milwaukee Sentinel*, November 4, 1915. Hick later claimed her first byline was on a story about Geraldine Farrar, but this one actually preceded it.

58 **soprano Geraldine Farrar. After a muddy:** Lorena Lawrence, "Geraldine Proves She's a Prima Donna," *Milwaukee Sentinel*, November 19, 1915.

58 **"I would die for Melba":** Lorena Lawrence, "Melba Charms Large Audience at the Auditorium, Diva Plants Kiss on Cheek of an Interviewer," *Milwaukee Sentinel*, December 4, 1915.

59 **a whole series of stories:** Lorena A. Hickok, "Wherein Girl Reporter Gets Her First Taste of Sunday Golf," June 11, 1922; "Uninitiated Girl Reporter 'Covers' Coppers Ball Game," September 26, 1922; "Dominoes More Fun, Less Work Than Boxing, Girl Reporter Opines," October 22, 1922; "Gopher Secrets Perfectly Safe When Girl Writer Sees Practice," November 5, 1922, all in *Minneapolis Morning Tribune*.

59 **"Santa, who has been overworking":** Lorena A. Hickok, "Juvenile Unbelievers Quick to Detect Fake Santa Claus," *Minneapolis Morning Tribune*, December 12, 1921.

59 She wrote touchingly: Lorena A. Hickok, "Life of Midget Actors Often Filled with Many Embarrassing Situations," *Minneapolis Morning Tribune*, March 30, 1922.

59 "a lump in my throat": Lorena A. Hickok, "'Men? All Alike,' Jailed Heiress of 15 Declares; Dejected Youngster Details Part in Holdup of Her Mother," *Minneapolis Morning Tribune*, June 4, 1922.

60 a World War I veteran: Lorena A. Hickok, "Leach Asks War Veterans to Aid Needy Comrades," *Minneapolis Morning Tribune*, December 16, 1921.

60 "We dispatched . . . the Invincible": Lorena A. Hickok, "'Red' Grange Carried Home on His Shield," *Minneapolis Morning Tribune*, November 16, 1924.

60 "Even here in enemy country": Lorena A. Hickok, "Calm Prevails at Ann Arbor; Dubious Pep Seems Omen Gophers Will Get Brown Jug," *Minneapolis Morning Tribune*, November 21, 1925.

60 "I guess there's just one more thing": Paul A. Dana, as told to Lorena A. Hickok, Associated Press staff writer, "Drifted 22 Hours with Woman in Sea," *New York Times*, November 15, 1928.

61 Eleanor was roundly criticized: Hick, *Reluctant First Lady*, 66.

61 They even docked her pay: Maurine H. Beasley, *Eleanor Roosevelt: Transformative First Lady* (Lawrence: University Press of Kansas, 2010), 59.

61 "Well, it won't be long now": Hick to Bess Furman, 1932 (n.d. on letter), Furman papers, Library of Congress.

CHAPTER FIVE: ELEANOR

63 "With my father": ER, *This Is My Story*, 6.

63 "intoxicated by the pure joy": Anna Eleanor Roosevelt, ed., *Hunting Big Game in the Eighties: The Letters of Elliott Roosevelt, Sportsman* (New York: Charles Scribner's Sons, 1933), 37.

63 his "pretty, companionable": Ibid., 172.

64 "sink through the floor": ER, *This Is My Story*, 17-18.

65 "We rarely fail": Anna Eleanor Roosevelt, *Hunting Big Game*, 176–77.

65 "got two elephants": Ibid., 119.

65 "my big tiger skin": Ibid., 81.

65 "he and I must keep": ER, *This Is My Story*, 20.

65 "I walked them off their feet": Ibid., 21.

66 "so often said 'no'": Ibid., 46.

66 three strong locks: Geoffrey Ward, *Before the Trumpet: Young Franklin Roosevelt, 1882–1905* (New York: Random House, 1985), 365: "The existence of triple locks on Eleanor's bedroom door was revealed to me by Laura Chanler White, who stayed in the room as a young woman and had their purpose explained to her."

66 "an almost exaggerated idea": ER, *This Is My Story*, 98.

67 "She always knew more": Ibid., 58.

67 the work was "shoddy": Ibid., 62.

67 had an "infectious ardor": Dorothy Strachey Bussy, quoted in Cook, *Eleanor Roosevelt*, 1.105-6

68 "every idea is brought": Ibid., 105.

68 "purity of heart": Ibid., 109–10.

68 "I still remember": ER, *This Is My Story*, 79.

69 "Do you love her?": *Olivia* (London: Hogarth Press, 1949), 47. The author, it was later revealed, was Dorothy Strachey Bussy.

69 "I am glad you liked *Olivia*": Cook, *Eleanor Roosevelt*, 1:120.

69 "There were perhaps": ER, *This Is My Story*, 63.

70 "Young girls have crushes": Cook, *Eleanor Roosevelt*, 1:116.

70 "I really marvel": ER, *This Is My Story*, 67.

70 "We simply fell off": Ibid., 83.

70 "had become one": Ibid., 96.

70 "I miss you": Cook, *Eleanor Roosevelt*, 1:122.

71 felt "deeply ashamed": ER, *This Is My Story*, 100–101.

71 "to go on a real spree": Ibid., 102.

71 "Though I was only nineteen": Ibid., 111.

71 "For ten years": Ibid., 163.

72 "I knew you were": Cook, *Eleanor Roosevelt*, 1:220.

72 "I still lived": ER, *This Is My Story*, 173.

72 "appalled by the independence": Ibid., 206.

72 was "somewhat shocked": Ibid., 181.

72 "All my executive ability": Ibid., 253.

72 "the budding of a life": Ibid., 323.

73 the words "toujours gai": Cook, *Eleanor Roosevelt*, 1:297.

74 "Their interests played": ER, *This Is My Story*, 325.

75 "as much as ever": ER to Marion Dickerman, February 5, 1926, FDRL.

76 a "rough stunt": Eleanor Roosevelt, *This I Remember* (New York: Harper & Brothers, 1949), 31–32.

76 Teapot Dome scandal: The Teapot Dome is a rock formation in Wyoming that looks like a teapot and marks one of the locations of the oil deposits.

76 "whose public service record": Cook, *Eleanor Roosevelt*, 1:352.

77 style for "my missus": Davis, *Invincible Summer*, 35.

77 "from her affectionate Uncle": Davis, *Invincible Summer*, 50.

79 "Hick dearest," she wrote from Maine: ER to Hick, June 23, 1933, FDRL.

CHAPTER SIX: GETAWAY

81 "Poor Hick," Eleanor had written: ER to Hick, June 8, 1933, FDRL. These are the letters that Hick retyped, presumably cutting some parts.

82 "I couldn't bear": ER to Hick, March 11, 1933, FDRL.

82 "Never in all the years": Hick, *Reluctant First Lady*, 156.

83 "Mr. Woollcott is": Eleanor Roosevelt, "My Day," February 27, 1941.

83 "Remember no one": ER to Hick, March 10, 1933, FDRL.

83 "I am so glad": ER to Hick, April 2, 1933, FDRL.

83 "My dear if you meet me": ER to Hick, March 9, 1933, FDRL.

84 "I never talked": ER to Hick, April 8, 1933, FDRL.

84 "Poor kid, blind faith": ER to Hick, April 7, 1933, FDRL.

84 "got on very well": ER to Hick, August 6, 1933, FDRL.

84 "I'm to talk to Betty": ER to Hick, April 5, 1933, FDRL.

84 "I went over everything": ER to Hick, June 1, 1933, FDRL.

85 "My heart aches": ER to Hick, April 12, 1933, FDRL.

85 "I am acutely conscious": ER to Hick, June 1, 1933, FDRL.

85 "a pretty unwise teacher": ER to Hick, May 27, 1933, FDRL.

85 "zest in life": ER to Hick, May 31, 1933, FDRL.

86 **"I must have looked funny"**: Hick, *Reluctant First Lady*, 122.

86 **"try[ing] on all"**: Eleanor Roosevelt, *It's Up to the Women* (New York: Frederick A. Stokes Co., 1933), 45.

86 **a dramatic departure**: Rodger Streitmatter, ed., *Empty Without You: The Intimate Letters of Eleanor Roosevelt and Lorena Hickok* (New York: Free Press, 1998), 27.

86 **just as it had loving women before them**: Susan Ware, *Partner and I: Molly Dewson, Feminism, and New Deal Politics* (New Haven, CT: Yale University Press, 1987). Also, Stephen, the main character in *The Well of Loneliness*, the 1928 novel by Radclyffe Hall, finally finds a measure of self-esteem as an ambulance driver in World War I. Gertrude Stein and Alice B. Toklas traveled together by car, and Stein drove an ambulance in World War I as well.

87 **"It is a word"**: Hick, *Reluctant First Lady*, 128.

88 **"vote for Franklin!"**: Ibid., 130.

88 **"as easily and confidently"**: Ibid. 130.

88 **as a "personal friend"**: *Chautauquan Daily*, July 25, 1933.

88 **"new social order"**: Eleanor Roosevelt at Chatauqua, July 25, 1933.

89 **by looking at the washing**: Hick, *Reluctant First Lady*, 134.

89 **"go around the country"**: John F. Bauman and Thomas H. Coode, *In the Eye of the Great Depression: New Deal Reporters and the Agony of the American People* (DeKalb: Northern Illinois University Press, 1988), 1.

CHAPTER SEVEN: PARTNERSHIP

93 **"bug-infested rags"**: Hick, *Reluctant First Lady*, 136–37.

93 **"I have the sense"**: Hick to ER, Wheeling, WV, n.d., FDRL.

94 **her partner, Nadia Danilevsky**: Cook, *Eleanor Roosevelt*, 2:133. Davis and Danilevsky met in Russia after the Revolution. Davis worked in Russia for the Quakers for eight years.

94 **began to elicit their stories**: "First Lady Leaves After Brief Visit to County," *Morgantown (WV) Post*, August 18, 1933.

95 **"the kind you or I"**: ER, *This I Remember*, 126–27.

95 **She told Eleanor**: *Morgantown Post*, August 18, 1933.

95 **"a swell guy"**: Fred Schroeder, "MRS. ROOSEVELT VISITS MINES HERE, Relief Projects in County Camps Given Attention," *Dominion News* (Morgantown, WV), August 18, 1933. For background on the West Virginia trip: Michael Golay, *America 1933: The Great Depression: Lorena Hickok, Eleanor Roosevelt, and the Shaping of the New Deal* (New York: Free Press, 2013).

95 **"Can you tell me"**: *Morgantown Post*, August 19, 1933.

96 **a freight car**: Ruby Black, *Eleanor Roosevelt: A Biography* (New York: Duell, Sloan & Pearce, 1940), 247.

96 **They thought hundreds**: Hick to ER, August 22, 1933, FDRL.

97 **"You and Eleanor"**: Hick, *Reluctant First Lady*, 140.

98 **"It is Paradise for us"**: ER typed essay, FDRL.

98 **as "our angel"**: Arthurdale was privatized in 1941. It is now a National Historic District, with a museum documenting the history of the first families. One original house is available for touring, but the rest are still in use and well maintained. Scotts Run has its own small museum in Osage, proudly documenting lives of mining families who lived in rare racial harmony.

98 "I seem . . . to have become": Hick to ER, from typed excerpts of a letter written in Philadelphia in August 1933, FDRL.
98 "scenery I've ever beheld": Hick to ER, August 22, 1933, FDRL.
98 "before he was born": Hick to ER, August 25, 1933, FDRL.
98 "makes me sick": Hick to ER, August 23, 1933, FDRL.
99 "35 bushels of pole beans": Hick to ER, August 22, 1933, FDRL.
99 "I talked to you": ER to Hick, August 25, 1933, FDRL.
99 "I am glad": ER to Hick, September 14, 1933, FDRL.
100 "Sorry the report": Hick to Kathryn Godwin, September 23, 1933, FDRL.
100 "It's the first time": Hick to ER, October 10, 1933, FDRL.
100 "Of course the long separation": ER to Hick, December 7, 1933, FDRL.
100 "Hick dearest," she wrote: ER to Hick, December 5, 1933, FDRL.
100 "Floyd Olson really is": Hick to Harry Hopkins, December 12, 1933, FDRL.
101 "a deep blue cloudless sky": Hick to ER, October 31, 1933, in Hick, *One Third of a Nation*, 59–60.
101 "keep them from starving": Ibid.
101 She wrote of two small boys: Ibid.
101 "flat brown country": Hick report to Hopkins, November 9, 1933, Hick, *One Third of a Nation*, 84–85.
101 The stories poured out: Hick to ER, November 11 and 12, 1933, ibid., 91.
101 "What a picture": ER to Hick, November 14, 1933, FDRL.
102 "from doing it!": ER to Hick, November 27, 1933, FDRL.
102 "I knew it wouldn't": ER to Hick, December 1, 1933, FDRL.
102 "Darling," Eleanor wrote: ER to Hick, November 28, 1933, FDRL.
102 "Good night, dear one!": Hick to ER, December 5, 1933, FDRL.
102 "Dear one," Eleanor wrote four: ER to Hick, December 9, 1933, FDRL.
103 "I know I'm not up to you": ER to Hick, December 23, 1933, FDRL.
103 "Dearest one bless you": ER to Hick, December 25, 1933, FDRL.
103 "Franklin said I could ask": ER to Hick, December 25, 1933, FDRL.

CHAPTER EIGHT: LA PRESIDENTA AND THE NEWSHAWK

105 "I want you to get this": Emma Bugbee, "Crowds Follow Mrs. Roosevelt in Island Slums," *New York Herald Tribune*, March 10, 1934.
105 "Photographs don't give": Hick, *One Third of a Nation*, 200.
106 "I cannot crawl": Emma Bugbee, "Mrs. Roosevelt Routs Escorts in Puerto Rico," *New York Herald Tribune*, March 9, 1934.
106 "only a crying baby": Emma Bugbee, "Mrs. Roosevelt Finds Life Busy in Mountains of Puerto Rico," *New York Herald Tribune*, March 12, 1934.
107 "a flowered chiffon with a spray": Emma Bugbee, "Reception Ends Mrs. Roosevelt's 300-Mile Day," *New York Herald Tribune*, March 13, 1934.
107 "Puerto Rico's greatest oppressor": "Liberals Oppose Welcome," *New York Herald Tribune*, March 12, 1934.
107 "You can't fool Mrs. Roosevelt": Emma Bugbee, "Mrs. Roosevelt Shops, Reviews Troops," *New York Herald Tribune*, March 14, 1934.
107 "I can never be": Hick to Bess Furman, n.d. but June 26, 1930, Furman papers, Library of Congress.
108 attended them "incense-burners": Maurine H. Beasley, *Eleanor Roosevelt and the*

Media: A Public Quest for Self-Fulfillment (Champaign: University of Illinois Press, 1987), 47.

108 "These things happened naturally": Bess Furman, *Washington By-Line* (New York: Alfred A. Knopf, 1949), 153.

108 "I rather think": ER to Hick, November 27, 1933, Streitmatter, *Empty Without You*, 45.

108 "Fog Interrupts Flight": *New York Herald Tribune*, March 15, 1934.

108 "a diamond monogrammed watch": Ibid., March 11, 1934.

109 "Mrs. Roosevelt," Bugbee wrote: Ibid., March 16, 1934.

109 "President Welcomes Wife": Ibid., March 18, 1934.

109 "It was announced": *Time*, February 19, 1934.

109 "get through with this": Hick to Kathryn Godwin, in Hickok, *One Third of a Nation*, 191–92.

109 "Mrs. Joe Doaks": Ibid.

109 "a rotund lady": Ibid.

110 the "amistad íntima": "La Dama Que Acompanara a la Sra. Roosevelt a la Isla," clipping, FDRL.

110 "would get all the publicity": Hick to Kathryn Godwin, in Hick, *One Third of a Nation*, 192.

110 "because you grow closer": ER to Hick, March 26, 1934, FDRL.

110 "We do do things": Hick to ER, December 5, 1933, FDRL.

111 "It will do us no harm": ER, *It's Up to the Women*, x.

111 "One of the girls": ER, *This Is My Story*, 11–12.

111 as a "bad habit": Ibid., 73–74.

112 "a combination of wet-nursin'": "Eugene Talmadge," Spartacus Educational, http://spartacus-educational.com/USAtalmadge.htm.

112 "I take it": David M. Kennedy, *Freedom from Fear: The American People in Depression and War, 1929–45* (New York: Oxford University Press, 1999), 193–94.

112 "No niggah's as good": Arthur M. Schlesinger Jr., *The Politics of Upheaval, 1935–36*, vol. 3 of *The Age of Roosevelt* (Boston: Houghton Mifflin, 1960), 521.

112 "Savannah must be": Hick to Hopkins, in Hick, *One Third of a Nation*, 151–52.

112 While at the *Minneapolis Tribune*: Lorena Hickok, *Minneapolis Tribune*, December 5, 1925.

112 "the 'Old South'": Hick to Harry Hopkins, January 11, 1934, FDRL.

113 "we've had a little Jew": ER to Esther Lape, Key West, 1925, FDRL.

113 "the country is still full": Cook, *Eleanor Roosevelt*, 2:316–17.

113 "Many of us do not appreciate": "A colored couple was married and immediately reports spread far and wide of their unhappiness, the wife, Beatrice, being known as the possessor of a hot temper. Some time after the marriage a lady who knew Beatrice met her in town and remarked: 'I hope you and your husband do not quarrel any more.' 'We sho' don do dat no mo'!' 'What caused you to stop it?' 'He's daid!'" "My Day," March 12, 1937.

114 in 1933 alone: Cook, *Eleanor Roosevelt*, 2:152–53.

114 "should be reading": ER to Hick, January 9, 1934, FDRL.

114 "three quiet evenings": ER to Hick, January 16, 1934, FDRL.

115 busybody and troublemaker: Cook, *Eleanor Roosevelt*, 2:155.

115 "Hick dearest," Eleanor wrote afterward: ER to Hick, January 23, 1934, FDRL.

115 "I had a little ache": Hick to ER, January 22, 1934, FDRL.

115 "trees and swamp": Hick, *One Third of a Nation*, 157.
115 a man with a blacksnake whip: Ibid., 157–58.
115 In North Carolina: Ibid., 194–96.
116 "When their slaves": Ibid., 186.
116 "take all that trouble": Ibid., 211.
117 "We are carrying on relief": Ibid., 231–33.
117 "As he came trailing": Ibid., 288–89.
118 "a holdup which netted them": Hick to ER, June 23, 1934, FDRL.
118 "I would have felt": ER to Hick, June 25, 1934, FDRL.
119 "I evidently answered": Cook, *Eleanor Roosevelt*, 2:166.
119 Their visit also led: Streitmatter, *Empty Without You*, 108, footnote 32.
119 member sent a "stern reproof": ER to Hick, April 20, 1934, FDRL.
119 "And now I'm going to bed": Hick to ER, April 20, 1934, FDRL.
119 "I thought about you": ER to Hick, January 14, 1934, FDRL.
120 "What wouldn't I give": ER to Hick, January 27, 1934, FDRL.
120 "I know I've got to fit in": ER to Hick, February 4, 1934, FDRL.
120 "The 'what might have happened aspect'": ER to Hick, telegram and letter, April 29, 1934, FDRL.
120 "Incidentally, sir, you have": Hick, *One Third of a Nation*, 238.
121 "You, Washington, the apartment": Hick to ER, July 3, 1934, FDRL.
121 "I can't understand": ER to Hick, July 10, 1934, FDRL.

CHAPTER NINE: GETTING AWAY WITH IT
124 "This is my vacation": Hick, *Reluctant First Lady*, 157–60.
124 was trying to "lose herself": "First Lady Striving to 'Lose Self,'" AP, July 13, 1934.
124 "looked as though": "First Lady Takes Her Coffee Black but Windmill's Apple Pie Breaks Through Resolve," clipping from Doris Faber papers, n.d., FDRL.
125 "I'll be glad": ER to Hick, February 4, 1934, FDRL.
125 "Yes, dear, I think you will": ER to Hick, June 28, 1934, FDRL.
125 "kept thinking of the mess": ER to Hick, June 3, 1934, FDRL.
126 was making Eleanor "boil": ER to Hick, June 25, 1934, FDRL.
126 "How could you": Hick, *Reluctant First Lady*, 161
126 her first published essay: Faber, *Life of Lorena Hickok*, 43–44, from an article in the *Lawrentian*, no. 19 (1913).
126 "Long busy days": Hick to ER, December 8, 1933, FDRL.
127 "I learned that nobody": ER, *This I Remember*, 142.
127 "It's a wonderful experience": Hick, *Reluctant First Lady*, 167.
127 "the first rays": Cook, *Eleanor Roosevelt*, 2:205.
127 "in Central Park": Hick, *Reluctant First Lady*, 166.
128 "Franklin was right": Ibid., 176.
128–29 "All you need": ER, *This Is My Story*, 143.
129 "If I had charge": *Berkeley Daily Gazette*, August 2, 1934.
129 "Darling, how I hated": ER to Hick, August 3, 1934, FDRL.
129 "There have been times": Hick to ER, August 8, 1934, FDRL.
129 "I'm afraid," Eleanor observed: ER to Hick, August 11, 1934, FDRL.
129 "I hope you are": Hick to ER, August 15, 1934, FDRL.
130 "I don't need anything": ER to Hick, August 21, 1934, FDRL.

130 "Oh dear one": ER to Hick, August 31, 1934, FDRL.

130 "Yes, I am happy here": ER to Hick, August 13, 1934, FDRL.

130 "Franklin was always": ER, *This I Remember*, 19.

130 "The sun is out": Cook, *Eleanor Roosevelt*, 2:107.

131 "one corner cupboard": April 18, 1934. Streitmatter, *Empty Without You*, has "probably won't argue" rather than "probably won't agree."

132 "My real trouble": ER to Hick, April 1, 1934, FDRL.

132 "the worst of the lot": Hick to ER, November 21, 1934, in Faber, *Life of Lorena Hickok*, 181.

CHAPTER TEN: NOW OR NEVER

133 She was pleased: Cook, *Eleanor Roosevelt*, 2:219.

133 "congressman-at-large": The position was created because of a growth in population not yet reflected in the apportionment of districts. From 1932 until 1945, when reapportionment was finally undertaken, a congressman-at-large represented the increase on an interim basis.

134 "I believe in certain things": Cook, *Eleanor Roosevelt*, 2:223.

134 "When politics is through with us": Ibid., 1:324.

134 "Are you going to stop": Ibid., 2:223.

135 "do not believe": Hick to Aubrey Williams, August 15, 1934, in Hick, *One Third of a Nation*, 306.

135 monumental Boulder Dam: Hick to Aubrey Williams, August 23, 1934, ibid., 316–17.

135 "This ain't a job": Hick to Hopkins, September 9, 1934, ibid., 331.

135 "All we need": Hick to ER, September 14, 1934, ibid., 335.

135 "Human patience," Hick wrote Hopkins: Hick to Hopkins, September 9, 1934, ibid., 330.

136 "They don't want to be 'rehabilitated'": Hick to ER, September 14, 1934, ibid., 335.

136 "Boys, this is our hour": Robert E. Sherwood, *Roosevelt and Hopkins* (New York: Harper & Brothers, 1948), 65.

CHAPTER ELEVEN: BLOWING OFF

139 slept through the entire thing: Hick, *Reluctant First Lady*, 41–42.

139 "Why do you have to *feel*": ER to Hick, June 25, 1936, FDRL.

140 reports for being "explosive": ER to Hick, September 25, 1935, FDRL.

140 "People keep asking them": Hick to ER, September 29, 1935, FDRL.

140 "We're getting a bad reputation": Hick report to Hopkins, October 10, 1935, FDRL.

141 "We're in this mess": Hick to ER, December 10, 1935, FDRL.

141 "And God help us": Hick to ER, October 16, 1935, FDRL.

142 object in tenderness: Interview with Martha Gellhorn by Emily Williams, oral historian, February 20, 1980.

142 "Poor Marty!" Eleanor wrote Hick: ER to Hick, June 11, 1935, FDRL.

142 "Since I backed her": Hick to Hopkins, May 31, 1935, FDRL.

142 "They told me": Carl Rollyson, *Nothing Ever Happens to the Brave: The Story of Martha Gellhorn* (New York: St. Martin's, 1990), 76.

143 Back in 1933, Hick: August 22 and 23, 1933, FDRL. Hick retyped and seemingly combined several long letters she wrote to Eleanor from West Virginia in 1933, then

edited them fiercely, crossing out entire passages of vivid writing. Presumably she was thinking of including them in her collection of reports to Hopkins. They have never been published.

144 "Get those families": Hick, *Reluctant First Lady*, 138.

144 "every last, horrible one": Hick to ER, September 17, 1935, FDRL.

144 "A set of harness": Hick to Hopkins, September 22, 1935, FDRL.

145 "That WAS an experience": Hick to ER, January 16, 1936, FDRL.

145 "chances of re-election?": ER to Hick, April 17, 1935, FDRL.

145 "Now I ask you": ER to Hick, April 27, 1935, FDRL.

145 "And they say": Hick to ER, February 7, 1935, FDRL.

146 "I've been ready": ER to Hick, April 28, 1935, FDRL.

146 "Hick darling, I'm sorry": ER to Hick, May 2, 1935, FDRL.

146 "It's sometimes rather tough": Hick to ER, July 31, 1936, FDRL.

147 "I think you can": ER to Hick, February 20, 1935, in Streitmatter, *Empty Without You*, 148.

147 "You have a feeling": ER to Hick, May 13, 1935, FDRL.

148 "Are you taking": ER to Hick, June 10, 1936, FDRL.

148 "I suppose I shall": Alicent Holt to Hick, June 14, 1936, in Cook, *Eleanor Roosevelt*, 2:365.

148 "a swell person": Hick to ER, July 27, 1936, FDRL.

148 "What I've tried to do": Hick to ER, August 2, 1932, FDRL.

148 "This is it": Hick to ER, June 27, 1936, FDRL.

149 "Dearest, how I wish": ER to Hick, July 11, 1936, Cook, *Eleanor Roosevelt*, 2:375.

149 "It is a strange world": ER to Hick, July 18, 1936, FDRL.

149 "It wouldn't be satisfactory": ER to Hick July 22, 1936, FDRL.

149 "I'm wondering if you": Hick to ER, July 31, 1936, FDRL.

150 "One can be": ER to Hick, August 3, FDRL.

150 "I'm back at my worst": ER to Hick, August 9, 1936, FDRL.

150 "All your fight": ER to Hick, September 25, 1936, FDRL.

150 "What happens tomorrow": "My Day," November 3, 1936.

151 "riotous cheering" greeted: *New York Times*, January 7, 1937.

151 "get a cross-section": Ibid., January 8, 1937.

CHAPTER TWELVE: LOOKING FOR A HOME

153 "This isn't my house": Cook, *Eleanor Roosevelt*, 1:395 (from Perkins Oral History, Columbia University).

153 "There was a sense": Davis, *Invincible Summer*, handwritten words in scrapbook pages, center section.

153 "It was one of the most pleasing": Gellhorn Oral History, February 20, 1980, FDRL.

154 "remarkably deft performance": Unpublished autobiography, Hickok papers, FDRL.

155 "a delightful oval room": Nigel Hamilton, *The Mantle of Command: FDR at War, 1941–1942* (Boston: Houghton Mifflin Harcourt, 2014), 136.

155 he had them blocked: According to Blanche Wiesen Cook, this was "no casual gesture." Eleanor had "placed a similar piece of furniture in front of shared doorways to end her mother-in-law's unannounced intrusions on the bedroom floor of their twin East 65th Street home." Cook, *Eleanor Roosevelt*, 2:33–34.

155 "It would be impossible": "My Day," January 12, 1938.

155 **contained Lincoln's bed:** In the Roosevelt years, this was called the "Lincoln bedroom," but that has since changed.

156 **Hick's little room:** All details of Hick's White House stays are from unpublished autobiography, Hickok papers, FDRL.

156 **"very amusing to go up":** "My Day," December 25, 1936.

157 **"All the preparations":** Curtis Roosevelt, *Too Close to the Sun: Growing Up in the Shadow of My Grandparents, Franklin and Eleanor* (New York: Public Affairs, 2008), 95–97.

158 **"felt very sad":** ER to Anna, Christmas Eve 1935, FDRL.

159 **establish a World Court:** Cook, *Eleanor Roosevelt*, 1:345.

159 **"The easy unconventionality":** *The WPA Guide to New York City* (New York: Pantheon, 1939), 131.

159 **Willa Cather, whose work:** Eleanor described Cather as "one of my favorite authors" in "My Day," July 10, 1947, and Hick once suggested that Eleanor should read Cather's "The Diamond Mine," a short story about a successful diva exploited by her family. Hick recommended the story in connection with the problems of her friend the actress Judith Anderson, but Eleanor's own situation sometimes resembled that of the story's protagonist.

160 **"about as rakish":** Rick Beard and Leslie Berlowitz, eds., *Greenwich Village: Culture and Counterculture* (New Brunswick, NJ: Rutgers University Press, 1990).

160 **"mecca for exhibitionists":** George Chauncey, "Long-Haired Men and Short-Haired Women: Building a Gay World in the Heart of Bohemia," in Beard and Berlowitz, *Greenwich Village.*

160 **"Now I am here":** ER to Hick, October 25, 1936, FDRL.

161 **bring a robe:** What she wrote was "bring a wrapper." The wrapper seems to have suggested an intimate time. On May 22, 1938, Eleanor wrote Hick that she was "glad to keep your wrapper as a hostage that you mean to come more often in the future!"

161 **"a man with whom":** Unpublished autobiography, Hickok papers, FDRL.

161 **"It seems to me, Hick":** Hick, *Reluctant First Lady,* 147.

162 **"The dresses are going":** Hick to ER, December 9, 1936, FDRL.

162 **"My God," Hick wrote:** Hick to ER, December 8, 1936, FDRL.

163 **"You two haven't":** Unpublished autobiography, Hickok papers, FDRL.

163 **"her reports on conditions":** Tugwell diary about Puerto Rico, Lash papers, FDRL.

164 **"Now if you could":** ER to Hick, August 3, 1935, FDRL. Dated August 30, but the context suggests that is a mistake.

164 **"amused at your idea":** Hick to ER, August 7, 1935, FDRL.

164 **"I don't worry about Marty":** Hick to ER, March 17, 1937, FDRL. Years later, in a homophobic tirade, Gellhorn insisted she barely knew or remembered Hick, except as someone very ugly. There is strong evidence to the contrary. "Probably one of the finest features of having returned to America and become a slave in the great forward movement of progress," Gellhorn wrote Hick on January 8, 1935, "is to have found you in the midst of it all. I consider you a definite addition to my life and am quite childishly delighted about the whole thing." Bauman and Coode, *Eye of the Great Depression,* 28.

164 **"To Hick, who could have":** *Democratic Digest* announcement of Hick's departure, April 1945.

164 **"I'd hate you to":** ER to Hick, September 10, 1936, FDRL.

165 **"War Correspondent Finds Many Troubles":** *New York Times,* December 8, 1935.

165 **"The White House":** Unpublished autobiography, Hickok papers, FDRL.

165 "Really some of it": Hick to ER, November 20, 1936, FDRL.

165 "Dear, whatever may have happened": Hick to ER, December 6, 1936, FDRL.

165 "depress me horribly": Hick to ER, December 7, 1936, FDRL.

166 "Poor, poor Mabel": Hick to ER, December 8, 1936, FDRL.

CHAPTER THIRTEEN: TRADING JOBS

169 "tell him with a little fire": ER to Hick, January 4, 1937, FDRL.

169 "Good Lord, are you always": Hick to ER, November 13, 1936, FDRL.

170 "pleased to have it settled": Hick to ER, November 17, 1936, FDRL.

170 "I read the notice": Hick to ER, November 21, 1937, FDRL.

170 "a painter of pictures": "My Day," October 21, 1937.

171 "very much in earnest": Ibid., January 26, 1937.

171 "as a rule": Ibid., March 6, 1937.

171 longed for more: Ibid., July 24, 1937. Eleanor had already expressed this idea at greater length in a *Ladies' Home Journal* article published on August 24, 1936.

172 "the same group": Ibid., February 10, 1937.

173 "That isn't my worry": ER to Hick, March 15, 1937, FDRL.

173 "Really this trip": Hick to ER, March 15, 1937, FDRL.

173 "Why must I": Hick to ER, November 11, 1936, FDRL.

173 pleasing all parties: ER to Hick, November 12, 1936, FDRL.

174 "All day I": Hick to ER, July 16, 1937, FDRL.

174 "Why can't someone": ER to Hick, January 21, 1937, FDRL.

175 "give Alicent what she wants": Hick to ER, August 27, 1937, FDRL.

175 "most painless house guest": Hick to ER, June 16, 1937, FDRL.

175 "It's this drifting": Hick to ER, September 8, 1937, FDRL.

175 "I didn't realize": ER to Hick, September 9, 1937, FDRL.

175 "Yes, I had a good time": Hick to ER, October 5, 1937, FDRL.

175 "Don't dress," Eleanor instructed: ER to Hick, December 18, 1937, FDRL.

176 "a lovely 'Christmas'": Hick to ER, December 22, 1937, FDRL.

176 grandmother's "visceral dislike": Curtis Roosevelt, personal communication with the author.

176 "I'm being perfectly honest": Hick to ER, January 19, 1939, FDRL.

176 "It won't help you": ER to Hick, January 19, 1938, FDRL.

176 "never in your life": Hick to ER, January 18, 1938, FDRL.

177 "WHY can't I": Hick to ER, December 28, 1937, FDRL.

CHAPTER FOURTEEN: THIS PLACE!

179 "If you like it": Hick to ER, in Cook, *Eleanor Roosevelt*, 2:518.

180 "He's such fun": Hick to ER, March 4, 1937, FDRL.

180 "the one dependable": Howard Haycraft, *Murder for Pleasure: The Life and Times of the Detective Story* (New York: Biblo & Tannen, 1968), ix.

180 "most insightful, perceptive": "Howard Haycraft Is Dead at 86; A Publisher and Mystery Scholar," *New York Times*, November 13, 1991.

181 "Golly—*this place!*": Hick to ER, May 15, 1937, FDRL.

181 "brief visit with a friend": "My Day," October 19, 1937.

182 "a grand week": ER to Hick, August 5, 1938, FDRL.

182 "I wouldn't live": Cook, *Eleanor Roosevelt*, 2:519.

182 a "personal triumph" she achieved: "My Day," August 4, 1938.
182 "A kind friend": Ibid., August 5, 1938.
183 "we have turned over": Ibid., December 22, 1938.
183 She looked forward: Ibid., August 25, 1937.
183 "like a drunken sailor": Tommy to Anna Roosevelt Boettiger (later Halsted), May 1937, Halsted papers, FDRL. Tommy began her letters to Anna with the salutation "Dear Gorgeous."
183 On another occasion: Tommy to Anna Roosevelt, September 10, 1937, Halsted papers, FDRL.
184 "When Earl first came": Joseph P. Lash, Love, Eleanor: Eleanor Roosevelt and Her Friends (New York: Doubleday & Co., 1982), 116.
184 she became godmother: Cook, Eleanor Roosevelt, 2:93.
184 "a little thing": ER to Anna, August 12, 1938, Halsted papers, FDRL.
185 "It leaves Nan": Tommy to Anna, summer 1938, ibid.
185 "so listless that I begin": ER to Anna, August 1938, ibid.
185 "a calm talk": ER to Anna, August 12, 1938, ibid.
185 "long and tragic talk": Davis, Invincible Summer, 150.
185 "[Nan] told me": ER to Nan and Marion, November 9, 1938, Dickerman papers, FDRL.
186 "You are dears": ER to Marion Dickerman, February 7, 1927, FDRL.
186 "I left the tables": ER to Hick, August 27 and 31, 1938, FDRL.
187 "I realize," she wrote Marion: ER to Marion Dickerman, May 17, 1939, in Davis, Invincible Summer, 155.
187 "I shall only come": ER to Nan and Marion, October 29, 1938, FDRL.
187 "Nancy has made": Tommy to Anna, September 5, 1938, Halsted papers, FDRL.
188 "I can't imagine": Tommy to Anna, November 12, 1938, FDRL.
188 "very sorry every minute": Davis, Invincible Summer, 153.
188 "My cottage difficulties": ER to Anna, November 13, 1938, Halsted papers, FDRL.
188 "It has done something": Ibid.
188 "She has been so": Tommy to Anna, November 1938, Halsted papers, FDRL.
189 Never before had she: Cook, Eleanor Roosevelt, 2:530.
189 "recovered from my disappointment": Ibid., 532.
189 "This is TOWARD": Ibid., 551.
189 "couldn't understand how": Hick to ER, November 17, 1938, FDRL.
189 "if some day": Hick to ER, October 12, 1938, FDRL.
189 "on a money-making basis": ER to Hick, October 15, 1938, FDRL.
190 "I don't want to go": Cook, Eleanor Roosevelt, 2:520.
190-91 "best agents for peace": "Mrs. Roosevelt Hails World Youth as Best Agents for Peace," New York Times, August 17, 1938.
191 "I felt what they said": ER to Hick, August 27, 1938, FDRL.
191 lead a chorus: Cook, Eleanor Roosevelt, 2:523.

CHAPTER FIFTEEN: TIME TEARS ON
193 "not telling anyone": ER telegram to Hick, May 1, 1939, FDRL.
193 "Bring warm wraps": Hick to ER, May 1, 1939, FDRL.
194 "my young niece": "My Day," May 2, 1939.
194 "It is very": Hick to ER, April 27, 1939, FDRL.

194 "I have seen the fireworks": "My Day," May 4, 1939.

195 "no one should go": "My Day," May 4, 1939.

195 "material comfort for those": Robert Morss Lovett, writing of the Columbian Exposition of 1893, quoted in the *New York Times*, April 30, 1939.

196 "My personal investigation": *New Yorker*, April 30, 1938.

196 "the World's Fair": "Spotlight at Fair Swings to Dedication of Palestine Pavilion," *New York Times*, May 29, 1939.

197 "Let us turn our eyes inward": Kennedy, *Freedom from Fear*, 386.

197 "Let us consecrate": Cook, *Eleanor Roosevelt*, 1:291.

197 "How can we be": "My Day," April 6, 1938.

198 "I think of those people": Gellhorn to ER, July 1937, FDRL.

199 "very moved by it": Gellhorn to ER, July 8, 1937, in Caroline Moorehead, ed., *Selected Letters of Martha Gellhorn* (New York: Henry Holt, 2006), 55.

199 There was a famous story: "Tales in Tidbits," syndicated column, *Hammond (IN) Times*, January 4, 1938.

199 "So long until tomorrow": "Edward J. Neil Dies of Wounds in Spain," *New York Times*, January 3, 1938.

199 It was "a waste": "My Day," January 6, 1938.

200 "It seems to me": Gellhorn to ER, February 1938, FDRL.

200 "one of two things": Susan Hertog, *Dangerous Ambition: Rebecca West and Dorothy Thompson* (New York: Ballantine, 2011), 254.

200 "waiting in an operating room": Gellhorn to ER, June 29, 1938, FDRL.

200 "War itself," Gellhorn wrote: Gellhorn to ER, 1938, FDRL.

201 "I do not believe": Gellhorn to ER, 1939, FDRL.

201 "For sheer eloquence": Kennedy, *Freedom from Fear*, 423.

201 "Roosevelt put his chin out": Ibid., 424.

CHAPTER SIXTEEN: AFRAID NO MORE

205 "What can one say?": Hick to ER, September 3, 1939, FDRL.

205 "who wouldn't be?": ER to Hick, June 14, 1939, FDRL.

206 "He is very nice": ER to Hick, June 8, 1939, FDRL.

206 she still hoped: ER to Hick, September 3, 1939, FDRL.

206 "We must not fight": "My Day," September 27, 1938, FDRL.

207 "afraid of many things": Typed essay by ER, to be submitted to *Look* magazine, March 1939, FDRL.

207 "My dear," Hick wrote Eleanor: Hick to ER, March 15, 1939, FDRL.

207 "slight stiffening of the backbone": Cook, *Eleanor Roosevelt*, 2:526.

208 commenting that "sometimes actions": Ibid., 564–65.

208 "with a special fire": Raymond Arsenault, *The Sound of Freedom: Marion Anderson, the Lincoln Memorial, and the Concert That Awakened America* (New York: Bloomsbury, 2009), 95.

208 "just as I was": Marion Anderson, *My Lord, What a Morning* (New York: Viking, 1956), 188.

209 "I am afraid": ER to Mrs. Henry M. Robert, president of the DAR, February 26, 1939.

209 "weight of the Washington affair": Arsenault, *Sound of Freedom*, 160.

209 "In this great auditorium": Ibid., 159.

209 "felt for a moment": Anderson, *My Lord, What a Morning*, 191.

NOTES

210 volume with each phrase: In 1963, Martin Luther King Jr. used the phrase "let freedom ring" as a repeating rhetorical device in his "I Have a Dream" speech at the same
location.
211 "I think the Youth Congress": ER to Hick, November 30, 1939, FDRL.
211 "a house full": Lash, *Love, Eleanor*, 285.
211 "we have found it a good thing": Ibid.
211 "I had a feeling": ER to Joe Lash, December 11, 1939, Lash papers, FDRL.
212 "My children could": ER to Hick, in Lash, *Love, Eleanor*, 314–15.
213 "It amuses me": Hick to ER, April 22, 1939, FDRL.
213 "confidence in you": Hick to ER, April 17, 1939, FDRL.
213 "with the white": *New York Times*, May 1, 1939.
214 "It made me": Hick to ER, January 8, 1938, FDRL.
215 "It was *bad*": Hick to ER, December 31, 1939, FDRL.
215 "This job is such fun": Hick to ER, February 20, 1940, FDRL.
215 "nearest thing to newspaper": Hick to ER, February 21, 1940, FDRL.
215 "Darling, I'm sorry": Hick to ER, March 8, 1940, FDRL.
215 in two words: "I groan": ER to Hick, February 11, 1940, FDRL.
215 A showdown of sorts: Leslie A. Gould, *American Youth Today* (New York: Random
House, 1940), 10–13, 26–27; Frank Freidel, *Franklin D. Roosevelt: A Rendezvous with
Destiny* (Boston: Little, Brown, 1990), 325.
216 "How dare you insult": Freidel, *Franklin D. Roosevelt*, 326.
216 "Why I Still Believe in the Youth Congress": Published in *Liberty*, April 1940.
217 "I *don't* believe": Hick to ER, March 14, 1940, FDRL.
217 "sane and dispassionate": Hick to ER, March 17, 1940, FDRL.
217 Back in 1917: Hick to ER, February 28, 1940, FDRL.
217 "I am sitting": "Hi" Austin Simons to Hick, Fort Leavenworth, KS, March 23, 1918,
Hickok papers, FDRL.
218 "you don't want to go to war": Doris Kearns Goodwin, *No Ordinary Time: Franklin
and Eleanor Roosevelt; The Home Front in World War II* (New York: Simon & Schuster,
1994), 84.
218 "role of elder statesman": ER, *This I Remember*, 212.

CHAPTER SEVENTEEN: A BETTER POLITICIAN THAN HER HUSBAND
221 "Love Eleanor"—Eleanor's telegram: Telegram from ER to Hick, July 18, 1940,
FDRL.
222 "I'm the only one": "Farley Stays In; Urges Unanimity," *New York Times*, July 16, 1940.
222 "the boys knew": *New York Times*, July 16, 1940.
222 "I have thought": Harold Ickes, *The Secret Diary of Harold L. Ickes*, vol. 3, *The Lowering
Clouds, 1939–1941* (New York: Simon & Schuster, 1954), 240.
223 The shouting, interspersed: "Roosevelt Leaves Third Term to Party; Releases
Delegates for a Free Choice; Move to Draft Him Set for Tonight," *New York Times*, July
17, 1940.
223 "the kind of man": Henry H. Adams, *Harry Hopkins: A Biography* (New York: G. P.
Putnam's Sons, 1977), 175.
224 "Harry has been": ER, *This I Remember*, 214–15.
224 "gone completely over": Goodwin, *No Ordinary Time*, 89.
224 "Well, would you": Ibid., 127.

225 **"tell her I mean it"**: Lorena Hickok and Eleanor Roosevelt, *Ladies of Courage* (New York: G. P. Putnam's Sons, 1954), 282.

225 **"a real sense of exhilaration"**: ER, *This I Remember*, 215.

225 **"Happy!" she replied**: "No Campaigning, First Lady States," *New York Times*, July 19, 1940.

226 **"watched with horror"**: Hickok and Roosevelt, *Ladies of Courage*, 283–84.

226 **"I don't know why"**: Goodwin, *No Ordinary Time*, 130.

227 **"on that occasion"**: Charles Michelson, *The Ghost Talks* (New York: G. P. Putnam's Sons, 1944), 159.

227 **"When it seemed"**: Senator George Norris to ER, July 19, 1940, FDRL.

227 **"She is truly"**: Tommy to Hick, July 25, 1940, FDRL.

227 **"I felt," she remembered**: ER, *This I Remember*, 218.

228 **to "sell Czechoslovakia"**: Freidel, *Franklin D. Roosevelt*, 354.

228 **"Golly he must be"**: Hick to ER, September 15, 1940, FDRL.

228 **"The more he hollers"**: Marion Elizabeth Rodgers, *Mencken: The American Iconoclast* (New York: Oxford University Press, 2005), 469.

228 **"a national evil"**: Goodwin, *No Ordinary Time*, 184.

229 **"The overwhelming majority"**: David Kaiser, *No End Save Victory: How FDR Led the Nation into War* (New York: Basic Books, 2014), 133.

229 **FDR happily obliged**: Freidel, *Franklin D. Roosevelt*, 355.

229 **"Along about 1 am"**: Hick to ER, November 7, 1940, FDRL.

230 **"very good in applauding"**: Kennedy, *Freedom from Fear*, 464.

230 **"I did not think"**: Churchill to Roosevelt, November 6, 1940, in Francis L. Loewenheim, Harold D. Langley, and Manfred Jonas, eds., *Roosevelt and Churchill: Their Secret Wartime Correspondence* (New York: E. P. Dutton, 1975), 119.

CHAPTER EIGHTEEN: IN RESIDENCE

231 **"One of my friends"**: "My Day," December 23, 1940.

231 **"He'd lie on the floor"**: Hick to ER, December 27, 1940, FDRL.

232 **"to answer endless letters"**: ER to Hick, November 15, 1940, FDRL.

232 **"Be a self-cranker"**: Dewson papers, FDRL.

232 **"the greatest she-politician"**: Michelson, *The Ghost Talks*, 36.

233 **"I am oblivious"**: Dewson to Felix Frankfurter, February 8, 1938, FDRL.

233 **"I honestly don't think"**: Hick to ER, November 16, 1940, FDRL.

234 **"What a newspaper career"**: Hick to ER, September 2, 1940, FDRL.

234 **"You are under her"**: ER to Hick, December 14, 1940, FDRL.

234 **"one of the most eloquent"**: Hickok papers, FDRL.

235 **So one day in March**: Hick to ER, March 18, 1940, FDRL.

236 **her $6,000 a year**: Streitmatter, *Empty Without You*, says it was $5,000, but Eleanor's letter of December 14 puts it at the higher amount.

236 **"Well, if that is the way"**: Unpublished autobiography, Hickok papers, FDRL.

236 **"That business of moping"**: Hick to ER, January 29, 1940, FDRL.

236 **"more interested in the *person*"**: Hick to ER, November 11, 1940, FDRL.

236 **"The personage is an accident"**: ER to Hick, November 15, 1940, FDRL.

237 **"I try to be a machine"**: Lash, *Love, Eleanor*, 331.

237 **"No other engagement"**: Ibid., 354.

237 **dreaded "getting accustomed"**: ER to Hick, November 8, 1940, FDRL.

237 "If you hear": ER to Hick, August 28, 1940, FDRL.
237–38 "I must say": "My Day," December 11, 1939.
238 "at his sparkling best": Goodwin, *No Ordinary Time*, 150.
238 "this situation seems": ER to Anna, from Rochester, MN, Halsted papers, FDRL. The letter is marked August 8, 1938, though the visit to the Mayo Clinic was in September.
239 "It is stupid": *San Antonio Light*, June 7, 1941.
239 "Many a ruffled feather": Unpublished autobiography, Hickok papers, FDRL.
239 "In residence today?": Ibid.

CHAPTER NINETEEN: IN IT, UP TO THE NECK
241 "the one and only person": Adams, *Harry Hopkins*, 206.
242 "warm and deep": Loewenheim, Langley, and Jonas, *Roosevelt and Churchill*, 155.
242 "The fact that": ER, *This I Remember*, 226.
242 "it was an important moment": "My Day," August 16, 1941.
243 "I found Mama": Penciled letter, May 30, 1941. Streitmatter, *Empty Without You*, puts this into a later letter.
243 "shut himself off": Goodwin, *No Ordinary Time*, 272.
243 "That big house": Geoffrey C. Ward, ed., *Closest Companion: The Unknown Story of the Intimate Friendship Between Franklin Roosevelt and Margaret Suckley* (New York: Houghton Mifflin, 1995), 148.
243 "Hick dearest," she wrote from Hyde Park: ER to Hick, September 7, 1941, FDRL.
244 "my idea of hell": Lash, *Love, Eleanor*, 357.
244 "He had great energy": ER, *This I Remember*, 229.
244 In 1938, in the midst: Freidel, *Franklin D. Roosevelt*, 271–72.
244 "I think you will": "My Day," October 25, 1940.
244 "Father struggled to her side": James Roosevelt, *My Parents: A Differing View* (Chicago: Playboy Press, 1976), 113.
245 "I know he would want": "My Day," September 27, 1941.
245 "He enjoyed life": ER to Eleanor Wotkyns, October 21, 1948, FDRL.
245 Sometimes at White House parties: Hick, *Reluctant First Lady*, 87.
245 "in a horrid frame of mind": Lash, *Love, Eleanor*, 361.
245 "I think Hall's illness": Hick to ER, October 11, 1941, FDRL.
246 "He had no more tricks left": Goodwin, *No Ordinary Time*, 283.
246 "TAKE ACTION!" she typed: Dorothy Thompson to ER, Thanksgiving 1941, Dorothy Thompson papers, Special Collections, Syracuse University Libraries.
247 remained "deadly calm": Goodwin, *No Ordinary Time*, 289.
248 "as though it had died": Unpublished autobiography, Hickok papers, FDRL.
249 "didn't see anything funny": Ibid.

CHAPTER TWENTY: RISKING EVERYTHING
251 "It just didn't seem": Goodwin, *No Ordinary Time*, 301.
251 there was his drinking: Ibid., 302.
251 "There is no question": ER interview for Robert D. Graff, ABC television series, 1961, FDRL.
252 "When I hear a man": Jon Meacham, *Franklin and Winston: An Intimate Portrait of an Epic Friendship* (New York: Random House, 2003), 146.
252 "They looked like": Goodwin, *No Ordinary Time*, 310–11.

252 "I grow deeply resentful": ER to Hick, March 23, 1942, FDRL. Senator Kenneth McKellar, Democrat from Tennessee, and Senator Harry Flood Byrd, Democrat from Virginia, were segregationists who opposed many New Deal reforms.

253 "At the end of this war": "My Day," January 28, 1942.

253 "better nutrition, better housing": Joseph P. Lash, *Eleanor and Franklin* (New York: W. W. Norton, 1971), 653.

253 "absurdity and contempt": *El Paso Herald-Post*, February 23, 1942.

253 "I still believe": Goodwin, *No Ordinary Time*, 324–25.

254 yet "very attractive": ER to Hick, May 30, 1934, FDRL.

254 "the best boss": Hick to Gladys Tillett, March 7, 1942, Tillett archive, University of North Carolina.

254 and felt "safer": Molly Dewson to James Farley, February 3, 1938, FDRL.

255 Norton told Hick: Hick to ER, February 27, 1942, FDRL.

255 "an intelligent tongue-lashing": *Chicago Defender*, April 28, 1945.

255 "made the boys mad": Norton to Hick, September 29, 1942, FDRL.

255 "exactly six meetings": "'No respect' for Hartley, Mrs. Norton Quits Committee," Associated Press, February, 1947.

255 Serving under Hartley: Norton to Hick, February 22, 1947, FDRL.

256 "which would have": Hick to ER, February 27, 1942. Later the Smith-Connally anti-strike act, which prohibited strikes in war-related industries, was passed by Congress, then vetoed by FDR. The veto was overridden by Congress.

256 presence of Marion Harron: Daniel R. Ernst, "Marion Janet Harron (1903–1972)," *Legal History Blog*, May 25, 2012, http://legalhistoryblog.blogspot.com/2012/05/marion -janet-harron-1903-1972.html.

257 "You don't even": Marion Harron to Hick, March 22, 1942, FDRL.

257 "how good the week": Marion Harron to Hick, May 12, 1942, FDRL.

257 "How in God's name": Marion Harron to Hick, January 6, 1944, FDRL.

257 "where my eyes travel": Marion Harron to Hick, February 2, 1944, FDRL.

258 confidante, as "the Lash": Joseph P. Lash, *A World of Love: Eleanor Roosevelt and Her Friends, 1943–62* (New York: Doubleday & Co., 1984), xxiii.

258 "Hickok is still here": Ibid., xix.

258 "Our friend, Hick": Ibid., xxxi.

258 "a great, ringing": Unpublished autobiography, Hickok papers, FDRL.

259 "I owed her that much": Geoffrey C. Ward and Ken Burns, *The Roosevelts: An Intimate History* (New York: Alfred A. Knopf, 2014), 385.

260 FDR liked having: Goodwin, *No Ordinary Time*, 361.

261 "Bring the Germans": Ibid., 363.

261 "one of those beautiful ships": Ibid., 368.

261 the *Democratic Digest: Democratic Digest*, January 1941 through December–January 1944–45, Library of Congress.

263 "Republicans and the worst Democrats": Hick to ER, November 5, 1942, FDRL.

263 "the one bright spot": Hick to Helen Douglas, November 11, 1942, FDRL.

264 "what he stands for": Hick to ER, November 5, 1942, FDRL.

264 that, "everything considered": Nigel Hamilton, *The Mantle of Command: FDR at War, 1941–42* (Boston: Houghton Mifflin Harcourt, 2014), 419.

264 "For weeks," she wrote: Ward, *Closest Companion*, 184.

265 the day Operation Torch: Hamilton, *Mantle of Command*, 349–77.

266 "We have landed": Goodwin, *No Ordinary Time*, 388.

266 "It never crossed my mind": Ibid., 316.

267 "These are days": "My Day," June 28, 1943.

267 Clapper wrote that "because of": Raymond Clapper, *Lowell (MA) Sun*, October 27, 1942.

268 "This is to impress you": ER to Hick, October 23, 1942, FDRL.

268 "Each empty building": "My Day," September 27, 1942.

268 "I don't want": ER, *This I Remember*, 275.

269 "a sweet baby": Goodwin, *No Ordinary Time*, 382.

269 "a boy playing the piano": "My Day," October 28, 1942.

269 "Every soldier I see": "My Day," November 5, 1942.

270 "They take refuge": Excerpt from ER's diary, October 26, 1942. FDRL.

270 "Darling," Hick wrote Eleanor from Washington: Hick to ER, October 26, 1942, FDRL.

270 "we are fighting together": "My Day," November 10, 1942.

271 On March 10, 1943: Goodwin, *No Ordinary Time*, 422–23.

272 "Never get into an argument": Hick. *Reluctant First Lady*, 148.

272 box of "lovely handkerchiefs": Hick to ER, December 23, 1942, FDRL.

272 "It is a pleasant thing": "My Day," December 26, 1942, FDRL.

272 "the most overwhelming disaster": The meeting was not FDR's finest hour. He began with a friendly joke about Governor Herbert Lehman (presumably because he was Jewish), was silent long enough to hear a blessing from the Orthodox rabbi in the group, then held forth for twenty-three of the twenty-nine minutes of the meeting. He said he knew from neutral country reports that the slaughter was happening, and said Hitler was a madman but that it would not do to alienate the entire German population by calling them murderers, then went on with some irrelevancies about the U.S. experience with Jews and Muslims in North Africa. He agreed to endorse the statement the delegation came up with.

273 Hardie Robbins took: Goodwin, *No Ordinary Time*, 398. Hick also wrote about this in her tribute to Eleanor in the *Democratic Digest*, June 1945.

CHAPTER TWENTY-ONE: A FIGHT FOR LOVE AND GLORY

275 "The screen was so placed": Unpublished autobiography, Hickok papers, FDRL.

276 As one of Churchill's aides: Goodwin, *No Ordinary Time*, 402.

276 "If anything happened": Ibid., 408.

277 "the sole occupant": Unpublished autobiography, Hickok papers, FDRL.

278 visit "your island": Lash, *World of Love*, 49.

278 "the one happy and personal thing": Ibid., 61.

278 "a journey undertaken": Ibid., 30.

279 had been "brutal": ER to Hick, July 9, 1943, ibid., 39.

279 "I wish so": Lash, *World of Love*, 56.

279 a "queer feeling": Ibid., 55.

280 "I marveled most": Ward and Burns, *The Roosevelts*, 419.

280 "When you get home": "My Day," September 2, 1943.

280 "These boys break": ER to Hick, September 1, 1943, FDRL.

280 Some of them told her: *Democratic Digest*, October 1943.

280 "I do camps": ER to Hick, September 12, 1943, FDRL.

281 "I'm surrounded by Generals": Lash, *World of Love*, 67.

281 "I have all the pomp": Ibid., 66.

281 "coolly and graciously": GI's letter of October 1943, sent to Harry Hopkins by Florence Kerr, Hopkins archive, FDRL.

282 "Happy tonight for we": Lash, *World of Love*, 70.

282 "The little white crosses": "My Day," September 22, 1943.

283 Very soon after Eleanor's return: Hick to ER, November 1, 1943, FDRL. "My dear: Word has come through that we still may win and get Mrs. Conkey and Ellen Woodward to that conference as delegates or alternates. I suspect you of having accomplished this, and I'm deeply grateful."

283 "We have reached": *Democratic Digest*, 1943.

284 "X marks the spot": Marion Harron to Hick, December 1943, FDRL.

CHAPTER TWENTY-TWO: WINNING WITH THE WOMEN

285 "Have a good trip dear": Hick to ER, March 5, 1944, FDRL.

285 "I too have thought": Hick to ER, March 7, 1944, FDRL.

286 At fifty-two, she was: There was some doubt about Hick's age. She thought she was fifty-two, but Aunt Ella insisted she was a year younger.

286 "Almighty or Franklin D. Roosevelt": Hick to Democratic Women's Committee office, October 4, 1942, University of North Carolina, Tillett archive.

287 "bright as sunshine, and as warm": Marion Harron to Hick, January 16, 1944, FDRL.

287 "those huge God-awful affairs": Hick to ER, March 5, 1944, FDRL.

287 "Your letters are short": Marion Harron to Hick, February 2, 1944, FDRL.

287 was a "little dog": Marion Harron to Hick, January 5, 1944, FDRL.

288 "We don't know when": "My Day," April 10, 1944.

289 "There's quite a boom": Hick to Eleanor, March 23, 1944, in Lash, *World of Love*, 127–28.

289 "Hard position when": ER to Hick, July 20, 1944, FDRL.

290 "every possible method": *New York Times*, July 20, 1944.

290 was the "final exam": *Democratic Digest*, August 1944, Library of Congress.

290 "true conservative" party: *New York Times*, July 20, 1944.

290 "Helen's speech was superb": Marion Harron to Hick, July 21, 1944, FDRL.

290 "praying to the gods": Marion Harron to Hick, July 30, 1944, FDRL.

290 "A perfect vacation": Marion Harron to Hick, August 20, 1944, FDRL.

290 "great comfort and joy": Marion Harron to Hick, August 25, 1944, FDRL.

291 "You see," Marion wrote poignantly: Marion Harron to Hick, August 30, 1944, FDRL.

291 "I'll be spending": Hick to ER, September 14, 1944, FDRL.

291 an elaborate analogy: Goodwin, *No Ordinary Time*, 482.

292 "The President," Eleanor reported: "My Day," April 7, 1944.

292 "His whole face": Goodwin, *No Ordinary Time*, 489.

293 "for a man of 62": Ibid., 494–97.

294 "Darling . . . I don't like to think": Hick to Eleanor, November 10, 1944, FDRL.

NOTES

CHAPTER TWENTY-THREE: THERE IS ONLY ONE PRESIDENT

295 "There are a lot of things": ER to Hick, November 1944, in Lash, *World of Love*, 151
295 "I have a feeling": Wallace to Morgenthau, ibid.
295 "There is no fundamental love": ER to Esther Lape, November 15 and 19, 1944, ibid., 150.
296 "so I won't have to go": ER to Hick, November 1944, ibid., 151.
296 "He got more": Goodwin, *No Ordinary Time*, 563.
297 James recalled coming home: James Roosevelt, *My Parents*, 68.
298 "Were you ever right!": Hick to ER, December 23, 1944, FDRL.
298 "fuss and feathers": William D. Hassett, *Off the Record with FDR, 1942–1945* (London: George Allen & Unwin, 1960), 312.
299 "Many thanks dear": Goodwin, *No Ordinary Time*, 583.
299 "the necessity of matching": ER, *This I Remember*, 340.
300 "At this stage": Kennedy, *Freedom from Fear*, 802.
300 "accepted a certain degree": ER, *This I Remember*, 342.
300 "I wish I could": Hick to ER, March 21, 1945, FDRL.
300 "I guess I did not": Dewson to Hick, October 23, 1941, FDRL.
300 "our friend 'Hick'": *Democratic Digest*, January 1942, Library of Congress.
301 "a gifted writer": *Democratic Digest*, April 1945, Library of Congress.
301 On April 11: Goodwin, *No Ordinary Time*, 600–603.
302 "Here is a flash": *New York Herald Tribune*, European edition, Paris, April 13, 1945.

CHAPTER TWENTY-FOUR: THE GREATEST CATASTROPHE FOR THE WORLD

303 Early on the fateful day: Goodwin, *No Ordinary Time*, 604.
303 "Darlings. Pa slept": Ward and Burns, *The Roosevelts*, 452.
303 "Harry," she told him: Goodwin, *No Ordinary Time*, 604.
304 "Boys," he told a group: David McCullough, *Truman* (New York: Simon & Schuster, 1992), 353.
304 "almost impersonal feeling": ER, *This I Remember*, 348–49.
305 "It seems sure": *Democratic Digest*, June, 1945.
305 "At midnight last night": My father, Robert Emmet Quinn, writing from Paris on April 13, 1945.
305 "dazed and incoherent letter": Hick to ER, April 13, 1945, FDRL.
305 "I'll bet there are darned few": Hick to Molly Dewson, May 3, 1945, FDRL.
306 "Darling . . . sometime I may": Hick to ER, April 14, 1945, FDRL.
306 taking a trip together: Goodwin, *No Ordinary Time*, 596.
307 "It is empty": ER to Hick, April 19, 1945, FDRL.

CHAPTER TWENTY-FIVE: SLIDING ON MARBLE FLOORS

311 "Eleanor Roosevelt . . . First Lady": *Democratic Digest*, June 1945, Library of Congress.
311 "For the first time": Ward and Burns, *The Roosevelts*, 459.
311 "active and important place": Hick to ER, April 13, 1945, FDRL.
311 "arms and legs": Lorena Hickok, unpublished essay, 1946, FDRL.
312 "No matter who": Tommy to Esther Lape, July 1945, FDRL.
312 "blowing soap bubbles": Tommy to Hick, January 1, 1946, FDRL.
312 "for persuasion and enlightenment": Esther Lape to ER, election day 1944, in Lash, *World of Love*, 149.

312 "You spoke of": ER to Esther Lape, November 15, 1944, ibid., 150.

312 "Somehow my family": ER to Hick, June 11, 1945, FDRL.

312 "I am quite shocked": Tommy to Esther Lape, July 1945, FDRL.

313 "She has the heart": Tommy to Hick, January 1, 1946, FDRL.

313 "the weight of suffering": "My Day," August 15, 1945.

313 she missed "Pa's voice": Goodwin, *No Ordinary Time*, 622.

313 she came to appreciate: Ibid., 619.

313 "get along with Congress": Hick to ER, April 13, 1945, FDRL.

313 "the loneliest man": ER to Hick, June 11, 1945, FDRL.

313 "I've been sorry for them": Hick to ER, June 13, 1945, FDRL.

314 "When I come home": ER to Hick, January 22, 1946, FDRL.

315 "good to work with": Eleanor Roosevelt, *On My Own* (New York: Harper & Brothers, 1958), 53.

315 "I take back everything": Joseph P. Lash, *The Years Alone* (New York: W. W. Norton, 1972), 56.

315 "more sick than she knows": Tommy to Esther Lape, July 1945, FDRL.

315 "good common sense": Gladys Tillett, April 30, 1947, FDRL.

315 "God I'm favored": Hick to ER, April 21, 1946, FDRL.

316 "that Mother dame": Faber, *Life of Lorena Hickok*, 297. This proved more true than Mary Norton knew. Marion lived with her mother until her mother's death, one year before her own. Ernst, "Marion Janet Harron (1903–1972)," *Legal History Blog*.

316 "I look at your slippers": Marion Harron to Hick, May 7, 1945.

316 "Marion has gone": Hick to ER, August 30, 1945, FDRL.

317 "an old, loyal": Hick to ER, July 3, 1943, FDRL.

317 like a bouncing cornflake: Faber, *Life of Lorena Hickok*, 297.

317 "iron her dishtowels": Ibid., 310.

318 "Now I shall have": "My Day," August 16, 1946.

319 "It was so much": Lash, *World of Love*, 259.

320 "At first," Eleanor wrote Gurewitsch: ER to David Gurewitsch, December 18, 1947, in Lash, *Years Alone*, 72.

320 took a few running steps: Lash, *Years Alone*, 72.

321 "It really isn't necessary": "My Day," July 14, 1948.

322 William O. Douglas turned him down: McCullough, *Truman*, 637. This account of the convention comes from 629–46.

323 "Gosh, my hat is off": Hick to Bess Furman, July 29, 1948, Library of Congress.

CHAPTER TWENTY-SIX: THE OPINION OF MANKIND

325 "telling us what dogs we are": Lash, *Years Alone*, 78.

325 "In spite of the fact": Edna P. Gurewitsch, *Kindred Souls: The Friendship of Eleanor Roosevelt and David Gurewitsch* (New York: St. Martin's, 2002), 36.

326 "be on the same side": ER to David Gurewitsch, October 25, 1948, in Lash, *World of Love*, 288.

326 "The work is hard": ER to Hick, November 28, 1948, FDRL.

327 "You have written this": Lash, *Years Alone*, 187–88.

327 "It is almost shockingly delightful": Ibid., 189.

328 "a nice, tame pet": Hick to Tommy, July 23, 1949, FDRL.

328 "the breath of life": Faber, *Life of Lorena Hickok*, 313.

328 "Both my husband": ER, *This I Remember*, 78.
329 "The Years Alone": E. J. Kahn, *New Yorker*, June 12 and 19, 1948.
330 praised her "unaffected approach": Lash, *Years Alone*, 185–86.
331 "The other afternoon": Ibid., 156–65.
331 "It was an emotional moment": Gurewitsch, *Kindred Souls*, 61.
332 She was in Allahabad: Lash, *Years Alone*, 200–201.
333 "I think on Election Day": "My Day," October 6, 1952.
333 would be a "big seller": Nannine Joseph to Hick, August 16, 1951, Joseph papers, University of Oregon archives.
333 "Thanks for helping": Mary Norton to Hick, December 19, 1951, FDRL.
334 "A big part": Mary Norton to Hick, August 16, 1952, FDRL.
334 "both our names": ER to Hick, July 26, 1952, FDRL.
334 they were "simply swell": ER to Hick, August 19, 1953, FDRL.
335 "He seems happy": ER to Hick, July 19, 1954, FDRL.
335 "How nearly are you": ER to Hick, May 19, 1955, FDRL.
335 "I will think of you": ER to Hick, July 31, 1955, FDRL.
335 "who remain with you": "My Day," April 14, 1953.
336 "My children would be": Lash, *Years Alone*, 182.
336 "I love you": Lash, *World of Love*, 440.
337 "I'm going to cling": Gurewitsch, *Kindred Souls*, 27.

CHAPTER TWENTY-SEVEN: A NEW WAY TO BE USEFUL

339 "an educational volunteer": Lash, *Years Alone*, 220.
340 "deep lines of experience": ER, *On My Own*, 150–51.
340 "sit down with anyone": Lash, *Years Alone*, 234.
340 "the time has come": Ibid., 235.
340 On one occasion: "She sent Hick out!" Lash, *World of Love*, diary entry, June 12, 1957, 464.
341 "She didn't talk down to you": This and subsequent quotes from Eleanor Seagraves come from personal communications with the author.
341 She liked being near Eleanor: Hick to Jeannette Brice, September 9, 1957, FDRL.
341–42 "In my innocence": Hick to Helen Douglas, September 9, 1957, University of Oklahoma archive.
342 an investigative trip to Russia: The first plan was a trip to China, but Eleanor couldn't obtain visas.
342 "write as a newspaper woman": "My Day," April 19, 1945.
343 "Can I tell our papers": Lash, *Years Alone*, 270–71.
344 "we have to face": Ibid., 273.
344 vehemently, "Don't worry": Gurewitsch, *Kindred Souls*, 130.
344 the Upper East Side of Manhattan: Eleanor kept the apartment on Washington Square in the Village until 1950, when she rented suites at the Park Sheraton Hotel in midtown. She rented an apartment on 62nd Street for a time, but was living at the Park Sheraton in 1958 when she moved into the town house she purchased with David and Edna Gurewitsch at 55 East 74th Street.
345 "Thanks for the check": The check was for $745, more than twice what she had received in royalties before. After that, there seemed to be checks almost monthly from the Helen Keller book, from *Ladies of Courage*, and from the other young adult books she was turning out.

345 "way over my head": Hick to Nannine Joseph, October 1, 1959, Joseph papers, University of Oregon archives.

346 "A case that comes": Eleanor Roosevelt, *You Learn by Living* (New York: Harper & Brothers, 1960), 82–83.

346 "She is by no means": Hick to Helen Douglas, December 27, 1961, Helen Douglas papers, University of Oklahoma.

346 "It's as though": Hick to Nannine Joseph, May 25, 1962, Joseph papers, University of Oregon archives.

347 "It can be awkward": Lash, *Years Alone*, 321.

347 "oodles of money": Ibid., 280.

347 "the slim young figure": "My Day," August 16, 1960.

348 "I will be surer": Lash, *Years Alone*, 298.

348 JFK was "absolutely smitten": Ibid., 297.

348 "I thought the speech magnificent": ER to Hick, January 23, 1961. FDRL.

348 "I think she knew": Hick to Esther Lape, November 21, 1962, FDRL.

348 "That time she stayed": Ibid.

349 "Apparently that virus": Hick to ER, September 13, 1962, FDRL.

349 muttered, "Utter nonsense": Lash, *Years Alone*, 331.

349 following a stroke: Ibid., and Edna Gurewitsch interview, "Remembering Mrs. Roosevelt: An Intimate Memoir," conducted by Geoffrey Ward, *American Heritage*, 1981.

350 Hick staged her own: These details come from Doris Faber, who interviewed Gordon Kidd.

CHAPTER TWENTY-EIGHT: LIVING ON

351 "I'm getting out of here": Hick to Helen Douglas, December 5, 1962, Helen Douglas papers, University of Oklahoma.

351 "A year from now": Hick to Helen and Melvyn Douglas, January 4, 1963, ibid.

351 "Grief can be": Hick to Jeannette Brice, April 3, 1963, Doris Faber papers, FDRL.

352 "I cannot forget": Hick to Esther Lape, November 21, 1962, FDRL.

352 "All of the boys": Hick to Helen Douglas, November 30, 1961, Helen Douglas papers, University of Oklahoma.

352 "I don't know": Hick to Helen Douglas, December 27, 1961, ibid.

352 "as though I were trapped": Hick to Helen Douglas, July 22, 1966, ibid.

353 "a fine mind": Hick to Helen Douglas, November 26, 1963, ibid.

353 "was just an intelligent": Hick to Melvyn Douglas, July 26, 1966, ibid.

353 "remarkable political savvy": Hick to Helen Douglas, November 24, 1964, ibid.

353 "Now almost blind": Hick, *Reluctant First Lady*, xvii, xviii.

354 "to avoid any sort": Memorandum attached to last will and testament, Doris Faber papers, FDRL.

355 "a fascinating book": *New York Times*, July 30, 1972.

355 Hick would have been pleased: Personal communication with the author.

POSTSCRIPT

357 Eleanor sometimes visited: Richard Peck, who had an apartment in the same house and was also one of the bank executors at the time of Hick's death. Personal communication with the author.

358 **Linda went to work:** Personal communications with both Patsy Costello and Linda Kavars. The fund-raising effort was so successful that it had been used to endow scholarships for women going into journalism or women's studies at Vassar College, Marist College, and SUNY New Paltz.

358 **Dr. JoAnne Myers:** They have since married.

INDEX

INDEX

Roosevelt, Ruth Googins, 126, 237, 312
Roosevelt, Sara, 30, 36–37, 40–41, 44, 71, 73, 74, 76, 77, 145, 153, 345, 374n
  death of, 243
Roosevelt, Theodore, 13, 18, 27, 39, 40, 63–64, 67, 126–27, 154
Roosevelt, Theodore, Jr., 76
Roosevelt family:
  Hyde Park mansion of, 18, 30, 76, 154, 155, 243
  Manhattan mansion of, 32, 36–37, 73
Roosevelt Home Club, 357
Roosevelt Presidential Library, 5
Roosevelt Special (FDR's 1932 campaign train), 11–12, 13, 14, 15–17, 19
Rosenman, Sam, 223
Roswell, Ga., 115
Rutherfurd, Lucy Mercer, 39–41, 72, 84, 259, 293, 296–97, 301, 304, 306, 365n
Rutherfurd, Winthrop, 41

Sagamore Hill, 18, 64
Saint-Gaudens, Augustus, 45
St. Paul's Cathedral, London, 268
San Francisco, Calif., 128, 129
Schiff, Dorothy, 342
Schumann-Heink, Ernestine, 58
Scotts Run valley, 93, 94, 96, 97, 113, 369n
Scripps-Howard newspapers, 342
Seagraves, Eleanor Roosevelt "Sistie," 184, 341, 350, 354, 355
Seagraves, Van, 354
Sea Lion, Operation, 218
Secret Service, U.S., 85, 86, 94, 123, 160
segregation, 207–8
Shangri-La (FDR's Catoctin Mountain camp), 265
Sheean, Vincent, 327
Sherwood, Robert, 246
Shirer, William L., 201, 299
Shoumatoff, Elizabeth, 301, 304
Sicily, Allied invasion of, 277
Simons, Austin, 217
Smith, Al, 15, 42, 76
Social Security, 134
Sorbonne, 325
South:
  de facto slavery in, 116
  federal relief programs in, 116–17
  lynchings in, 114
  racism in, 112–13, 115–17, 207–8
South Carolina, 116, 293

South Dakota, 2, 50, 93, 148
Southern Conference on Human Welfare, 207
Souvestre, Émile, 67
Souvestre, Marie, 29, 67–69, 74
Soviet Union, 196, 198, 325
  atomic weapons acquired by, 343
  ER's trips to, 342–43, 347
  German nonaggression pact with, 201, 211
  Jews in, 343
  refugee crisis and, 314–15
  in "winter war" in Finland, 216
  in World War II, 264, 277
Spain, 196
Spanish Civil War, 164, 198–99, 244, 268, 330
Spanish Earth, The (film), 198
Spellman, Francis Joseph Cardinal, ER attacked by, 330–31
Stalin, Joseph, 196, 201, 211, 264–65
  at Tehran Conference, 277, 285
  at Yalta Conference, 299, 343
Stalingrad, Battle of, 277
Starnes, Joe, 210–11
Stein, Gertrude, 160, 369n
Stevenson, Adlai, 332–33, 347–48
Stimson, Henry, 265, 270–71
Student Union, 211
Suckley, Daisy, 243, 260, 264, 295, 296, 301–2
Sullivan, Anne, 341, 342
Supreme Court, U.S.:
  FDR's castigation of, 151
  FDR's proposed expansion of, 172, 180, 197
  New Deal legislation overturned by, 151, 172, 256
Sweet, Mr., 140–41

Talmadge, Eugene, 112, 116
Tammany Hall, 27, 60
Tarbell, Ida, 159–60
Taubman, Howard, 330
Teamsters Union, 293–94
Teapot Dome scandal, 76
Tehran Conference, 277, 283, 285
Thompson, Dorothy, 200, 246, 305
Thompson, Malvina "Tommy," 118, 131–32, 170, 182, 183, 216, 248, 278, 279, 328, 352
  death of, 335–36
  and ER's break with Cook and Dickerson, 185, 187–89, 207
  on ER's friendships, 258
  and ER's post–White House career, 312–13